ILLUSTRATOR CS4

for Windows and Macintosh
Visual QuickStart Guide

Elaine Weinmann
Peter Lourekas

 Peachpit Press

For Simona

Visual QuickStart Guide
Illustrator CS4 for Windows and Macintosh
Elaine Weinmann and Peter Lourekas

Peachpit Press
1249 Eighth Street
Berkeley, CA 94710
510/524-2178
510/524-2221 (fax)

Find us on the Web at: www.peachpit.com
To report errors, please send a note to errata@peachpit.com
Peachpit Press is a division of Pearson Education

Copyright © 2009 by Elaine Weinmann and Peter Lourekas
Cover Design: Peachpit Press
Interior Design: Elaine Weinmann
Production: Elaine Weinmann and Peter Lourekas
Illustrations: Elaine Weinmann and Peter Lourekas, except as noted

ISBN-13: 978-0-321-56345-3

ISBN-10: 0-321-56345-X

9 8 7 6 5 4 3 2 1

Printed and bound in the United States of America

Acknowledgments

We're grateful to many people for their individual contributions to this book.

Nancy Aldrich-Ruenzel, publisher of Peachpit Press, has enthusiastically supported our projects for over a decade.

Susan Rimerman, our editor, keeps the many wheels in motion for us at Peachpit.

Victor Gavenda, longtime editor at Peachpit, tech edited this book in Windows with his usual keen intelligence and wit.

Production editor Lisa Brazieal gave us speedy answers to our production questions and did an expert job of spearheading the prepress production before sending our files off to Courier Printing.

Many other Peachpit Press staff members do important work, such as Nancy Davis, editor-in-chief; Gary-Paul Prince, PTG tradeshow and conventions manager; and Keasley Jones, business manager.

Illustrator pro artists Michael Bartalos, J.D. King, Koichi Fujii, Chris Lyons, Daniel Pelavin, and Nancy Stahl kindly permitted us to reproduce some of their work. We know it will be a source of inspiration to our readers. (For credits, see Appendix B.)

Elaine Soares, photo research manager, and Lee Scher, photo research coordinator, of the Image Resource Center at Pearson Education, the parent company of Peachpit Press, quickly procured the stock graphics from Shutterstock.com that we requested.

As book packagers, we know that no book is complete without some final polishing. Rebecca Pepper, copy editor, scoured our pages for errors with great care and made intelligent corrections.

Steve Rath generated the index and Suzie Nasol did the last round of proofreading.

This book would have no reason for being without the software that is its subject matter. We commend Adobe Systems, Inc. and the Adobe Illustrator CS4 team, and in particular Silas Lepcha, Adobe senior prerelease program associate, for making significant improvements to what was already a great product.

And finally, we're blessed with loyal friends and family, who are understanding when we're in deadline mode, give our lives some semblance of balance, and are present for us to love and enjoy even more when we reemerge.

Elaine Weinmann and Peter Lourekas

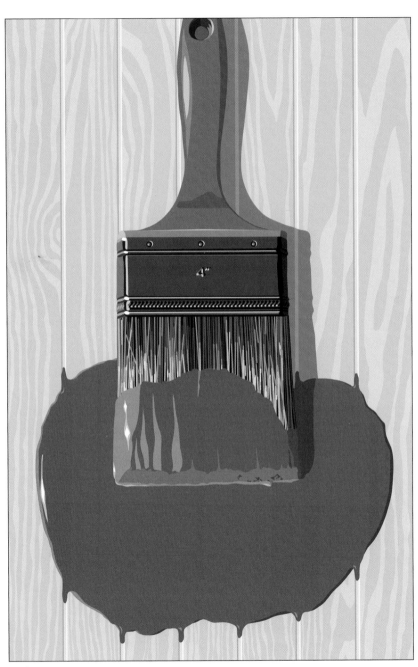

©Chris Lyons

Chapters at a glance

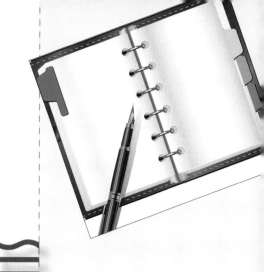

CONTENTS

★ Indicates topics which cover new (Illustrator CS4) features

Contents

10 Fill & Stroke

11 Transform

12 Reshape

13 Layers

14 Appearances

15 Effects

16 Graphic Styles

©Chris Lyons

REGISTER THIS BOOK!

Purchasing this book entitles you to more than just a couple of pounds of paper. If you register the book with Peachpit Press, you're also entitled to download copies of some of the images used in the book, which you can use to practice with as you follow the step-by-step tutorials. To get started, follow this link: www.peachpit.com/illustratorcs4vqs. This takes you to the book's page at the Peachpit Press website. Once there, click Register your book to log in to your account at peachpit.com. If you don't already have an account, it takes just a few seconds to create one, and it's free!

After logging in, you'll need to enter the book's ISBN code, which you'll find on the back cover. Next you're asked a security question to access

the images. The answer is found in the book. Click Submit, and you're in! You'll be taken to a list of your registered books. Find *Illustrator CS4 Visual QuickStart Guide* on the list, and click Access to protected content to get to the download page.

Please note that these images are low-resolution (not suitable for printing), and they are copyrighted by their owners, who have watermarked them to discourage unauthorized reproduction. They are for your personal use only, not for distribution.

Of course, you're not restricted to using the downloadable photos that accompany the text. For any given set of instructions, you can substitute a photo of your own or choose a different photo from the assortment offered.

In this chapter, we'll show you how to get up and running in Adobe Illustrator. After learning how to launch the program, you'll learn how to create a new document; preview, open, and create templates; create and modify multiple artboards; save and close your document; and quit/exit Illustrator.

Launching Illustrator

To create a document after launching Illustrator, see page 3.

To launch Illustrator in Macintosh:

Do one of the following:

On the startup drive, open the Applications > Adobe Illustrator CS4 folder, then double-click the Adobe Illustrator CS4 application icon. **Ai**

Click the Illustrator application icon **Ai** in the Dock.**A** (To create an icon, drag the application icon from the application folder to the Dock.)

To launch Illustrator by opening a file, double-click an Illustrator file icon **B** or drag an Illustrator file icon over the application icon in the Dock.

➤ By default, a welcome screen opens when Illustrator launches.**C** You can check Don't Show Again to prevent it from appearing upon relaunch; to redisplay it at any time, choose Help > Welcome Screen.

A Click the Adobe Illustrator CS4 application icon in the Dock.

B Double-click an Illustrator file to open it and launch Illustrator. All of the files shown above were created and saved in Illustrator (note the three different formats).

1

IN THIS CHAPTER

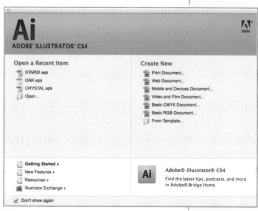

C This is the welcome screen for Illustrator.

A new document window doesn't appear automatically when you launch Illustrator. To create a new document after launching the application, follow the instructions on the next page.

To launch Illustrator in Windows:

Do one of the following:

Open My Computer, double-click the icon for the hard drive in which Illustrator is installed; the default drive is Local Disk (C:). Follow the path Program Files\Adobe\Adobe Illustrator CS4, then double-click the Adobe Illustrator CS4 icon.

Double-click an Illustrator file icon **A** to launch Illustrator and open that file.

Click the Start button on the taskbar, choose All Programs, then click Adobe Illustrator CS4. **B**

➤ By default, a welcome screen opens when Illustrator launches. **C** You can check Don't Show Again to prevent it from appearing upon relaunch; to redisplay it at any time, choose Help > Welcome Screen.

A Double-click an Illustrator file to open it and launch Illustrator. All of the files shown above were created and saved in Illustrator (note the three different formats).

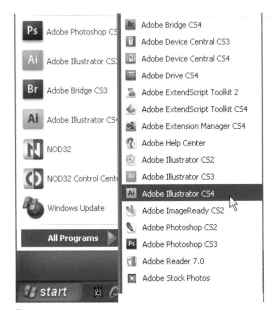

B Click the Start button, then locate and click the Adobe Illustrator CS4 application.

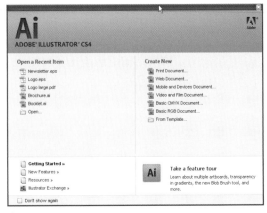

C This is the welcome screen for Adobe Illustrator CS4 in Windows.

Creating a new document

To create a new document: ★

1. Do either of the following:

   Choose File > **New** (Cmd-N/Ctrl-N).

   If the Adobe Illustrator CS4 welcome screen is displaying, on the right side under **Create New**, click **Print Document** or **Web Document**.

2. The New Document dialog opens.**A** Type a **Name** for the new document.

3. From the **New Document Profile** menu, choose a preset for the medium in which you plan to output your file.

4. Each artboard in a document defines a separate printable area. For now, create only one artboard by leaving the **Number of Artboards** value at 1 (at this setting, the artboard Grid, Rows, and Spacing options are dimmed).

5. Do either of the following:

   From the **Size** menu, choose a preset from the list of available sizes for the profile you chose in step 3.

   Choose a measurement unit from the **Units** menu (use Pixels for Web output only), then enter custom Width and Height values.

6. For the **Orientation**, click the portrait (vertical) or landscape (horizontal) button.

7. The **Bleed** values control the width of the print area for items that extend beyond the artboard. Ask your print shop what values to enter; you can do so either now in this dialog or later in the Document Setup or Print dialog.

8. Expand the dialog by clicking the **Advanced** button, if neccessary, then do the following:

   Choose a **Color Mode** for the document: CMYK for print output, or RGB for video or Web output.

   Choose a resolution for **Raster Effects**, depending on your output requirements (effects are discussed in Chapter 15).

   Leave the **Preview Mode** setting as Default.

9. Click OK. A new document window will open at the maximum size for your display, and the full artboard will display at its maximum zoom level for that window size. If the Application frame is displayed (see pages 21–22), the document will be docked as a tabbed window.

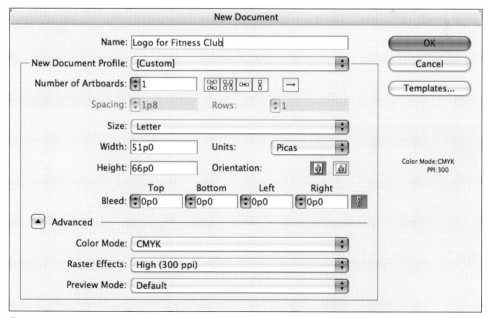

A In the New Document dialog, type a name, then choose a preset or custom settings.

Using templates

A template is an Illustrator document that opens automatically as an unsaved copy. Illustrator includes many industry-standard templates that can be used as a starting point for creating custom projects. They contain artboards, crop marks, objects, styles, symbols, custom swatches, and more. You can get an inkling of what the templates look like via the previews in Bridge (instructions below). If you're new to Illustrator, this is a also good way to see what the program can do. On the following page, we'll show you how to open a normal Illustrator document as a template and how to create a custom template.

To preview and open an Illustrator template:

1. Launch Bridge by clicking the Go to Bridge button [Br] at the top left corner of the Application bar. ★

2. Click the Folders tab in the left panel, navigate to and open the Adobe Illustrator CS4/Cool Extras/en_US/Templates folder in the Mac OS, or Program Files\Adobe\Adobe Illustrator CS4\Cool Extras\en_US\Templates in Windows. Double-click any of the folders inside the Templates folder, then browse through the images. **A**

3. Double-click a template file. It will open as a new, untitled document—content, specifications, and all—and can be edited like any other document. **B–C** The original file is left intact.

4. Save the new file (see page 11).

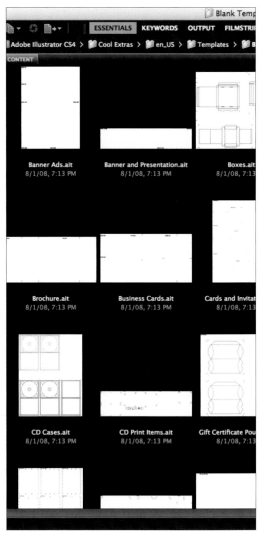

A You can preview the Adobe Illustrator CS4 templates in Bridge.

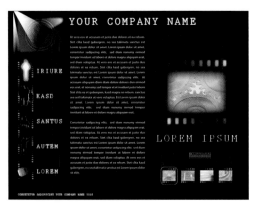

B This template for a website is in the Film folder.

C This business card template is in the Tech folder.

You're not limited to using the templates that ship with Illustrator. You can also open any existing Illustrator file as an untitled document.

To open an existing Illustrator file as an untitled document:

1. Do either of the following:

   Choose File > **New from Template** (Cmd-Shift-N/Ctrl-Shift-N).

   Under Create New on the Adobe Illustrator CS4 welcome screen, click **From Template**.

   The New from Template dialog opens.

2. Locate and select an existing Illustrator file, then click **New** to open the file as an untitled document.

3. If a Missing Profile alert prompt appears, see page 16.

4. Save the file (see page 11).

You can also save any of your own Illustrator files as templates. Regardless of what kind of project you're working on—CD label, business card, book cover, Web or package design—using a template will save you setup time as you create new documents.

When creating a file to be saved as a template, you can choose settings and layout aids such as guides, a zoom level, and multiple artboards, and you can also incorporate such Illustrator features as brushes, swatches, symbols, graphic styles, crop marks, and, of course, path objects. Note: You'll probably want to revisit these instructions later, when you're better acquainted with Illustrator and have created some artwork.

To create a template:

1. Create a new file or open an existing file.

2. Do any of the following:

   Create path objects, swatches, graphic styles, symbols, etc.

   Choose specifications for one or more artboards.

   Set a zoom level.

   Create and save custom views.

   Create layers.

   Create ruler or object guides.

   Define transparency flattener, PDF, and print presets.

   Create text boxes containing instructions for the lucky user of your template.

3. Save the file via File > **Save as Template** (keep the format as Illustrator Template (ait). You can save it in the default location, which is the folder listed in step 2 on the preceding page. That's all there is to it.

USING THE STATUS BAR

► To see information about the current file, rest the pointer on the status bar at the bottom of the document window.

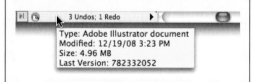

► Depending on which category is chosen on the Show submenu on the status bar menu, the bar displays the current Version Cue Status, tool name, date and time, number of available undos, or document color profile. (Option-click/Alt-click the status bar menu to access the moon phase, shopping days 'til Christmas, and other vital statistics.)

THE ANATOMY OF A DOCUMENT

To compare the currently active artboard to the paper size for the currently chosen printer, choose View > Fit Artboard in Window (Cmd-0/Ctrl-0) and View > Show Print Tiling. To display the artboard boundaries if they're currently hidden, choose View > Show Artboards (Cmd-Shift-H/Ctrl-Shift-H). To learn more about the Illustrator workspace, see Chapter 3. To cycle among multiple artboards in a document, see page 26.

The current document title, zoom level, color mode (CMYK or RGB), and view (Preview, Outline, Pixel Preview, or Overprint Preview) are listed on the title bar. And if View > Proof Colors is on, the current proof profile is also listed.

Pool table.ai* @ 50% (CMYK/Preview) ✕

The artboard (within the solid line) defines the maximum printable area. Only one artboard can be active at a time. You can print and export artboards individually or sequentially. (In this document, the size of the printable page matches the size of the artboard.)

The red rectangle defines the bleed region, which can be specified in the New Document dialog when you create your file, in the Document Setup dialog at any time, or in the Print dialog. To create a bleed, your artwork must extend into the canvas area.

The inner dotted rectangle represents the actual printable area. It takes into account the printer's nonprintable margins at the edge of the paper, and is controlled by the specifications of the currently chosen printer (see Chapter 31).

The outer dotted rectangle represents the paper size.

You can create and stash objects on the canvas area* (the area outside the artboards), and drag them into any artboard when needed. Objects on the canvas save with the file but won't print unless they extend partially onto an artboard, within the current bleed region.

*In Adobe Photoshop, the image is contained in what is known as the live canvas area, whereas in Illustrator, the artboard is the "live" area and the "nonlive" area surrounding it is called the canvas area. Mighty confusing, when you consider that both programs are in the Adobe Creative Suite!

Adding artboards to a document

Every Illustrator document has one or more movable artboards, which contain the artwork. You chose dimensions for the default artboard in the New Document dialog. Using the Artboard tool, you can add more artboards, as well as scale them individually (you can have different-sized artboards within the same document), change their orientation, and move them around.

If you were to create a corporate identity package for a client, for example, you could create a business card, stationery, and a brochure on separate artboards within the same document. Any colors or graphic, paragraph, or character style definitions that you create for one artboard will be available for all the other artboards in the same file. You can also use multiple artboards to create such projects as a multipage PDF file, graphics for a Web page, or components of a package design.

To add an artboard to your document: ★

1. With a document open in Illustrator, press Cmd- –/Ctrl- – to zoom out, if necessary, then hold down the Spacebar and drag to display the current artboard and some of the canvas area to the right of it.

2. Do either of the following:

   Choose the **Artboard** tool 🔲 (Shift-O).

   On the Control panel, click **Document Setup**, then click **Edit Artboards**.

   Your original artboard is now selected. Note that the canvas area surrounding it is gray (if it's not, see page 10).

3. Drag to create a new artboard to the right of the existing one.**A** (Multiple artboards are assigned numbers based on the sequence in which they are created.)

4. To scale the new artboard, see step 4 on page 9.

5. To exit artboard editing mode, press Esc (the last tool will reselect) or click a different tool.

➤ To quickly display all the artboards in the document window, choose View > Fit All in Window (Cmd-Option-0/Ctrl-Alt-0).

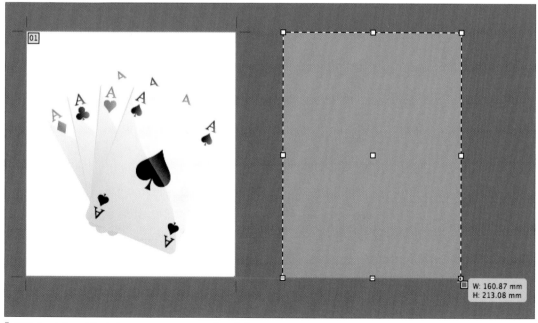

W: 160.87 mm
H: 213.08 mm

A With the Artboard tool, drag to create a new artboard. (Here, we are using a Smart Guide to align the new artboard with the existing one (see pages 96–97).

To duplicate an artboard but not its contents: ★

1. Do either of the following:

   Choose the **Artboard** tool ⊡ (Shift-O), make sure the **Move/Copy Artwork with Artboard** button 🔁 on the Control panel is deactivated, then Option-drag/Alt-drag an artboard.

   Click in an existing artboard, click the **New Artboard** button 🔳 on the Control panel, position the artboard preview rectangle in the window, then click to place it (or Option-click/Alt-click to create multiple copies of it).

2. Press Esc or choose a different tool.

To duplicate an artboard and its contents: ★

1. Choose the **Artboard** tool ⊡ (Shift-O).

2. Activate the **Move/Copy Artwork with Artboard** button 🔁 on the Control panel, then Option-drag/Alt-drag the artboard.**A–B**

3. Press Esc or choose a different tool.

It's as easy to delete an artboard as it is to create one. Only the artboard is deleted, not the artwork contained within it.

To delete an artboard: ★

1. Choose the **Artboard** tool ⊡ (Shift-O).

2. Do one of the following:

   In the upper right corner of the artboard to be deleted, click the **Delete** icon.⊠

   Click the artboard to be deleted, then press **Delete/Backspace**.

   Click the artboard to be deleted, then Click the **Delete Artboard** button 🗑 on the Control panel.

   Note: One artboard must remain in your document.

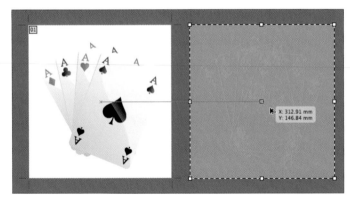

A To copy the artboard and its contents, activate the Move/Copy Artwork with Artboard button on the Control panel, then with the Artboard tool, Option-drag/Alt-drag the artboard.

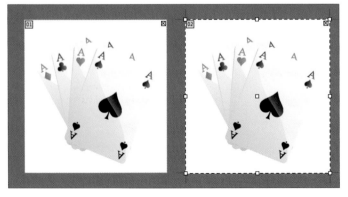

B The duplicate artboard and its contents appear.

Modifying artboards

To change the position, scale, or orientation of an artboard: ★

1. Press Cmd-Option-0/Ctrl-Alt-0 to fit all the artboards in the document window.

2. Choose the **Artboard** tool ▯ (Shift-O), then click an artboard to select it.

3. To reposition the artboard, drag inside it. You can use Smart Guides (Cmd-U/Ctrl-U) to align the top or side of the artboard to other artboards (see pages 96–97).

   Note: Normally, the artwork moves along with the artboard that contains it. If you want to reposition the artboard relative to the artwork, click the **Move/Copy Artwork with Artboard** button ⬇ on the Control panel to deactivate it, then move the artboard. **A** Reactivate the button when you're done.

4. To scale the artboard, do any of the following:

   From the **Preset** menu on the Control panel, choose a predefined size.

To scale the artboard **manually**, drag a side or corner handle. You can use the on-object readouts for exact dimensions.* **B** To scale the artboard proportionally, Shift-drag. Note: If Constrain Proportions is checked in the Artboard Options dialog, the proportions will be preserved automatically; see the next page.

Enter new values in the **W** and/or **H** fields on the Control panel. Use any unit abbreviation; Illustrator will translate the value into the current unit of measure.

5. To change the orientation of the artboard, click the **Portrait** 📱 or **Landscape** 📱 button on the Control panel.

6. Press Esc.

➤ To cycle among multiple artboards when the Artboard tool is selected, hold down Option/Alt and click an arrow key on your keyboard.

A To move an artboard without moving its contents, deactivate the Move/Copy Artwork with Artboard button on the Control panel, then with the Artboard tool, drag the artboard.

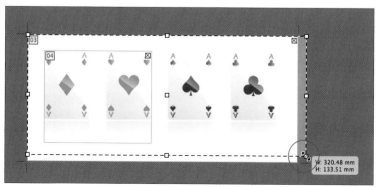

B To scale an artboard manually, drag one of its handles with the Artboard tool.

*If the readouts aren't displaying, go to Illustrator/Edit > Preferences > Smart Guides, and check Measurement Labels.

To choose artboard options: ★

1. To open the Artboard Options dialog, do either of the following:

   Choose the Artboard tool, then click the **Artboard Options** button ⊞ on the Control panel.

   Double-click the **Artboard** tool.⬚

2. *Optional:* For the currently selected artboard, you can choose a Preset; change the Width, Height, or Orientation; or change the horizontal or vertical Position.

3. Check any of the following options, which will apply to all the artboards in your document:

   Constrain Proportions to preserve the proportions of your artboards as they're scaled manually.

   The features of the artboard that you want to **Display**: **Show Center Mark** displays a point in the center of each artboard; **Show Cross Hairs** displays a line marking the center of each side of the artboard; and **Show Video Safe Areas** displays guides that mark the viewable area for video output.

   Fade Region Outside Artboard to have the area outside the artboards display as dark gray (not white) while the Artboard tool is selected.

   Update While Dragging to have an artboard area display as gray as the artboard is dragged.

4. Click OK.

➤ Beware! The Delete button in the Artboard Options dialog deletes the currently selected artboard.

➤ Most of the options found in the Artboard Options dialog are also available on the Control panel when the Artboard tool is selected.

CHOOSING DISPLAY OPTIONS VIA THE CONTROL PANEL ★

With the Artboard tool selected, you can turn specific artboard features on or off via the Display Options menu on the Control panel. When an option has a check mark, you can also turn just that option on or off quickly by clicking the icon adjacent to the menu.

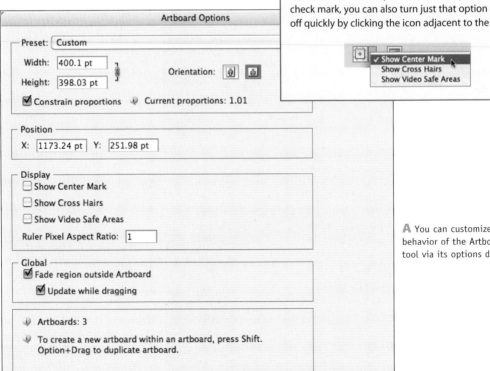

A You can customize the behavior of the Artboard tool via its options dialog.

Saving files

When saving an Illustrator file, you can choose from these seven formats: Adobe Illustrator (ai), Illustrator EPS (eps), Illustrator Template (ait), Adobe PDF (pdf), FXG (fxg), SVG Compressed (svgz), and SVG (svg). Files in these formats can be reopened and edited in Illustrator.

We recommend sticking with the Adobe Illustrator (ai) format if you're going to print your file directly from Illustrator or if you're going to import it into a program that reads this format, such as Adobe InDesign. If you're going to display your file online or export it to an application that doesn't read native Illustrator files, you'll need to save a copy of it in a different format such as Adobe PDF; see Chapter 32.

To save a file in the Adobe Illustrator (ai) format:

1. If the file has never been saved, choose File > Save (Cmd-S/Ctrl-S). If the file has already been saved in a different format, choose File > Save As. In either case, the Save As dialog opens.

2. Enter a name in the Save As/File Name field.

3. Navigate to the desired folder or drive.

4. In the Mac OS, choose Format: **Adobe Illustrator (ai)**.

   In Windows, choose Save as Type: **Adobe Illustrator (ai)**.

5. Click Save. The Illustrator Options dialog opens. Leave Illustrator CS4 as the choice on the Version menu. (For the legacy formats, see the sidebar on this page.)

6. Under **Fonts**, enter a percentage in the **Subset Fonts When Percent of Characters Used Is Less Than** field to save fonts used in the illustration as part of the document. If not all the characters in a particular font are being used in your artwork, this option allows you to embed just a subset of characters, as opposed to the whole font, to help reduce the file size. For example, at a setting of 50%, the entire font will be embedded only if more than 50% of its characters are used in the file, and the Subset option will apply if fewer than 50% of the font's characters are used in the file.

   Characters in embedded fonts will display and print on any system, even where they aren't installed, but keep in mind that the higher the

Subset Fonts percentage, the more characters will be embedded, and the larger the file size will be. At 100%, all the font characters are embedded.

7. Under **Options**, you can check:

   Create PDF Compatible File to make your file readable by other applications that support the PDF format, such as Photoshop. This option increases the size of your Illustrator file.

   Include Linked Files to save a copy of any linked files with the document. Read about linking in Chapter 22.

   If a profile was chosen in the Edit > Assign Profile dialog, check **Embed ICC Profiles** to embed those profiles in the file so it will be properly color-managed.

   Use Compression to compress vector data (and PDF data, if included) to help reduce the file storage size.

8. Click OK.

➤ Both the Save As and Save a Copy commands let you save a copy of a file as a variation or in a different format. When you use Save As, the file with the new name stays open onscreen, while the file with the original name closes but is preserved on disk. The Save a Copy command (see the following page) keeps the original file open onscreen, while the copy with the new name is saved to disk.

SAVING IN OTHER CS VERSIONS

To save a CS4 file in an earlier Illustrator CS format, in the Illustrator Options dialog (step 5 on this page), choose the desired format from the Version menu. Saving to an earlier CS version can cause unexpected text reflows. Hopefully, you won't find a need to save a file in a pre-CS version of Illustrator, as those versions can't save such elements as multiple artboards, live effects, Live Paint groups, and transparency.

If you save a document that contains multiple artboards to a previous version of Illustrator (e.g., CS3) and click Save Each Artboard as a Separate File in the Illustrator Options dialog, the result will be a separate file for each artboard, along with a master file in which each artboard has been converted to a guide.

The prior version of a file is overwritten each time the Save command is executed. Do yourself a favor and save often—don't be shy about it! And be sure to create backups of your work frequently, too.

To resave a file:

Choose File > **Save** (Cmd-S/Ctrl-S).

When you use the Save a Copy command, the original version of the file stays open onscreen, and a copy of it is saved to disk.

To save a copy of a file:

1. Choose File > **Save a Copy** (Cmd-Option-S/ Ctrl-Alt-S). The Save a Copy dialog opens.

2. To save the file in the Illustrator (ai) format, see the preceding page; for other formats, see Chapter 32.

To revert to the last saved version:

1. Choose File > **Revert**.

2. Click **Revert** in the alert dialog.

Ending a work session

To close a document:

1. To close a **tabbed** document, click the ✖ on the window tab. ★

   To close a **floating** document in the Mac OS, click the close (red) button in the upper left corner of the document window (Cmd-W). In Windows, click the close box in the upper right corner of the document window (Ctrl-W).

2. If the file was modified since it was last saved, an alert dialog will appear. 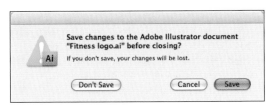 Click Don't Save to close the file without saving your changes; or click Save to resave the file before closing it; or click Cancel to back out of the deal.

To quit/exit Illustrator:

1. In the Mac OS, choose Illustrator > **Quit Illustrator** (Cmd-Q).

   In Windows, choose File > **Exit** (Ctrl-Q) or click the close box for the application window.

2. All open Illustrator files will close. If you edited any of those files since they were last saved, an alert dialog will appear. To resave the file(s), click Save, or to quit/exit Illustrator without saving your edits, click Don't Save.

A If you try to close a file that's been modified since it was last saved, this prompt appears.

SHORTCUTS TO THE SAVE DIALOGS		
	Mac OS	Windows
Save the edits in a previously saved file (no dialog opens), or open the Save As dialog if the file hasn't yet been saved	Cmd-S	Ctrl-S
Open the Save As dialog	Cmd-Shift-S	Ctrl-Shift-S
Open the Save a Copy dialog	Cmd-Option-S	Ctrl-Alt-S

CLOSING ALL FILES QUICKLY ★

Close all tabbed windows	Control-click/right-click a window tab and choose Close All from the context menu
Close all floating windows (Mac OS only)	Option-click the close button on one of the document windows
Close all tabbed and floating windows	Press Cmd-Option-W/ Ctrl-Alt-W

Choosing the proper color settings for Illustrator is a crucial step before creating graphics. In this chapter, you'll learn how to use color settings to manage and maintain color consistency between documents and output devices; synchronize the color settings of all the programs in the Adobe Creative Suite; change document color profiles; and finally, soft-proof your artwork onscreen for your chosen output device.

Introduction to color management

Problems with color can creep up on you when the various hardware devices and software packages you use treat color differently. If you were to open an Illustrator graphic in several different imaging programs or Web browsers, the colors might look completely different in each case, and may not look the same as they did on your screen in Illustrator. Print the graphic, and the results could be different yet again. In some cases, you might find such color changes to be slight and unobjectionable, but in other instances, they can wreak havoc with your design and turn your project into a disaster.

A color management system can solve most of these problems by acting as a color interpreter. Such a system knows how each device and program understands color, and by using color profiles (mathematical descriptions of the color space of each device) makes the proper adjustments so the colors in your files look the same as you move them from one program or device to another. Illustrator, Photoshop, and other programs in the Adobe Creative Suite use the standardized ICC (International Color Consortium) profiles to tell your color management system how specific devices use color. Whether you're planning a traditional print run or will be using the same graphic for multiple purposes (such as for Web and print), your work will benefit if you use color management.

In Illustrator, you'll find most of the color management controls in the Edit > Color Settings dialog. It gives you access to preset management settings for various publishing situations, including press and Web output, and also lets you choose custom settings. There are two main areas in the basic dialog:

➤ The **Working Spaces** govern how RGB and CMYK colors are displayed in your document and serve as the default color profiles for new Illustrator documents.

Continued on the following page

MANAGE COLOR

2

IN THIS CHAPTER

➤ The **Color Management Policies** for RGB and CMYK color files govern how the program deals with color when opening files that don't have an attached color profile, or when a file's profile doesn't match the current color settings in Illustrator.

Choosing the correct color settings will help keep your document colors consistent from the onscreen version to final output. The abundance of options in the Color Settings dialog may appear complex at first, but you and your documents will benefit if you take the time to learn about them.

Note: For high-end print output, ask your print shop to recommend specific color management settings to ensure that your color management workflow runs smoothly.

Display types

There are two basic types of computer displays: CRT (cathode ray tube, as in a traditional TV set) and LCD (liquid crystal display, or flat panel). The display performance of a **CRT** fluctuates due to its analog technology and the fact that its display phosphors (which produce the glowing dots that you view onscreen) tend to fade over time. CRT displays can be calibrated reliably for only around three years.

An **LCD** display uses a grid of fixed-sized liquid crystals that filter color coming from a backlight source. Although you can adjust only the brightness on an LCD (not the contrast), the LCD digital technology offers more reliable color consistency than a CRT, without the characteristic flickering of a CRT. The newest LCD models provide good viewing angles, display accurate color, use the desirable daylight temperature of 6500K for the white point (an industry-standard color temperature), and are produced under tighter manufacturing standards than CRTs. Moreover, in most cases the color profile that is provided with an LCD display (and that is installed in your system automatically) describes the display characteristics accurately.

➤ Both types of displays lose calibration gradually, so you may not notice a change until the colors are way off. To maintain good color consistency, try to stick to a regular monthly calibration schedule.

Calibrating your display

The first step toward achieving color consistency is to calibrate your display by adjusting the contrast and brightness, gamma, color balance, and white point.

In the Mac OS, Illustrator relies on the Calibrate utility, which is found in the Displays panel (Color tab) in System Preferences. This utility generates an ICC profile that the operating system refers to in order to display colors accurately onscreen.

If you're using a Windows machine, or if you want to generate a more complete profile in the Mac OS (which we recommend doing), you'll need to use a hardware calibrator. Calibrate your display with it, and save the settings as an ICC profile. Thereafter, that profile will be available to the Adobe color management system and will be used by all the color-managed applications in the Adobe Creative Suite. For more information about calibrating a display, see Illustrator Help or our *Photoshop CS4: Visual QuickStart Guide*.

WHAT ARE COLOR SPACES AND PROFILES?

Each device, such as a camera or computer display, can capture and reproduce a particular range (gamut) of colors; this is known as its color space. The mathematical description of the color space of each device is called the color profile. The color management system uses the color profile to define the colors in your document. Illustrator uses the document profile to display and edit artwork colors; or if the document doesn't have a profile, Illustrator uses the current working space instead (which is the color space profile you will choose in the Color Settings dialog).

Choosing color settings

To choose color settings:

1. Choose Edit > **Color Settings** (Cmd-Shift-K/ Ctrl-Shift-K). The Color Settings dialog opens (**A**, page 17).

2. Choose a preset from the **Settings** menu. The four basic presets are summarized as follows:

   Monitor Color sets the RGB working space to your display profile. This is a good choice for video output, but not for print output.

   North America General Purpose 2 meets the requirements for screen and print output in the United States and Canada. All profile warnings are off.

   North America Prepress 2 manages color to conform with common press conditions in the United States and Canada. The default RGB color space that is assigned to this setting is Adobe RGB. When CMYK documents are opened, their values are preserved.

   North America Web/Internet is designed for online output. All RGB images are converted to the sRGB color space.

3. At this point you can click OK to accept the predefined settings or you can proceed with the remaining steps to choose custom settings.

4. The **Working Spaces** menus control how RGB and CMYK colors will be treated in a document that lacks an embedded profile. You can either leave these settings as is or choose other options. The RGB options that we recommend using are discussed below (see the second tip on the following page). For the CMYK setting, you should ask your output service provider which working space to choose.

   Adobe RGB (1998) encompasses a wide range of colors and is useful when converting RGB images to CMYK images. This working space is recommended for inkjet printing, but not for online output.

   ColorMatch RGB contains a smaller range of colors than Adobe RGB (1998) but, because it matches the color space of Radius Pressview displays, is suitable for print work.

   ProPhoto RGB contains a very wide range of colors and is suitable for output to high-end dye sublimation and inkjet printers.

   sRGB IEC61966-2.1 is a good choice for Web output, as it reflects the settings for an average computer display. Many hardware and software manufacturers are using this as the default space for scanners, low-end printers, and software.

5. From the RGB and CMYK menus in the Color Management Policies area, choose a color management policy for Illustrator to use when the profile in a document doesn't match the current color settings in Illustrator:

   Off to prevent files from being color-managed when imported or opened.

   Preserve Embedded Profiles if you will be working with both color-managed and non-color-managed documents. This option ties each color file's profile to the individual file. Remember, in Illustrator, each open document can keep its own profile.

   Convert to Working Space if you want all your documents to reflect the same color working space. This is usually the best choice for Web work.

   For **Profile Mismatches**, check **Ask When Opening** to have Illustrator display an alert if the color profile in a file you're opening doesn't match the working space for the application. If you choose this option, you can override the current color management policy when opening a document.

   Check **Ask When Pasting** to have Illustrator display an alert when a color profile mismatch occurs as you paste a color image into your document. If you choose this option, you can override the current current color management policy when pasting.

   And for files that have **Missing Profiles**, check **Ask When Opening** to have Illustrator display an alert offering you the opportunity to assign a profile to files as you open them.

6. *Optional:* If you've chosen custom color settings that you want to save for later use, click Save. To have your custom file name display on the Settings menu, save it in the default

Continued on the following page

location. In the Mac OS, that location is Users/[user name]/Library/Application Support/Adobe/Color/Settings; in Windows, it's C:\Documents and Settings\[user name]\Application Data\Adobe\Color\Settings.

7. Click OK.

➤ To reuse your saved settings, choose the file name from the Settings menu in the Color Settings dialog. To load a settings file that wasn't saved in the Settings folder (and therefore isn't listed on the Settings menu), click Load, then locate the desired file.

➤ We discourage using the Monitor RGB and ColorSync RGB color spaces because they rely on a profile that is specific to each computer system. This means your document could look different on each system, which defeats the whole point of using color management.

RESPONDING TO THE PROFILE ALERTS

➤ When you open an Illustrator document, if its embedded color profile doesn't match the current RGB or CMYK working space, the Embedded Profile Mismatch alert dialog opens. We suggest that you click either of the first two options in the dialog, then click OK.

➤ If you open an Illustrator document that doesn't contain an embedded color profile, the Missing Profile alert dialog opens. Here too, we suggest that you click either of the first two options in the dialog, then click OK.

COMPENSATING FOR COLOR BLINDNESS ★

At some point you may need to design graphics, such as signage, that are fully accessible to color-blind viewers. In fact, some countries require graphics in public spaces to comply with the Color Universal Design (CUD) guidelines. To simulate how your document will look to a color-blind viewer, use the View > Proof Setup > Color Blindness – Protanopia-Type and Color Blindness – Deuteranopia-Type commands in Adobe Illustrator.

In case you're not familiar with those two terms, for a protanope, the brightness of red, orange, and yellow is dimmed, making it hard for such a person to distinguish red from black or dark gray. Protanopes also have trouble distinguishing violet, lavender, and purple from blue because the reddish components of those colors appear dimmed. Deuteranopes are unable to distinguish between colors in the green-yellow-red part of the spectrum and experience color blindness similar to that of protanopes, but without the problem of dimming.

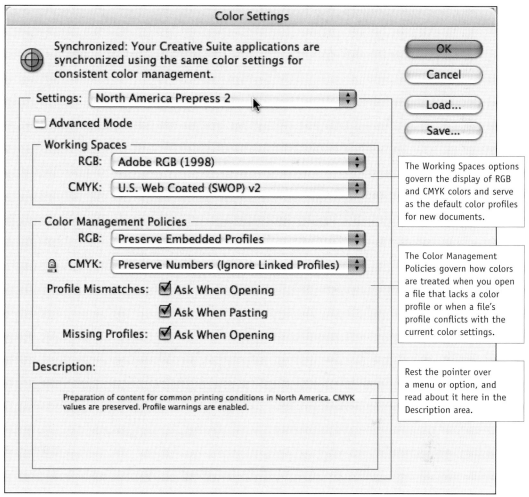

Color Settings

Synchronized: Your Creative Suite applications are synchronized using the same color settings for consistent color management.

OK

Cancel

Settings: North America Prepress 2

Load...

Save...

☐ Advanced Mode

Working Spaces

RGB: Adobe RGB (1998)

CMYK: U.S. Web Coated (SWOP) v2

The Working Spaces options govern the display of RGB and CMYK colors and serve as the default color profiles for new documents.

Color Management Policies

RGB: Preserve Embedded Profiles

🔒 CMYK: Preserve Numbers (Ignore Linked Profiles)

Profile Mismatches: ☑ Ask When Opening

☑ Ask When Pasting

Missing Profiles: ☑ Ask When Opening

The Color Management Policies govern how colors are treated when you open a file that lacks a color profile or when a file's profile conflicts with the current color settings.

Description:

Preparation of content for common printing conditions in North America. CMYK values are preserved. Profile warnings are enabled.

Rest the pointer over a menu or option, and read about it here in the Description area.

A When you choose a preset from the Settings menu in the Color Settings dialog, the options below the menu are chosen for you automatically. You can customize any preset by choosing settings.

Synchronizing the color settings

When the color settings in another Adobe Creative Suite program, such as Photoshop, don't match the current settings in Illustrator, an alert displays at the top of the Color Settings dialog in Illustrator. If you don't own the complete Adobe Creative Suite, you'll have to start up each of your Adobe applications and fix its color settings by hand. If you're fortunate enough to have the whole suite, you can use the Suite Color Settings dialog in Bridge to synchronize the color settings of all the suite programs that you have installed.

To synchronize color settings using Bridge:

1. In Bridge, choose Edit > **Creative Suite Color Settings** (Cmd-Shift-K/Ctrl-Shift-K). The Suite Color Settings dialog opens,**B** showing the same list of settings as found in the Color Settings dialog when Advanced Mode is unchecked.

2. Click one of the settings to select it, then click Apply. Bridge will change (synchronize) the color settings of the other Adobe Creative Suite applications to match the preset you've chosen.

A This alert in the Color Settings dialog informs us that the color settings in our Creative Suite applications aren't synchronized.

B Use the Suite Color Settings dialog to synchronize the color settings of all the Adobe Creative Suite applications that you have installed.

Changing the document profile

When a file's profile doesn't match the current working space or is missing a color profile altogether, you can use the Assign Profile command to assign the correct one. You may notice visible color shifts if the color data of your file is reinterpreted to match the new profile, but rest assured, the color data in the actual document is preserved.

To change or delete a file's color profile:

1. Choose Edit > **Assign Profile**. The Assign Profile dialog opens.**A**

2. Do one of the following:

   To remove a color profile from your document, click **Don't Color Manage This Document**. The current working space will now control the appearance of colors in your artwork.

   If your document doesn't have an assigned profile or if its profile is different from the current working space, click **Working** [document color mode and the name of the current working space] to assign that profile.

   To assign a different profile to your document, click **Profile**, then choose the desired profile from the menu. This won't change or convert any color data in your artwork.

3. Click OK.

EMBEDDING A PROFILE WHEN SAVING

When you use the File > Save As command to save a file in a format that supports embedded profiles, such as Adobe Illustrator (ai), the Illustrator Options dialog opens. There, you can check Embed ICC Profiles to embed a profile with the document, if one has been assigned.

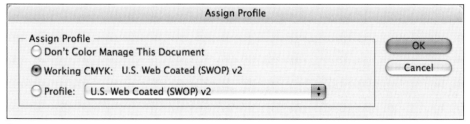

A Use the Assign Profile dialog to either delete a file's color profile or assign a new one. The profile chosen here will also be listed as the Document Profile in the Color Management panel of the File > Print dialog.

Proofing a document onscreen

Specifying a color management setup is all well and good, but once you start creating some Illustrator artwork, you will need to get an idea of how it's going to look in print or online. You can do this by viewing a soft proof of your document onscreen. Although this method is less accurate than actually making a print or viewing your Web graphics on various displays, it can give you a general idea of how your artwork will look in different settings. You can choose either preset or custom settings.

To proof your document onscreen:

1. From the View > **Proof Setup** submenu, choose the type of output display to be simulated:

   To simulate output from your current CMYK printing device, choose the **Working CMYK** profile.

   For a document that is in RGB Color mode, both Windows and Macintosh users can choose **Windows RGB**, the industry-standard display gamma of 2.2.

   To create a proofing model for a specific output device, choose **Customize**. The Proof Setup dialog opens.**A** From the **Device to Simulate** menu, choose the color profile for your target output device, then check or uncheck **Preserve CMYK (or RGB) Numbers**. This option is available only when the document color mode of the current file matches the mode of the output device profile that is currently chosen on the Device to Simulate menu (e.g., if the document color mode is CMYK and the proofing profile is a CMYK profile). With this option checked, colors will look as if they're not converted to the proofing space. With this option unchecked, Illustrator colors will appear as though converted, and you'll need to choose a **Rendering Intent** (see the sidebar). Click OK.

2. *Optional:* The Display Options (On-Screen) are available for some profiles. Simulate Paper Color simulates the soft white of actual paper, based on the current proof profile, and Simulate Black Ink simulates the dark gray that many printers produce when printing black.

3. Click OK.

4. View > **Proof Colors** will be checked automatically, allowing you to see the soft proof onscreen. Uncheck it when you're ready to turn off soft-proofing.

A Use the Proof Setup dialog to choose custom options for soft-proofing.

THE RENDERING INTENTS

► Perceptual changes colors in a way that seems natural to the human eye, while attempting to preserve the appearance of the overall document. This is a good choice for continuous-tone images.

► Saturation changes colors with the intent of preserving vivid colors but compromises color fidelity in order to do so. This is a good choice for charts and business graphics, which usually contain a limited number of colors.

► Absolute Colorimetric maintains color accuracy only of colors that fall within the destination color gamut (i.e., the color range of your printer), but in so doing sacrifices the accuracy of colors that are out of gamut.

► Relative Colorimetric, the default intent for all the Adobe presets in the Color Settings dialog, compares the white, or highlight, of your document's color space to the white of the destination color space (the white of the paper, in the case of a printer), shifting colors where needed. This is the best Rendering Intent choice for documents in which most of the colors fall within the color range of the destination gamut, because it preserves most of the original colors.

Illustrator CS4 includes new interface features, such as an Application bar and document tabs, which you will learn about in this chapter. You will also learn how to change document zoom levels, switch among multiple artboards, move an area of a document in view, change screen display modes, choose a document view (e.g., Preview, Outline), save and choose custom view settings, and save and manage custom workspaces. By the end of the chapter, you'll be equipped to configure your workspace to suit your usual workflow.

Features of the Illustrator workspace ★

Upon launching Illustrator, Mac OS users will notice something new right away: By default, a movable Application frame appears onscreen. In both the Mac OS and Windows, the Application frame houses the new Application bar and tabbed document windows, as well as the Control panel and all the other panels. A note to Windows users: We will also refer to the Windows application window as the "Application frame."

Document windows can be docked as tabs inside one window or can be left to float freely as in previous versions. We recommend that you give the new tabbed window format a try, and in the Mac OS, keep the new Application bar, Control panel, and other panels neatly ensconced inside the Application frame. The Application frame can be hidden in the Mac OS, **A** but not in Windows.

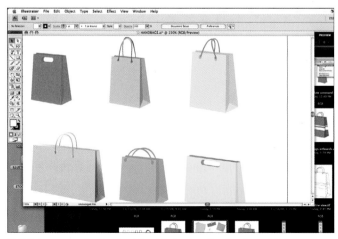

A This is a screen in the Mac OS, with the Appplication frame hidden.

The Application frame conveniently blocks out the Desktop and displays your artwork against a light gray background, which provides a good backdrop for color work. Without the frame, if your Desktop is cluttered or brightly colored, you'll have to spend time enlarging your document windows to hide the visual noise. Another advantage to using the Application frame is that in Normal Screen mode, the viewing area for your document resizes dynamically as you hide or show the panels or collapse or expand the panel docks.

➤ To minimize the Application frame in Windows, click the Minimize button; in the Mac OS, double-click the Application bar.

To show or hide the Application frame in the Mac OS: ★

To show the Application frame, check Window > **Application Frame**;A or to hide it, uncheck the command.

➤ You can resize the Application frame at any time by dragging an edge or corner.

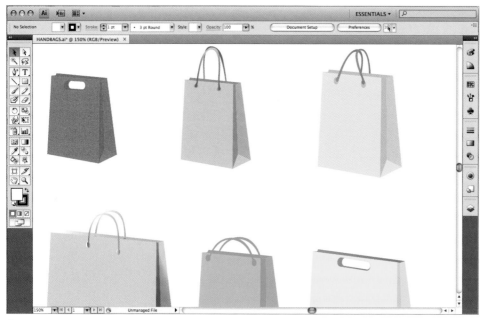

A In the Mac OS, we like to work with the Application frame showing.

To use the Application bar ★

Use the button and menus on the Application bar to manage your workspace.B If the Application bar is hidden in the Mac OS, choose Window > **Application Bar**. In Windows, the main Illustrator menus also display on the Application bar.

To search for info at Adobe.com and other websites, enter a word or phrase in the Search for Help field, then press Return/Enter.

Button for switching to Adobe Bridge | Arrange Documents menu for arranging multiple documents onscreen | The current workspace | Menu for accessing, saving, and deleting workspaces

B These controls are available on the Application bar in the Mac OS.

Using tabbed document windows ★

Whether you're a Windows or Mac OS user (with the Application frame showing or not), you can dock multiple open document windows as a series of tabs, and then display any document by clicking its tab. This will help keep them neatly organized and, best of all, readily accessible. If you become accustomed to working with the Application frame, you'll naturally want to dock your documents as tabs anyway.

To dock document windows as tabs:

Do any of the following:

To dock a document window manually, drag its title bar to the tab area (just below the Control panel) of the Application frame or just below the title bar of another floating document window, and release when the blue drop zone bar appears. **A**

If one or more documents are already docked as tabs and you want to dock all floating document windows into the Application frame or into the active document window, Control-click/right-click a tab and choose **Consolidate All to Here** from the context menu. **B** Or on the Arrange Documents menu ▦ on the Application bar, click the **Consolidate All** (first) icon. ▦

To set a preference so all future documents that you open dock as tabs automatically, go to Illustrator/Edit > Preferences > User Interface and check **Open Documents as Tabs**.

➤ To cycle among open documents, press Cmd-~/ Ctrl-Tab. To cycle among multiple artboards, see page 26.

To turn a tabbed document window into a floating one:

Do either of the following:

Control-click/right-click a document tab and choose **Move to New Window**. **C**

Drag a tab downward off the tab bar.

➤ We recommend that you not float any document windows when the Application frame is displayed—it defeats the whole point of using the frame.

➤ To resize a floating document window, drag any edge or corner of the window. Tabbed windows fit within the Application frame automatically.

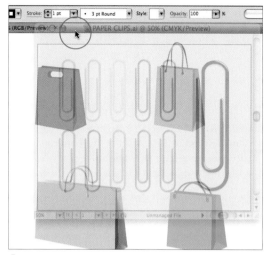

A To dock a floating document window as a tab manually, drag its title bar to the tab area of the Application frame (or just below the title bar of another document window), and release when the blue drop zone bar appears.

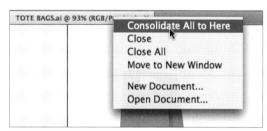

B To dock all open floating windows, Ctrl-click/right-click an existing document tab and choose Consolidate All to Here.

C Here, documents are docked as tabs in a floating window, whereas in the figure on the previous page, a document is docked in the Application frame.

Arranging document windows ★

By using icons on the Arrange Documents menu on the Application bar, you can quickly display multiple documents in various tabbed layouts, such as two documents side by side or top to bottom, or four or six documents in a grid formation.

To display multiple tabbed document windows:

On the Application bar, click the **Arrange Documents** menu icon ▦ to open the menu, release the mouse, then click one of the available icons (availability depends on how many documents are currently open).**A**

➤ If any open documents are floating when you choose an Arrange Documents option, they will be docked as tabbed windows.

Just as effortlessly, you can go to back to displaying one document at a time.

To redisplay one tabbed document window:

Do either of the following:

Control-click/right-click a tab and choose **Consolidate All to Here** from the context menu.

On the Arrange Documents menu ▦ on the Application bar, click the **Consolidate All** (first) icon.▦

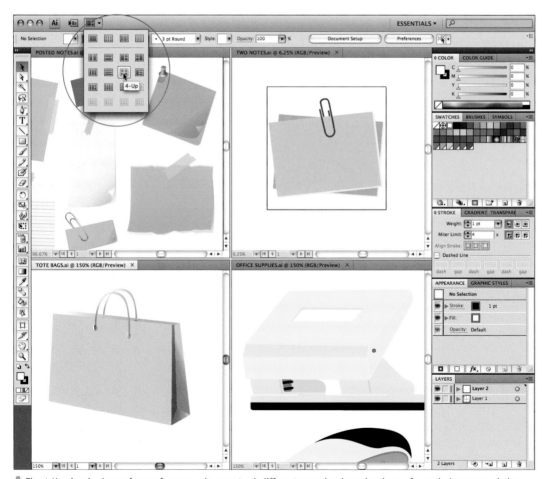

A The 4-Up view is chosen for our four open documents. A different zoom level can be chosen for each document window.

Changing zoom levels

By changing the zoom level for the document window, you can display multiple artboards, one artboard, or a magnified detail of your artwork. The current zoom level is listed as a percentage (3.13%–6400%) on the document tab or title bar and in the lower left corner of either the Application frame or a floating document window. ★ The zoom level doesn't affect the output size.

There are many ways to change the zoom level in a document. The fastest method is via the keyboard, because you can do it with any tool selected. Pick a few methods that you like, memorize them, and ignore the rest.

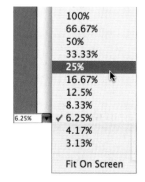

A Choose a preset percentage from the zoom menu in the lower left corner of the Application frame or document window.

To change the zoom level:

Do any of the following:

Use any of the shortcuts listed in the sidebar at right.

Make sure no objects are selected, then Control-click/right-click the document and choose Zoom In or Zoom Out.

Choose a preset percentage from the zoom menu in the lower left corner of the document window/Application frame.**A** Or choose Fit on Screen from the menu to fit the entire artboard within the current document window size.

Double-click the zoom field in the lower left corner of the document window/Application frame, type the desired zoom level, then press Return/Enter. To try out a zoom value without exiting the zoom field, press Shift-Return/Shift-Enter.

➤ To move a different part of your magnified artwork into view, see the next page.

➤ You can change the zoom level while the screen is redrawing.

➤ You can also change the zoom level or bring a different part of your document into view by using the Navigator panel, but there are faster methods, and after a while, we get kind of "paneled out."

SHORTCUTS FOR ZOOMING IN AND OUT

	Mac OS	Windows
Fit Artboard in Window	Cmd-0 (zero)	Ctrl-0 (zero)
Fit All in Window	Cmd-Option-0 (zero)	Ctrl-Alt-0 (zero)
Actual Size	Cmd-1	Ctrl-1
Zoom in	Cmd- + (plus) or Cmd-Spacebar click or drag	Ctrl- + (plus) or Ctrl-Spacebar click or drag
Zoom out	Cmd- – (minus) or Cmd-Option-Spacebar click	Ctrl- – (minus) or Ctrl-Alt-Spacebar click

USING THE ZOOM TOOL

Although the Zoom tool ⌕ (Z) might seem the most likely method for changing the zoom level, once you get accutomed to faster methods, such as the shortcuts listed above, you'll probably forgo using it. In any case, if you want to use it, choose it, then do any of the following:

➤ In the document window, click in the center of, or drag a marquee across, the area you want to magnify. The smaller the marquee you drag, the greater the degree of magnification.

➤ Option-click/Alt-click in the document window to reduce the zoom level.

➤ Drag a marquee and then, without releasing the mouse, press and hold down the Spacebar, move the marquee over the area you want to magnify, and release the mouse.

Switching among artboards

To simply activate an artboard, click anywhere on it with the Selection tool (V). The methods below fit the artboard you choose in the document window. You can switch among multiple artboards in your document just as you might navigate between pages in a layout program.

To switch among multiple artboards: ★

In the Artboard Navigation controls area in the lower left corner of the document window or Application frame, do either of the following:

From the **Artboard Navigation** menu, choose an artboard number.**A** The number of the currently displayed artboard is listed in the field.

Click the **First**, **Previous**, **Next**, or **Last** arrow.

The artboard you selected will zoom to fit in the document window.**B**

➤ The Artboard Navigation controls display in both normal document view and artboard editing mode (when the Artboard tool is selected).

➤ Artboards are numbered based on the sequence in which they are created. If you want your artboards to be numbered from left to right, create each new one to the right of or below the existing ones.

Moving an area of a document into view

To move a different area of a document into view:

Choose the **Hand** tool 🖐 (H) or hold down the Spacebar to turn another tool into a temporary Hand tool, and drag the illustration to the desired position.**C**

➤ You can also move the illustration by clicking any of the scroll arrows at the edge of the document window.

A Choose an artboard number from the Artboard Navigation menu.

C Spacebar-drag to move your magnified artwork in the document window.

B The chosen artboard displays in the document window.

Changing the screen mode

The three screen modes control the display of various Illustrator interface features.

To change screen modes: ★

Press F to cycle through the screen modes, or from the **Screen Mode** menu at the bottom of the Tools panel,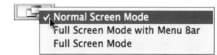 choose one of the following:

Normal Screen Mode  (the default mode) to display the Application frame (if turned on), menu bar, Application bar, document tabs, and panels, with the Desktop visible behind everything. This is the only mode in which a tabbed document window resizes dynamically as you hide or show the panels or resize a panel dock (in the Mac OS, when the Application frame is displayed).

A Choose from the Screen Mode menu at the bottom of the Tools panel.

Full Screen Mode with Menu Bar **C** to display the document in a maximized window with the menu bar, Application bar, scroll bars, and panels visible, but not the document tabs or document title bar (nor the Application frame, in the Mac OS).

Full Screen Mode to display the illustration in a maximized window with only the scroll bars visible, and the Application frame, menu bar, Application bar, document tabs, title bar, panels, and Dock/Taskbar hidden.

B In Normal Screen mode, we pressed Tab to hide all the panels, and the tabbed window enlarged automatically to fill the entire display. If we were to redisplay the panels (by pressing Tab), the window would shrink down to its former size.

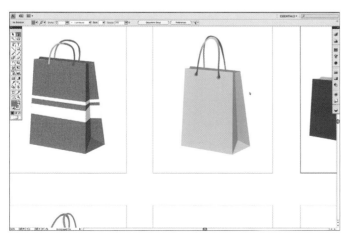

C This is Full Screen Mode with Menu Bar.

Switching views

A document can be displayed and edited in four different views: Preview, Outline, Pixel Preview, and Overprint Preview. In all views, the other View menu commands—Hide/Show Edges, Artboard, Print Tiling, Slices, Guides, and Grid—are accessible. (Overprint Preview view is discussed on page 387.)

To switch views:

Do any of the following:

From the View menu, choose **Preview A** to display objects with all their fill and stroke colors and all placed images, or choose **Outline** to display all objects as wireframes with no fill or stroke colors.**B** You can press Cmd-Y/Ctrl-Y to toggle between the two views. The screen redraws more quickly in Outline view.

Make sure no objects are selected (click a blank area), then Control-click/right-click in the document window and choose Outline or Preview.

To activate a 72-ppi preview for Web graphics, choose View > **Pixel Preview C** (or press

> **SNAPPING TO PIXELS**
>
> When you choose Pixel Preview view (and also View > Actual Size), you can get a good idea of what your vector graphics will look like if you rasterize them for the Web—but it's more than just a preview. When you choose this view, View > Snap to Pixel is turned on automatically, and edges of objects will snap to the nearest pixel edge as you move or reshape them. Snap to Pixel reduces the need for anti-aliasing and helps make the edges of objects look crisp. Note: Anti-aliasing adds pixels along the edges of objects to make them look smoother but can also diminish their crispness.

Cmd-Option-Y/Ctrl-Alt-Y), and also choose View > **Actual Size** (Cmd-1/Ctrl-1). See also the sidebar above.

➤ Cmd-click/Ctrl-click the visibility (eye) icon for a layer (not an individual object) on the Layers panel 👁 to toggle between Preview and Outline views for just that layer (see Chapter 13).

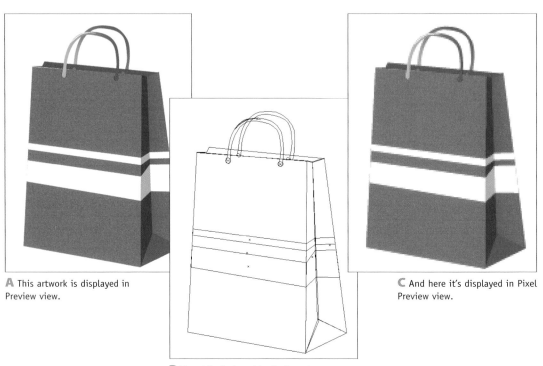

A This artwork is displayed in Preview view.

C And here it's displayed in Pixel Preview view.

B Here it's displayed in Outline view.

Creating custom views

You can save up to 25 custom views, and you can switch among them by using either the View menu or assigned shortcuts. Each custom view can include a zoom level, the display of a specific artboard, and a choice of Preview or Outline view.

To define a custom view:

1. Do all of the following:

   Choose a **zoom** level for your document.

   If the document contains multiple artboards, choose an **artboard** via the Artboard Navigation controls.★

   Put your illustration into **Preview** or **Outline** view (Cmd-Y/Ctrl-Y).

2. Choose View > **New View**. The New View dialog opens.**A**

3. In the Name field, type a descriptive name for the new view for easy identification (as in "160% view, Preview, Artboard 4").

4. Click OK. The view is now listed on, and can be chosen from, the bottom of the View menu.

➤ To assign a keyboard shortcut to a custom view, open the Edit > Keyboard Shortcuts dialog, choose Menu Commands from the menu, expand the listing for View, scroll down to the Custom View listings, and click one. Click in the Shortcut column, and press a keyboard combination that is not already in use.

To rename or delete a custom view:

1. Choose View > **Edit Views**.

2. In the Edit View dialog, click the view to be renamed or deleted.**B**

3. Do either of the following:

   Change the name in the **Name** field.

   Click **Delete** to delete the view.

4. Click OK. The View menu will update to reflect the changes.

➤ If you want to rename more than one view, you have to click OK and then reopen the dialog for each one. It's a primitive little system.

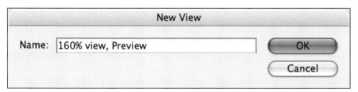

A Type a Name for a custom view in the New View dialog.

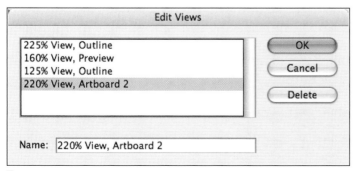

B In the Edit Views dialog, highlight a view, then change the Name or click Delete.

Configuring the panels

Most edits made in Illustrator require the use of one or more panels. Clever design features make the panels easy to store, expand, and collapse so they don't intrude on document space when you're not using them. Although such a flexible system may seem a bit complex at first, in no time the mechanics will become second nature to you. Note: The individual panels are illustrated in the next chapter.

Hide or show all the panels: Press Tab to hide or show all open panels, including the Tools panel, or press Shift-Tab to hide or show all the panels except the Tools panel.

Make hidden, docked panels reappear: ★ With the panels hidden as per the instructions in the preceding paragraph, move the pointer to the very edge of the Application frame or your monitor. The panel docks (but not freestanding panels) will redisplay temporarily. Move the pointer away from the panels, and they'll disappear again.

In the predefined workspaces (which are accessed from the Workspace menu on the Application bar), panels are arranged in docks on the right side of your screen **A**—except for the Tools panel, which is on the left side. Each dock can hold one or more panels or panel groups. Next, we'll show you how to reconfigure the panel groups and docks to suit your workflow.

Show or hide an individual panel: To show a panel, choose the panel name from the Window menu. The panel will display either in its default group and dock or in its last location. To bring a panel to the front of its group, click its tab (panel name). Some panels can also be shown or hidden via keyboard shortcuts, which are listed on the Window menu.

Show or hide an individual panel (icon): Click the icon or panel name. If Auto-Collapse Icon Panels is checked in Illustrator/Edit > Preferences > User Interface and you open a panel from an icon, it collapses back to the icon when you click elsewhere. With this preference unchecked, the panel stays expanded. To collapse a panel back to an icon, click the Collapse to Icons button ▐▶ on the panel bar, or click the panel icon.

Maximize or minimize a panel (non-icon) or group (to toggle the full panel to just a panel tab, or vice versa): Double-click the panel tab; or click the title bar (gray bar next to the panel tabs).

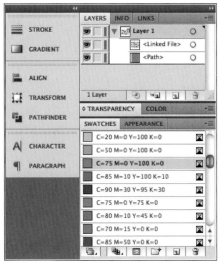

A Two docks are shown above. Panels in the left dock are collapsed to icons with names; panels in the right dock are expanded and are organized into three groups. The Transparency/Color group is minimized vertically.

B We clicked the Collapse to Icons button to collapse the whole right dock to icons. The panel groups were preserved.

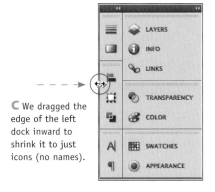

C We dragged the edge of the left dock inward to shrink it to just icons (no names).

Use a panel menu: Click the ⬛ icon to open a menu for whichever panel is in front in its particular group.

Close a panel or group: ★ To close (but not collapse) a panel, right-click/Control-click the panel tab and choose Close from the context menu. To close a whole panel group, choose Close Tab Group from the context menu. To close a group that's an icon, expand the dock first by clicking the Expand Panels button.⬛ (To reopen a closed panel, use the Window menu or shortcut.)

Collapse a whole dock to icons or to **icons with names:** Click the Collapse to Icons button ⬛ or the dark gray bar at the top of the dock (**B**, preceding page). To further collapse the dock to just icons (no names), drag the vertical edge of the dock inward horizontally (**C**, preceding page); to expand the dock, click the dark gray bar again.

Widen or narrow a dock and panels: Position the mouse over the vertical edge of the dock (⬌ cursor), then drag sideways.

Lengthen or shorten a panel or group (in the Mac OS, when the Application frame is hidden): Position the mouse over the bottom edge of the panel or group, and when you see this cursor,⬍ drag upward or downward. Panels in the same group will scale accordingly.

Move a panel to a different slot, same group: Drag the panel tab (name) to the left or right.

Move a panel to a different group: Drag the panel tab over the title bar of the desired group, and release when the blue drop zone border appears.**A**

Move a panel group upward or downward in a dock: Drag the title bar, and release the mouse when the horizontal blue drop zone bar appears in the desired location.**B**

Create a new dock: Drag a panel tab or title bar sideways over the vertical edge of the dock,**C** and release when you see the blue vertical drop zone bar.

Make a panel or group free-floating: Drag the panel tab, icon, or title bar out of the dock. You can stack free-floating panels and groups together from top to bottom.

Reconfigure a dock (icon): Use methods similar to those for an expanded group. Drag the group "title" bar (double dotted line) ⬛ to the edge of a dock to create a new dock; or drag the title bar

Continued on the following page

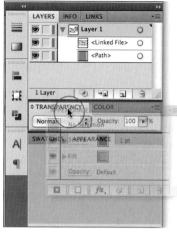

A A blue drop zone border appears as we drag a panel into a different group.

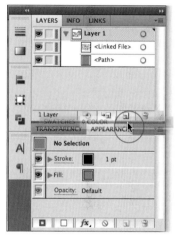

B A blue horizontal drop zone bar appears as we move a panel group upward within the same dock.

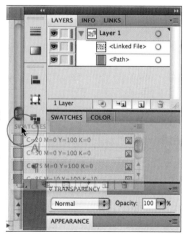

C A blue vertical drop zone bar appears as we drag a panel out of a dock and create a new dock for it.

between groups to restack it (look for a horizontal drop zone line); or drag the title bar into another group to combine it with that group (look for a blue drop zone border).**A–B**

➤ To reset the panels to their default locations and visibility states, choose Essentials from the Workspace menu on the Application bar.

➤ To redock floating panels into the Application frame, drag the dark gray bar at the top of the panel group to the right edge of the Application frame, and release when the mouse is at the edge and you see a vertical blue drop zone line.★

Choosing and saving workspaces

When you choose a predefined Illustrator workspace, panels and panel groups that are most suitable for a particular sphere of work appear onscreen. Among the specialty workspaces are Automation, Painting, Printing and Proofing, Typography, and Web. On the following page, you'll learn how to create and save your own workspaces.

To choose a predefined workspace: ★

From the **Workspace** menu on the Application bar, choose a predefined workspace.**C**

➤ The arrangement of panels on a computer with dual displays is saved as a single workspace. You could put all the panels in one display, or put the ones you use most often in one display and those you use less often in the other.

A A blue horizontal drop zone bar appears as we move the Gradient panel group upward into the Color/Swatches panel group.

B Now the Gradient panel is a member of the Color/Swatches/Gradient panel group.

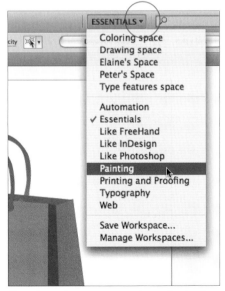

C On the Workspace menu on the Application bar, user-defined workspaces are listed first, followed by the preset workspaces.

If the predefined workspaces don't suit you, you can hide, show, collapse, or expand any of the panels or docks, or reconfigure the dock. Even better, instead of tediously repeating these steps each time you start a work session, save your custom settings as a workspace, then simply choose the saved workspace name from the Workspace menu on the Application bar. You can use any of the preset workspaces on the Workspace menu as a starting point, and save variations for each type of work you do.

To save a workspace:

1. Configure your workspace by doing any or all of the following:

   Position all the panels where you want them, including the Tools panel and any library panels (such as a PANTONE color book), in the desired groups and in the desired locations in the dock.

   Expand the panels that you use frequently in one dock, and collapse the ones you use less frequently to icons in another dock.

   Resize any of the panels, including any of the ones that open from the Control panel.

   Choose a **View** (thumbnail or swatch **size**) from any panel menu, including any that open from the Control panel. For example, you can choose a different View for the Swatches panel that opens from the Control panel than for the ones that open from the Window menu.

   Open any **tearoff toolbars** for tool groups that you use frequently (such as the toolbar for the type tools).

2. From the Workspace menu on the Application bar, choose **Save Workspace**. ★

3. In the Save Workspace dialog, 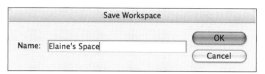 enter a Name for the workspace, such as your own name or a descriptive title.

4. Click OK. Your workspace (and any other user-saved workspaces) will be listed on, and can be chosen from, the Workspace menu on the Application bar.

A Type a name for your new workspace in the Save Workspace dialog.

To rename, delete, or duplicate a workspace:

1. From the Workspace menu on the Application bar, ★ choose **Manage Workspaces**.

2. In the Manage Workspaces dialog, **A** do any of the following:

   To **rename** a workspace, click the workspace name, then type the desired name in the field.

   To **duplicate** a workspace, click an existing workspace, then click the New Workspace button. Rename the duplicate workspace, if desired (a good idea).

   To **delete** a workspace, click the workspace name, then click the Delete Workspace button.

3. Click OK.

➤ If no workspaces are selected in the Manage Workspaces dialog when you click the New Workspace button, the new workspace will be based on the current state of your display, panels, etc.

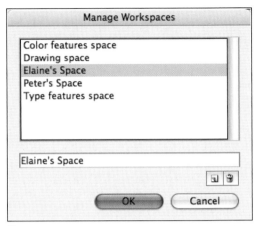

A Use the Manage Workspaces dialog to rename or delete your custom workspaces.

EDITING AN EXISTING WORKSPACE

If you want to edit an existing workspace, follow the instructions on the preceding page, except reenter the same name in the Save Workspace dialog. When the alert dialog appears, click Yes to overwrite the existing workspace.

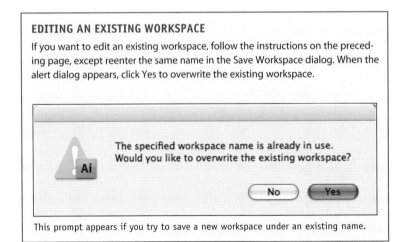

This prompt appears if you try to save a new workspace under an existing name.

This chapter will help you become more intimately acquainted with the Illustrator interface features that you will be using continually as you work: the panels. In the preceding chapter, you learned how to arrange them onscreen. Here, you will see what the individual panels look like and be introduced to the specific function of each one—from choosing color swatches (Swatches panel) to styling type (Character and Paragraph panels, among others), to editing layers (the Layers panel). Note: In-depth instructions for using specific panels are amply provided throughout this book.

You can read through this chapter with or without glancing at or fiddling with the panels onscreen, and then use it as a reference guide as you work. The panel icons are shown on the next page to help you identify them quickly. After that, you'll find instructions for using the Tools panel and a brief description of each tool, an introduction to the Control panel, then information about the other panels, in alphabetical order.

PANELS

4

IN THIS CHAPTER

CHOOSING VALUES IN PANELS AND DIALOGS

8 pt

Or choose a preset value from the menu.

Click the up or down arrow to change the value by one increment at a time.

Or enter a new value in the field.

▶ To change a value incrementally, click in a field in a panel or dialog, then press the up or down arrow key.

▶ To access a pop-up slider in a panel or dialog (e.g., to choose an Opacity percentage from the Control panel), click the arrowhead. To close a slider, click anywhere outside it or press Enter/Return. If you click an arrowhead to open a slider, then change your mind, you can press Esc to close it and restore the last chosen setting.

▶ You can change numerical values in some panels and dialogs quickly by using a scrubby slider: Drag slightly to the left or right over the option name or icon. Examples include controls on the Character and Paragraph panels and settings in the Effect Gallery.

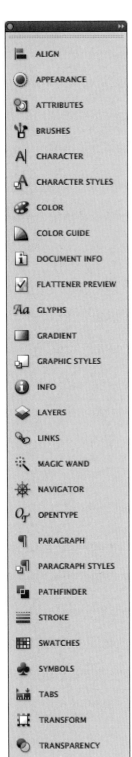

The Illustrator panel icons

Identifying the panel icons

A When collapsed, each panel has a unique icon.

Each panel in Photoshop has a unique icon. **A** Try to memorize the icons—at least the ones for the panels you use most often—so you'll be able to identify and access them quickly as you work.

USING THE CONTEXT MENUS

When you right-click/Control-click in the document window—depending on where you click and which tool happens to be selected—a menu of context-sensitive commands pops up onscreen. Many panel thumbnails, names, and features also have related context menus. If a command is available on a context menu (or can be executed quickly via a keyboard shortcut), we'll let you know, to spare you from having to trudge to the main menu bar.

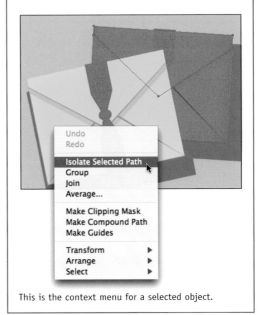

This is the context menu for a selected object.

The Tools panel

Using the Tools panel

The Tools panel contains 77 tools that are used for object creation and editing, as well as color controls and a screen mode menu. If the Tools panel is hidden, choose Window > Tools to display it. To move the Tools panel, drag the top (dark gray) bar.

Click once on a visible tool to select it, or click and hold on a tool that has a tiny arrowhead to choose a related tool from a pop-out menu. Some tools, such as the Paintbrush and Pencil tools, have a related options dialog box, which you can open by double-clicking the tool.

To create a standalone tearoff toolbar, **A–B** click the arrowhead, then release the mouse when it's over the vertical tearoff bar on the far right side of a tool pop-out menu. Move a tearoff toolbar by dragging its top bar. To restore a tearoff toolbar to the Tools panel, click its close box.

To access a tool quickly, use the assigned letter shortcut. They are listed in parentheses on the next two pages, as well as in the tool tips onscreen.* **C** Some tools can also be accessed temporarily via a toggle key. For example, pressing Cmd/Ctrl accesses a temporary Selection tool. You'll learn more tool toggles as you proceed through this book.

To turn tool pointers into a crosshair for precise positioning, go to Preferences > General and check Use Precise Cursors. Or if you prefer to turn the pointer into a crosshair temporarily, press the Caps Lock key and leave the preference off.

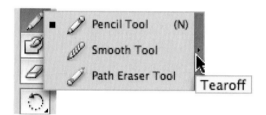

A Open a tearoff toolbar by choosing a tearoff bar.

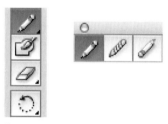

B A tearoff toolbar is created.

C Use tool tips to learn tool shortcuts.

HIDING AND SHOWING PANELS AND TOOLBARS	
Hide or show all currently open panels and tearoff toolbars, including the Tools panel.	Tab
Hide or show all currently open panels and tearoff toolbars, but not the Tools panel.	Shift-Tab

*If the tool tips aren't displaying, go to Illustrator/Edit > Preferences > General and check Show Tool Tips.

The Tools panel illustrated

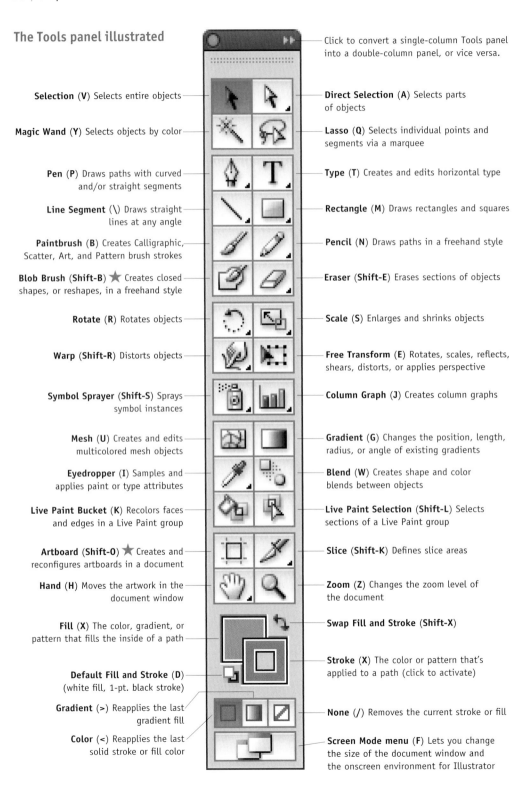

Click to convert a single-column Tools panel into a double-column panel, or vice versa.

Selection (V) Selects entire objects

Direct Selection (A) Selects parts of objects

Magic Wand (Y) Selects objects by color

Lasso (Q) Selects individual points and segments via a marquee

Pen (P) Draws paths with curved and/or straight segments

Type (T) Creates and edits horizontal type

Line Segment (\) Draws straight lines at any angle

Rectangle (M) Draws rectangles and squares

Paintbrush (B) Creates Calligraphic, Scatter, Art, and Pattern brush strokes

Pencil (N) Draws paths in a freehand style

Blob Brush (Shift-B) ★ Creates closed shapes, or reshapes, in a freehand style

Eraser (Shift-E) Erases sections of objects

Rotate (R) Rotates objects

Scale (S) Enlarges and shrinks objects

Warp (Shift-R) Distorts objects

Free Transform (E) Rotates, scales, reflects, shears, distorts, or applies perspective

Symbol Sprayer (Shift-S) Sprays symbol instances

Column Graph (J) Creates column graphs

Mesh (U) Creates and edits multicolored mesh objects

Gradient (G) Changes the position, length, radius, or angle of existing gradients

Eyedropper (I) Samples and applies paint or type attributes

Blend (W) Creates shape and color blends between objects

Live Paint Bucket (K) Recolors faces and edges in a Live Paint group

Live Paint Selection (Shift-L) Selects sections of a Live Paint group

Artboard (Shift-O) ★ Creates and reconfigures artboards in a document

Slice (Shift-K) Defines slice areas

Hand (H) Moves the artwork in the document window

Zoom (Z) Changes the zoom level of the document

Fill (X) The color, gradient, or pattern that fills the inside of a path

Swap Fill and Stroke (Shift-X)

Stroke (X) The color or pattern that's applied to a path (click to activate)

Default Fill and Stroke (D) (white fill, 1-pt. black stroke)

Gradient (>) Reapplies the last gradient fill

None (/) Removes the current stroke or fill

Color (<) Reapplies the last solid stroke or fill color

Screen Mode menu (F) Lets you change the size of the document window and the onscreen environment for Illustrator

The tearoff toolbars

Convert Anchor Point
Converts corner points
to smooth, and vice
versa (Shift-C)

Add Anchor Point (+) **Delete Anchor Point** (–)

DRAWING TOOLS

Polar Grid Creates circular grids

Arc Creates curved line segments **Spiral** Creates spiral lines **Rectangular Grid** Creates rectangular grids

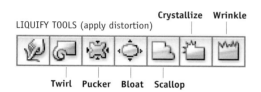

Reflect Creates a mirror image of an object (O)

Crystallize **Wrinkle**

LIQUIFY TOOLS (apply distortion)

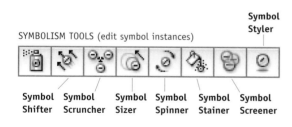

Twirl **Pucker** **Bloat** **Scallop**

Symbol Styler

SYMBOLISM TOOLS (edit symbol instances)

Symbol Shifter **Symbol Scruncher** **Symbol Sizer** **Symbol Spinner** **Symbol Stainer** **Symbol Screener**

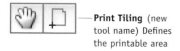

Measure Measures the distance between two points

Print Tiling (new tool name) Defines the printable area

Group Selection
Selects whole groups

TYPE TOOLS

Area Type Creates and edits type inside an object horizontally **Vertical Type** Creates and edits vertical type

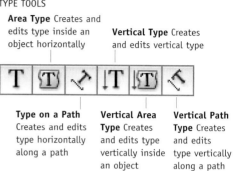

Type on a Path Creates and edits type horizontally along a path **Vertical Area Type** Creates and edits type vertically inside an object **Vertical Path Type** Creates and edits type vertically along a path

OBJECT CREATION TOOLS

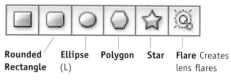

Rounded Rectangle **Ellipse** (L) **Polygon** **Star** **Flare** Creates lens flares

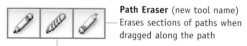

Path Eraser (new tool name) Erases sections of paths when dragged along the path

Smooth Smooths path segments

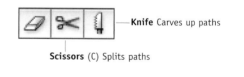

Knife Carves up paths

Scissors (C) Splits paths

Reshape Reshapes sections of paths

Shear Skews objects

GRAPH TOOLS

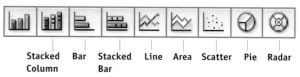

Stacked Column **Bar** **Stacked Bar** **Line** **Area** **Scatter** **Pie** **Radar**

Slice Select Selects slices (who knew!?)

The Control panel

The Control panel houses many frequently used controls conveniently under one roof, and changes contextually depending on what type of object is selected (a couple of variations are shown below). For example, you can use this panel to apply fill and stroke colors; change an object's opacity; apply basic type attributes, such as font and point size; align and distribute multiple objects; access controls for editing symbols, Live Trace, and Live Paint objects; and embed or edit linked images.

When no objects are selected, you can choose default fill, stroke, brush, style, and opacity settings for the current document, as well as quickly access the Document Setup dialog or Preferences dialog by clicking a button on the panel. ★

To move the Control panel to the top or bottom, respectively, of the Application frame or your screen, choose Dock to Top or Dock to Bottom from the panel menu at the right end of the panel. Or if you prefer to make the panel free-floating, drag the gripper bar on the far left side.

And finally, to control which options display on the panel, uncheck or check any of the items that are listed on the lower part of the panel menu.

OPENING TEMPORARY PANELS

► You can click a blue underlined word or letter on the Control panel to open a related panel. For example, clicking Stroke opens a temporary Stroke panel, and clicking Opacity opens a temporary Transparency panel.

► Click the stroke or fill color square on the Control panel to open a temporary Swatches panel, or Shift-click either square to open a temporary Color panel.

► You can open other temporary panels by clicking a thumbnail or arrowhead. For example, clicking the Brush thumbnail or arrowhead opens a temporary Brushes panel, and clicking the Style thumbnail or arrowhead opens a temporary Graphic Styles panel.

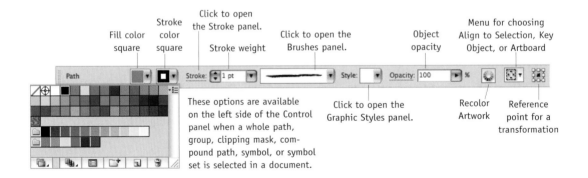

Fill color square | Stroke color square | Click to open the Stroke panel. | Stroke weight | Click to open the Brushes panel. | Object opacity | Menu for choosing Align to Selection, Key Object, or Artboard

These options are available on the left side of the Control panel when a whole path, group, clipping mask, compound path, symbol, or symbol set is selected in a document.

Click to open the Graphic Styles panel.

Recolor Artwork | Reference point for a transformation

Horizontal and vertical location of selected object, relative to the reference point | Width of selected object | Maintain Aspect Ratio | Height of selected object

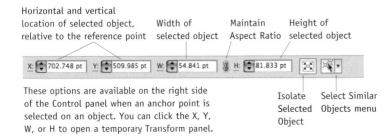

These options are available on the right side of the Control panel when an anchor point is selected on an object. You can click the X, Y, W, or H to open a temporary Transform panel.

Isolate Selected Object | Select Similar Objects menu

The other panels illustrated

Align panel 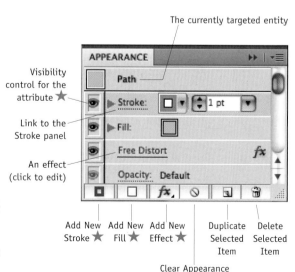 Shift-F7

Buttons on the top two rows of the Align panel let you align and/or distribute two or more objects along their centers or along their top, left, right, or bottom edges. Buttons at the bottom of the panel let you redistribute (equalize) the spacing between three or more objects. Align buttons also appear on the Control panel when multiple objects are selected.

SHOWING OR HIDING EXTRA OPTIONS

Some panels have extra options, which you can display or show by clicking the double arrow on the panel tab.

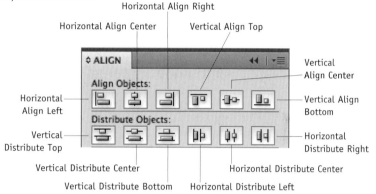

Horizontal Align Right

Horizontal Align Center

Vertical Align Top

Vertical Align Center

Horizontal Align Left

Vertical Align Bottom

Vertical Distribute Top

Horizontal Distribute Right

Vertical Distribute Center

Horizontal Distribute Center

Vertical Distribute Bottom

Horizontal Distribute Left

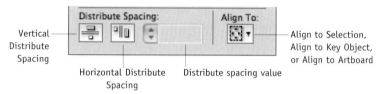

Vertical Distribute Spacing

Align to Selection, Align to Key Object, or Align to Artboard

Horizontal Distribute Spacing

Distribute spacing value

Appearance panel 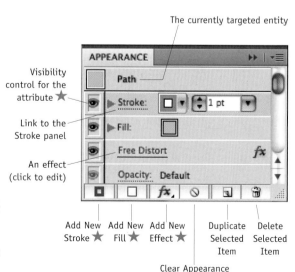 Shift-F6

Appearance attributes are an object's fill color, stroke color, Stroke panel settings, effects, and Transparency panel settings. The Appearance panel lists every appearance attribute and its specific settings for the layer, group, or object that is currently targeted on the Layers panel. You can use the panel to edit or remove existing attributes, add extra fill or stroke attributes, apply effects, and edit the attributes of a graphic style (in conjunction with the Graphic Styles panel).

The new in-panel editing feature lets you edit attributes quickly. For example, if you click a link (blue underlined word), a related panel opens temporarily: Click Stroke to open the Stroke panel, Opacity to open the Transparency panel, or the name of an effect to open its dialog. You can also click the stroke or fill color square, then click the thumbnail or arrowhead to open the Swatches panel, or Shift-click it to open the Color panel.

The currently targeted entity

Visibility control for the attribute ★

Link to the Stroke panel

An effect (click to edit)

Add New Stroke ★

Add New Fill ★

Add New Effect ★

Duplicate Selected Item

Delete Selected Item

Clear Appearance

Attributes panel 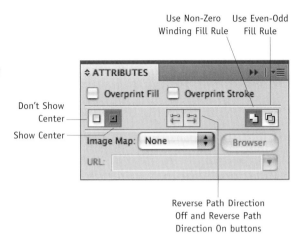 Cmd-F11/Ctrl-F11

The "catchall" Attributes panel lets you choose overprint options for an object, show or hide an object's center point, switch the fill between color and transparency in a compound path, change an object's fill rule, choose a shape for an image map area, and enter a Web address for an object to designate it as a hot point on an image map. Click Browser to launch the currently installed Web browser.

Brushes panel 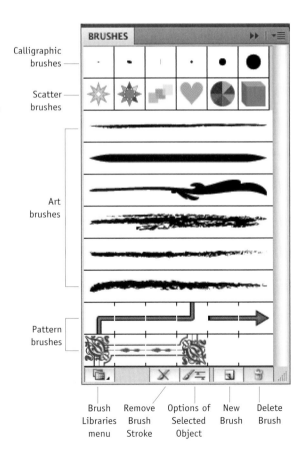 F5

Four varieties of decorative brushes can be applied to paths: Calligraphic, Scatter, Art, and Pattern. You can do this either by choosing the Paintbrush tool and a brush and then drawing a shape, or by applying a brush to an existing path.

To personalize your brush strokes, you can create and edit your own brushes. And brushes are live: If you modify a brush that's being used in a document, you'll be given the option via an alert dialog to update the paths with the revised brush. Brushes on the Brushes panel save with the current document.

To open a temporary Brushes panel, click the Brush thumbnail or arrowhead on the Control panel.

Character panel Cmd-T/Ctrl-T

Use the Character panel to apply type attributes: font, font style, font size, leading, kerning, tracking, horizontal scale, vertical scale, baseline shift, character rotation, underline, and strikethrough. The panel also lets you select a language for hyphenation. To choose values on the panel, see the sidebar on page 35.

When a type tool is selected, the Control panel also provides some basic type controls (see below), and a temporary Character panel opens if you click Character on the Control panel.

SHORTCUTS FOR SHOWING THE TYPE PANELS

Seven Illustrator panels are used for formatting type: Character, Character Styles, Glyphs, OpenType, Paragraph, Paragraph Styles, Tabs. Open them via the Window > Type submenu, or for quick access to any of the four listed below, use its assigned shortcut.

	Mac OS	Windows
Character	Cmd-T	Ctrl-T
OpenType	Cmd-Option-Shift-T	Ctrl-Alt-Shift-T
Paragraph	Cmd-Option-T	Ctrl-Alt-T
Tabs	Cmd-Shift-T	Ctrl-Shift-T

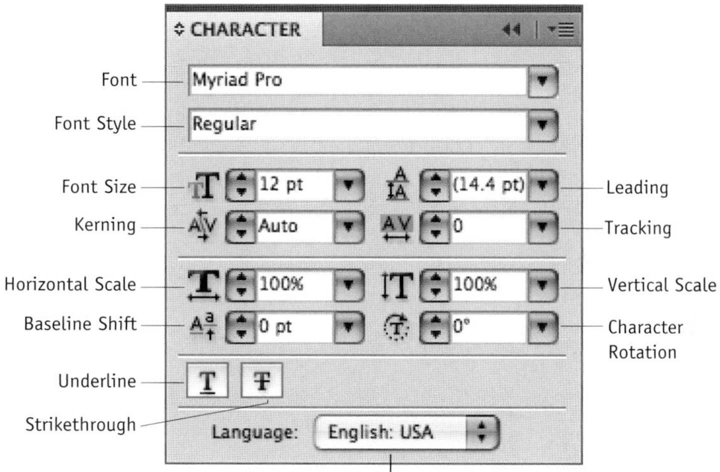

Hyphenation Language for the current document

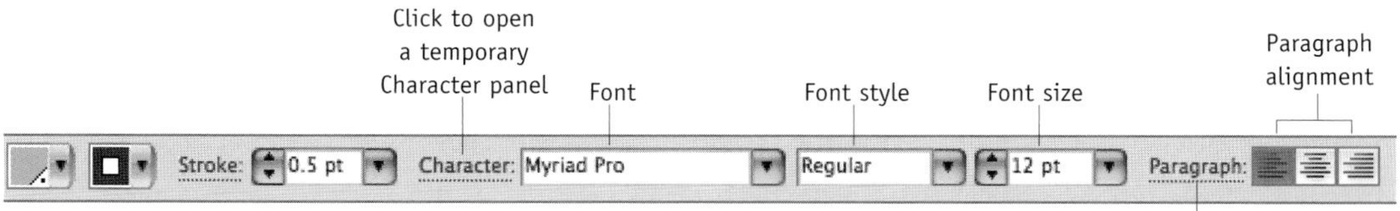

These controls (among others) appear on the Control panel when type or a type object is selected.

Character Styles panel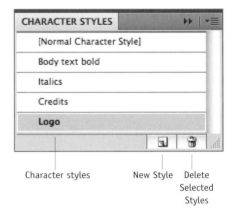

A character style is a collection of character settings, including font, font style, font size, leading, tracking, and kerning. Unlike paragraph styles, which apply to whole paragraphs, character styles are used to quickly format small bits of type—such as bullets, boldfaced words, italicized words, or large initial caps—to distinguish them from the main text. When you edit a character style, any text that it's associated with updates accordingly. The Character Styles panel lets you create, apply, edit, store, duplicate, and delete styles. (Compare with the Paragraph Styles panel on page 50.)

Character styles · New Style · Delete Selected Styles

Color panel ☕ F6

Use the Color panel to remix global process or spot color tints, choose Web-safe colors, or switch between the current fill and stroke colors. Choose a color model for the panel, such as RGB or CMYK, from the panel menu. Quick-select a color, black, white, or None from the spectrum bar at the bottom of the panel. To open a temporary Color panel, Shift-click the fill or stroke color square or arrowhead on the Control panel or Appearance panel.

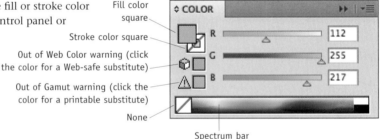

Fill color square

Stroke color square

Out of Web Color warning (click the color for a Web-safe substitute)

Out of Gamut warning (click the color for a printable substitute)

None

Spectrum bar

Color Guide panel ▨ Shift-F3

Use the Color Guide panel to generate variations (harmonies) of the current color. As is the case with the Swatches panel, you can click a color variation to apply it to selected objects. You can also save variations from the Color Guide panel as a group to the Swatches panel.

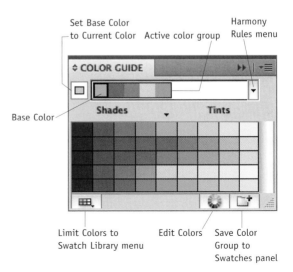

Set Base Color to Current Color · Active color group · Harmony Rules menu

Base Color

Limit Colors to Swatch Library menu · Edit Colors · Save Color Group to Swatches panel

Document Info panel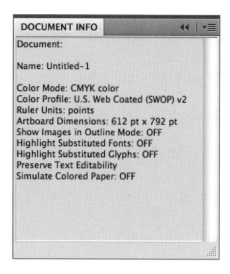

Like the Info panel, the Document Info panel is noninteractive. It merely lists information about artwork in your document, depending on the category chosen on the panel menu: Document (all data), or individual Objects, Brushes, Gradient Objects, Fonts, Linked Images, or Embedded Images, etc. With Selection Only chosen, the panel lists only data pertaining to the currently selected object.

Flattener Preview panel

Artwork that contains semitransparent objects will require flattening before it is output to print. Using the Highlight options in the Flattener Preview panel, you can preview which objects in your document will be affected by flattening, adjust the flattening settings, then click Refresh to preview the effect of the new settings in your artwork.

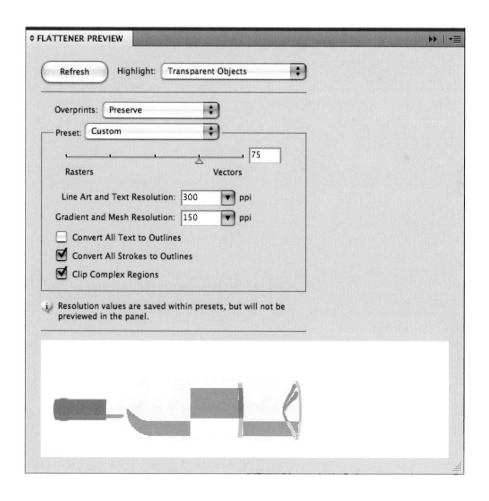

Glyphs panel

By using the Glyphs panel, you can find out which character variations (alternate glyphs) are available for any given character in a specific OpenType font and insert glyphs from that font into your text (including those that can't be inserted via the keyboard).

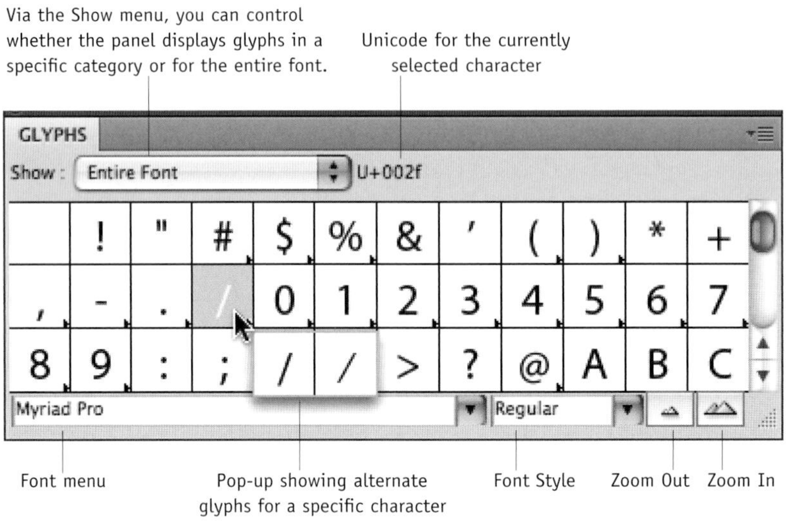
Via the Show menu, you can control whether the panel displays glyphs in a specific category or for the entire font.
Unicode for the currently selected character
GLYPHS
Show :
Entire Font
U+002f
Myriad Pro
Regular
Font menu
Pop-up showing alternate glyphs for a specific character
Font Style
Zoom Out
Zoom In

Gradient panel Cmd-F9/Ctrl-F9

Use the Gradient panel to apply, create, and edit gradients, which are soft blends between two or more colors. You can adjust the amount of a color by dragging its stop, choose a different color or opacity value for a selected stop, click below the gradient slider to add new colors, move a midpoint diamond to change the location where two adjacent colors are mixed equally, reverse the gradient colors, or change the overall gradient type or angle. For a radial gradient, you can also change the aspect ratio to make the gradient more oval or more round.

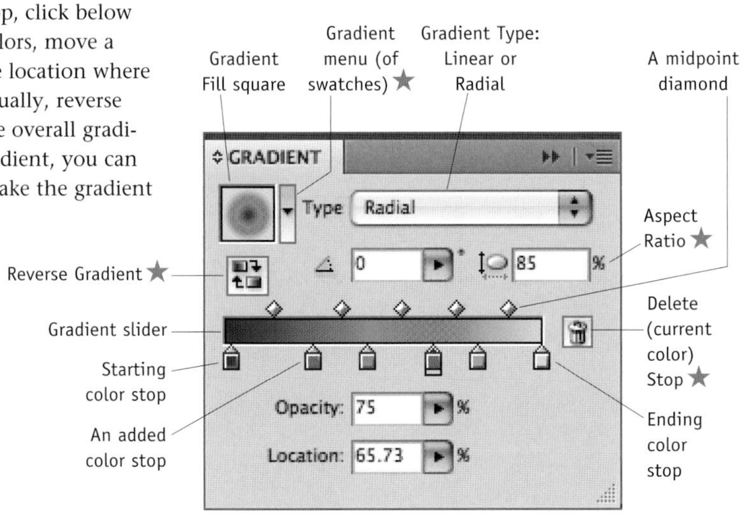
Gradient Fill square
Gradient menu (of swatches) ★
Gradient Type: Linear or Radial
A midpoint diamond
GRADIENT
Type
Radial
Aspect Ratio ★
Reverse Gradient ★
Gradient slider
Starting color stop
An added color stop
Delete (current color) Stop ★
Ending color stop
Opacity: 75 %
Location: 65.73 %
0
85 %

Graphic Styles panel 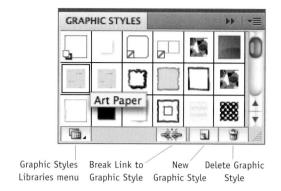 Shift-F5

The Graphic Styles panel lets you store and apply collections of appearance attributes, such as multiple solid-color and pattern fills, multiple strokes, transparency and overprint settings, blending modes, brush strokes, and effects. Like paragraph styles for type, graphic styles let you apply attributes quickly and with consistency. To open a temporary Graphic Styles panel, click the Style thumbnail or arrowhead on the Control panel.

Graphic Styles Libraries menu   Break Link to Graphic Style   New Graphic Style   Delete Graphic Style

Info panel 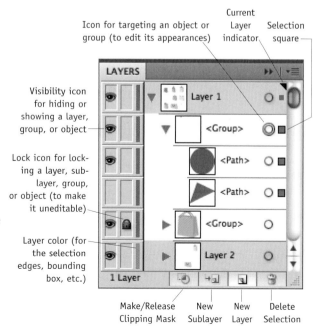 Cmd-F8/Ctrl-F8

If no objects are selected in the current document, the Info panel lists the horizontal and vertical location of the pointer in the document window (for most tools). When an object is selected, the panel lists the location of the object relative to the ruler origin, its width and height, and color data about its fill and stroke. When a type tool and type object are selected, the panel displays type specifications. The Info panel opens automatically when the Measure tool is used and lists the distance and angle the tool has calculated.

Horizontal (X) and Vertical (Y) location of the currently selected object

Object Width (W) and Height (H)

Fill info (color breakdown, or the pattern or gradient name)

Stroke info (color breakdown, or the pattern name)

Layers panel F7

The indispensable Layers panel lets you add and delete layers and sublayers from a document. You can also use this panel to select, restack, duplicate, delete, hide or show, lock, unlock, merge, change the view for, create a clipping set for, or target a layer, sublayer, group, or individual object. When your artwork is finished, it can be flattened into one layer, or objects can be released to separate layers for export as a Flash animation.

Icon for targeting an object or group (to edit its appearances)

Current Layer indicator

Selection square

Visibility icon for hiding or showing a layer, group, or object

Lock icon for locking a layer, sublayer, group, or object (to make it uneditable)

Layer color (for the selection edges, bounding box, etc.)

Make/Release Clipping Mask   New Sublayer   New Layer   Delete Selection

Links panel

When you place an image into an Illustrator document, you can either embed the image into the file (and thereby increase the file size) or merely link the image to the file. The Links panel lets you monitor the status of linked images, relink to a missing image, open a linked image in its original application, update a modified image, and convert a linked image to an embedded one.

You can also embed a linked image by clicking the Embed button on the Control panel, or edit it in its original application by clicking the Edit Original button.

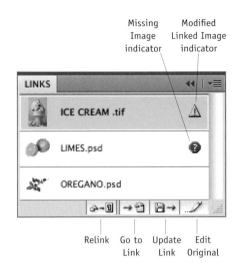

Missing Image indicator

Modified Linked Image indicator

Relink   Go to Link   Update Link   Edit Original

Magic Wand panel

The Magic Wand tool selects objects that have the same or similar fill color, stroke color, stroke weight, opacity, or blending mode as the currently selected object. Using the Magic Wand panel, you can choose parameters for the tool. The Tolerance is the range within which the tool selects objects containing that attribute. For example, if you were to check Opacity, choose an opacity Tolerance of 10%, then select an object that has an opacity of 50%, the tool would find and select objects in the document that have an opacity of 40%–60%.

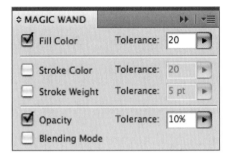

Navigator panel

The Navigator panel has two functions: It lets you move an illustration in the document window, and it lets you change the document zoom level. In addition to using the zoom controls at the bottom of the panel, you can also drag or click in the proxy preview area to move the illustration in the document window, or Cmd-drag/Ctrl-drag in the proxy preview area to zoom that area into view.

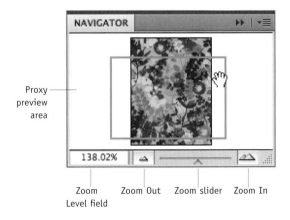

Proxy preview area

Zoom Level field   Zoom Out   Zoom slider   Zoom In

OpenType panel O_T
Cmd-Option-Shift-T/Ctrl-Alt-Shift-T

Among the Roman OpenType font families that ship with Illustrator, the fonts that contain an expanded character set with a large assortment of alternate glyphs are labeled "Pro." By clicking a button on the OpenType panel, you can specify which alternate characters (glyphs) will appear in your text when you type the appropriate key(s), such as ligatures, swashes, titling characters, stylistic alternates, ordinals, and fractions. You can also use the panel to specify options for numerals, such as a style (e.g., tabular lining or oldstyle) and a position (e.g., numerator, denominator, superscript, or subscript).

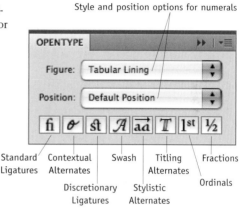

Style and position options for numerals

Standard Ligatures · Contextual Alternates · Swash · Titling Alternates · Fractions

Discretionary Ligatures · Stylistic Alternates · Ordinals

Paragraph panel ¶ Cmd-Option-T/Ctrl-Alt-T

Use the Paragraph panel to apply specifications that affect entire paragraphs, including horizontal alignment, indentation, space before or after paragraphs, and automatic hyphenation. Via the panel menu, you can also choose hanging punctuation, justification, hyphenation, and composer options. (The Left, Center, and Right alignment buttons are also available on the Control panel when a type object is selected.) To open a temporary Paragraph panel, click Paragraph on the Control panel.

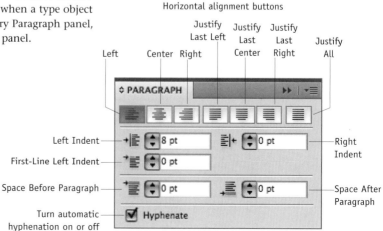

Horizontal alignment buttons

Left · Center · Right · Justify Last Left · Justify Last Center · Justify Last Right · Justify All

Left Indent
First-Line Left Indent
Space Before Paragraph
Turn automatic hyphenation on or off

Right Indent
Space After Paragraph

Paragraph Styles panel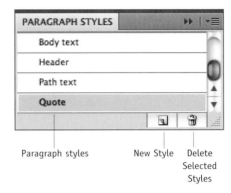

A paragraph style is a collection of paragraph specifications (including horizontal alignment, indentation, space before paragraph, word spacing, letter spacing, hyphenation, and hanging punctuation), plus character attributes, such as the font and font size. When you apply a paragraph style to selected paragraphs, the type is reformatted according to the specifications in that style. When you edit a paragraph style, the type it's assigned to updates accordingly. Using paragraph (and character) styles, you can typeset text more easily and quickly, and they also enable you to keep the formatting consistent throughout your document. You'll use this panel to create, apply, edit, store, duplicate, and delete paragraph styles.

Pathfinder panel
Cmd-Shift-F9/Ctrl-Shift-F9

The Shape Mode buttons on the top row of the Pathfinder panel create nonoverlapping paths or editable, flexible compound shapes from multiple selected objects. (The buttons have new names and a new default function in Illustrator CS4.) The Expand button converts a compound shape into either a path or a compound path (the latter if the Pathfinder command produced a cutout shape). The Pathfinder buttons on the bottom row of the Pathfinder panel produce flattened, cut-up shapes from multiple selected objects.

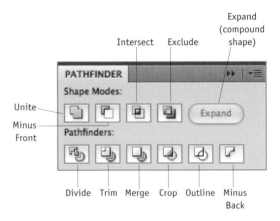

Separations Preview panel

The Separations Preview panel lets you see how the C, M, Y, and K color components in a CMYK document will separate to individual printing plates during the commercial printing process. You can use the panel to check that a color is properly set to knock out colors beneath it in the artwork, or to check whether a color is properly set to overprint on top of the other colors. You can monitor the use of spot colors in the artwork and verify that any spot color is set to knock out colors beneath it. And you can determine whether a specific black is a rich black (a mixture of C, M, Y, and K inks) or a simple black comprised of only the K component.

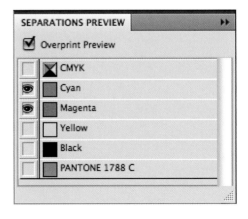

Stroke panel ≣ Cmd-F10/Ctrl-F10

The stroke attributes affect how the path (edge) of an object looks. By using the Stroke panel, you can change the stroke weight, the cap (end) and join (bend) styles, and the alignment on selected objects, and you can also create dashed lines or borders. To open a temporary Stroke panel, click Stroke on the Control or Appearance panel.

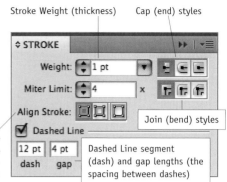

Stroke Weight (thickness)   Cap (end) styles

Join (bend) styles

Align Stroke to Center, Align Stroke to Inside, or Align Stroke to Outside (of the path)

Dashed Line segment (dash) and gap lengths (the spacing between dashes)

Swatches panel ▦

Use the Swatches panel to choose and store default and user-defined solid colors, patterns, gradients, and color groups to be applied to objects in your artwork. If you click a swatch, it becomes the current fill or stroke color, depending on whether the fill or stroke square is currently active on the Tools panel and Color panels.

Double-click a swatch to open the Swatch Options dialog, where you can change the swatch name or change the color type to global process, nonglobal process, or spot. Via the panel menu, you can merge swatches and perform other tasks. To open a temporary Swatches panel, click the fill or stroke square or arrowhead on the Control or Appearance panel.

A nonglobal process color

A spot color

A global process color

A color group

Swatch Libraries menu   Show Swatch Kinds menu   Swatch Options   New Color Group   New Swatch   Delete Swatch

Symbols panel ♣ Cmd-Shift-F11/Ctrl-Shift-F11

Using symbols (Illustrator objects that are stored on the Symbols panel), you can quickly and easily create a complex collection of objects, such as a bank of trees or clouds. To create one instance of a symbol, you simply drag from the Symbols panel onto the artboard; to create multiple instances quickly, you use the Symbol Sprayer tool.

The other symbolism tools let you change the proximity (density), position, stacking order, size, rotation, transparency, color tint, or graphic style of multiple symbol instances in a symbol set. When you use these tools, the link to the original symbol is maintained. If you edit the original symbol, all instances of that symbol in the document update automatically. Symbols on the panel are available for use in any document.

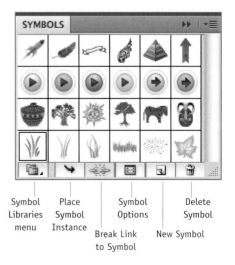

Symbol Libraries menu   Place Symbol Instance   Symbol Options   Delete Symbol

Break Link to Symbol   New Symbol

Tabs panel 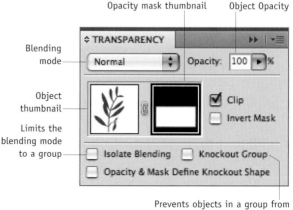 Cmd-Shift-T/Ctrl-Shift-T

If you want to create columns of text that align perfectly, regardless of the current font or font size, you must use tabs. By using the Tabs panel, you can insert, move, and change the alignment for custom tab markers (tab stops), as well as specify optional leader and align-on characters.

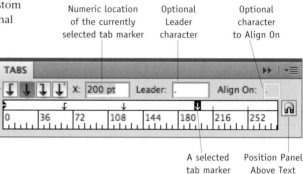

Numeric location of the currently selected tab marker

Optional Leader character

Optional character to Align On

Left-, Center-, Right-, and Decimal-Justified alignment buttons for horizontal type (or Top-, Center-, and Bottom-Justified buttons for vertical type)

A selected tab marker

Position Panel Above Text

Transform panel 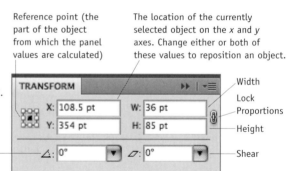 Shift-F8

The Transform panel displays location, width, and height information about the currently selected object. You can use the panel to move, scale, rotate, or shear a selected object or objects from a reference point of your choosing. To open a temporary Transform panel, click the X, Y, W, or H on the Control panel (or click the word "Transform," if those fields aren't displayed). A reference point icon and X, Y, W, and H fields also appear on the Control panel when one or more paths are selected.

Reference point (the part of the object from which the panel values are calculated)

The location of the currently selected object on the *x* and *y* axes. Change either or both of these values to reposition an object.

Width

Lock Proportions

Height

Rotate

Shear

Opacity mask thumbnail

Object Opacity

Transparency panel
Cmd-Shift-F10/Ctrl-Shift-F10

You can use the Transparency panel to change the blending mode or opacity of any layer, group, or individual object. To open a temporary Transparency panel, click Opacity on the Control or Appearance panel.

The Make Opacity Mask command on the panel menu generates an editable opacity mask, which hides parts of a layer or group. This technique isn't covered in this book.

You can also change the opacity of an object via the Control panel.

Blending mode

Object thumbnail

Limits the blending mode to a group

Prevents objects in a group from showing through one another

In this chapter, you will open files via the Open command and via Bridge, a separate application that serves as a conduit among Adobe Creative Suite programs. You'll also learn how to customize the Bridge window and use it to preview, open, label, rate, group, find, rename, delete, move, copy, and assign keywords to files.

Opening files from Illustrator

You can follow the instructions on this page to open Illustrator files using the Open command in Illustrator. Or if you'd prefer to use Bridge to open files—as we do and recommend—turn the page and start reading from there. (To learn how to import files from other programs into Illustrator, see Chapter 22.)

To open a file from Illustrator:

1. Do either of the following:

Choose File > **Open** (Cmd-O/Ctrl-O).

If you've just launched Illustrator and the Adobe Illustrator CS4 welcome screen is displaying, click **Open**.

2. In the Mac OS, to list files only in the formats that Illustrator can read, choose Enable: All Readable Documents; in Windows, to list all files, readable and not, choose Files of Type: All Formats, or choose a specific format.

3. Locate and click a file name, then click Open. If an alert dialog about a color profile appears, see the sidebar on page 16; for the Font Problems dialog, see the first step 3 on page 60; and for an alert dialog about imported images, see page 283.

➤ To reopen a recently opened file, choose it from the File > Open Recent Files submenu.

➤ If you open an Illustrator CS3 document that contains crop areas, those areas will be converted to artboards in CS4. You may be prompted to specify how the crop areas are to be converted.

To open a file from the Macintosh Desktop or Windows Explorer:

Double-click the icon for an Illustrator file. The file name will include one of the following extensions: .ai, .eps. ait., .pdf., .fxg, .svgz, or .svg.

In the Mac OS, you can also open a file by dragging its icon over the Adobe Illustrator CS4 appplication icon on the Dock.

Illustrator will launch if it isn't already running.

BRIDGE

5

Launching Bridge

The Bridge application is available to any Adobe Creative Suite program. Its excellent navigation controls and large thumbnail previews make locating and opening files a snap. Bridge also includes many other useful features, such as the ability to organize file thumbnails into collections and collapsible stacks, assign keywords to files, and view file data (metadata). You don't need to master all the Bridge features at once. Learn the basics in the first half of this chapter, then explore additional features when the mood or need arises.

To launch Bridge:

Do one of the following:

On the Application bar in Illustrator, click the **Go to Bridge** button Br (Cmd-Option-O/Ctrl-Alt-O).

In Applications/Adobe Bridge CS4 in the Mac OS or in Program Files\Adobe\Adobe Bridge CS4 in Windows, double-click the **Bridge** application icon. Br

In the Mac OS, click the **Bridge** icon Br on the **Dock**.

Features of the Bridge window

First, we'll identify the main sections of the Bridge window, starting from the top (**A**, next page). The two rows of buttons and menus running across the top of the window are collectively called the "toolbar." The second row of the toolbar is also called the "Path bar." ★ In the default workspace, the main window is divided into three panes: a large pane in the center and a vertical pane on either side. Each pane contains one or more panels, which are accessed via tabs: Favorites, Folders, Filter, Collections, Content, Preview, Metadata, and Keywords. Panels in the side panes let you manage files, filter the display of thumbnails, and display file data; the large central panel displays file thumbnails. You can hide, show, or resize any of the panels or move any panel into a different pane. And finally, at the bottom of the Bridge window are controls for changing the thumbnail size and configuration.

The following is a brief description of the individual panels.

The **Favorites** panel displays a list of folders that you've designated as favorites, for quick and easy access (see the sidebar on page 59).

The **Folders** panel contains a scrolling window with a hierarchical listing of all the top-level and nested folders on your hard drive (see page 58).

By clicking various listings in the **Filter** panel on or off, you can control which files in the current folder display in the Content panel (see page 68).

The **Collections** panel displays the names (and folder icons) for collections, which are user-created groups of image thumbnails. ★ Like many Bridge features, collections are useful for organizing and helping you locate files (see pages 65–66).

In the center pane of the Bridge window, the **Content** panel displays thumbnails for files (and, optionally, for nested folders) within the current folder. In the lower right corner of the Bridge window, you can click a View Content button to control whether, and in what format, metadata displays in the Content panel. ★ The Content panel is used and illustrated throughout this chapter.

The **Preview** panel displays a large preview of the currently selected file (or folder) thumbnail. If you select a video file, the Preview panel will display a controller for playing the video. If you select a multipage PDF file, you can click the Next Page or Previous Page button to preview pages in the file. You can also cycle through multiple artboards in a file, or preview multiple selected thumbnails, to compare them (see pages 56–59).

Detailed information about the currently selected file displays in two locations in the **Metadata** panel: a quick summary in the placard at the top and detailed listings in categories below. The File Properties category, for example, lists such data as the file name, format, date created, and date modified. To expand or collapse a category, click the arrowhead. You can use the IPTC Core category in the Metadata panel to attach creator, description, copyright, and other information to the currently selected file. Click the field next to a listing, enter or modify the file description information, press Tab to cycle through and edit other data, then click the Apply button ◼ in the lower right corner. For a closeup of this panel, see the sidebar on page 59; see also Bridge Help.

Use the **Keywords** panel to assign descriptive keywords to files, such as an event, name, location, or other criteria. You can find file thumbnails via a keyword search, or display files based on keywords by using the Filter panel (see pages 68–69).

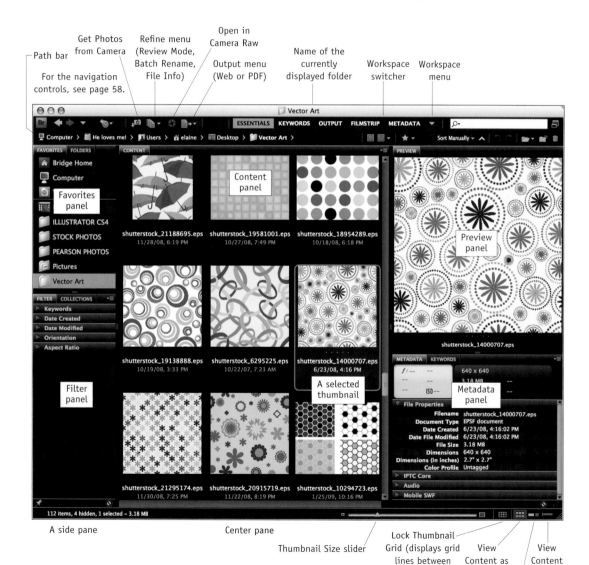

Browse Quickly
by Preferring
Embedded Images

Thumbnail
Quality and
Preview menu

Filter Items
by Rating
menu

Sort By
menu

Rotate
selected
thumbnails

Open
Recent
File menu

Create
a New
Folder

Descending Order/
Ascending Order

Get Photos
from Camera

Refine menu
(Review Mode,
Batch Rename,
File Info)

Open in
Camera Raw

Output menu
(Web or PDF)

Name of the
currently
displayed folder

Workspace
switcher

Workspace
menu

Path bar

For the navigation
controls, see page 58.

Content
panel

Favorites
panel

Preview
panel

Filter
panel

A selected
thumbnail

Metadata
panel

A side pane

Center pane

Thumbnail Size slider

Lock Thumbnail
Grid (displays grid
lines between
full thumbnails)

View
Content as
Thumbnails

View
Content
as List

View Content as Details

A Features of the Bridge window are identified above.
You'll learn their function throughout this chapter.

Choosing a workspace for Bridge

To reconfigure the Bridge window quickly, choose one of the predefined workspaces. (To create and save custom workspaces, see pages 60–62.)

To choose a workspace for Bridge: ★

Do one of the following:

In the workspace switcher on the toolbar, click **Essentials, Keywords, Filmstrip, Metadata** (List View for the thumbnails), **Preview, Light Table, Folders**, or a user-saved workspace. **A** (To display more workspace names, pull the vertical bar to the left. **B**)

From the **Workspace** menu on the workspace switcher, choose a workspace **C** (and **A–C**, next page).

Press the **shortcut** for one of the first six workspaces on the switcher (as listed on the Workspace menu): Cmd-F1/Ctrl-1 through Cmd-F6/Ctrl-6. The shortcuts are assigned automatically to the first six workspaces on the switcher, based on their current left-to-right order.

➤ The Output workspace has a different purpose from the other workspaces.*

To change the order of workspaces on the switcher: ★

Drag a workspace name to the left or right.

Control-click/right-click a workspace name and choose a different name from the context menu.

A Click a workspace on the workspace switcher. Workspace menu

B To reveal more workspace names, drag the vertical bar to the left.

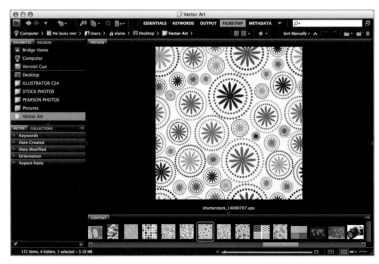

C In the Filmstrip workspace, you can click a thumbnail, then keep pressing the left or right arrow key to cycle through the thumbnails in the current folder. This workspace also features a large preview of the currently selected thumbnail.

*To learn about the Output workspace, see our Visual QuickStart Guide to Photoshop.

A In the Essentials workspace, all the panels are showing, and the Center pane is wider than the side panes.

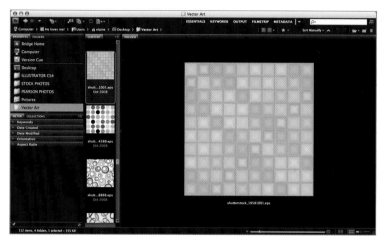

B In the Preview workspace, the Metadata and Keywords panels are hidden to make room for a large preview, and the thumbnails are displayed vertically (rather than horizontally, as in the Filmstrip workspace).

C The Light Table workspace allows you to display the largest number of thumbnails in a folder, because the Content panel takes up the entire Bridge window.

➤ To resize the thumbnails for any workspace, see Figure C on page 61.

Previewing graphics in Bridge

Bridge CS4 has new controls on the toolbar for navigating to and opening folders, in addition to the existing controls in the Folders and Favorites panels that you may already be familiar with.

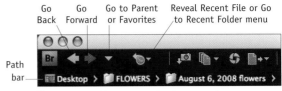

A Bridge CS4 offers new navigation controls.

To select and preview graphics in Bridge: ★

1. Do any of the following:

In the **Folders** panel, navigate to the folder you want to open. Scroll upward or downward, or expand or collapse any folder by clicking the arrowhead.

Display the contents of a folder by clicking its icon in the **Folders** panel or by double-clicking its thumbnail in the **Content** panel. Note: If folder icons aren't displaying, check View > Show Folders.

Click the **Go Back** button ◄ or the **Go Forward** button ► at the top of the Bridge window to step back or forward through recently viewed folders.**A**

Click a folder that you've placed in the **Favorites** panel.

Choose from a list of Favorites or Recent Folders on the **Go to Parent or Favorites** menu ▼ at the top of the Bridge window.

Click a folder name on the **Path** bar (Window > Path Bar).

From one of the menus ▷ on the Path bar, choose a folder. If another submenu displays, click yet another folder; repeat until you get to the desired folder.

➤ To display all the thumbnails for files in the current folder, including the files in any nested subfolders, choose Show Items from Subfolders from its menu.▷ To restore the original hierarchy, click the Cancel button.◉

2. In the **Content** panel, do either of the following:

Click a thumbnail. A colored border will appear around it, and data about the file will be listed in the Metadata panel. An enlarged preview of the graphic will also display in the Preview panel, if that panel is showing.

To select multiple files, Cmd-click/Ctrl-click nonconsecutive thumbnails; or click the first thumbnail in a series of consecutive thumbnails, then Shift-click the last one.**B**

The Preview panel displays an enlargement of one or more selected thumbnails, so you can shop and compare.

B Cmd-click/Ctrl-click multiple thumbnails in the Content panel to select them for previewing.

3. If the file for the currently selected thumbnail contains multiple artboards, you can cycle through them by clicking the left or right arrow below the preview or by entering the desired artboard number in the field.**A**

➤ If a thumbnail has a number in the upper left corner, it's part of a group of thumbnails called a stack. To display all the thumbnails in a stack, click the number; to collapse the stack, click the number again (to learn more about stacks, see page 63).

➤ To cycle through thumbnails in the current folder in the Filmstrip workspace, press the arrow keys on the keyboard.

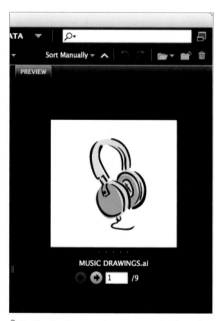

A In the Preview panel, you can cycle through multiple artboards in an Illustrator document by clicking the left or right arrow or by entering the desired artboard number in the field.

PLAYING FAVORITES

➤ Via check boxes in the Favorite Items area of Adobe Bridge CS4/Edit > Preferences > General, you can control which folders appear in the top part of the Favorites panel.

➤ To add a folder to the user-created list of folders in the lower part of the Favorites panel, drag the folder from the Content panel (in the center pane) or from the Desktop into the Favorites panel, and release the mouse when the + (plus sign) pointer displays; or click the folder and choose File > Add to Favorites.

➤ To remove a folder from the list of Favorites, click it, then choose File > Remove from Favorites.

VIEWING A FILE'S METADATA ★

If you click the thumbnail for an Illustrator document, on the Metadata panel, you will see information about the file, in expandable categories.

Drag this bar upward (or downward) to make the panel taller (or shorter).

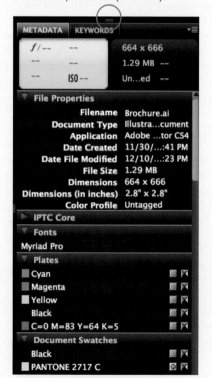

Opening files from Bridge

You can open as many files in Illustrator as currently available RAM and scratch disk space allow. (To learn how to import files from other programs into Illustrator, see Chapter 22.)

To open files from Bridge into Illustrator:

1. In the Content panel, display the thumbnail for the documents you want to open.

2. Do either of the following:

   Double-click a thumbnail.

   Click a thumbnail or select multiple thumbnails, then click one of them or press Cmd-O/Ctrl-O.

   Illustrator will launch, if it isn't already running, and the documents will appear onscreen.

3. The Font Problems dialog will appear if the file(s) being opened uses a font that's unavailable to your system. Click **Open** to have the document open with a substitute font, or click **Cancel**. If a missing font subsequently becomes available to the system, it will also become available on the font lists in Illustrator, and the type will redisplay correctly without any action required on your part.

   If an alert about a color profile appears, see the sidebar on page 16; and if an alert about a linked image file appears, see page 283.

➤ Mac OS: By default, the Bridge window stays open after you use it to open a file. To close the Bridge window as you open a file, hold down Option as you double-click a thumbnail.

➤ To locate a file in the Finder/Explorer, click its thumbnail in Bridge, then Control-click/right-click and choose Reveal in Finder/Reveal in Explorer. The folder that the file resides in will open in a window in the Finder/Explorer and the file icon will be selected.

To reopen a recently opened file:

Do either of the following:

In Bridge, choose the file name from the **Open Recent Files** menu 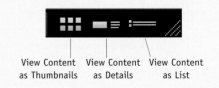 on the right side of the Path bar. ★

Customizing the Bridge window

To choose colors for the Bridge interface:

1. Choose Adobe Bridge CS4 (Edit, in Windows) > **Preferences** (Ctrl-K/Cmd-K). The Preferences dialog opens.

2. On the left side, click **General**, and in the **Appearance** area, do any of the following:

   Move the **User Interface Brightness** slider to set a gray value for the side panes.

   Move the **Image Backdrop** slider to set a gray value for the center pane and the Preview panel.

   Choose an **Accent Color** for the border that surrounds selected folders, thumbnails, and stacks.

3. *Optional:* If you want to use tool tips in Bridge to identify thumbnails, click Thumbnails on the left side of the Preferences dialog, then check Show Tooltips.

4. Click OK.

➤ To learn more about the Bridge Preferences, see Bridge > Help.

USING THE VIEW CONTENT BUTTONS ★

To control the format in which metadata displays in the Content panel, do the following:

➤ In the lower right corner of the Bridge window, click a View Content button: View Content as Thumbnails (minimal file data), View Content as Details (more file data), or View Content as List (small icons with columns of data). With View Content as List chosen, you can change the column order by dragging any column header to the left or right.

➤ When the content is viewed as thumbnails, you can toggle the display of metadata on or off by pressing Cmd-T/Ctrl-T.

View Content   View Content   View Content
as Thumbnails   as Details   as List

To further customize the Bridge workspace, you can resize, move, or hide any of the panels. And if you save your new layout as a user-created workspace by following the instructions on the next page, you'll be able to access it again quickly at any time.

To customize the Bridge panes and panels:

Do any of the following:

To make a panel or panel group **taller** or **shorter**, drag its horizontal bar upward or downward.**A**

To make a whole pane **wider** or **narrower**, drag its vertical bar sideways;**B** the adjacent pane resizes accordingly.

To **minimize** any panel except Content to just a tab, double-click its tab; double-click the tab again to maximize the panel.

To move a panel into a different **group**, drag the panel tab (name), and release the mouse

when the blue drop zone border appears around the desired group.

To display a panel in its **own group**, drag its tab between two panels, and release the mouse when the horizontal blue drop zone line appears.

To resize the thumbnails, drag the **Thumbnail Size** slider **C** or click the **Smaller Thumbnail Size** button ▢ or **Larger Thumbnail Size** button.▢

➤ To hide (or show) the side panes, press Tab or double-click the vertical bar between the panes. To display only the Content panel in a compact window, click the Compact Mode button ⬜ in the upper right corner of the Bridge window; click it again to restore the full window.

A You can move the horizontal bar upward to shorten the Favorites/Folder panels and lengthen the Filter panel.

B You can move the vertical bar for the right pane to the left to widen the Preview and Metadata panels.

C Use the Thumbnail Size slider to resize the thumbnails in the center pane.

Saving custom workspaces

If you save your customized workspaces, you'll be able to access them again quickly at any time, and will avoid having to set up your workspace each time you launch Bridge.

To save a custom workspace for Bridge: ★

1. Choose a size and location for the overall Bridge window onscreen, arrange the panel sizes and groups as desired, choose a thumbnail size for the Content panel, choose a sorting order from the Sort By menu at the top of the Bridge window (see page 68), and click the desired View Content button.

2. From the **Workspace** menu on the workspace switcher, choose **New Workspace**. The New Workspace dialog opens.**A**

3. Enter a Name for the workspace, check Save Window Location as Part of Workspace and/or Save Sort Order as Part of Workspace (both are optional), then click Save.

   Note: Your new workspace will be listed first on the workspace switcher, and will be assigned the first shortcut (Cmd-F1/Ctrl-1). To change the order of workspaces on the bar, drag any workspace name sideways to a different slot. The shortcuts are assigned automatically based on the current left-to-right order of the workspaces.

Resetting the Bridge workspace

When you make a manual change to a saved workspace, the change sticks with the workspace even when you switch back and forth between workspaces. For example, if you were to change the thumbnail size for the Filmstrip workspace, click the Essentials workspace, then click back on the Filmstrip workspace, the new thumbnail size would still display (in Filmstrip). Via the commands for resetting workspaces, you can restore the default settings to a specific predefined or user-saved workspace or to all the predefined (standard Adobe) workspaces.

To reset the Bridge workspace: ★

Do either of the following:

To restore the default settings to one workspace, display that workspace, then choose **Reset Workspace** from the Workspace menu.

To restore the default settings to all the predefined (Adobe) workspaces, choose **Reset Standard Workspaces** from the Workspace menu.

A Use the New Workspace dialog to name your workspace and choose options for it.

Using thumbnail stacks

Before learning about stacks, start with the simple technique of dragging thumbnails to change their location in the Content panel.

To rearrange thumbnails manually:

Drag a thumbnail (or select, then drag multiple thumbnails) to a new location. The Sort By menu header switches to "Sort Manually." Thumbnails remain where you place them unless you change the sorting order or perform a stacking operation.

An easy way to limit how many thumbnails display at a given time is to organize them into stacks. We suggest doing so in categories, such as by subject matter or theme, by type of artwork (e.g., freehand drawings, type, templates), by project (e.g., work for individual clients, personal work), or by state of completion (e.g., rough or finished).

To group thumbnails into a stack:

1. Shift-click or Cmd-click/Ctrl-click to select multiple thumbnails.**A** The thumbnail listed first in your selection becomes the "stack thumbnail" (displays on top of the stack).

2. Choose Stacks > **Group as Stack** (Cmd-G/ Ctrl-G) or Control-click/right-click and choose Stack > **Group as Stack**. A stack looks like two playing cards in a pile, and instead of all the individual thumbnails, you see just the stack thumbnail on top.**B** The number in the upper left corner (the "stack number") indicates how many thumbnails the stack contains.

To select thumbnails in a stack:

To **select and display** all the thumbnails in a stack, click the stack number. Click the number again to collapse the stack. The stack remains selected.

To **select** all the thumbnails in a stack while keeping the stack **collapsed**, click the stack border (bottom "card") or Option-click/Alt-click the stack thumbnail (the top one in the stack).

To rearrange thumbnails in a stack:

To **move** a thumbnail to a new position in an expanded stack, click it to deselect the other selected thumbnails, then drag it to the desired location (as shown by the vertical drop zone line).

To move a whole stack:

1. Collapse the stack, then Option-click/Alt-click the stack thumbnail.

2. Drag the stack thumbnail (not the border).

➤ If you drag the top thumbnail of an unselected stack, you'll move just that thumbnail, not the whole stack.

To add a thumbnail to a stack:

Drag a thumbnail over a stack thumbnail (you'll see a drop zone border) or into an open stack.

To remove a thumbnail from a stack:

1. Click the stack number to expand the stack.

2. Click the thumbnail to be removed (to deselect the other thumbnails), then drag it out of the stack.

To ungroup a whole stack:

1. Click the stack number to expand and select all the thumbnails in the stack.

2. Choose Stacks > **Ungroup from Stack** (Cmd-Shift-G/Control-Shift-G) or Control-click/ right-click and choose Stack > **Ungroup from Stack**. The stack number and border disappear.

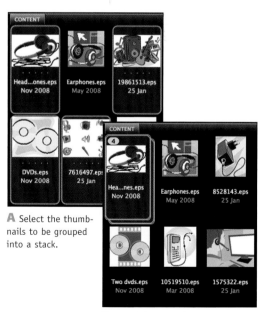

A Select the thumbnails to be grouped into a stack.

B A stack is created.

Searching for files

To find files via Bridge: ★

1. In Bridge, choose Edit > **Find** (Cmd-F/Ctrl-F). The Find dialog opens.**A**

2. From the **Look In** menu in the Source area, choose the folder to be searched (the current folder is listed, by default). To select a folder that's not on the list, choose Look In: Browse, locate the desired folder, then click Choose/OK.

3. From the menus in the **Criteria** area, choose search criteria (e.g., file name, date created, label, rating, particular camera settings), choose a parameter from the adjoining menu, and enter data in the field. To include additional criteria in the search, click the ⊕, then choose and enter more search criteria.

4. From the **Match** menu, choose "If any criteria are met" to find files based on one or more criteria, or choose "If all criteria are met" to narrow the selection to files that meet all the chosen criteria.

5. *Optional:* Check Include All Subfolders to also search through any subfolders within the folder you chose in step 2.

6. *Optional:* Check Include Non-indexed Files to search through files that Bridge hasn't yet indexed (any folder Bridge has yet to display). This will slow down the search.

7. Click Find. The search results will display in the Content panel and also in a temporary folder called Search Results: [name of source folder],**B** which is listed both on the Path bar and on the Reveal Recent File or Go to Recent Folder menu 🔲 on the Bridge toolbar.

8. To save a copy of the search results to a permanent file group, see the following page, or to cancel the search results, click the ⊠.

➤ To discard the current search results and perform a new search, click New Search.

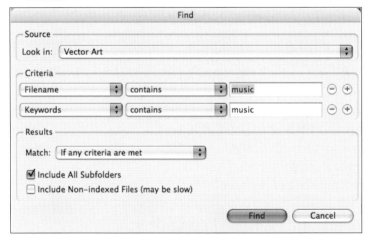

A Use the Find dialog to search for and locate files according to various criteria.

QUICK SEARCH

If you know the name of the file you're looking for, type it in the search field 🔍▾ on the right end of the Bridge toolbar, then press Return/Enter.

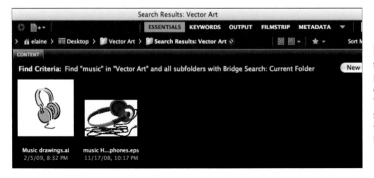

B After you click Find, the search results (from the temporary Search Results folder) display in the Content panel. The parameters used for the search and the name of the folder that was searched are listed as the Find Criteria.

Creating and using collections

The collection features in Bridge offer a useful way to group and access file thumbnails (without actually relocating them). There are two kinds of collections: a Smart Collection created from the results of a Find search, and a collection created by dragging thumbnails manually into a collection folder.

To create a Smart Collection: ★

1. Click the tab for the Collections panel (if you don't see this panel, choose Window > Collections Panel).

2. Perform a search by using the Edit > **Find** command (see the preceding page). When the search is completed, click the **Save as Smart Collection** button ▦ at the top of the Content panel or at the bottom of the Collections panel.**A**

3. A New Smart Collection folder appears in the top part of the Collections panel.**B** To rename it, type a name in the highlighted field, then press Return/Enter.

To display a collection: ★

Click its icon in the Collections panel.

The smart thing about Smart Collections is that you can run a new search for a collection based on either new criteria or a new search folder, and the collection contents update automatically.

To edit a Smart Collection: ★

1. In the **Collections** panel, click the icon for an existing Smart Collection.

2. Click the **Edit Smart Collection** button ▦ at the top of the Content panel or in the lower left corner of the Collections panel.**C**

3. The Edit Smart Collection dialog opens. Enter a new folder to be searched and/or new search criteria, then click Save.

4. The results of the new search will display in the Content panel, and new thumbnails, if any, will replace the old ones in the same collection. Note: If you move a thumbnail out of a Smart Collection folder or move the actual file from the folder that was used in the search, it is removed from the collection.

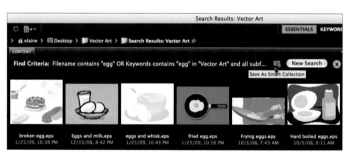

A Click the Save as Smart Collection button to create a Smart Collection.

B The new Smart Collection displays on the Collections panel. Enter a new name in the highlighted field.

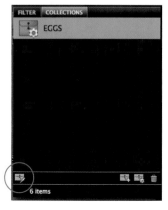

C To edit a Smart Collection, click a Smart Collection folder on the Collections panel, then click the Edit Smart Collection button at the bottom of the panel.

Bridge also lets you create a nonsmart collection without running a search, and you can add to the collection simply by dragging thumbnails into it.

To create a nonsmart collection: ★

1. Do either of the following:

   On the **Content** panel, select thumbnails to be placed into a collection. On the **Collections** panel, click the **New Collection** button, then click Yes in the alert dialog.

   When viewing files in **Review mode** (Cmd-B/Ctrl-B), drag any files you don't want in the collection out of the carousel, then click the **New Collection** button.

2. On the panel, type a name for the collection,**A** then press Return/Enter.

To add files to a nonsmart collection: ★

1. Display the **Collections** panel.

2. Drag one or more thumbnails to an existing collection folder.**B**

A Click the New Collection button to create a new collection, then type a name for the collection in the highlighted field.

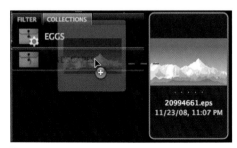

B Drag one or more thumbnails from the Content panel to a folder in the Collections panel.

To remove a thumbnail from a collection: ★

1. On the **Collections** panel, click a collection folder to display its contents.

2. Select the thumbnails to be removed, then click the **Remove from Collection** button at the top of the Content panel **C** (or Control-click/right-click a thumbnail and choose Remove from Collection).

➤ Beware! If you apply the Delete command to a thumbnail in either type of collection, the actual file it represents is deleted from your hard drive.

If you rename a file or move it from its original location, Bridge tries to update the link to any nonsmart collections that contain the file. If the program is unable to do so, here's what to do.

To relink a missing file to a collection: ★

1. On the **Collections** panel, click a folder to which you want to relink a file or files.

2. Next to the Missing File Detected alert at the top of the Content panel, click **Fix.D**

3. In the **Find Missing Files** dialog, click Browse, locate and select the missing file, then click Open (Skip ignores the current missing file and proceeds to the next one). Click OK.

C Click Remove from Collection to take the selected thumbnail(s) out of the currently selected collection.

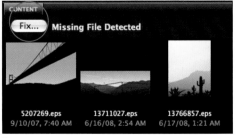

D Click Fix to relink a file that's missing from a collection.

Labeling and rating thumbnails

If you assign thumbnails a star rating and/or color label, you'll be able to filter their display based on the presence or absence of that rating or label and find them easily via the Filter panel (see the following page) and the Find command. You can also apply a Reject rating to thumbnails that you want to hide from the Content panel but aren't quite ready to delete the actual files for from your hard drive.

To label and rate thumbnails:

1. Select one or more thumbnails in the **Content** panel.

2. Do any of the following:

   From the **Label** menu, choose a **Rating** (number of stars) and/or a **Label** (color-coded strip, which appears below the thumbnail).

   Control-click/right-click a thumbnail in the **Content** panel, and from the **Label** submenu on the context menu, choose a category. (You can rename the categories in the Labels panel of the Preferences dialog.)

   Control-click/right-click in the **Preview** panel and choose a star rating and/or label.

   Click a thumbnail, then click any one of the five **dots** below it; stars will appear. To **remove** a star, click the star to its left. To remove all the stars from a thumbnail, click to the left of the first star. (If you don't see the dots or stars, enlarge the thumbnails.)

   Press one of the keyboard **shortcuts** listed on the Label menu or context menu.

   To label the losers with a red "Reject" label, choose Label > **Reject** (Option-Delete/Alt-Del). If Show Reject Files is unchecked on the View menu, all rejected thumbnails will be hidden.

➤ If tool tips get in the way of your adding or removing stars, go to Adobe Bridge CS4/Edit > Preferences > Thumbnails and uncheck Show Tooltips.

➤ To remove the ratings from a selected thumbnail or thumbnails, choose Label > No Rating or press Cmd-0/Ctrl-0 (zero).

To redisplay all rejected thumbnails:

Choose View > **Show Reject Files**. All thumbnails with a Reject rating will redisplay.

A This thumbnail has an Approved (green) rating.

B We clicked the third dot on this thumbnail to assign a 3-star rating...

C ...but then we changed our minds, so we clicked to the left of the stars to remove them.

D This poor thumbnail has a Reject rating.

Choosing a sorting order

The sorting order that is currently chosen on the Sort By menu controls the order in which thumbnails display in the Content panel. The sorting order of thumbnails is also important for batch and automate operations, which process files based on the current sequence of thumbnails. The current sorting order applies to all folders and thumbnails, not just to one folder in particular. By choosing a sorting order and by using the Filter panel (see below), you'll be able to locate the thumbnails you need more quickly and efficiently.

To choose a sorting order:

From the **Sort By** menu on the Path bar,★ choose a sorting order (such as By Date Created).**A** Thumbnails will be rearranged in the Content panel (thumbnails in stacks are exempt).

➤ Click the Ascending Order ◢ or Descending Order ◥ arrowhead to swap the sorting order.

Using the Filter panel

The Filter panel lists data specific to files in the current folder, such as the label, star rating, file type, date created, and date modified. By checking specific criteria in the panel, you can control which thumbnails display in the current folder. A thumbnail must match all checked criteria in order to display.

To filter out which thumbnails display:

Do either of the following:

On the **Filter Items by Rating** menu on the Bridge toolbar,**B** check the desired criteria.★

In the **Filter** panel, check a listing within any category, such as Labels or Ratings, to display thumbnails that meet that criterion;**C** to display thumbnails that meet additional criteria, check other listings in the **same** category. To display even fewer thumbnails, check listings in **other** categories. (To redisplay hidden thumbnails, remove the check mark by clicking the listing again.) To display only files with a Reject rating, check Reject in the Ratings category.

➤ To apply the currently checked criteria to other folders you display, activate (click) the Keep Filter When Browsing 📌 button at the bottom of the panel.

➤ To remove all check marks from the Filter panel, click the Clear Filter ⊘ button at the bottom of the panel; or press Cmd-Option-A/Ctrl-Alt-A.

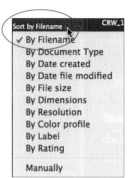

A Choose a sorting order for your Bridge thumbnails from the Sort By menu on the Path bar.

B Filter the display of thumbnails via the Filter Items by Rating menu.

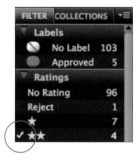

C Because we checked the two-star option under Ratings in the Filter panel, only thumbnails matching that criterion (that have two stars) display in the Content panel.

DYNAMIC PANEL ★

The Filter panel is dynamic, meaning that the categories listed on it (such as File Type, Keywords, Date Created, and Date Modified) change depending on what data is available for files in the current folder. For example, if you haven't applied ratings to any thumbnails in the current folder, there won't be a Ratings category. Should you apply a rating to a thumbnail, the Ratings category will appear. (Click an arrowhead to expand or collapse a category.)

Assigning keywords to files

Keywords (identifying text) are used by search utilities to locate files and by file management programs to organize them. In Bridge, you can create main-level keyword categories (such as events, people, places, things, themes, etc.), and nested subkeywords within those categories, and then assign them to your files. You can also locate files in Bridge by using the Find command with Keywords as a search criterion or by checking specific keywords in the Keywords category in the Filter panel.

To create keywords:

1. To create a new main-level keyword category, in the Keywords panel, click the **New Keyword** button, then type a keyword.A ★

2. To create a nested subkeyword, click a main-level keyword category, click the **New Sub Keyword** button, type a word, then press Return/Enter. You can also create sub-subkeywords. ★

➤ You can move (drag) any subkeyword into a different main-level keyword category.

To assign keywords:

1. Select one or more Illustrator file thumbnails. If the file has been assigned keywords already, they will be listed at the top of the panel; you can assign additional ones.

2. Check the box for one or more subkeywords.B (Although you can assign a main-level keyword to a file, it won't be very useful in a search.)

➤ The keywords for a file are also listed under Keywords in the Filter panel and in the File > File Info dialog.

➤ If keywords are contained in a file that you import into Bridge, they will be listed in the Other Keywords category in the Keywords panel. If you want to add them as permanent subkeywords, Control-click/right-click each one and choose Make Persistent from the context menu.

➤ You can also assign keywords via the File Info dialog. Select one or more thumbnails, then from the Refine menu on the Bridge toolbar, choose File Info. In the Description tab of the dialog, enter the desired keywords, separated by semicolons or commas (watch out for typing errors!). ★

A We created a new main-level keyword called "Places," kept the category selected, then used the New Sub Keyword button to add new subkeywords to it.

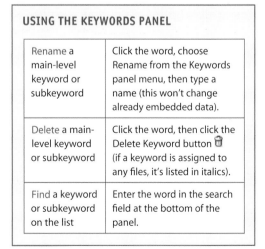

B We clicked the thumbnail for an Illustrator file, then assigned subkeywords to it by checking categories.

USING THE KEYWORDS PANEL

Rename a main-level keyword or subkeyword	Click the word, choose Rename from the Keywords panel menu, then type a name (this won't change already embedded data).
Delete a main-level keyword or subkeyword	Click the word, then click the Delete Keyword button (if a keyword is assigned to any files, it's listed in italics).
Find a keyword or subkeyword on the list	Enter the word in the search field at the bottom of the panel.

Exporting the Bridge cache

Each time a folder is displayed in the Content panel in Bridge, the program automatically creates a cache file, containing information about the files in the folder, such as the data for displaying ratings, labels, and high-quality thumbnails. Having the cache helps speed up the display of thumbnails when you choose that folder again. If you want to include this display information with files you copy to a removable disk or to a shared folder on a network, you'll need to copy the cache files—but before you can do so, you have to build the cache files and export them to the current folder.

To export the cache to the current folder: ★

1. Choose Adobe Bridge CS4/Edit > Preferences > Cache. In the Cache area, check **Automatically Export Cache to Folders When Possible**, then click OK.

2. Choose Tools > Cache > **Build and Export Cache**. In the alert dialog, check **Export Cache to Folders**, then click OK.

3. Two hidden cache files—one named .BridgeCache (metadata cache) and one named .BridgeCacheT (thumbnail cache)—will be placed in the currently displayed folder.

   Note: If you use the File > Move To (or Copy To) command in Bridge to move (or copy) selected thumbnails, the folder cache you just created will also move or copy, thanks to the export option that you turned on in Preferences > Cache.

➤ To display the generic cache file icons in the Content panel, choose View > Show Hidden Files.

Thumbnail cache files sometimes cause display problems, in which case purging them may resolve the issue. The purge will cause Bridge to regenerate the thumbnail previews for the current folder.

To purge the cache files:

To purge the cache files from the current folder, choose Tools > Cache > **Purge Cache for Folder** "[current folder name]." Two new (hidden) cache files will be generated.

To purge the cache files from multiple selected thumbnails, Control-click/right-click and choose **Purge Cache for Selection**. ★

Managing files using Bridge

To create a new folder:

1. Via the Folders panel or the Path bar, navigate to the folder in which you want the new folder to appear.

2. Click the **New Folder** button 🗀 at the right end of the Bridge toolbar, type a name in the highlighted field below the new folder, then press Return/Enter.

To delete files:

1. Click a thumbnail (or Cmd-click/Ctrl-click multiple thumbnails or Shift-click a series of thumbnails).

2. Press Cmd-Delete/Ctrl-Backspace, then click OK in the alert dialog. Beware! You can also delete a whole folder full of files. To retrieve a deleted file or folder, double-click the Trash icon/Recycle Bin for the operating system, then drag the item into the Content panel in Bridge.

To rename a file:

1. Click a thumbnail, then click the file name. The name will become highlighted.

2. Type a new name (don't try to delete the extension), then press Return/Enter or click outside the name field.

To move or copy files to other folders:

Method 1 (by dragging)

1. Click the **Folders** panel tab. Display the subfolder that you want to move files to, and expand any folders, if necessary.

2. Select one or more thumbnails in the **Content** panel, then drag them over a folder name in the **Folders** panel to move them, or hold down Option/Ctrl and drag them over a folder name to copy them.

Method 2 (by using the context menu)

1. Select one or more thumbnails in the **Content** panel.

2. Control-click/right-click one of the selected thumbnails, then from the **Move To** or **Copy To** submenu on the context menu, do either of the following:

   Select a folder name under **Recent Folders**.

   Select **Choose Folder**. Locate a folder in the Choose a Folder dialog, then click Choose/OK.

In Illustrator, the paths you create consist of anchor points connected by straight and/or curved line segments. Paths can be closed, such as polygons and ovals, or open, such as arcs and straight lines. In the instructions below, we show you how to select and delete unwanted objects. Following that are instructions for using the Rectangle, Rounded Rectangle, Ellipse, Polygon, Star, Line Segment, and Spiral tools, which enable you to produce geometric objects quickly and easily.

In the next chapter, you will learn to draw in a loose, freehand manner. After learning these basics, learn how to select paths for editing (Chapter 8), copy and align them (Chapter 9), apply colors to them (Chapter 10), and change their shape (Chapters 11 and 12). Other ways to create objects, such as by using the Pen tool and the type tools, and by tracing, are covered in later chapters.

Selecting and deleting objects

You'll be creating lots of different shapes in this chapter, and your artboard may start to become crowded with junk. To remove an object you've just created, choose Edit > Undo (Cmd-Z/Ctrl-Z). To remove an object that's been lying around, follow these instructions.

To select and delete objects:

1. Choose the **Selection** tool ▶ (V), then click the object you want to delete, or drag a marquee around multiple objects.

2. Press Delete/Backspace.

➤ If you have used the Direct Selection tool to select points on an object, you can press Delete/Backspace twice to delete the whole object.

GEOMETRIC OBJECTS

CHOOSING AN ARTBOARD FIRST ★

➤ If your document contains multiple artboards, before creating any objects, display the artboard you want to add the objects to (choose from the Artboard Navigation menu at the bottom of the document window).

➤ Once your document contains multiple layers, you will also need to choose a layer before creating an object (see Chapter 13).

CHOOSING COLORS QUICKLY

Methods for choosing and applying fill and stroke colors are explained fully in Chapter 10. In the meantime, if you want to choose a fill and stroke color for the tools you will be using in this chapter, see "A quick color primer" on page 79.

Creating rectangles and ellipses

To create a rectangle or an ellipse by dragging:

1. Choose the **Rectangle** tool ▧ (M) or the **Ellipse** tool ◯ (L).

2. Drag diagonally.**A** As you drag, a wireframe representation of the rectangle or oval displays. When you release the mouse, the rectangle or oval will be selected, and the current fill and stroke settings will be applied to it.**B**

   You can also use these modifiers:

   To draw the object from its center, Option-drag/ Alt-drag.

   To move the rectangle or ellipse as you draw it (before releasing the mouse), Spacebar-drag.

   To draw a square with the Rectangle tool or a circle with the Ellipse tool, Shift-drag.

To create a rectangle or an ellipse by specifying dimensions:

1. Choose the **Rectangle** tool (M) or the **Ellipse** tool (L).

2. Click on an artboard. The Rectangle or Ellipse dialog opens.**C**

3. Enter **Width** and **Height** values. To create a circle or a square, enter a value in the Width field, then click the word Height (or vice versa)—the value in one field will copy to the other one.

4. Click OK.**D**

➤ Values in dialogs in the current document display in the measurement units currently chosen in the Document Setup dialog. To open that dialog, click a blank area of the artboard to deselect all, then click Document Setup on the Control panel. ★

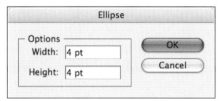

C Enter values in the Ellipse (or Rectangle) dialog.

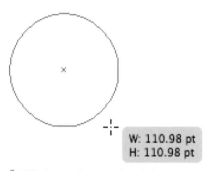

A Shift-drag to draw a perfect circle.

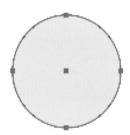

B The current fill and stroke settings are applied to the ellipse automatically.

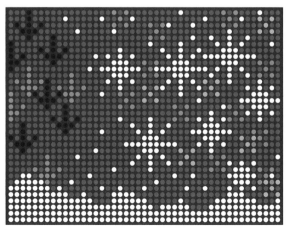

D This is a grid of dots (ellipses), in four different colors, on top of a solid dark blue rectangle. To copy objects, see page 98.

To create a rounded rectangle:

1. Choose the **Rounded Rectangle** tool.⬚

2. Drag diagonally. As you drag, a wireframe representation of the rounded rectangle displays.**A** When you release the mouse, the rounded rectangle will be selected and the current fill and stroke settings will be applied to it.**B–C**

➤ As you create an object with the Rounded Rectangle tool, keep the mouse button down and keep pressing the up arrow to make the corners more round, or the down arrow to make them more square. Press (don't hold) the left or right arrow to toggle between square and round corners.

➤ To draw a rounded rectangle of a specific size, choose the Rounded Rectangle tool, click on an artboard, then enter Width, Height, and Corner Radius values. The Corner Radius option (0–8192 pt), which controls the degree of curvature in the corners of rounded rectangles, can also be specified in Preferences > General. When changed in one location, the value updates in the other location automatically.

A An object is drawn with the Rounded Rectangle tool.

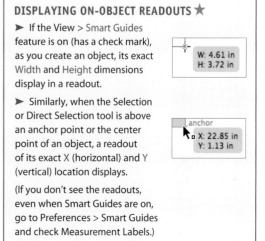

B The rounded rectangle remains selected after it's drawn.

C This retro pattern contains rounded rectangles of various sizes and colors (see pages 131–132).

DISPLAYING ON-OBJECT READOUTS ★

➤ If the View > Smart Guides feature is on (has a check mark), as you create an object, its exact Width and Height dimensions display in a readout.

| | W: 4.61 in |
| | H: 3.72 in |

➤ Similarly, when the Selection or Direct Selection tool is above an anchor point or the center point of an object, a readout of its exact X (horizontal) and Y (vertical) location displays.

| anchor |
| X: 22.85 in |
| Y: 1.13 in |

(If you don't see the readouts, even when Smart Guides are on, go to Preferences > Smart Guides and check Measurement Labels.)

Here's a quick introduction to one of the many commands on the Effect menu: Round Corners. Effects produce editable appearances, which are nonpermanent changes. To learn more about effects, see Chapter 15.

To round the corners of an existing object:

1. Select one or more objects.**A**

2. Choose Effect > Stylize > **Round Corners**.

3. In the dialog, check **Preview**. Enter a **Radius** value (the radius of the curve, in points),**B** then press Tab to preview that setting.

4. Click OK.**C** If you want to edit the Round Corners setting for the object at any time, display the **Appearance** panel, then click Round Corners.

   Note: Make sure the New Art Has Basic Appearance option is checked on the Appearance panel menu, so any new objects you create won't have the current Appearance panel settings.

Creating polygons

With the Polygon, Star, and Spiral tools, as with the other tools discussed in this chapter, all you have to do is drag in an artboard or enter values in the tool's dialog.

To create a polygon by clicking:

1. Choose the **Polygon** tool.

2. Click where you want the center of the polygon to be located. The Polygon dialog opens.**D**

3. Enter a **Radius** value (0–8192 pt) for the distance from the center of the object to the corner points.

4. Choose a number of **Sides** for the polygon by clicking the up or down arrow or by entering a number (3–1000). The sides will be of equal length.

5. Click OK.**E** A polygon will appear where you clicked on an artboard, and the current fill and stroke settings will be applied to it automatically (see Chapter 10).

A Three objects are selected.

B A Radius value is entered in the Round Corners dialog.

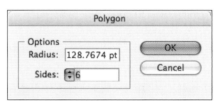

C Now the corners are rounded.

D Radius and Sides values are entered in the Polygon dialog.

E A polygon is created. This object has a dark brown stroke and a fill of None.

To create a polygon by dragging:

1. Choose the **Polygon** tool.

2. Drag in an artboard, starting from where you want the center of the polygon to be located.

   While dragging, do any of the following:

   To scale the polygon, drag away from or toward the center.

   To rotate the polygon, drag in a circular direction.

   To constrain the bottom side of the polygon to the horizontal axis, hold down Shift.

   To add sides to or delete sides from the polygon, press or hold down the up or down arrow key.

   To move the polygon without scaling it, hold down the Spacebar.

3. When you release the mouse, the polygon will be selected, and the current fill and stroke settings will be applied to it.

➤ To align a new object with an existing object as you draw it, use Smart Guides (see pages 96–97).

Creating stars

To create a star by clicking:

1. Choose the **Star** tool.

2. Click where you want the center of the star to be located. The Star dialog opens.**A**

3. Enter **Radius 1** and **Radius 2** values (0–8192 pt). The higher value is the distance from the center of the star to its outermost points; the lower value is the distance from the center of the star to the innermost points. The greater the difference between the two values, the thinner the arms of the star.

4. Choose a number of **Points** for the star by clicking the up or down arrow, by clicking in the field and pressing the up or down arrow key, or by entering a number (3–1000).

5. Click OK.**B**

➤ You can rotate the completed star by using its bounding box (see page 133).

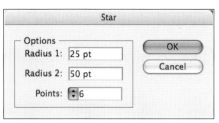

A Radius and Points values are entered in the Star dialog.

B A star is born.

BASIC BUILDING BLOCKS

You can create illustrations by using basic geometric objects as building blocks, such as ellipses, rectangles, and rounded rectangles.

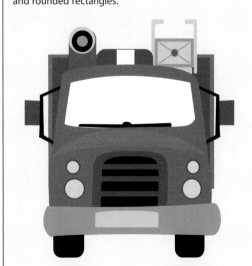

To create a star by dragging:

1. Choose the **Star** tool.

2. Drag in an artboard, starting from where you want the center of the star to be located.

   While dragging, do any of the following:

   To scale the star, drag away from or toward its center.

   To rotate the star, drag in a circular direction.

   To constrain two points of the star to the horizontal axis, drag with Shift held down.**A**

   To add points to or delete points from the star, press the up or down arrow key.**B**

   To move the star, drag with the Spacebar held down.

   To make each pair of shoulders (opposite segments) parallel to each other, drag with Option/Alt held down.

   To increase or decrease the length of the arms of the star while keeping the inner radius points constant, drag away from or toward the center with Cmd/Ctrl held down.**C**

3. When you release the mouse, the star will be selected and the current fill and stroke settings will be applied to it.**D**

➤ Hold down ~ (tilde) while dragging quickly with the Star or Polygon tool to create progressively larger copies of the shape. The more rapidly you drag, the farther apart the copies will be from one another. You can change the stroke colors and settings for the copies afterward.

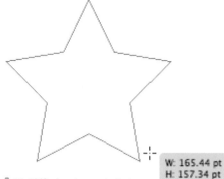

W: 165.44 pt
H: 157.34 pt

A We Shift-drag to constrain two points of the star to the horizontal axis.

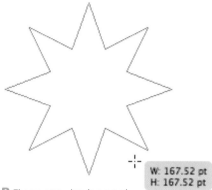

W: 167.52 pt
H: 167.52 pt

B The up arrow key is pressed to add points to the star.

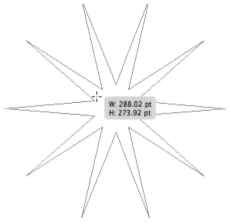

W: 288.02 pt
H: 273.92 pt

C Cmd/Ctrl is held down while dragging to make the arms of the star longer.

D To create a dotted stroke, as has been applied to these ellipses, stars, and lines, see page 117.

Next, we'll show you how to use the Line Segment and Spiral tools (on the Line Segment tool pop-out menu), which create independent objects or groups of objects.

Creating line segments

The Line Segment tool creates straight lines. Each time you release the mouse and drag again with this tool, a new, separate path is created.

To draw a line segment by dragging:

1. Choose the **Line Segment** tool ❭ (\).

2. Drag to draw a line.**A–B** As you do so, you can do any of the following:

   To extend the line outward from both sides of the origin point, drag with Option/Alt held down.

   To constrain the line to the nearest 45° increment, drag with Shift held down.

   To move the line, drag with the Spacebar held down.

➤ To create multiple lines of varied lengths from the same center point at different angles, drag in a circular direction with ~ (tilde) held down. Move the mouse rapidly to spread the lines apart.

To draw a line segment by entering values:

1. Choose the **Line Segment** tool ❭ (\).

2. Click where you want the segment to begin. The Line Segment Tool Options dialog opens.

3. Enter the desired line Length.

4. Enter an Angle or move the dial.

5. *Optional:* Check Fill Line to assign the current fill color to the line (see Chapter 10), in addition to the current stroke color, which is assigned automatically. If you reshape the line later into a curve or an angle, the fill color will be revealed. With Fill Line unchecked, the line will have a fill of None, but you can apply a fill color (and also change the stroke color) after exiting the dialog.

6. Click OK.

➤ To restore the factory-default settings to the Line Segment Tool Options dialog, Option-click/ Alt-click the Reset button (Cancel becomes Reset).

DÉJA VU

When you open the options dialog for the Rectangle, Ellipse, Rounded Rectangle, Polygon, Star, Line Segment, or Spiral tool (by clicking an artboard with the tool), the last used settings display — whether the last object was created by dragging or by using the dialog. To quickly create additional objects using the current options settings, simply click on an artboard with the tool, then press Return/Enter.

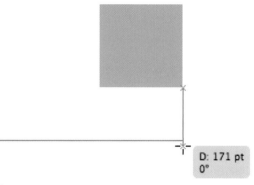

A Shift is held down as a line is drawn, to constrain it to the horizontal axis. Smart Guides (in green) are also being used to align the line to another object (see pages 96–97).

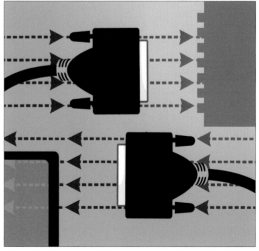

B To add an arrow brush to a line, see pages 292–293. To create a dashed stroke, see page 117.

Creating spirals

To create a spiral by dragging:

1. Choose the **Spiral** tool.

2. Drag in the document window, starting from where you want the center of the spiral to be located.

3. While dragging, do any of the following: **A**

   To scale the spiral, drag away from or toward the center.

   To control how tightly the spirals wind toward the center (the Decay value), Cmd-drag/Ctrl-drag slowly away from or toward the center.

   To add segments to or delete segments from the center of the spiral, press the up or down arrow key.

   To rotate the spiral, drag in a circular direction.

   To move the spiral, drag with the Spacebar held down.

4. When you release the mouse, the spiral will be selected, and the current fill and stroke settings will be applied to it.**B–C**

➤ You can also create a spiral or arc by entering values (click with the tool on an artboard to open the dialog), but it's not the most intuitive method in the world.

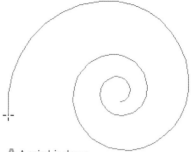

A A spiral is drawn.

B The Streamer brush from the Borders_ Novelty brush library is applied to the spiral. To learn about brushes, see Chapter 23.

C Spirals can be altered in several ways, such as by applying brush strokes, shearing, and applying effects. You will learn these techniques later in the book.

If you enjoy sketching in a loose, freehand manner, the Pencil, Paintbrush, and Blob Brush tools will be up your alley. Each tool has its own special attributes, which are explored in this chapter. Paths drawn with these tools can be reshaped by using any of the techniques in Chapters 11 and 12. In fact, in addition to being object-creation tools, the Pencil and Blob Brush tools also have a reshaping function.

A quick color primer

Before using the freehand drawing tools, learn how to quickly set the fill color, stroke color, and stroke width. You can use either the Control panel or the new in-panel editing feature of the Appearance panel.

To choose a fill or stroke color: ★

1. Choose the **Selection** tool ▶ (V), then click an object or drag a marquee around multiple objects.

2. Do either of the following:

   On the **Control** panel, click the fill or stroke square or arrowhead, **A** then on the temporary Swatches panel, click a swatch.

   On the **Appearance** panel, ◉ click the square for the Fill or Stroke listing, click the color square or arrowhead, ★ then on the temporary Swatches panel, click a swatch. **B**

   Note: To choose a fill or stroke color of None, click the **None** button ⬜ on the Swatches panel.

To choose a stroke width: ★

   Do either of the following:

   On the Control panel, click the up or down **Stroke Weight** arrow.

   On the Appearance ◉ panel, click the Stroke square, then click the up or down **Weight** arrow on the temporary Stroke panel that opens.

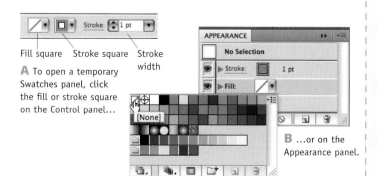

Fill square   Stroke square   Stroke width

A To open a temporary Swatches panel, click the fill or stroke square on the Control panel...

B ...or on the Appearance panel.

FILL AND STROKE DEFINED

► The fill, which is applied to the inside of a closed or open object, can be a solid color, a pattern, a gradient, or None (of the above).

► The stroke, which is applied to the path of a closed or open object, can be a solid color, a dashed stroke, or None. A Scatter, Calligraphic, Art, or Pattern brush can be applied to it, but not a gradient.

Note: To learn more about choosing and applying fill and stroke colors, see Chapter 10.

Note: For optimal results, use a pressure-sensitive tablet and a stylus with the Pencil, Paintbrush, and Blob Brush tools. Don't worry, it's recommended but not mandatory.

Drawing with the Pencil tool

The Pencil tool has three distinct functions: Drag in a blank area of the artboard, and a new, open path is created (instructions below); drag along the edge of an existing, selected path (open or closed), and the path is reshaped (see page 151); or drag from an endpoint of an existing open path, and new segments are added to the path (see page 149).

Note: To choose options for the Pencil tool, see page 82.

To draw with the Pencil tool:

1. Choose the **Pencil** tool ✐ (N).

2. Choose a stroke color and width, and a fill color of None.

3. Draw lines (a dotted line will appear while you draw). You can release the mouse between strokes. That's all there is to it. (Well, except for the artistic part!)

4. Choose View > Preview to see the line with the current Stroke settings,**A** or Outline to see it as a wireframe representation.

5. *Optional:* Keep the artwork selected, show the Brushes panel ❦ (F5) or click the Brush thumb-nail or arrowhead on the Control panel, [●▾] then click a brush on the panel.**B** (You can also choose a brush for the tool before drawing the artwork.)

➤ To create a closed path with the Pencil tool, start drawing the path, then finish drawing it with Option/Alt held down.

➤ To close an existing Pencil path with a straight segment, choose the Selection tool (V), click the line, then choose Object > Path > Join (Cmd-J/Ctrl-J).

➤ If you want to draw straight lines or smooth curves, you could go mad trying to do it with the Pencil tool! Use the Line Segment, Arc, or Pen tool instead.

A An iPod is drawn with the Pencil tool. If you don't know what subject matter to draw, look around the room you're in right now, and draw the contour of any object you see.

B The Tapered Stroke brush in the Artistic_Ink brush library produces strokes like these.

Drawing with the Paintbrush tool

If you use a stylus and a pressure-sensitive tablet, the Paintbrush tool will respond to pressure. The harder you press on the tablet, the wider the stroke.

Note: To choose options for the Paintbrush tool, see the instructions on the following page. To learn about choosing and customizing different types of brushes, see Chapter 23.

To draw with the Paintbrush tool:

1. Choose the **Paintbrush** tool ✐ (B).

2. Choose a stroke color and width, and a fill color of None.

3. Show the **Brushes** panel ❦ (F5) or click the Brush thumbnail or arrowhead on the Control panel, ● ▪ then click a brush on the panel.

4. Do either of the following:

   To draw open paths, draw separate lines.**A**

   To draw a closed path, drag to draw the path, then Option-drag/Alt-drag to close it (release Option/Alt last).

5. Choose View > Preview to see the path with the current stroke settings, or Outline to see it as a wireframe representation.**B**

A These objects were drawn with an Art brush chosen for the Paintbrush tool.

B Assorted fill colors were applied to the objects.

Choosing options for the Pencil and Paintbrush tools

The Pencil or Paintbrush tool can be customized in two ways: by choosing settings on the Control panel and via the tool's options dialog. Changes to the tool options settings affect only lines you subsequently draw, not existing ones.

To choose options for the Pencil or Paintbrush tool:

1. Do either of the following:

   Double-click the **Pencil** tool ✏ (or press N to choose the tool, then press Return/Enter).

   Double-click the **Paintbrush** tool 🖌 (or press B to choose the tool, then press Return/Enter).

2. In the Tolerances area of the options dialog: **A**

   Choose a **Fidelity** value (.5–20). **B–C** A low Fidelity setting produces many anchor points and paths that accurately follow the movement of your mouse; a high setting produces fewer anchor points and smoother, but less accurate, paths.

   Choose a **Smoothness** value (0–100). The higher the Smoothness, the fewer the irregularities in the path.

3. Check any of the following options:

   Fill New Pencil Strokes or **Fill New Brush Strokes** to have new paths (whether open or closed) fill automatically with the current fill color. The default setting is off.

   Keep Selected to have the paths stay selected after they're created. This saves you a step if you are likely to add to a path right after drawing it, or if you tend to draw using many separate lines. **D**

   Edit Selected Paths to activate the reshaping function of the tool (see page 151). The Within: [ ] Pixels value is the minimum distance the pointer must be from a path for the tool to reshape it. Uncheck this option if you want to be able to draw multiple lines or brush strokes near one another without reshaping any existing selected paths.

4. Click OK.

➤ Click Reset in the Pencil or Paintbrush Tool Options dialog to restore the default settings to the tool.

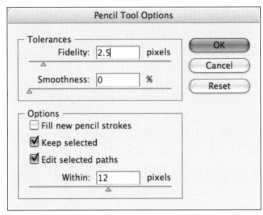

A The Pencil tool has its own options dialog.

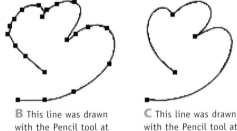

B This line was drawn with the Pencil tool at a low Fidelity setting.

C This line was drawn with the Pencil tool at a high Fidelity setting.

D Each stroke in this drawing is a separate path.

Drawing with the Blob Brush tool

The new Blob Brush is a versatile, dual-purpose tool. It lets you draw closed path objects in a loose, freehand style, and also lets you reshape existing closed paths, regardless of which tool they were created with. The tool is similar to a traditional felt-tip marker, with two advantages: it enables you to reshape your strokes after they're drawn and it's odor-free! If you like to draw artwork "by hand," you'll probably take an instant liking to it. "Blob Brush tool" is a cumbersome name to say aloud, but it's a fun tool to use.

On this page, you'll learn how to create objects with the Blob Brush tool; on the next page, you'll choose options for the tool; and on page 152, you'll master its reshaping function.

To draw with the Blob Brush tool: ★

1. Choose the **Blob Brush** tool 🖉 (Shift-B).

2. On the Control panel, click the **Stroke** thumbnail or arrowhead 🔲▾ to open a temporary Swatches panel, then click a solid-color swatch on the panel.

3. Position the brush cursor over an artboard. Press [to decrease the brush tip size or] to increase it.

4. Draw chunky lines, as you would with a traditional marking pen.**A–B** The lines can crisscross one another. When you release the mouse, a new closed compound path is created.

   Note: This tool produces different results from those you get with the other freehand tools, such as the Paintbrush, which create stroked paths.

5. *Optional:* Without changing the stroke color, draw a connecting line from one end of a Blob Brush shape to the other end, to connect them.

6. Choose the Selection ▸ or Direct Selection ▸ tool, then click the new shape. The original stroke color on the object will convert automatically to a fill color, and the stroke color will convert to None.

A A briefcase is drawn with the Blob Brush tool.

B Other areas of "shading" were drawn with the Blob Brush.

Choosing options for the Blob Brush tool

To choose options for the Blob Brush tool: ★

1. Double-click the **Blob Brush** tool icon 🖌 on the Tools panel. The Blob Brush Tool Options dialog opens.**A**

2. Do any of the following:

   Check **Keep Selected** to have the Blob Brush path stay selected after it's created; or check **Selection Limits Merge** to have your Blob Brush strokes merge with only currently selected objects, and to prevent nonselected objects with the same fill color from being merged (to merge shapes with the Blob Brush, see page 152).

   Choose a **Fidelity** value. A low Fidelity setting produces many anchor points and paths that follow your mouse movements accurately; a high setting produces fewer anchor points and smoother, but less accurate, paths.

   Choose a **Smoothness** value to preserve or smooth out irregularities in the path.

3. For Size, Angle, and Roundness,**B–C** see steps 4–7 in the instructions on pages 298–299 for editing a Calligraphic brush (the Diameter option in the Calligraphic Brush Options dialog is equivalent to the Size option here).

4. Click OK.

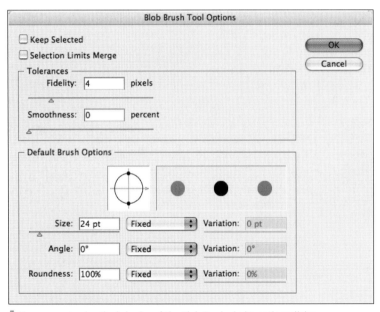

A You can customize the behavior of the Blob Brush via its options dialog.

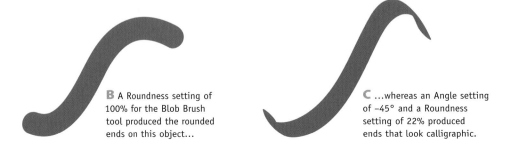

B A Roundness setting of 100% for the Blob Brush tool produced the rounded ends on this object...

C ...whereas an Angle setting of –45° and a Roundness setting of 22% produced ends that look calligraphic.

As a prerequisite to learning the many editing techniques in Illustrator, you need to learn how to select (and deselect) objects, because objects must be selected before they can be edited. The many selection controls in Illustrator include five tools, a host of Select menu commands, and a special feature of the Layers panel. You'll learn all of these methods in this chapter, as well as how to group objects, isolate groups and objects for editing, and save your selections. Once you master these fundamental skills, you'll be ready to learn how to copy and align objects (in the next chapter), and then plunge into all the fun stuff, such as recoloring, transforming, reshaping, and applying effects.

The five selection tools

These descriptions of the basic functions of the selection tools will help prepare you for the step-by-step instructions that follow:

Use the **Selection** tool ▶ (V) to select or move a whole object or group (or to scale or rotate an object via its bounding box), **A** and to select all the points on an object. (See page 87.)

Continued on the following page

A The Selection tool selects
whole objects.

Use the **Direct Selection** tool (A) to select one or more individual anchor points or segments on a path. A If you click a curve segment with this tool, the direction handles and anchor points for that segment will become visible. (Straight segments don't have direction handles—they just have anchor points.) (See page 88.)

Although the **Group Selection** tool can be used to select all the anchor points on a single path, its main purpose in life is selecting groups of objects that are nested inside larger groups. Click once with this tool to select an object, click twice to select that object's group, click three times to select the next group that was added to the larger group, and so on. The Group Selection tool is found on the Direct Selection tool pop-out menu, but the easiest way to access it is by holding down Option/Alt when the Direct Selection tool is selected.

➤ An easier way to edit a group is to put it in isolation mode. An advantage of this method is that it prevents you from editing other objects unintentionally. (See pages 90–91.)

Use the **Lasso** tool (Q) to select anchor points and segments by dragging a freeform marquee around them. B (See page 92.)

The **Magic Wand** tool (Y) selects objects containing the same or a similar fill color, stroke color, stroke weight, opacity, or blending mode as the object you click on, depending on the current tool settings on the Magic Wand panel. C (See page 93.)

Note: In the illustrations on this page, the bounding box is hidden (Cmd-Shift-B/Ctrl-Shift-B).

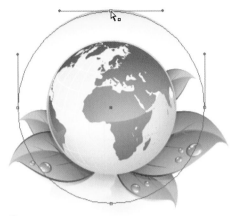

A The Direct Selection tool selects individual anchor points and segments on a path.

B The Lasso tool selects anchor points and segments via a freeform marquee.

C The Magic Wand tool selects objects containing the same or a similar fill color, stroke color, stroke weight, opacity, or blending mode as the object you click.

Using the Selection tool

To select an object or objects:

1. Turn on View > **Smart Guides** (Cmd-U/Ctrl-U). Also go to Illustrator/Edit > Preferences > Smart Guides, and make sure **Object Highlighting** is checked.

2. Choose the **Selection** tool ▶ (V).

3. Do one of the following:

   Because Smart Guides are enabled with the Object Highlighting option, the path will be highlighted as you move the pointer over it. Click the path.**A**

   If the object has a color fill, your document is in Preview view, and the Object Selection by Path Only option is off (see the sidebar at right), click the fill.

   Position the pointer outside the object (or objects) you want to select, then drag a marquee across all or part of it.**B** The whole path will become selected, even if you marquee just a portion of it.**C**

With the Selection tool, you can add objects to or subtract objects from a selection.

To add objects to or subtract objects from a selection:

Choose the **Selection** tool ▶ (V), then Shift-click on or Shift-drag a marquee around any unselected objects to include them in the selection, or do the same for any selected objects to deselect them.

OBJECT SELECTION BY PATH ONLY

With Object Selection by Path Only checked in Illustrator/Edit > Preferences > Selection & Anchor Display, in order to select an object, you must click a segment or anchor point on the path. With this option unchecked, you don't have to be as precise about where you click: if the object contains a fill (not None) and the document is in Preview view, you can click on the fill (or the path).

A A path is selected with the Selection tool (in the figures on this page, the bounding box is hidden).

B A few paths are marqueed with the Selection tool.

C The paths within the marquee became selected.

Using the Direct Selection tool

As a prerequisite to reshaping objects (Chapter 12), you need to learn how to select individual points and segments. It's important to be precise about which components you select.

To select or deselect anchor points or segments with the Direct Selection tool:

1. Go to Preferences > Selection & Anchor Display, and check **Highlight Anchors on Mouse Over** (you can also choose preferences for the anchor and/or handle display; see page 362). And in the Smart Guides panel of the dialog, make sure **Object Highlighting** is checked. Click OK.

2. Turn on View > **Smart Guides** (Cmd-U/Ctrl-U).

3. Choose the **Direct Selection** tool ▶ (A).

4. Do one of the following:

   To select a segment, click the path.**A**

   To select anchor points, pass the pointer over an anchor point (the point enlarges temporarily), then click.**B–C**

   Position the pointer outside the object or objects, then drag a marquee across the anchor points or segments you want to select (a temporary marquee defines the area as you drag).**D** Only the points or segments you marqueed will become selected.**E**

5. *Optional:* To select additional anchor points or segments, or to deselect selected anchor points or segments individually, Shift-click them or Shift-drag a marquee around them.

➤ To access the last-used selection tool (Selection or Direct Selection) temporarily when using a nonselection tool, hold down Cmd/Ctrl.

Selecting objects by using a command

The Select commands select objects whose characteristics are similar to those of the last or currently selected object. Each command is named by the attributes it searches for.

To select objects by using a command:

Do any of the following:

Select an object to base the search on, or deselect all objects to base the search on the last object that was selected. From the Select > **Same** submenu, choose one of the available commands, such as Fill & Stroke, Fill Color,

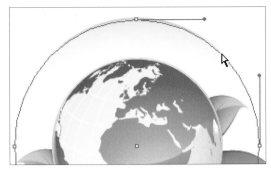

A A curve segment is clicked with the Direct Selection tool.

B As you move the pointer over an anchor point, it becomes enlarged temporarily. Click the point to select it.

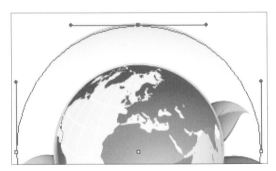

C Selected anchor points are solid; unselected ones are hollow.

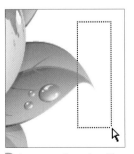

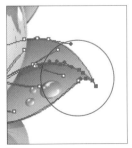

D A marquee is made with the Direct Selection tool.

E Only anchor points within the marquee became selected.

Opacity, Stroke Color, or Stroke Weight. **A** Most of these commands are also on the **Select Similar Options** menu  on the Control panel **B** (the menu isn't available for all objects).

Select an object or objects, then from the Select > **Object** submenu, **C** choose one of the following: **All on Same Layers** to select all the objects on the layer the object resides on (or if the currently selected objects are on more than one layer, from those layers); or choose **Direction Handles** to select all the direction handles on the currently selected object or objects (see Chapter 12).

With or without selecting an object first, from the Select > **Object** submenu, choose one of the following: **Brush Strokes** to select all objects that have a brush stroke; **Clipping Masks** to select masking objects (to display the edges of a masking object); **Stray Points** to select lone points that don't belong to any paths (so they can be deleted); or **Text Objects** to select all the type objects in the document.

Selecting objects via the Layers panel

The following basic instruction for selecting objects via the Layers panel is a sneak preview of Chapter 13 (specifically, pages 170–172).

To select objects by using the Layers panel:

1. Display the **Layers** panel 🌐 (F7).

2. Do either of the following:

   If the listing for the object that you want to select isn't visible on the Layers panel, click the expand/collapse triangle for its top-level layer, sublayer, or group to reveal it. Next, at the far right side of the panel, click the selection area for the object you want to select. A colored square appears (each layer is assigned a unique color automatically). **D**

   To select all the objects on a layer or sublayer, click the selection area for the whole layer.

RESELECTING SIMILAR OBJECTS QUICKLY

Say you used a command on the Select Similar Options menu on the Control panel and you want to use it again. Select an object, then click the Select Similar Objects button 🖌️ (next to the menu).

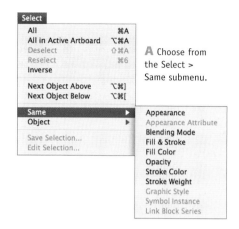

A Choose from the Select > Same submenu.

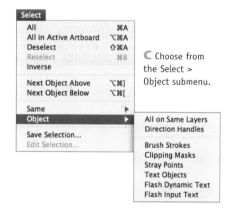

B Or choose from the Select Similar Options menu on the Control panel.

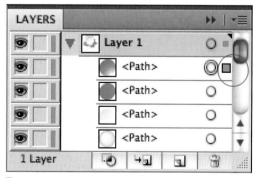

C Choose from the Select > Object submenu.

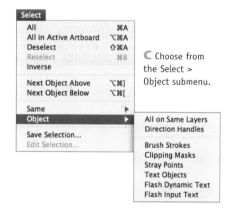

D Click the selection area for an object on the Layers panel.

Working with groups

By gathering objects into a group, you'll be able to select, isolate, copy, paste, or edit them as a unit. You can group different kinds of objects together (e.g., type objects with placed images), and you can edit individual objects in a group without having to ungroup them first.

To put objects in a group:

1. Do either of the following:

   Choose the Selection tool . Then, in the document window, Shift-click or drag a marquee around all the objects to be grouped.

   Shift-click the selection area at the far right side of the Layers panel to make a selection square appear for each object to be put in a group (click the expand/collapse arrow, if necessary, to display the object listings). Or to select all the objects on a layer, click the selection square for the layer.

2. Control-click/right-click in the document window and choose **Group** from the context menu (Cmd-G/Ctrl-G).**A** All the objects in the group will be put on the same layer.

The easiest and fastest way to edit individual objects in a group is with the group in isolation mode.

To edit grouped objects in isolation mode: ★

1. Go to Illustrator/Edit > Preferences > General and make sure **Double Click to Isolate** is checked.

2. Choose the Selection tool or hold down Cmd/Ctrl, then double-click a group in your artwork.**B**

3. A dark gray **isolation mode** bar appears at the top of the document window, listing the name of the selected layer and group (an Isolation Mode listing also appears on the Layers panel). Objects outside the group are temporarily dimmed and uneditable.

4. You can select and edit objects in an isolated group with the Selection tool, or select and edit individual paths with the Direct Selection tool.**C** You can also double-click any nested group (within the larger group) to isolate it, or click <Group> or the arrowhead on the isolation mode bar to navigate through nested groups.

5. To exit isolation mode, click the isolation mode bar or press Esc.

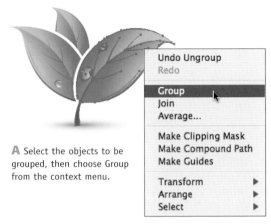

A Select the objects to be grouped, then choose Group from the context menu.

Isolation mode bar

B We double-clicked the leaf group on the right to put it into isolation mode; the other objects are dimmed.

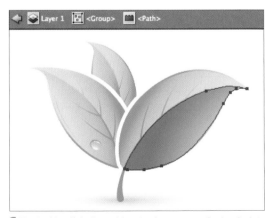

C We double-clicked an object in the group to further isolate it. The name of the object appears on the isolation mode bar.

Before creating an object or placing an image into an Illustrator document, you can choose which group you want it to belong to.

To add a new object to a group:

1. Choose the Selection tool ▶ (V), then double-click a group to isolate it.**A**

2. Draw a new object or objects.**B** A listing for each new object you create will appear at the top of the nested group on the Layers panel.

3. *Optional:* On the Layers panel, expand the group that you added an object to, then drag the new object name to a different stacking position in the group list.

4. Click the gray isolation mode bar at the top of the document window to exit isolation mode.

To add an existing object to a group:

1. With the Selection tool ▶ (V), click the object to be added to a group.

2. Choose Edit > **Cut** (Cmd-X/Ctrl-X).

3. Double-click the group to isolate it.

4. Choose Edit > **Paste** (Cmd-V/Ctrl-V), drag the object to reposition it, then click the gray isolation mode bar at the top of the document window to exit isolation mode.

➤ You can also add an existing object to a group by using the Layers panel; see page 173.

Sometimes a group has to be disbanded—er, ungrouped.

To ungroup a group:

1. To select the group, choose the Selection tool ▶ (V), then either click the group in the document window or click the selection area for the group listing on the Layers panel.

2. Do either of the following:

   Control-click/right-click the artboard and choose **Ungroup** from the context menu.

   Choose Object > **Ungroup** (Cmd-Shift-G/ Ctrl-Shift-G).

   The group listing disappears from the Layers panel.

➤ Keep choosing the same command to ungroup nested groups (groups within larger groups).

➤ To learn how to select groups and grouped objects by using the Layers panel, see page 172.

A We double-clicked the leaf group on the right to put it into isolation mode; the other objects are dimmed.

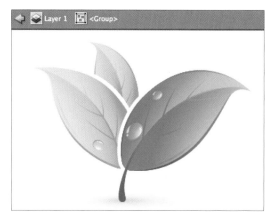

B Two new objects (the water droplets) were added to the isolated group.

Isolating nongrouped objects

In addition to editing grouped objects in isolation mode, you can edit individual objects. This is a great way to work with individual components when your artwork contains overlapping shapes, because it makes all nonisolated objects temporarily dimmed and uneditable. Note: Throughout this book, when we instruct you to select an object for editing, bear in mind that in most cases you can simply isolate an object instead, if you prefer.

To isolate a nongrouped object: ★

1. Go to Illustrator/Edit > Preferences > General and make sure **Double Click to Isolate** is checked.

2. Choose the Selection tool ▶ (V) or hold down Cmd/Ctrl, then double-click an object.

3. A dark gray **isolation mode** bar appears at the top of the document window, listing the name of the selected object.**A**

4. Edit the object.

5. To exit isolation mode, click the gray isolation mode bar at the top of the window or press Esc.

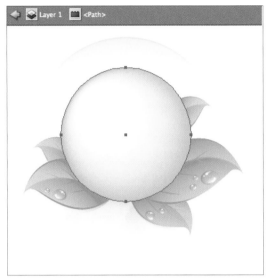

A We double-clicked a circle object to isolate it.

Using the Lasso tool

Let's say you need to select a few points on one path and a couple of points on a nearby path. You could grab the Direct Selection tool and click the points individually (tedious) or you could marquee them (works only if the points in question fall conveniently within the rectangular marquee). With the Lasso tool, you can wend your way around to encircle just the points and segments you want to select. This is especially helpful for creating selections among paths that are in close proximity. Don't try to use it to select whole paths.

To select or deselect points or segments with the Lasso tool:

1. Deselect (click a blank area of the artboard).

2. Choose the **Lasso** tool 🔫 (Q), then drag to encircle just the segments or points you want to select.**B–C** You can drag right across a path. You don't need to close the lasso selection; simply release the mouse when the desired points have been lassoed.

3. *Optional:* Shift-drag around any unselected points or segments to add them to the selection, or Option-drag/Alt-drag around any selected points or segments to deselect them.

B Wend your way around parts of objects with the Lasso tool.

C Only the points and segments you marquee will become selected.

Using the Magic Wand tool

The Magic Wand tool selects all the objects in a document that have the same or a similar fill color, stroke color, stroke weight, opacity, or blending mode as the object you click on, depending on which options are currently checked on the Magic Wand panel.

To choose options for the Magic Wand tool:

1. To show the Magic Wand panel, double-click the **Magic Wand** tool ✴ (Y) or choose Window > **Magic Wand**.

   If all three sections of the panel aren't showing, click the up/down arrowhead on the panel tab to make them appear.

2. On the left side of the panel, **A** check which attributes you want the tool to select: Fill Color, Stroke Color, Stroke Weight, Opacity, or Blending Mode.

3. For each option you checked in the preceding step (except Blending Mode), choose a Tolerance range. Choose a low value to select only objects with colors, weights, or opacities that match (or are very similar to) the one you will click with the tool; or choose a high value to allow the tool to select a broader range of those attributes. For Fill Color or Stroke Color, choose a range (depending on the document color mode, the range is 0–255 for RGB or 0–100 for CMYK); for Stroke Weight, choose a width Tolerance (0–1000 pt); and for Opacity, choose a percentage (0–100).

4. To permit the Magic Wand tool to select objects on all layers, make sure Use All Layers has a check mark on the panel menu (the default setting), or uncheck this option to permit the tool to select objects on just the current layer.

➤ The Reset command on the Magic Wand panel menu resets all fields on the panel to their default values and unchecks all the options except Fill Color.

IN THE CROSSHAIRS

If Use Precise Cursors is checked in Illustrator/Edit > Preferences > General, the Lasso and Magic Wand tool pointers will be crosshairs -¦- instead of the tool icon, which is helpful for precise positioning.

To use the Magic Wand tool:

1. Choose the **Magic Wand** tool ✴ (Y).

2. To create a new selection, click an object in the document window. Depending on the current settings on the Magic Wand panel, other objects containing the same or a similar fill color, stroke color, stroke weight, opacity, or blending mode may become selected. **B–C**

3. Do either of the following:

   To add to the selection, Shift-click another object.

   To subtract from the selection, Option-click/Alt-click a selected object.

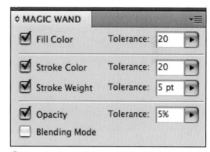

A Use the Magic Wand panel to choose default settings for the tool.

B The first two water droplets have an opacity of 100%, whereas the third one has an opacity of 50%. With Fill Color and Opacity checked for the Magic Wand tool, the fill of the leftmost object is clicked. Only the middle drop, which has the same fill color and opacity as the first, became selected.

C This time the Magic Wand tool was used with the Opacity option off. All three objects became selected, because opacity was ignored as a factor.

Saving selections

Via the Save Selection command, you can save any selection under a custom name, then reselect those objects quickly by choosing that name from the Select menu.

To save a selection:

1. Select one or more objects.

2. Choose Select > **Save Selection**.

3. In the Save Selection dialog,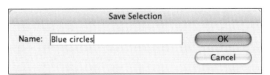 enter a descriptive name, then click OK. To reselect those objects at any time, simply choose the selection name from the bottom of the **Select** menu.

➤ To rename or delete a saved selection, choose Select > Edit Selection. Click a selection name, then change it or click Delete.**B**

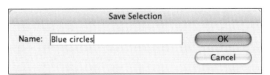

A By saving your selections, they will be easy to reselect.

Selecting and deselecting all objects

To select all the objects in a document:

Choose Select > **All** (Cmd-A/Ctrl-A). All unlocked objects in your document will become selected, regardless of whether they're on an artboard or in the scratch area. This command doesn't select hidden or locked objects or objects on hidden layers (for which the visibility icon on the Layers panel is off).

➤ If the text cursor is flashing in a text block, the Select > All command will select all the text in the block instead of all objects in the document.

To prevent objects from being modified, you must make sure they're deselected.

To deselect all objects on all layers:

Do either of the following:

Choose Select > **Deselect** (Cmd-Shift-A/Ctrl-Shift-A).

Choose any selection tool (or hold down Cmd/Ctrl), then click a blank area of the document.

➤ To deselect an individual object within a multiple-object selection, Shift-click it with the Selection tool. To deselect an object within a group, see page 172.

The Inverse command deselects all selected objects and selects all unselected objects.

To invert a selection:

Choose Select > **Inverse**.

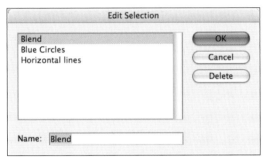

B Use the Edit Selection dialog to rename or delete any of your saved selections.

Once you have created multiple objects in a document, you'll undoubtedly find a need to reposition them. You may also find a need to copy or align them. In this chapter, you'll learn how to move objects with the aid of Smart Guides; duplicate, align, and distribute objects; and create and use ruler guides, guide objects, and the grid to position objects manually.

Moving objects

In these instructions, you will learn the simplest and most straightforward method for moving objects: by dragging. In conjunction with a great feature called Smart Guides (see the next page), dragging will serve most of your moving needs.

To move an object or group by dragging:

1. Choose the Selection tool ▶ (V).

2. Do either of the following:

   Drag the object's path (you can do this in Outline or Preview view).

   If the document is in Preview view, the object has a fill, and Object Selection by Path Only is off in Illustrator/Edit > Preferences > Selection & Anchor Display, you can drag the object's fill.**A** This can also be done with the Direct Selection tool.

➤ Hold down Shift while dragging an object to constrain the movement to a multiple of 45° (or to the current Constrain Angle in Illustrator/Edit > Preferences > General, if that value isn't 0).

➤ To learn other techniques for moving objects, such as the Transform panel, Control panel, and Transform Each command, see pages 138–141.

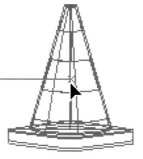

A With the aid of a Smart Guide, a group is dragged along the horizontal axis.

Aligning objects by using Smart Guides

Smart Guides are nonprinting labels or lines that appear onscreen temporarily when you create, move, duplicate, or transform an object. For example, alignment guides are "magnetic" guides that appear onscreen when you move an object. You can use them, say, to move an object along the horizontal or vertical axis, or to align the edge of an object with the edge of an artboard or the edge of another object. You can also use Smart Guides when repositioning an artboard in your document. In Illustrator CS4, Smart Guides are even easier to use than before, because they let you snap objects to guides or to other objects, as opposed to the pointer. This feature is easier done than said, so give it a try.

To use Smart Guides to align objects: ★

1. Make sure the View > **Smart Guides** (Cmd-U/ Ctrl-U) feature is on (has a check mark), and that View > Snap to Grid is off.

2. To establish the necessary preferences for Smart Guides, go to Illustrator/Edit > Preferences (Cmd-K/Ctrl-K) > **Smart Guides**, and check all six option boxes.*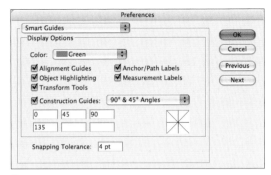 Switch to the **Selection & Anchor Display** panel, check **Snap to Point**, then click OK.

3. Choose the **Selection** tool ▸ (V), then as you drag an object, release the mouse when the object snaps to any of the following:

   An **alignment guide** that denotes the edge of another object.**B**

   The **center point** of another object.**C**

   An **anchor point** on the edge of another object (**A**, next page).

   ➤ The measurement label (in the gray rectangle) indicates the current horizontal distance (dX) and vertical distance (dY) the group has been moved from its original location.

A Check all six Display Options check boxes in the Smart Guides panel of the Preferences dialog.

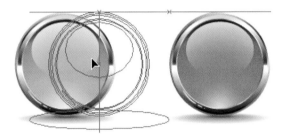

B A horizontal alignment guide appears at the moment when the edge of the group we're moving aligns with the top edge of another group.

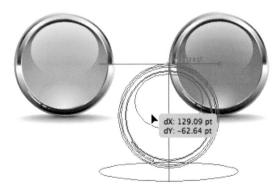

C We're aligning the center point of a group with the intersection of two alignment guides — in this case, from the center points of two other objects. Note the measurement label in the gray box.

---

*Although you won't be using all of the Smart Guides options in this task, you may find it convenient to activate them all so they're available for other tasks.

➤ Smart Guides vanish as quickly as they appear. To create guides that stay onscreen, see page 103.

➤ The Smart Guides preferences are described in detail on page 366. For example, you can establish specific angles for Smart Guides; or if you need the guides to contrast better with colors in your artwork, you can choose a different color from the Color menu. To use the Transform Tools option for Smart Guides, see page 135.

➤ Smart Guides provide useful information even when the mouse is just hovering over an object. **B**

A Because the Snap to Point option is on (in the Selection & Anchor Display panel of the Preferences dialog), when the pointer of an object we drag is over an anchor point on another object, it becomes a white arrowhead.

HIDING OR SHOWING AN OBJECT'S CENTER POINT

To hide (or show) the center point on one or more selected objects, display the Attributes panel 🗐 (Cmd-F11/Ctrl-F11), then click the Don't Show Center button (or the Show Center button) on the panel. To show or hide the center point for all the objects in the document, choose Select > All (Cmd-A/Ctrl-A) first. Note: If the Show Center buttons aren't visible on the panel, click the up/down arrowhead on the panel tab.

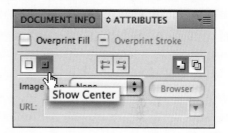

The center point on this object is visible...

...whereas here the center point is hidden.

B Object highlighting (the blue border) and anchor/path labels (green text labels) display when the pointer is over the edge or an anchor point of an object, mouse button up. The measurement label on the right is indicating the *X,Y* location of that anchor point.

Duplicating objects

To duplicate an object or group, you can use any of the following techniques:

➤ Dragging (instructions on this page)

➤ Arrow keys (sidebar at right)

➤ The Clipboard (the following page)

➤ The Offset Path command (page 100)

➤ A transform tool (page 134 and pages 136–137), the Transform panel (pages 138–139), the Transform Each command (page 140), or the Transform effect (page 141)

➤ The Layers panel (page 174)

To duplicate an object or group in the same document:

1. Choose the Selection tool ► (V).

2. Option-drag/Alt-drag an object's path or fill (not its bounding box). **A–B** The pointer will turn into a double arrowhead. Release the mouse before releasing Option/Alt.

   To reposition the duplicate object along the horizontal or vertical axis, use alignment Smart Guides (see the two preceding pages).

➤ To repeat the last transformation (such as the making of a duplicate), press Cmd-D/Ctrl-D.

➤ To duplicate an object in a group, start dragging with the Direct Selection tool, then continue dragging with Option/Alt held down; the copy will be a member of the same group. If you want the duplicate to appear outside the group, copy it by using the Direct Selection tool and the Clipboard instead (see the next page).

When you drag an object between files, a copy of the object appears in the target document automatically.

To drag and drop an object or group between files: ★

1. Open two documents as tabbed windows.

2. Choose the Selection tool ► (V).

3. Drag an object or group to the tab of the target document, pause until the target document window displays, then release the mouse where you want the duplicate object to appear.

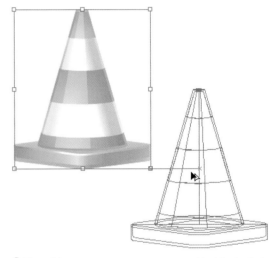

USING AN ARROW KEY TO COPY OBJECTS

Choose the Selection tool, select an object, then press Option-Shift-arrow/Alt-Shift-arrow to copy the object and move the copy in the direction of the arrow by 10 times the current Keyboard Increment setting in Preferences > General. The default increment is 1 pt.

A The quickest way to copy a group or an object is simply to Option-drag/Alt-drag it. Note the double-arrowhead pointer.

B A copy of the group is made.

If you select an object or a group and choose the Cut or Copy command, the object or group is placed onto the Clipboard, a temporary storage area in memory. The contents of the Clipboard are replaced each time you choose Cut or Copy.

The Paste command places the current Clipboard contents on the currently selected layer in the center of the currently active document window. The Paste in Front and Paste in Back commands paste an object in the same horizontal and vertical *(x/y)* location from which it was cut or copied, in front of or behind the current selection, and are useful for positioning an object in a particular stacking position.

Objects are copied to the Clipboard in the PDF and/or AICB format, depending on the current settings in Illustrator/Edit > Preferences > File Handling & Clipboard (see page 371). The same Clipboard contents can be pasted an unlimited number of times.

To duplicate or move objects between documents via the Clipboard:

1. Open two documents.

2. With the Selection tool ▶ (V), select the object or group to be copied or moved.

3. Do either of the following:

   To place a copy of the object or group on the Clipboard while leaving the original in the current document, choose Edit > **Copy** (Cmd-C/Ctrl-C).

   To place the object or group on the Clipboard and delete it from the current document, choose Edit > **Cut** (Cmd-X/Ctrl-X).

4. Click the tab for the target document.

5. Choose Edit > **Paste** (Cmd-V/Ctrl-V).

➤ To restack the pasted object in front of or behind another object, use the Layers panel (see page 173).

REMEMBERING LAYERS

To paste an object to the top of the same layer or sublayer rather than to a different layer, turn the Paste Remembers Layers option on via the Layers panel menu. Note: If this option is on and you copy an object, delete the object's layer, then use the Paste command, the object will paste onto a brand new layer.

HIDING THE BOUNDING BOX

On page 133, you'll learn how to transform an object or group via its bounding box. In the meantime, if you want to hide (or show) the bounding box, which displays on all selected objects, choose View > Hide Bounding Box (or Show Bounding Box) or press Cmd-Shift-B/Ctrl-Shift-B.

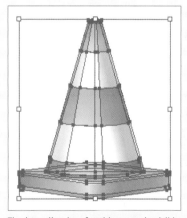

The bounding box for this group is visible.

Whereas here the bounding box is hidden.

The Offset Path command duplicates a path and offsets the duplicate around or inside the original path by a specified distance. The command also reshapes the duplicate automatically so it fits nicely around the original path. The fill and stroke attributes of the duplicate match those of the original object. You might not use this command on a regular basis, but it can come in handy when you need a precisely scaled copy of an object.

To offset a duplicate of a path:

1. Select an object.

2. Choose Object > Path > **Offset Path**. The Offset Path dialog opens.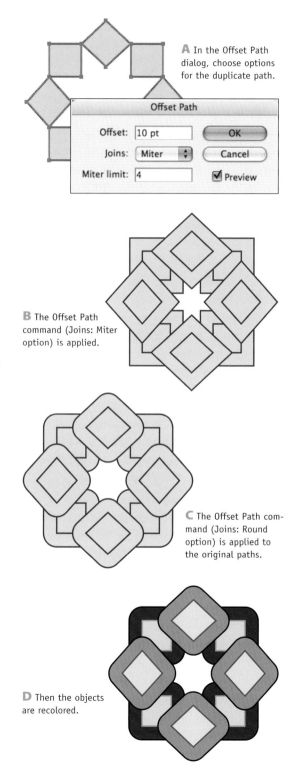 Check Preview.

3. In the Offset field, enter the distance the duplicate path is to be offset from the original. Be sure your Offset value is larger or smaller than the stroke weight of the original path so the duplicates will be visible.

For a closed path, if a positive value is chosen, the new path will be larger than the original; if a negative value is chosen, the new path will be smaller. For an open path, both positive and negative values create a wider closed path, in the same shape as the original stroke.

4. Choose a **Joins** (bend) style: **Miter** (pointed), **B Round** (semicircular), **C** or **Bevel** (square-cornered) for the shape of the joints in the duplicate.

5. *Optional:* Change the Miter Limit (1–500) value for the point at which a miter (pointed) corner becomes a beveled corner. A high Miter Limit creates long, pointy corners; a low Miter Limit creates beveled corners.

6. Click OK. The offset path will be a separate path from, and stacked behind or in front of, the original path.**D** Regardless of whether the original object was open or closed, the resulting offset path will be closed.

➤ The Offset Path command can also be applied as an editable effect via Effect > Path > Offset Path (to learn about effects, see Chapter 15).

A In the Offset Path dialog, choose options for the duplicate path.

B The Offset Path command (Joins: Miter option) is applied.

C The Offset Path command (Joins: Round option) is applied to the original paths.

D Then the objects are recolored.

Aligning and distributing objects

To line up objects neatly in a row or column (e.g., buttons for a Web page or blocks of point type), rather than trying to position them by eye, use the convenient controls on the Align or Control panel.

To align or distribute objects: ★

1. To align, select two or more objects or groups; to distribute, select three or more objects. (Or if all the objects are in the same group, you can isolate the group before selecting the objects.) Display the **Align** panel ■ (Shift-F7) **A** or the **Control** panel.**B** If the Align Objects buttons aren't showing on the Control panel, choose Align from the Control panel menu.

2. On the Align panel menu, check **Use Preview Bounds** to have Illustrator factor in an object's stroke weight and any effects when calculating the alignment or distribution, or turn this option off to have Illustrator ignore the stroke weight and any effects. This option can also be turned on or off in Preferences > General. (By default, the stroke extends partially outside the edge of a path.)

3. Do either of the following:

   From the Align To menu, 🔲▾ choose **Align to Selection** (the default setting) to reposition some or all of the selected objects within the bounding box of the overall selection, depending on which Align Objects button you will click in the next step.

   To specify which object in the selection remains stationary (becomes the "key" object), click it now; the selection border of the key object is now wider than the others. Or alternatively, choose **Align to Key Object** ★ from the Align To menu to have the topmost of the selected objects in the stacking order (Layers panel) become the key object.

Continued on the following page

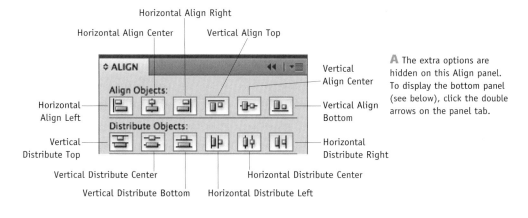

Horizontal Align Right

Horizontal Align Center   Vertical Align Top

♦ ALIGN

Align Objects:

Horizontal Align Left

Distribute Objects:

Vertical Distribute Top

Vertical Align Center

Vertical Align Bottom

Horizontal Distribute Right

A The extra options are hidden on this Align panel. To display the bottom panel (see below), click the double arrows on the panel tab.

Vertical Distribute Center   Horizontal Distribute Center

Vertical Distribute Bottom   Horizontal Distribute Left

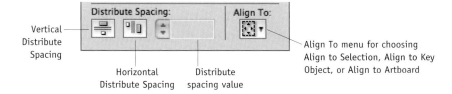

Distribute Spacing: Align To:

Vertical Distribute Spacing

Horizontal Distribute Spacing   Distribute spacing value

Align To menu for choosing Align to Selection, Align to Key Object, or Align to Artboard

B The Align buttons are also available on the Control panel when multiple objects are selected.

➤ To cancel the key object, choose Align to Selection from the Align To menu or choose Cancel Key Object from the panel menu.

4. On the Align panel or Control panel, click one or more of the **Align Objects** buttons **A–B** and/or **Distribute Objects** buttons.**C**

Or for **Distribute Spacing**, click one of the selected objects to designate it as the key object. Choose or enter the desired distance to be placed between the objects by using the Distribute Spacing menu or field, then click either or both of the two Distribute Spacing buttons.

➤ Change your mind? To apply a different Align panel option, first nix the last one by using the Undo command (Cmd-U/Ctrl-U).

➤ If you choose Align to Artboard from the Align To menu ▦▾ on the Align or Control panel, and depending on which Align Objects button you click, at least two of the selected objects will align with the top, right, bottom, or left edge of the artboard. Or if you were to click, say, the Vertical Distribute Top button, the top of the topmost object would align to the top of the artboard, the bottom of the bottommost object would align to the bottom of the artboard, and the remaining objects would be distributed between them.

A These are the original objects.

B The Vertical Align Bottom button is clicked.

C The Horizontal Distribute Center button is clicked.

Creating ruler guides

For most purposes, Smart Guides work quite well for arranging objects, but they do disappear. If you need guides that stay onscreen, create ruler guides by following these instructions. Ruler guides don't print.

To create ruler guides:

1. Choose View > Guides > **Show Guides** (Cmd-;/ Ctrl-;), or if the command is listed as Hide Guides, leave it be.

2. *Optional:* To create a new top-level layer to contain the guides, Option-Shift-click/Alt-Shift-click the New Layer button ▣ on the Layers panel. In the dialog, name the layer "Guides," then click OK. Keep the Guides layer selected.

3. If the rulers aren't visible at the top and left sides of the document window, choose View > **Show Rulers** (Cmd-R/Ctrl-R).

4. Drag a guide or guides from the horizontal or vertical ruler onto your artboard,**A–B** noting its location by the dotted line on the opposite ruler. (The higher the zoom level, the finer the ruler increments.) Each guide is listed separately on the Layers panel as <Guide>.

➤ To learn about locking, unlocking, and clearing guides, see page 105.

➤ Option-drag/Alt-drag from the horizontal ruler to create a vertical guide, or from the vertical ruler to create a horizontal guide.

MAKE IT SNAPPY

➤ With View > Snap to Point on, as you drag an object near a guide or an anchor point, the black pointer turns white and the part of the object that's under the pointer snaps to that guide or point. You can change the Snap to Point value (the maximum distance between the pointer and the target within which the snap occurs) in Preferences > Selection & Anchor Display. The default value is 2 px.

➤ With View > Pixel Preview on, View > Snap to Grid becomes View > Snap to Pixel, and Snap to Pixel is turned on automatically. This feature causes any new objects you create or any existing objects you drag or transform to snap to the invisible pixel grid. Also, anti-aliasing is removed from any horizontal or vertical edges of those objects (the edges become more crisp).

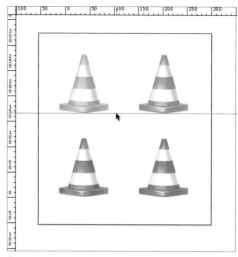

A A guide is dragged from the horizontal ruler.

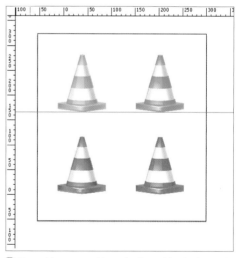

B The guide appears (the color for guides is chosen in Illustrator/Edit > Preferences > Guides & Grid).

Creating guide objects

Thus far we have shown you how to work with two kinds of guides: Smart Guides and ruler guides. Next, you'll learn how to convert a standard path into a guide object (guide objects don't print). The process is reversible, meaning a guide object can be converted back to a standard object at any time.

To turn an object into a guide:

1. Select an object,**A** a group of objects, or an object within a group (but not a symbol, an object in a blend, or a Live Paint group). You can copy the object and work off the copy, if you like. Note: If the object you turn into a guide is part of a group, the guide will become part of the group.

2. Do either of the following:

Choose View > Guides > **Make Guides** (Cmd-5/Ctrl-5).**B**

Control-click/right-click the artboard and choose **Make Guides** from the context menu.

➤ You can transform or reshape a guide object, provided guides aren't locked (see the next page). The guide object can be selected (and hidden) via the Layers panel (see Chapter 13); look for the <Guide> listing. Remember to relock it afterward.

When you release a guide object, its former fill and stroke attributes are restored.

To turn a guide object back into an ordinary object:

1. On the Layers panel, make sure none of the guides to be released have a lock icon.

2. Do either of the following:

To release **one** guide, in the document window, Cmd-Shift-double-click/Ctrl-Shift-double-click the edge of the guide.

To release **one or more** guides, make sure guides are unlocked (to unlock them, Control-click/right-click and choose Lock Guides from the context menu to uncheck the command). Choose the Selection tool (V), Shift-click or marquee the guides to be released, then Control-click/right-click and choose **Release Guides** from the context menu (Cmd-Option-5/Ctrl-Alt-5).

A A three-sided polygon (triangle) is selected.

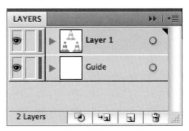

B We used the Make Guides command to convert the path to a guide object, then aligned the objects to the three sides of the guide. (We put our guide on a separate layer.)

Locking and unlocking guides

To select or move ruler guides or guide objects, you must make sure they're unlocked first.

To lock or unlock all guides:

Deselect all objects, then Control-click/right-click in the document window and choose **Lock Guides** from the context menu (Cmd-Option-;/Ctrl-Alt-;).

➤ To hide (or show) guides, choose Hide Guides (or Show Guides) from the context menu.

You can lock or unlock (or hide or show) ruler guides and guide objects individually, because each one has its own <Guide> listing on the Layers panel.

To lock or unlock one guide:

1. Make sure the Lock Guides command is off (see the preceding set of instructions).

2. On the Layers panel, click in the edit (lock) column for any guide to be locked or unlocked. The padlock icon appears or disappears.

Clearing guides

To clear one guide:

1. Make sure either all guides are unlocked or the guide you want to remove is unlocked.

2. Choose the Selection tool (V), then click the ruler guide or guide object to be removed.

3. In the Mac OS, press Delete; in Windows, press Backspace or Del.

4. To relock all the remaining guides, deselect all objects, then Control-click/right-click in the document window and choose Lock Guides.

The Clear Guides command removes all the ruler guides and guide objects in your document.

To clear all guides:

Choose View > Guides > **Clear Guides.**

TIPS FOR WORKING WITH GUIDES

➤ If you drag all your guides into one guides-only layer, you will be able to lock or unlock all of them at once by clicking the lock icon for that layer, or lock or unlock any guide individually via its own lock icon.

➤ To make it easier to tell when your guides are selected, make the selection color for the layer that contains the <Guide> listings different from the guide color. Double-click the layer name, then in the Layer Options dialog, choose a Color from the menu. Alternatively, you can change the color for the guides in the Guides: Color area of Illustrator/Edit > Preferences > Guides & Grid.

Using the grid

The grid is like nonprinting graph paper. You can use it as a framework to arrange objects on, either by eye or by using the Snap to Grid feature. The first step, logically, is to display the grid.

To show or hide the grid:

Do either of the following:

Choose View > **Show Grid** or **Hide Grid** (Cmd-'/ Ctrl-').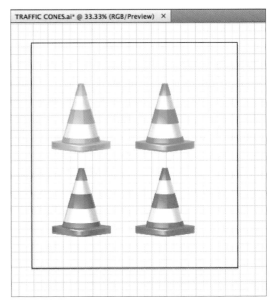

Deselect all, then Control-click/right-click and choose Show Grid or Hide Grid from the context menu.

➤ You can change the grid style (lines or dots), color, or spacing in Preferences > Guides & Grid. With the Grids in Back option checked in that dialog (the default setting), the grid displays behind all objects, not in front.

To snap objects to the grid:

1. Choose View > **Snap to Grid** (Cmd-Shift-'/ Ctrl-Shift-') to make the check mark appear.

2. Move an object near a gridline; the edge of the object will snap to the gridline. This feature works whether the grid is displayed or not.

   Note: When the Snap to Grid command is on, Smart Guides don't display. If you like to use Smart Guides to align objects, as we do, when you're done using the grid, remember to hide it, and also remember to turn off Snap to Grid.

A The grid is showing in this document.

In the preceding four chapters you mastered creating, selecting, and positioning objects. In this chapter, you will apply colors or patterns to add a finishing touch. You will be introduced to the basic color controls in Illustrator and gain an understanding of what type of colors are suitable for print or Web output. You will fill the inside or edge of an object with a solid color or pattern using various panels and tools, save and organize swatches in the Swatches panel, copy swatches between files, choose stroke attributes, use the Color Guide and Kuler panels, replace and edit colors in your artwork, invert colors, colorize grayscale images, blend fill colors between objects, and create and edit patterns.

Color in Illustrator

The fill is applied to the inside of an object; it can be a solid color, pattern, or gradient (or None). The stroke is applied to an object's path; it can be a solid color (or None), a dashed stroke, or a Scatter, Calligraphic, Art, or Pattern brush stroke, but not a gradient. Dashed strokes are created by using the Stroke panel; brushes are applied by using the Brushes panel. The path that you apply a fill and/or stroke to can be open or closed.

The fill and stroke colors in the current or most recently selected object, or new colors that you have chosen if no objects are selected, display on the Tools, Color, Control, and Appearance panels.**A** The current fill and stroke colors are applied to new objects automatically as they are created.

Continued on the following page

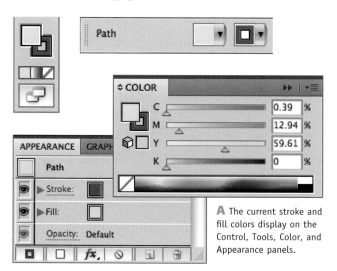

A The current stroke and fill colors display on the Control, Tools, Color, and Appearance panels.

FILL & STROKE

10

In this chapter, you will use the Color, Swatches, Color Guide, Kuler, and Appearance panels; the Color Picker; swatch library panels; and the Eyedropper tool to create and apply colors and patterns. And you'll use the Control, Stroke, and Appearance panels to change the stroke weight, style (dashed or solid), alignment (position on the path), and endcaps.

Beyond this chapter, there are many color features to explore. In Chapter 14, you will apply multiple fill and stroke attributes; in Chapter 18, you will apply colors with the Live Paint Bucket tool; in Chapter 24, you will create and save gradients; and in Chapter 29, you will use the powerful Live Color dialog to assign new colors or color groups to selected artwork.

Colors for your output medium

Before you start using the panels, picker, and dialogs, you need to know what types of colors are suitable for your artwork and the output medium.

Colors for commercial printing

A **spot** color is a predefined mixture of specific inks that is printed via a separate printing plate. For example, your print shop would create PANTONE 7489C (a medium green) by mixing 60 cyan, 0 magenta, 80 yellow, and 7 black. To choose a spot color, you flip through a fan book for a matching system (such as PANTONE); pick a named, numbered spot color; then locate that color in Illustrator. You can use just spot colors if your document doesn't contain any continuous-tone images. Your budget may limit the number, however, because each added spot color incurs an extra charge.

In commercial **process** printing, tiny dots of the four process colors—cyan (C), magenta (M), yellow (Y), and black (K)—are printed from four separate plates. On the printout, your eyes blur the dots together and read them as solid colors. But if you were to examine a photograph in a magazine or catalog with a magnifying lens or loupe, you would see the actual dots. You can choose premixed process colors from a matching system, such as TRUMATCH or PANTONE Process, or enter your own process color percentages in the Color panel **A** or Color Picker.**B** The four-color process printing method must be used if your artwork contains continuous tones, such as photographic images or gradients. (See also **A**, next page.)

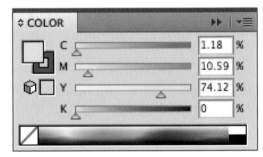

A Use the CMYK color model for print output. CMYK colors can be mixed by using the Color panel...

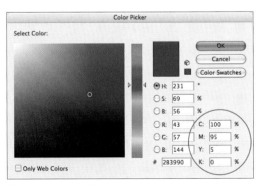

B ...or the Color Picker.

If the budget for the project allows, you can have it all: process printing, plus one or two spot colors, say, for a key graphic, such as a logo.

Colors for the Web

For Web output, you should choose **RGB** colors (the acronym stands for red-green-blue).**B** For the vast majority of viewers whose monitors display millions of colors, the RGB colors you choose will look close to the way you intend them to.

If you must cater to the handful of viewers who use 8-bit monitors, choose colors using the Web Safe RGB color model on the Color panel (choose that option from the panel menu). With your artwork restricted to Web-safe colors, no color substitutions will occur in a viewer's browser. If you mix a non-Web-safe color, an Out of Web Color Warning button 🟩 appears on the Color panel; click the cube or the swatch, and the color is converted to its closest Web-safe cousin.

When the New Document dialog was open, as you created a document, you had the option to choose CMYK or RGB as the Color Mode. Any colors you mix or choose in your document conform automatically to the current mode, which is listed in the document tab or title bar. When you change the document color mode, all the colors in the document convert to the new mode. The gamut of RGB colors is wider than the gamut of CMYK colors.

To change the document color mode:

1. To be on the safe side, create a copy of your file by using the File > Save As command (Cmd-Shift-S/Ctrl-Shift-S).

2. Choose File > Document Color Mode > **CMYK Color** (for print output) or **RGB Color** (for Web or video output).

➤ If you need to reverse a document color mode change, don't rechoose the prior color mode. Instead, use Edit > Undo.

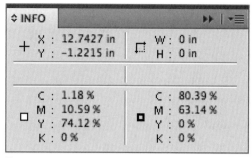

A The Info panel lists the color breakdowns for the fill and stroke in the currently selected object. If the currently selected objects contain different color values, those read-out areas will be blank.

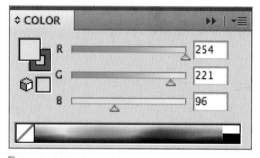

B Use the RGB color model for Web output.

STAYING IN THE MODE

➤ Any process colors that you create in a document will conform to the current document color mode, regardless of which mode you choose from the Color Mode menu in the Swatch Options dialog (see page 128). In other words, you can create either process CMYK colors or RGB colors in a document, but not both.

➤ Embedded placed and pasted images are converted to the current document color mode automatically.

➤ The Object > Rasterize dialog displays a color option for just the current document color mode.

Using the basic color controls

Just to get the ball rolling, we'll show you how to quickly apply a fill or stroke color and change the stroke width. One of the methods below uses a new in-panel editing feature of the Appearance panel.

To apply a fill or stroke color, gradient, or pattern from a temporary Swatches panel:

1. Select or isolate an object or objects.

2. Do either of the following:

   On the **Control** panel, click the fill or stroke square or arrowhead,**A** then on the temporary Swatches panel, click a solid-color, gradient, or pattern swatch.**B–C**

   On the **Appearance** panel,◉ click the square for the fill or stroke listing,**D** click the color square or arrowhead,**E** ★ then on the temporary Swatches panel, click a swatch.

To apply a fill or stroke color of None:

1. Select or isolate an object or objects.

2. Do either of the following:

   On the **Control** panel, click the fill or stroke square or arrowhead; or on the **Appearance** panel,◉ click the square for the fill or stroke listing, then click the color square or arrowhead. Click the **None** button ◻ on the temporary Swatches panel or press /.

   On the **Color** panel,◪ click the fill or stroke square, then click the **None** button ◻ or press /.

➤ There is also a None button on the Tools panel.

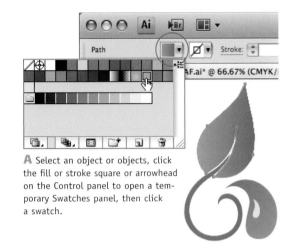

A Select an object or objects, click the fill or stroke square or arrowhead on the Control panel to open a temporary Swatches panel, then click a swatch.

B Our new fill color choice appears in the object.

C Next, we changed the stroke color.

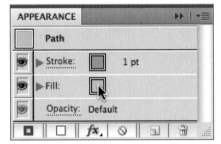

D Click the fill or stroke color on the Appearance panel.

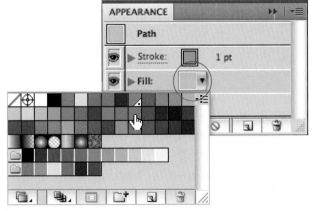

E Next, click the fill or stroke square or arrowhead to open a temporary Swatches panel, then finally, click a color swatch.

In addition to the methods described on the preceding page, there are other ways to quickly choose and apply solid colors, such as by using the Color Picker or the Color Guide panel.

To apply a solid fill or stroke color using the Color Picker:

1. Select or isolate an object; or to choose colors for an object you're about to create, deselect all.

2. On the Tools or Color panel, double-click the **fill** or **stroke** square to open the Color Picker.

3. Click a hue on the vertical bar in the middle of the dialog, then click a variation of that color in the large square.**A** (If your document is going to be printed and the Out of Gamut icon ⚠ appears, click the swatch below the icon to substitute the closest printable color.)

4. Click OK.

▶ If the fill or stroke colors differ among selected objects, a question mark **?** appears in the fill and/or stroke square on the Tools, Color, and Control panels. You can go ahead and apply a new fill or stroke color to the selection.

▶ A gradient can't be applied as a stroke color. For a workaround to this limitation, see page 310.

To view and choose solid-color variations:

Just for the heck of it, display the **Color Guide** panel, then click a variation of the current color on the panel (see pages 124–126).**B**

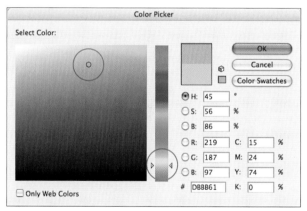

A In the Color Picker, click a hue on the vertical bar, then click a variation of that color in the large square.

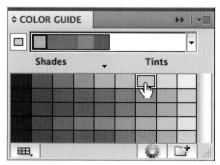

B On the Color Guide panel, click a variation of the current color.

SEEING THINGS IN BLACK AND WHITE

▶ To apply a white fill and a black stroke of 1 pt., click the Default Fill and Stroke button on the Tools panel or press D.

▶ To apply a white or black fill or stroke separately, click the White or Black selector in the bottom right corner of the Color panel (shown below) or click the White or Black swatch on the Swatches panel.

Saving colors as swatches

The Swatches panel is used for storing and applying solid process and spot colors, patterns, gradients, and color groups. Swatches that you add to the panel save only with the current file. To learn more about this panel, see pages 120–123.

To save the current fill or stroke color as a swatch:

1. Select an object that contains the color to be saved as a swatch; or with no objects selected, choose a color via the Color Picker (see the preceding page) or specify values via the Color panel (see page 115).

2. Display the **Swatches** panel, ⊞ expanded in a dock or as a floating panel, so it stays open.

3. Do one of the following:

    Drag the fill or stroke square from the **Color** panel 🎨 to the Swatches panel. **A**

    Drag a color from the **Color Guide** panel 📑 to the Swatches panel.

    Click the fill or stroke square on the Color or Tools panel, then Option-click/Alt-click the **New Swatch** button 🔲 at the bottom of the Swatches panel.

    The new swatch appears on the panel.

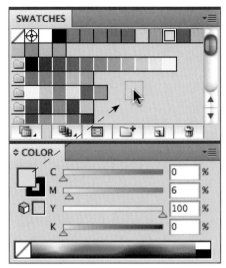

A To save a color as a swatch, drag from the color square on the Color panel to the Swatches panel.

➤ To choose options for a new swatch as you save it, in lieu of step 3 at left, click the New Swatch button on the Swatches panel. Type a Swatch Name, keep the Color Type as Process Color, check or uncheck Global, keep the Color Mode as is, then click OK.

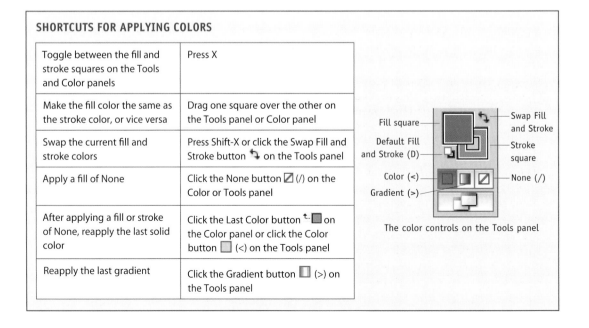

SHORTCUTS FOR APPLYING COLORS

Toggle between the fill and stroke squares on the Tools and Color panels	Press X
Make the fill color the same as the stroke color, or vice versa	Drag one square over the other on the Tools panel or Color panel
Swap the current fill and stroke colors	Press Shift-X or click the Swap Fill and Stroke button ⤢ on the Tools panel
Apply a fill of None	Click the None button ⬚ (/) on the Color or Tools panel
After applying a fill or stroke of None, reapply the last solid color	Click the Last Color button ⤺▪⬛ on the Color panel or click the Color button ⬛ (<) on the Tools panel
Reapply the last gradient	Click the Gradient button ⬛ (>) on the Tools panel

Fill square

Swap Fill and Stroke

Default Fill and Stroke (D)

Stroke square

Color (<)

None (/)

Gradient (>)

The color controls on the Tools panel

Applying colors from a library

In these instructions, we'll show you how to access and apply spot or processs colors from a matching system (such as PANTONE) or from one of the predefined Adobe color libraries.

To access colors from a library:

1. *Optional:* Select an object or objects to apply a color to, and click the fill or stroke square on the Tools or Color panel.

2. From the **Swatch Libraries** menu 🔳. at the bottom of the Swatches panel, choose a library name. If you want to open a library from a matching system (for print output), choose that system from the Color Books submenu on the Swatch Libraries menu (see the sidebar at right); or to reload default swatches, choose from the Default Swatches submenu.

   The chosen library will open in a floating panel. Scroll or enlarge the panel, if necessary, to reveal more colors.

3. If you click a swatch in a Color Books library or click a color group icon 📁 in any library, that color or color group appears on the Swatches panel automatically. Otherwise, do either of the following:

   On the library panel, click a swatch or Cmd-click/Ctrl-click multiple swatches, then choose **Add to Swatches** from the library panel menu.**A**

   Drag a swatch or a selection of multiple swatches from the library panel to the Swatches panel.

4. To view other libraries, starting with the ones from the same submenu, click the **Load Next Swatch Library** ▶ or **Load Previous Swatch Library** ◀ button on the library panel.

➤ To have a library panel reappear when you relaunch Illustrator, choose Persistent from the library panel menu. To close a whole library panel, click its close box; to close a single library on the panel, Control-click/right-click its tab and choose Close from the context menu.

➤ You can't modify swatches on a library panel (note the non-edit icon ✗ in the lower right corner). However, you can edit any swatch once it's been added to the Swatches panel.

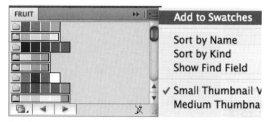

A Select swatches or color groups on a library panel, then choose Add to Swatches from the library panel menu to add them to the Swatches panel.

➤ To locate a particular color, choose Show Find Field from the library panel menu, then type the desired number in the field.

THE COLOR BOOK BRANDS

ANPA colors are used in the newspaper industry.

DIC Color Guide and TOYO Color Finder colors are used in Japan.

FOCOLTONE colors are designed to reduce registration problems and the need for trapping.

HKS process colors and HKS spot colors (no "Process" in the name) are used in Europe.

PANTONE process colors and PANTONE spot colors (no "Process" in the name) are widely used for printing projects in North America.

TRUMATCH process colors include 40 tints and shades of each hue, organized differently from PANTONE colors.

AVOID NASTY COLOR SURPRISES

As you learned in Chapter 2, the Color Settings command in Illustrator uses monitor and printer device profiles and output intents in conjunction with the system's color management utility to ensure accurate color matching between the onscreen display of your artwork and its final output. Unfortunately, even with the best color management system in place, you can't proof process and spot colors for commercial printing onscreen—however tempted you may be to trust what you see. Instead, always pick spot colors and look up process color formulas in a printed fan book for a color matching system. And before you give the go-ahead for a print run, be sure to tell your print shop that you need to see a color proof (or two, if you end up making changes).

Changing the tint percentage

You can achieve a pleasing range of tints (and keep your project within budget) with just one black and one spot color printing plate by applying an assortment of tint percentages of the spot color. You can also change the percentage of a global process color.

To change the tint percentage of a spot or global process color:

1. On the Swatches panel, ⊞ click either a **spot** color (a swatch with a dot in the lower right corner ▣) or a **global process** color (a swatch with a white triangle in the corner ▢).

2. Do either of the following:

   On the Color panel, ▨ move the **T** (Tint) slider **A** or click the **Tint** ramp at the bottom of the panel.

   To open a temporary Color panel, Shift-click the fill square on the Control panel; or on the Appearance panel, ◉ click, then Shift-click the fill square. Move the **T** (Tint) slider or click the **Tint** ramp at the bottom of the panel.**B** ★

   ➤ If Select Same Tint % is checked in Illustrator/ Edit > Preferences > General, the Fill & Stroke, Fill Color, and Stroke Color commands on the Select Similar Options menu ▨▾ (Control panel) will select only objects containing the same color and tint percentage as the selected object. With this option unchecked, the commands will select all tint percentages of the same color.

PRINTING SPOTS AS SPOTS

When color-separating a file from Illustrator, you can choose to either preserve spot colors as they are or convert them all to process colors. To ensure that each spot color in your document color separates correctly to a separate plate, choose File > Print, click Output on the left side, choose a Separations option from the Mode menu, and leave Convert All Spot Colors to Process unchecked.

CHANGING THE REGISTRATION COLOR

The [Registration] color is used for crop marks and other marks that a commercial printer uses to align the printing plates. If your print shop requests that this color be changed (perhaps your artwork is very dark and the marks would show up better if they were white), click the Registration swatch, then drag the Tint slider on the Color panel.

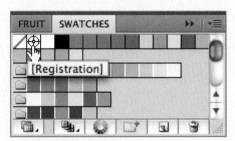

The [Registration] color appears on every plate when a file is color-separated.

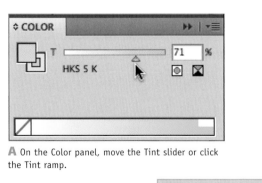

A On the Color panel, move the Tint slider or click the Tint ramp.

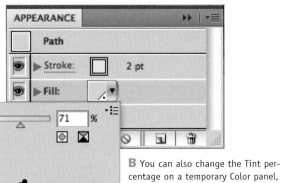

B You can also change the Tint percentage on a temporary Color panel, accessed from the Appearance panel (or the Control panel).

Mixing colors numerically

Follow these instructions to mix an RGB color for Web output or a CMYK color for print output by specifying numeric values.

To mix a color numerically:

1. Select or isolate an object; or to choose colors for an object you're about to create, deselect all.

2. Do one of the following:

   On the **Color** panel, click the fill or stroke square.

   On the **Control** panel, Shift-click the fill or stroke square or arrowhead to open a temporary Color panel.

   On the **Appearance** panel, Shift-click the fill or stroke square or arrowhead to open a temporary Color panel.*

3. Choose a color model from the Color panel menu:

   Grayscale to convert the fill and stroke colors in any selected objects to grayscale, or to choose a gray shade.

   RGB to mix a color for video or Web output, or for output to a desktop color printer.

   HSB to mix a color according to its hue (location on the color wheel), saturation (purity), and brightness values; this model has no practical use for print output.

   CMYK to create a process color for commercial printing.

   Web Safe RGB to mix colors for Web output using hexadecimal values.

4. Move the available sliders (0–255 for RGB; 0–100% for CMYK) or enter values. **A** For print output, refer to a printed fan book for a matching system, such as PANTONE Process Coated for exact color percentages.

5. *Optional (recommended):* To save the new color as a swatch, click the New Swatch button on the Swatches panel, check or uncheck Global in the Swatch Options dialog, then click OK.

➤ To cycle through the color models on the Color panel, Shift-click the color bar.

➤ You can also enter HSB, RGB, or CMYK percentages via the Color Picker. To open it, double-click the fill or stroke square on the Tools or Color panel.

*If the square isn't active, click and then Shift-click it.

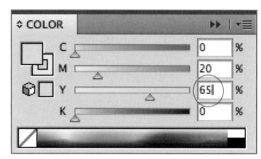

A On the Color panel, click the fill or stroke square, choose a color model from the panel menu, then move the sliders — or as shown here, enter percentages from a swatch book.

SELECTING TYPE FOR RECOLORING

➤ To recolor all the type in a block, select it with the Selection tool.

➤ To recolor just a portion of a type block, select those characters or words with one of the type tools.

STAYING WITHIN THE GAMUT

An Out of Gamut warning ⚠ below the fill and stroke squares on the Color panel signifies that the current RGB or HSB color has no CMYK equivalent and therefore can't be printed on a commercial press. If you click the icon or swatch, Illustrator will substitute the closest equivalent printable color.

Changing stroke attributes

In addition to changing the color of a stroke, you can also change its weight (width), position on the path, and style (dashed or solid, rounded or sharp corners, flat or rounded ends). First, the width.

To change the width of a stroke: ★

1. Select or isolate one or more objects, or select some type.

2. Do either of the following:

   Display the full Stroke panel (see the sidebar at right), then in the **Weight** area, click the up or down arrow, enter a value, or choose a preset value.**A**

   In the **Stroke Weight** area of the Control or Appearance panel, click the up or down arrow, enter a value, or choose a preset value.**B** (To access the Stroke Weight area on the Appearance panel, click the stroke square.)

➤ Shift-click the up or down Stroke Weight arrow to change the value by a larger interval.

➤ You can enter a stroke weight in points (pt), picas (p), inches (in), millimeters (mm), centimeters (cm), or pixels (px). When you press Return/Enter or Tab, the value is converted automatically to the current Stroke unit in Illustrator/Edit > Preferences > Units & Display Performance.

➤ A stroke that is narrower than .25 pt. may not print.

➤ Don't apply a wide stroke to small type; the letterforms will look distorted.

To change the alignment of a stroke on a path:

1. Select one or more closed objects. To see the effect of the align options, make the stroke fairly wide, or zoom in on your artwork.

2. Display the Stroke panel (see the sidebar on this page).

3. Click the **Align Stroke to Center,☐ Align Stroke to Inside,☐ or Align Stroke to Outside** button.☐ **C–E** Note: If the buttons aren't showing, keep clicking the arrowheads on the panel tab until they appear.

> **DISPLAYING THE STROKE PANEL**
>
> ➤ Click the Stroke panel icon ☰ in a panel dock.
>
> ➤ Press Cmd-F10/Ctrl-F10.
>
> ➤ On the Control panel or Appearance panel, click the underlined word Stroke. ★

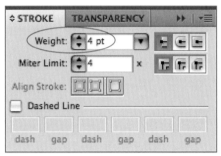

A Use the Weight controls on the Stroke panel...

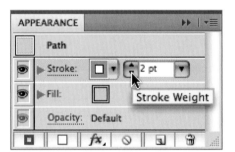

B ... or on the Appearance panel, click the stroke square, then click the up or down Stroke Weight arrow to change the stroke width.

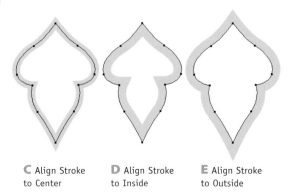

C Align Stroke to Center   **D** Align Stroke to Inside   **E** Align Stroke to Outside

Using the Dashed Line feature, you can easily create a dashed stroke, with uniform or varied dash lengths and spacing.

To create a dashed (or dotted) stroke:

1. Select or isolate an object. Make sure the stroke has a color and that its weight is greater than zero.

2. Make sure the full options are showing on the Stroke panel.☰ If not, click the arrowheads on the panel tab until they appear.

3. Click a **Cap** button for the dash shape (see the following page).

4. Check **Dashed Line**.

5. Enter a value in the first **Dash** field (for the length of the first dash), then press Tab.**A–B**

   ► Although the Stroke unit in Illustrator/Edit > Preferences > Units & Display Performance (Points is the default) is used in the Dash and Gap fields, you can enter values in another unit, such as centimeters (cm) or pixels (px).

6. *Optional:* Enter a value in the first Gap field (the length of the first gap following the first dash), then press Tab to proceed to the next field or press Return/Enter to exit the panel. If you don't enter a gap value, the dash value will also serve as the gap value.

7. *Optional:* To create dashes of varying lengths, enter values in the other dash fields. If you don't do this, the first dash value will be used for all the dashes. Ditto for the gaps.

► To create a dotted line, click the second Cap button, enter a dash value of 0, and enter a gap value that's equal to or greater than the stroke weight. For example, for a stroke weight of 15 pt., you would enter a dash value of 0 and a gap value of 20–30 pt.

► To save a dashed stroke as a graphic style, drag a path to which that stroke is applied to the Graphic Styles panel (see page 207).

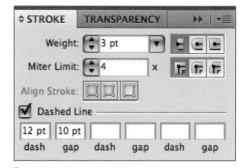

A The Dashed Line settings chosen here will create 12-pt. dashes, with 10-pt. gaps between them.

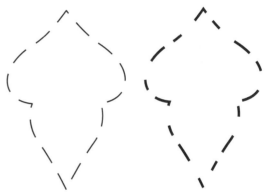

Weight 1 pt., dash 14, gap 9, Butt cap

Weight 2 pt., dash 8, gap 15, dash 15, gap 8, Butt cap

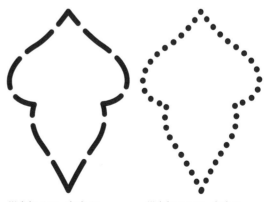

Weight 4 pt., dash 24, gap 8, Round cap

Weight 4.6 pt., dash 0, gap 7.8, Round cap and join

B These dashed strokes were created using various settings.

To change the stroke caps or joins:

1. Select or isolate an object, and apply a fairly wide stroke to it.

2. Make sure the full options are showing on the Stroke panel.☰ If not, click the arrowheads on the panel tab until they appear.

3. Click a Cap button to modify the endpoints of a solid line or all the dashes in a dashed line:**A–B**

   Butt Cap ⊑ to create square-cornered ends in which the stroke stops at the endpoints, or to create thin, rectangular dashes. Use this option when you need to align your paths very precisely.

   Round Cap ⊑ to create semicircular ends or elliptical dashes.

   Projecting Cap ⊑ to create square-cornered ends in which the stroke extends beyond the endpoints, or to create rectangular dashes.

4. Click a Join button to modify the bends on corner points (not on curve points) of the path:

   Miter Join 🔲 to produce pointed bends.

   Round Join 🔲 to produce semicircular bends.

   Bevel Join 🔲 to produce beveled bends. The sharper the angle of the path, the wider the bevel.

5. *Optional:* Change the Miter Limit (1–500) value to control how long a mitered (pointed) corner must be for it to become a beveled corner. Don't worry about how it works; just use a high Miter Limit value (greater than 15) to create sharp, pointy corners or a low Miter Limit value (less than 4) to create beveled corners.

➤ To learn the difference between corner and curve points, see page 273.

A You can use tool tips to identify the Cap and Join buttons on the Stroke panel.

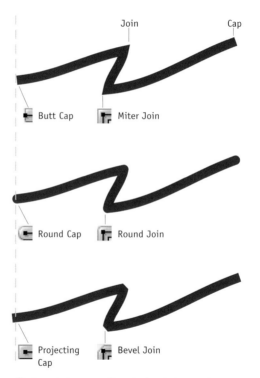

B The Join buttons affect the bends in a stroke, whereas the Cap buttons affect the ends.

Using the Eyedropper tool

When you click an object with the Eyedropper tool, it samples the object's color and stroke attributes, displays them on the Color, Stroke, and Appearance panels, and applies them to any currently selected objects—all in one quick step.

To sample and apply colors with the Eyedropper tool:

1. *Optional:* To specify which attributes the Eyedropper tool picks up, double-click the tool.🖋 The Eyedropper Options dialog opens. Check which attributes are to be picked up and applied (all are checked by default), uncheck the attributes to be ignored, then click OK.

2. *Optional:* Select an object or objects. They will be recolored instantly with the attributes you will sample with the Eyedropper (in step 4).

3. Choose the **Eyedropper** tool 🖋 (I).

4. Click an object in your artwork that contains the desired attributes.**A** It can be any kind of object (even a color in a placed image), and it can contain a solid color, pattern, or gradient. The object doesn't have to be selected. Depending on the current Eyedropper options, the sampled colors will appear in the fill and/ or stroke squares on the Tools, Color, and Appearance panels,★ and the sampled stroke settings will appear on the Stroke panel.

   If you selected any objects before using the Eyedropper tool, the sampled attributes will be applied to those objects.**B**

➤ Option-click/Alt-click an object to do the opposite of the above—apply color attributes from the currently selected object to the object you click.**C–D**

➤ To have the Eyedropper tool sample only the color it is clicked on (no other attributes), click the fill or stroke square on the Tools or Color panel, then Shift-click the color to be sampled.

➤ To preserve a sampled color for future use, drag it from the fill or stroke square on the Color panel to the Swatches panel.

A Select an object or objects, then with the Eyedropper tool, click an object that contains the desired attributes.

B The attributes you sample will be applied instantly to the selected object.

C Or Option-click/ Alt-click with the Eyedropper tool to apply attributes from the currently selected object to the one you click.

D These are the results after we Option/Alt clicked with the Eyedropper tool.

Using the Swatches panel

Via the Swatches panel menu, you can control the categories and size of swatches the panel displays.

To choose display options for the Swatches panel:

1. To control which categories of swatches display on the Swatches panel, ▦ from the **Show Swatch Kinds** menu ▦. at the bottom of the panel, choose **Show All Swatches** for all types (colors, gradients, patterns, and groups);**A Show Color Swatches** for just solid colors and color groups; **Show Gradient Swatches** for just gradients; **Show Pattern Swatches** for just patterns; or **Show Color Groups** for just color groups.

2. From the panel menu, choose a view for the currently chosen category of swatches: **Small Thumbnail View**, **Medium Thumbnail View**, **Large Thumbnail View**, **Small List View**, or **List View**. Medium and Large Thumbnail views are useful for identifying gradients and patterns. In the two list views, icons representing the color type and mode for each solid color also display.**B**

3. *Optional:* From the panel menu, choose Sort by Name to sort the swatches alphabetically by name or numerically by their color contents; or choose Sort by Kind (when all swatch categories are displayed) to sort swatches in the following order: solid colors, gradients, patterns, color groups.

➤ To locate a particular swatch, choose Show Find Field from the panel menu, click in the field, then start typing the swatch name. Choose the command again to hide the field.

➤ You can drag a swatch, or multiple selected swatches, to another location on the panel.

➤ To learn the difference between global and nonglobal colors, see page 128.

Global process colors have a white corner but no dot.   Nonglobal process color are plain.   Spot colors have a dot.

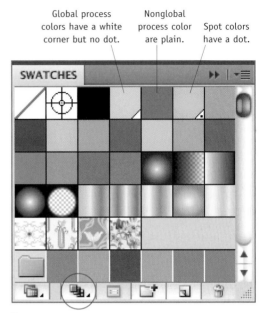

A All four kinds of swatches are displayed on this Swatches panel because Show All Swatches is chosen on the Show Swatch Kinds menu. This is Large Thumbnail view.

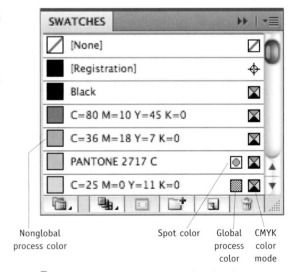

Nonglobal process color   Spot color   Global process color   CMYK color mode

B When the Swatches panel is in a list view, icons representing the color type and document color mode display on the right side.

Color groups are a very useful organizational tool for the Swatches panel. If you're coordinating a group of solid colors for a client, for a specific design, or by a particular theme, you'll be able to locate them more easily if they're in a group.

When the panel is in a thumbnail view, the colors in each group are lined up in a tidy row, starting with the folder icon, and you can identify a group name via its tool tip. When the panel is in a list view, the name of the color group is listed next to the folder icon, followed by a nested listing of the colors in the group.

To create a color group from swatches:

1. On the Swatches panel, ▦ Shift-click to select contiguous solid-color swatches or Cmd-click/ Ctrl-click to select multiple swatches (sorry, no gradients or patterns).**A**

2. Click the **New Color Group** button ◲ at the bottom of the panel. The New Color Group dialog opens.

3. Enter a Name, keep the Create From setting as **Selected Swatches**, then click OK. The new swatches group appears on the panel.**B**

➤ You can also create a color group based on harmonies via the Color Guide panel (see pages 124–126) or the Live Color dialog (see Chapter 30).

➤ To rename a group, double-click its folder icon, change the name in the dialog that opens, click OK, then click Yes in the alert dialog.

➤ To restack a color group among the other color groups, drag its icon upward or downward.

To create a color group from artwork:

1. With the Selection tool or via the Layers panel, select the artwork that contains the desired colors for a color group.**C**

2. Click the **New Color Group** button ◲ on the Swatches panel.

3. In the New Color Group dialog, enter a name for the group, click **Selected Artwork** (check the available options, if desired), then click OK.**D**

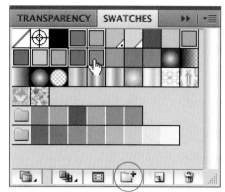

A Select the solid-color swatches to be put into a group, then click the New Color Group button.

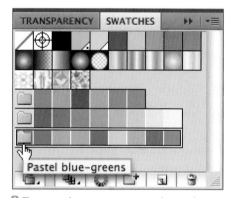

B The new color group appears on the panel.

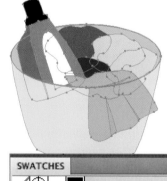

C Select the artwork that contains the desired colors for a color group, then click the New Color Group button on the Swatches panel.

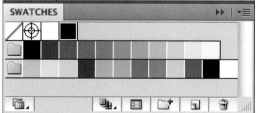

D The new color group appears on the panel.

To copy swatches between Illustrator files:

1. Open the file into which you want to load swatches.

2. From the **Swatch Libraries** menu 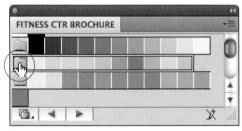, at the bottom of the Swatches panel, choose **Other Library**. The Select a Library to Open dialog opens.

3. Locate and click the Illustrator file you want to copy swatches from, then click Open. A library of swatches appears onscreen, bearing the name of the source file.

4. Do one of the following:

   Drag a swatch from the source library panel into the Swatches panel.

   Click a color group icon on the source library panel.**A–B**

   Cmd-click/Ctrl-click or Shift-click multiple swatches, then choose Add to Swatches from the library panel menu.

5. If the Swatch Conflict dialog appears, see the sidebar on this page.

RESOLVING SWATCH CONFLICTS

The Swatch Conflict dialog appears as you copy swatches between files if a global process color that you're attempting to copy has the same name as an existing swatch in the current document but different color percentages. Click Merge Swatches to preserve the existing swatch and percentages, or click Add Swatches to add the new swatch (a number will be appended to its name). If the conflict dialog appears as you append colors by dragging an object between files, click Add Swatches if you want to prevent colors in the copied objects from changing.

► To have the current Options setting apply to any other name conflicts that crop up, and to prevent the alert dialog from opening repeatedly, check Apply to All in the Swatch Conflict dialog.

► To append spot and global process colors from one file to another quickly, copy and paste or drag and drop an object from one Illustrator document window to another. The object's colors will appear on the Swatches panel of the target document.

A A library of swatches is opened from another file, then a color group is clicked.

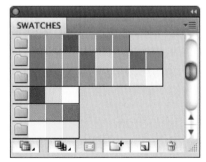

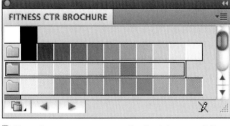

B The color group appears on the Swatches panel for the current document.

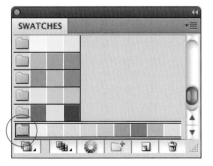

To duplicate a swatch:

1. On the Swatches panel, click the swatch you want to duplicate, then click the **New Swatch** button  on the panel. The New Swatch dialog opens.

2. Change the name, if desired, check Global or not (see page 128), then click OK.

➤ To bypass the dialog as you duplicate a swatch, click the swatch, then Option-click/Alt-click the New Swatch button (or drag the swatch over the button).

To delete swatches:

1. Do either of the following:

   Click a swatch in, or the icon for, a color group that you want to delete, or Shift-click or Cmd-click/Ctrl-click to select multiple swatches or color groups.

   To select only the swatches that aren't being used in your artwork, choose Show All Swatches from the Show Swatch Kinds menu, then choose Select All Unused from the Swatches panel menu.

2. Do one of the following:

   Click the **Delete Swatch** button at the bottom of the Swatches panel, then click Yes in the alert dialog.

   To bypass the prompt, Option-click/Alt-click the Delete Swatch button.

➤ If you delete a global process color that's being used in your artwork, you will no longer be able to edit the color globally for those objects. If you delete a spot color that's currently applied to an object, a nonglobal process color equivalent of the deleted color is applied to the object (see page 128).

➤ To restore a deleted swatch or swatches, choose Undo immediately. Or if you unintentionally delete a nonglobal solid color (but not a global process or spot color), gradient, or pattern that's being used in the current file and it's too late to use Undo, you can retrieve it by selecting an object that contains it, then dragging the fill and/or stroke square from the Color panel to the Swatches panel.

➤ If you want to restore swatches from a default library or any other library, see page 113.

By saving your favorite swatches and color groups to custom libraries, you'll be able to load them onto the Swatches panel for use in any document.

To save a library of swatches:

1. Make sure the Swatches panel contains only the swatches or color groups to be saved in a library.

   ➤ If you want to remove the swatches that aren't being used in your artwork, follow the instructions for deleting swatches on this page; use the second method in step 1.

2. From the **Swatch Libraries** menu at the bottom of the Swatches panel, choose **Save Swatches.A** The Save Swatches as Library dialog opens.

3. Type a name for the library in the Save As field, keep the default location, and click Save.

4. The new library is now listed on, and can be opened from, the **User Defined** submenu on the Swatches Libraries menu, along with any other user-defined libraries.

A To save the current swatches on the panel as a library, choose Save Swatches from the Swatches Libraries menu.

Using the Color Guide panel

By using the Color Guide panel, you can generate color schemes based on harmony rules and types of variations and save the resulting colors as a group to the Swatches panel. This panel might prove useful if you want to apply a set of coordinated colors quickly, if your projects require you to work with an approved group of colors, or if you simply want to see how a new range of hues, tints, or saturation values would look in your artwork.

To get acquainted with the Color Guide panel, start by choosing options for it.

To choose variation options for the Color Guide panel:

1. Show the **Color Guide** panel ![panel icon] (Shift-F3), then choose **Color Guide Options** from the panel menu. The Variation Options dialog opens.**A**

2. Click the up/down arrow to set the number of variation **Steps** (columns of colors) to be displayed on either side of the central column on the panel, and move the **Variation** slider to control how much the colors can vary from those in the central column.

3. Click OK.**B**

➤ To make the swatches larger, enlarge the Color Guide panel by dragging its left or right edge.

To apply color variations via the Color Guide panel:

1. From the **Limit Color Group to Swatch Library** menu ![icon] at the bottom of the Color Guide panel, choose None.

2. To make a color appear on the panel, do either of the following:

   Select an object,**C** click the fill or stroke square on the Tools or Color panel, then in the upper left corner of the Color Guide panel, click the **Set Base Color to Current Color** button.![icon]

   With no objects selected, click the fill or stroke square on the Tools or Color panel, click a swatch on the Swatches panel, or mix a color on the Color panel.

3. The active color group displays at the top of the Color Guide panel. To control what types of variations are derived from the active color group, choose a variation type from the panel menu:

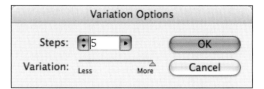

A In the Variation Options dialog box, specify the number of Steps (variations to be displayed) and the degree of Variation for colors on the Color Guide panel.

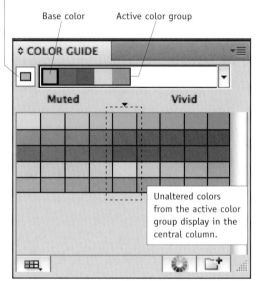

B The options for this Color Guide panel are set to four Steps (four on either side of the central column) and the maximum amount of Variation (More).

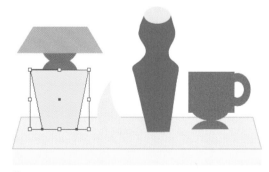

C An object is selected.

Show Tints/Shades adds progressively more black to variations on the left side of the central column and progressively more white to variations on the right.

Show Warm/Cool adds progressively more red to variations on the left and progressively more blue to variations on the right.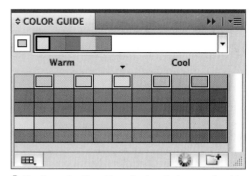

Show Vivid/Muted adds progressively more gray to variations on the left and increases the saturation progressively for variations on the right.

4. Do either of the following:

To recolor a selected object, click a color in the active group at the top of the panel or click a variation in the main part of the panel.

Drag a variation swatch over any unselected object.**B**

➤ Clicking a variation on the Color Guide panel makes that color the current color. If you then click the Set Base Color to Current Color button, the active color group changes and new variations are generated.

➤ To limit the harmony and variation colors on the Color Guide panel to colors in a library, from the Limit Color Group to Swatch Library menu, ▦ choose a library name (e.g., Color Books > PANTONE Solid Coated). The library name will be listed at the bottom of the panel, and only colors from that library will display as variations on the panel and on the Harmony Rules menu (see the next page). To remove the current restriction, choose None from the same menu.

➤ To replace a spot color in a selected object with a different spot color, click a variation that has a dot in the lower right corner.

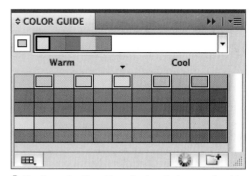

A We chose the Show Warm/Cool variation type for this Color Guide panel.

B To use some of the new variations, we dragged five colors individually over objects in the artwork to create a progression from warm to cool (the colors are shown selected in the panel above, in the order in which they were used).

Another way to change the variations on the Color Guide panel is by choosing one of the preset harmony rules, such as Complementary, Analogous, or High Contrast. A new color group and variations are generated from the same base color, in accordance with the chosen rule.

To create a color group and variations based on a harmony rule:

1. To establish the base color on the Color Guide panel, follow step 2 in the second set of instructions on page 124.

2. On the **Color Guide** panel, click the **Harmony Rules** arrowhead (to the right of the active color group) to open the menu.**A** The current base color is shown as the first color in each rule. Click a rule. The menu closes, and a new color group for that base color, in accordance with that rule, displays at the top of the panel. Below that, you'll see the new variations that Illustrator generated from the new color group.**B**

3. *Optional:* At any time, you can change the base color to generate a new color group and variations based on the current harmony rule, or choose a different rule.

4. To recolor an object, select it, then click a variation.**C**

The active color group changes when you change the base color, choose a new harmony rule, or click a swatch on the Swatches panel. Whenever you create an active color group that you like, you can preserve it for future use.

To save the active color group:

On the Color Guide panel, click the **Save Color Group to Swatches Panel** button. The new group appears on the Swatches panel.

➤ To save a single variation instead of a whole color group, drag that variation from the Color Guide panel to the Swatches panel.

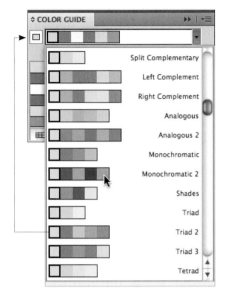

A Choose from the Harmony Rules menu on the Color Guide panel. (The base color will stay the same, but the color group will change to abide by the new rule.)

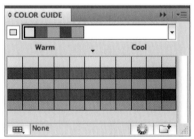

B A new color group and variations appear on the panel, based on the chosen harmony rule.

C Some of the new color variations, based on the current harmony rule, were dragged onto objects in this artwork.

Using the Kuler panel

Kuler (pronounced "cooler") is a free, Web-hosted Adobe application that lets you create and upload color groups, called color themes. By using the Kuler panel, you can access and browse through various color themes and then, with a click of a button, add the currently selected theme to the Swatches panel in Illustrator. To use the Kuler panel efficiently, take advantage of its built-in search feature.

To access color themes via the Kuler panel: ★

1. Display the Kuler panel by choosing Window > Extensions > **Kuler**.

2. In the field at the top of the panel, enter the theme name (or an exact keyword tag or creator name, if you happen to know it), then press Return/Enter to run the search.

   ➤ You can sort of free-associate here, based on the theme you're aiming for (e.g., "sunset," "Paris," "Monet," "wine," "grapes"). If you get few or no results, the criterion you've entered is probably too narrow. For example, "Navajo rug" yielded only one theme, but "Navajo" yielded many color themes.**A**

3. To view more results based on the same search criterion, click the **View Next Set of Themes** button ⬇ at the bottom of the panel.

4. To make a color group from Kuler appear on the Swatches panel in Illustrator, click the group on the Kuler panel, then click the **Add Selected Theme to Swatches** button ⊞ at the bottom of the panel.

5. *Optional:* To customize the new color group, double-click the color group icon on the Swatches panel, then follow the instructions on pages 353–354.

   ➤ To save your search criteria for quick access in the future, choose Custom from the menu on the left side of the Kuler panel. In the dialog, enter the criteria to be saved, then click Save. To run a search based on the saved criteria, choose the name from the same menu.

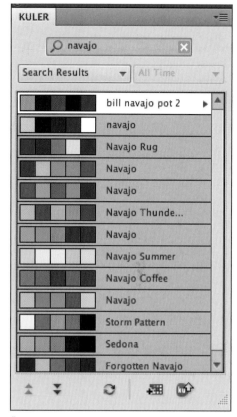

A Use the Kuler panel to browse through color themes online and to add select themes to your Swatches panel in Illustrator.

➤ To view more information about a selected color theme on the Kuler website, click the triangle for that theme and choose View Online in Kuler. If an alert about the Flash Player crops up, follow the instructions to install the required player.

➤ To learn more, go to kuler.adobe.com. There, you can generate themes from photographs, upload your favorite themes to make them available to other users, etc.

Replacing colors in your artwork

Via the Select Similar Options menu, you can quickly select multiple objects that have an attribute in common, such as the same fill color, then apply a new color to all the selected objects.

To replace a color, stroke attribute, or opacity setting throughout a document:

1. Select an object that contains the spot color(s), nonglobal process color(s), stroke weight, or other attribute that you want to change.

2. From the **Select Similar Options** menu 🖼️▾ on the Control panel, choose an option, such as Fill Color, Stroke Color, or Fill & Stroke Color.

3. To change any attributes, such as the one(s) chosen in the prior step, do one or more of the following:

   Click the fill or stroke square on the Tools or Color panel, then click a different swatch on the Swatches or Color Guide panel or in an open swatch library panel, or mix a new color by using the Color panel.

   Choose a new stroke Weight or other stroke attributes (Stroke or Appearance panel).

   Change the Opacity percentage on the Control or Appearance panel.

4. Deselect all (Cmd-Shift-A/Ctrl-Shift-A).

A nonglobal process color swatch is one for which Global is unchecked in the Swatch Options dialog.

To change a color from nonglobal to global, or vice versa:

1. Double-click a global or nonglobal process color swatch on the Swatches panel. Global process color swatches have a white corner and no dot; nonglobal process colors are plain (no corner, no dot).

2. The Swatch Options dialog opens.**A** Check or uncheck Global, then click OK.

When you edit the values in a global process color, the color updates automatically in all the objects where it's being used—whether those objects are selected or not.

To edit the values in a global process color:

1. Double-click a global process color swatch on the Swatches panel.

2. In the Swatch Options dialog, check Preview, modify the color by moving the sliders, then click OK. Tint percentages are preserved.

To replace a global process color that's being used in multiple objects, instead of recoloring one object at a time, simply replace the current color swatch with a new one, and it will update automatically in all the objects where it's being used (even when no objects are selected). Existing tint percentages are preserved.

To replace a global process color swatch:

1. Deselect all objects.

2. Do one of the following:

   From the Swatch Libraries menu 🗔▾ on the Swatches panel, choose a library name. Click a color on the library panel, then Option-drag/ Alt-drag it over the global process color swatch on the Swatches panel to be replaced.

   Click the fill or stroke square on the Color panel, then mix a new color using the Color panel (or double-click either square, then mix a color via the Color Picker); or click a color on the Color Guide panel. (Be sure to create a new color, not just a tint variation of an existing one.) Option-drag/Alt-drag the fill or stroke square over the global process color swatch on the Swatches panel to be replaced.

   On the Swatches panel, Option-drag/Alt-drag one swatch over another.

➤ If you Option-drag/Alt-drag a nonglobal process color swatch over a global process swatch, the resulting swatch will be a global process color.

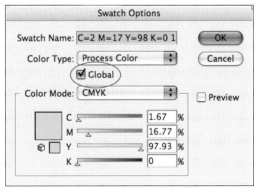

A Double-click a swatch to open the Swatch Options dialog, then check or uncheck Global.

Inverting colors

The Invert Colors command on the Edit menu converts multiple nonglobal process colors in selected objects to their opposite values on the color scale. The command doesn't convert spot colors, global process colors, gradients, or patterns.

To invert colors:

To invert multiple nonglobal process colors, select one or more objects (or an imported image),**A** then choose Edit > Edit Colors > **Invert Colors.B**

Colorizing grayscale images

1. Open or place a grayscale EPS, JPEG, PCX, PDF, PSD, or TIFF image into an Illustrator document.**C** To learn about the File > Open and File > Place commands, see Chapter 22.

   Note: You can't colorize a linked EPS image, but you can colorize an embedded EPS file (to embed an image, uncheck the Link option in the Place dialog).

2. Click the grayscale image that you have imported into Illustrator, click the fill square on the Colors or Tools panel, then apply a color via the Color, Swatches, or Color Guide panel, or via the Color Picker.**D** Gray areas will be recolored; white background areas will remain opaque white.

➤ Another option is to convert an imported, embedded image to grayscale via Edit > Edit Colors > Convert to Grayscale, then colorize it by following step 2 in the instructions above.

A This is the original placed image.

B The Invert Colors command is applied.

C This grayscale Photoshop image was placed into an Illlustrator document.

D We colorized the image by clicking a brown solid color on the Swatches panel.

Blending fill colors

To blend fill colors between objects:

1. Select three or more objects that contain fill colors (make sure none of them have a fill of None), or isolate a group.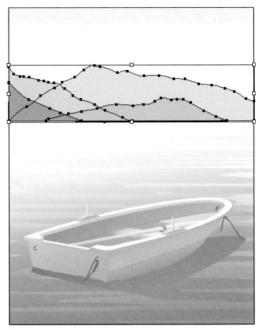 The more objects you use, the more gradual the blend will be.

   The two objects that are either farthest apart or frontmost and backmost can contain only nonglobal colors or different tints of the same spot color, not global process colors, patterns, or gradients (and they can't be type objects).

2. From the Edit > **Edit Colors** submenu, choose:

   Blend Front to Back to use the fill colors of the frontmost and backmost objects (in the stacking order) as the starting and ending colors in the blend. This works irrespective of the *x/y* location of the objects in the artwork.**B**

   Blend Horizontally to use the fill colors of the leftmost and rightmost objects as the starting and ending colors in the blend.

   Blend Vertically to use the fill colors of the topmost and bottommost objects as the starting and ending colors in the blend.

   Selected objects that are stacked between the frontmost and backmost objects, or that are located between the leftmost and rightmost objects or between the topmost and bottommost objects, will be assigned intermediate blend colors. The stroke colors and widths will remain the same, and the objects will stay on their respective layers.

A A group is put in isolation mode.

B The Blend Front to Back command is applied.

Creating and editing fill patterns

When creating a pattern, as an optional step you can use a rectangle to control the amount of white space around the pattern, or to crop away parts of objects that you want to exclude.

To define a pattern:

1. *Optional:* To define an area for the pattern, choose the Rectangle tool ▢ (M), then drag a rectangle. To help prevent a printing error, make it no larger than an inch (6 picas) square. Apply a fill and stroke of None to the rectangle if you don't want it to be an element in the pattern, or apply a fill color to it if you do. On the Layers panel, ☜ (F7) click in the edit (second) column for the rectangle object to lock it; the padlock icon 🔒 appears.

2. Draw an object or objects of any type to be used for the pattern. For example, you could create geometric objects with the Rectangle, Ellipse, Polygon, Spiral, or Star tool; the objects can contain brush strokes. To copy an object along an axis, Option-Shift-drag/Alt-Shift-drag it with the Selection tool. To position the objects precisely, you can use Smart Guides (see pages 96–97) or the Align buttons (see pages 101–102). Note: Complex attributes in a pattern, such as gradients, can cause printing problems.

3. Deselect all. If necessary, click the edit (lock) icon on the Layers panel for the rectangle object, to unlock it.

4. With the Selection tool ▸ (V), marquee all the objects for the pattern. **A**

5. Do either of the following:

   Choose Edit > **Define Pattern**.

   Drag the selection onto the **Swatches** panel, deselect the objects, then double-click the new swatch.

6. The New Swatch or Swatch Options dialog opens. Type a Swatch Name, then click OK. The new pattern appears on the Swatches panel. **B**

7. The new pattern can be applied to any object. **C**

➤ To transform (e.g., scale) a pattern fill without transforming the object, see page 137.

➤ Creating a symmetrical pattern takes patience and skill. To learn more, enter "create seamless geometric patterns" in the Search for Help field on the Application bar.

A The objects for a pattern are selected.

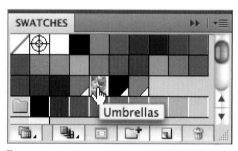

B The pattern swatch appears on the Swatches panel.

C The new pattern is used as a fill in an object.

You can edit any pattern, including any of the predefined Illustrator patterns.

To edit a pattern:

1. Drag a pattern swatch from the Swatches panel or a pattern swatch library panel onto a blank area of the artboard.

2. Double-click the group to isolate it, then modify the pattern objects. Use the Direct Selection tool ⟋ (A) to select individual paths. **A**

3. Click the isolation mode bar to exit that mode.

4. Choose the Selection tool ⟍ (V), then Option-drag/Alt-drag the group over the original pattern swatch. **B** The pattern will update in any objects in which it's being used. **C**

➤ To add an edited pattern as a new swatch, drag the selection onto the Swatches panel without holding down Option/Alt, then double-click the new swatch to rename it.

➤ To shift the pattern fill or stroke in an object without moving the object, hold down ~ (tilde) and drag inside it with the Selection tool.

➤ To expand a pattern into individual objects, select an object that contains the pattern, then choose Object > Expand. In the Expand dialog, check Fill. The former fill pattern will be divided into the original shapes that made up the pattern tile, nested as groups below a clipping mask (listed on the Layers panel as <Clipping Path>). Each nested group may also contain its own clipping path. You can release a mask (Object > Clipping Mask > Release), change its shape, or delete it altogether.

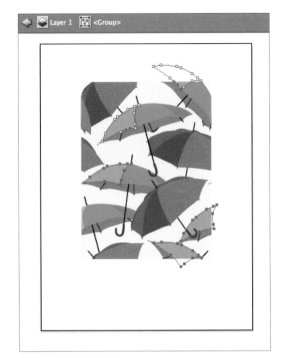

A Drag the pattern to be edited from the Swatches panel to the artboard, double-click the group to isolate it, then edit the objects. (We changed the orange shapes to light brown.)

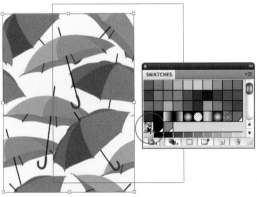

B Exit isolation mode, select all the objects, then Option/Alt drag them back over the original swatch.

C The edited pattern updates in the object in which it is being used.

Via a transform method, you can rotate, scale, reflect, distort, shear, or apply perspective to an object.

The methods include manipulating the object's bounding box, as well as using the multipurpose Free Transform tool, the individual transformation tools, the Transform panel, the Control panel, the Transform Each command, and the Transform effect.

Transforming via the bounding box

One of the fastest ways to transform an object is by using its bounding box. Note that with this method, you can't move the reference point or make copies.

To transform an object via its bounding box:

1. With the Selection tool, select one or more objects or double-click an object to isolate it. A rectangular bounding box with eight handles will appear around the object(s). If not, press Cmd-Shift-B/ Ctrl-Shift-B (View > Show Bounding Box).

2. Do one of the following:

   To **scale** the object along two axes, drag a corner handle; to scale it along one axis, drag a side handle. Or Shift-drag to scale the object proportionally; Option-drag/Alt-drag to scale it from its center; **A–B** or Option-Shift-drag/Alt-Shift-drag to scale it proportionally from its center.

   To create a **reflection** (mirror image) of the object, drag a side handle all the way across it. **C–D**

   To **rotate** the object, move the pointer slightly outside a corner handle (the pointer will be a curved double arrow), then drag in a circular direction.

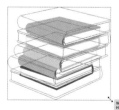

A Option-drag/Alt-drag an object or group to scale it from its center.

B The object is enlarged.

C To reflect an object, drag a handle of its bounding box all the way across it.

D The object is reflected.

Using the Free Transform tool

The multipurpose Free Transform tool lets you rotate, scale, reflect, distort, shear, or apply perspective to an object. However, unlike the other transformation tools, with this tool, you can't move the reference point or make copies.

To use the Free Transform tool:

1. Select one or more objects or a group, **A** or isolate a single object. Also copy the object if you want to transform a copy of it instead of the original.

2. Choose the **Free Transform** tool ![icon] (E).

3. To **scale** the object(s) along two axes, drag a corner handle; to scale along one axis, drag a side handle. Shift-drag to scale the object proportionally; Option-drag/Alt-drag to scale it from its center; or Option-Shift-drag/Alt-Shift-drag to scale it proportionally from its center.

   To **rotate** the object, position the pointer outside it, then drag in a circular direction. Shift-drag to rotate in 45° increments.

   To **shear** the object, start dragging a side handle, then hold down Cmd/Ctrl and continue to drag. **B** To constrain the shear, drag a side handle, then Cmd-Shift-drag/Ctrl-Shift-drag. To shear the object from its center, start dragging, then hold down Cmd-Option/Ctrl-Alt and continue to drag.

   To **reflect** the object, drag a side handle all the way across it; to reflect the object from its center, Option-drag/Alt-drag a side handle.

   To **distort** any object except editable type, start dragging a corner handle, then hold down Cmd/Ctrl and continue to drag. **C**

   To apply **perspective** to any object except editable type, start dragging a corner handle, then hold down Cmd-Option-Shift/Ctrl-Alt-Shift and continue to drag. **D** The perspective transformation will occur along the *x* or *y* axis, depending on the direction in which you drag.

A This is the original object.

B The object is sheared.

C Then it is distorted.

D Finally, a perspective transformation is applied.

As we showed you on pages 96–97, Smart Guides can be a great help when aligning objects or points to one another. In these instructions, Smart Guides are used as an object is transformed.

To use Smart Guides when transforming an object:

1. In Preferences (Cmd-K/Ctrl-K) > Smart Guides, make sure **Transform Tools** is checked.

   Optional: You can also choose a different Angles set for the guides or enter custom angles.

2. Make sure View > **Smart Guides** is on (Cmd-U/Ctrl-U).

3. Select the object(s) or group to be transformed or isolate a single object.

4. Choose the **Free Transform** ⛶ tool (or the **Rotate** (R) ⟳, **Reflect** (O) ⧓, **Scale** (S) ⬓, or **Shear** tool ⬀; see the instructions on the following page).

5. Drag the mouse to transform the object; Smart Guides will appear onscreen temporarily. **A–C** Move the pointer along a Smart Guide to apply the transformation on that axis. The angle of rotation or other readout will appear onscreen as you apply the transformation.

PREFERENCES FOR TRANSFORMATIONS

When performing transformations, there are three options in Illustrator/Edit > Preferences (Cmd-K/Ctrl-K) > General that you should know about:

► When transforming objects, the default Horizontal angle is 0° and the default Vertical angle is 90°. The default starting point for measuring the degree of an angle is the horizontal (x) axis (the three o'clock position). To create a new default setting, enter a custom Constrain Angle.

► If Transform Pattern Tiles is checked when you transform an object that contains a pattern fill or stroke, the pattern will transform as well.*

► Via the Scale Strokes & Effects check box, you can control whether an object's stroke and effects scale when an object is scaled.*

This option can also be turned on or off on the Transform panel menu.

A Smart Guides are used with the Reflect tool.

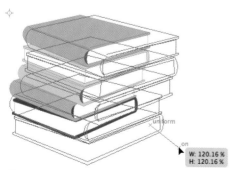

B Smart Guides are used with the Scale tool.

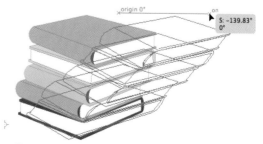

C Smart Guides are used with the Shear tool.

Using the Rotate, Reflect, Scale, and Shear tools

To transform an object by using the Rotate, Reflect, Scale, or Shear tool:

1. Select one or more objects or a group, or isolate a single object.

2. Choose the **Rotate** (R) ↻, **Reflect** (O) ◁, **Scale** (S) ⬛, or **Shear** tool.▱

3. When using the tool, you have two reference point options. You can either let the object transform from its center (the default behavior), or you can set a custom reference point by clicking near the object (the pointer will turn into an arrowhead). In either case, before dragging, move the mouse (button up) far away from the center or reference point for better control.**A–B**

   Depending on the tool you have chosen, do one of the following (and don't forget to use Smart Guides):

   To **scale** the object, drag away from or toward it.

   To **rotate** the object, drag around it.

   To **shear** the object,**C–D** drag away from it.

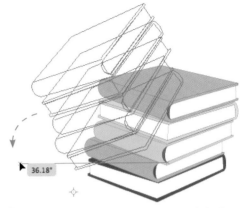

A We click to establish a reference point with the Rotate tool, reposition the mouse, then drag in a circular direction.

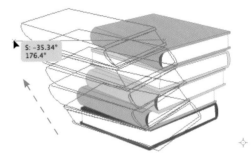

B We click to establish a reference point with the Shear tool, reposition the mouse, then drag diagonally to the left.

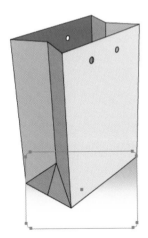

C The shadow object is selected...

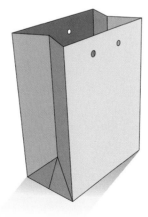

D ...and then it's sheared along the horizontal axis.

To **reflect** the object, click to establish a reference point, then drag to define the axis of reflection (or Shift-click to place the second point along the nearest 45° angle).**A–B**

To transform a **copy** of the object, start dragging, then hold down Option/Alt and continue to drag (release the mouse first).

To transform the object at a multiple of **45°** or to **scale** it **proportionally**, start dragging, then hold down Shift and continue to drag (release the mouse button first).**C**

To transform a **copy** of the object along a multiple of **45°**, or to **copy** and **scale** it proportionally, start dragging, then hold down Option-Shift/Alt-Shift and continue to drag.

To **flip** and **scale** the object simultaneously, drag completely across it with the Scale tool.

➤ To transform a pattern but not the object when using the Rotate, Reflect, Scale, or Shear tool, drag with ~ (tilde) held down.

TRANSFORMING VIA A DIALOG

➤ To apply a transformation via a dialog, select one or more objects or a group, then Control-click/right-click in the document window and choose Transform > Rotate, Reflect, Scale, or Shear from the context menu. When the dialog opens, check Preview. After choosing values, you may check Copy instead of OK to exit the dialog and transform a copy of the selected object(s). (To transform an object from a reference point of your choosing instead of the center, with the Rotate (R) ↻, Reflect (O) ◪, Scale (S) ◳, or Shear tool ◩, Option-click/Alt-click on or near the object.)

➤ If an object's fill or stroke contains a pattern and you want the pattern to transform along with the object, check both Patterns and Objects in the transform dialog; or to scale just the pattern and not the object, uncheck Objects. These options are also available on the Transform panel menu.

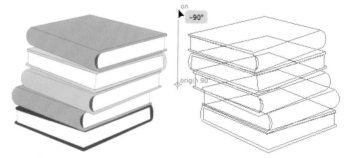

A We click to establish a reference point with the Reflect tool...

B ...then drag upward with Shift held down.

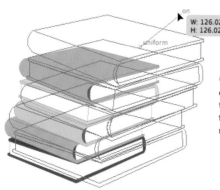

C We click to establish a reference point with the Scale tool, reposition the mouse, then drag toward the upper right with Shift held down.

Using the Transform and Control panels

Use the Transform panel to move, scale, rotate, or shear an object by an exact value or percentage.

To move, scale, rotate, or shear an object using the Transform panel:

1. Select one or more objects or a group, or isolate a single object.

2. Do either of the following:

    Show the **Transform** panel ⊞ (Shift-F8).

    To open a temporary Transform panel, click the blue **X**, **Y**, **W**, or **H** link on the Control panel. Or if your application frame or window is too narrow for those letters to display, click the **Transform** link.

3. Choose a reference point for the transformation by clicking a handle on the reference point locator on the left side of the panel.**A**

4. From the Transform panel menu, choose **Transform Object Only**, **Transform Pattern Only**, or **Transform Both** (to transform both the object and the pattern).

5. If you're going to scale the object, via the **Scale Strokes & Effects** option on the panel menu, you can control whether the object's stroke and effects will also scale (this option can also be turned on or off in Illustrator/Edit > Preferences > General).

6. Enter or choose values as per the instructions below, applying them via one of the shortcuts listed in the sidebar on this page:

    To move the object horizontally, change the **X** value. Increase the value to move the object to the right, or lower it to move it to the left.

    ► Be sure to see the sidebar on the following page for an easy way to change values on the Transform panel.

    To move the object vertically, change the **Y** value. Increase the value to move the object upward, or lower it to move it downward.

    To scale the object, enter the desired **width** (W) and/or **height** (H) as a percentage or as absolute values. To scale the object proportionally, click the Constrain Proportions button ▯ first (a bracket appears next to the button).

SHORTCUTS FOR APPLYING TRANSFORM PANEL VALUES

Apply value and exit the panel	Return/Enter
Apply value and select the next field	Tab
Apply value and reselect the same field	Shift-Return/ Shift-Enter
Apply value, exit the panel, and clone the object	Option-Return/ Alt-Enter
Highlight the next field and clone the object (Mac only)	Option-Tab

A Reference point locator (to set which part of the object Transform panel values are calculated from)

Width and height of selected object

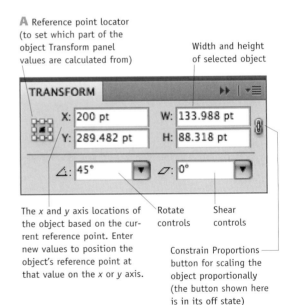

The x and y axis locations of the object based on the current reference point. Enter new values to position the object's reference point at that value on the x or y axis.

Rotate controls

Shear controls

Constrain Proportions button for scaling the object proportionally (the button shown here is in its off state)

Enter or choose a positive **Rotate** value to rotate the object counterclockwise, or a negative value to rotate it clockwise.

To shear (slant) the object to the right, enter or choose a positive **Shear** value; to shear to the left, enter or choose a negative Shear value.

7. From the panel menu, you can also choose **Flip Horizontal** or **Flip Vertical**.

➤ To apply a transformation as an editable and removable effect, see page 141.

➤ With Use Preview Bounds checked in Illustrator/ Edit > Preferences > General (the default setting), the W and H values on the Transform, Control, and Info panels are calculated based on the full dimensions of an object, including the stroke width and any applied effects. With this option off, the dimensions of the basic wireframe path are listed instead.

Note: If your application frame or window is too narrow to display the X, Y, W, and H controls on the Control panel and you can't widen it, click the Transform link and enter values on the temporary Transform panel in lieu of following these instructions (see the preceding page).

To move or scale an object using the Control panel:

1. Select an object or group, or isolate a single object.

2. On the **Control** panel, **A** do either or both of the following:

To move the object, enter or choose new **X** (horizontal) and/or **Y** (vertical) values.

To scale the object, enter or choose **W** (width) and/or **H** (height) values.

➤ Click in a field on any panel and press the up or down arrow on the keyboard to change the value incrementally.

The Constrain Proportions button is in its on state.

X: 127.832 pt   Y: 705.574 pt   W: 303.988 pt   H: 263.259 pt

A On the Control panel, reposition an object or group by changing the X and/or Y values, or scale it by changing the W and/or H values.

Using the Transform Each command

The transformation tools transform multiple objects relative to a single, common reference point, whereas the Transform Each command modifies one or more selected objects relative to their individual center points. **A** To make your artwork look less regular and more hand-drawn, try applying this command to a bunch of objects with the Random option checked.

To perform multiple transformations via the Transform Each command:

1. Select one or more objects (preferably two or more). Objects in a group can't be transformed individually.

2. Control-click/right-click and choose Transform > **Transform Each** (Cmd-Option-Shift-D/ Ctrl-Alt-Shift-D).

3. Check Preview, and move the dialog out of the way, if necessary.

4. Do any of the following **B**:

   Click a different **reference** point ▦ (the point from which the transformations are calculated).

   Move the **Horizontal** or **Vertical Scale** slider (or enter a percentage then press Tab) to scale the objects horizontally and/or vertically from their individual reference points.

   Choose a higher **Horizontal Move** value to move the objects to the right or a negative value to move them to the left; and/or choose a higher **Vertical Move** value to move the objects upward, or vice versa.

   Enter a **Rotate: Angle** value and press Tab, or rotate the dial.

   Check **Reflect X** or **Reflect Y** to flip the objects.

   Check **Random** to have Illustrator apply random transformations within the range of the values you've chosen for Scale, Move, or Rotate. For example, at a Rotate Angle of 35°, a different angle between 0° and 35° will be used for each selected object. Uncheck and recheck Preview to get different random effects.

5. Click OK or Copy.

This is the original arrangement of objects.

The objects are rotated 15° via the Rotate tool.

The objects are rotated 15° via the Transform Each command, with the Random option unchecked.

A The results of the Transform Each command are compared with results from using the Rotate tool.

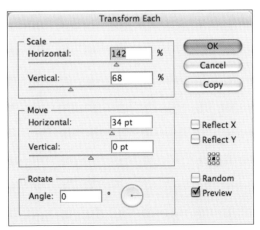

B The Transform Each dialog lets you Scale, Move, Rotate, or Reflect an object randomly or using exact values.

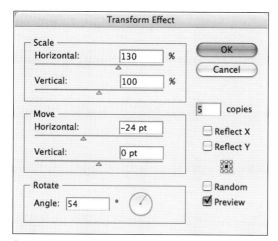

A Use the Transform Effect dialog to apply editable transformations.

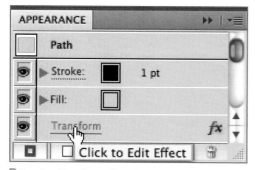

B To edit a Transform effect, double-click the Transform listing on the Appearance panel.

Using the Transform effect

When applied via the Transform Effect dialog, your transformation settings can be modified long after you close the dialog, and even after you close and reopen the file!

To use the Transform effect:

1. Select one or more objects.

2. From the Add New Effect menu *fx.* on the Appearance panel ★ or from the Effect menu on the menu bar, choose Distort & Transform > **Transform**.

3. The Transform Effect dialog looks and functions like the Transform Each dialog, with two exceptions: In the Transform Effect dialog, you can specify a number of **Copies**, and when **Random** is checked, the same random value is applied to every selected object.A Follow the instructions for the Transform Each dialog on the previous page, including exiting the dialog.

4. To edit the transformation at any time, select the object, then double-click Transform on the Appearance panel ◉ B to reopen the Transform Effect dialog. To learn more about appearances, see Chapter 14.

Repeating a transformation

By using the Transform Again command, you can quickly repeat the last transformation (using the last-used values) on any selected object. If you copied an object while transforming it, Transform Again will produce another transformed copy.

To repeat a transformation:

1. Transform an object or group. **A**

2. Keep the object selected, or select another object or group.

3. Control-click/right-click and choose Transform > **Transform Again** (Cmd-D/Ctrl-D). **B–C**

RESETTING THE BOUNDING BOX

If you rotate an object by using a tool or by dragging the corner of the bounding box, the bounding box will no longer align with the x/y axes of the page. If you like, you can square off the bounding box to the horizontal axis while preserving the new orientation of the object. Select the object, then Control-click/right-click and choose Transform > Reset Bounding Box (or choose Object > Transform > Reset Bounding Box). To show or hide the bounding box, press Cmd-Shift-B/Ctrl-Shift-B.

A To create a sunburst, the first step was to rotate and copy a triangle (24°) via the Rotate dialog.

B Then the Transform Again command was applied 14 times by pressing Cmd-D/Ctrl-D.

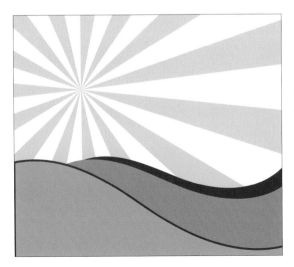

C This landscape contains three curved objects in front of a sunburst. To clip the outer edges in an illustration like this one, draw a rectangle across the objects, select all the objects, then press Cmd-7/Ctrl-7 to create a clipping mask (see Chapter 26).

In Chapters 6 and 7 you learned how to draw paths without thinking about their individual components. In this important chapter, you'll learn how to reshape a path's contour by manipulating the nuts and bolts that all paths are composed of: direction handles, anchor points, and segments. Once you learn how to change the position, number, or type (smooth or corner) of anchor points on a path, you'll be able to create just about any shape imaginable.

Other techniques covered in this chapter include learning how to quickly reshape all or part of a path with the Pencil, Paintbrush, Blob Brush, Path Eraser, Eraser, and Reshape tools; align anchor points; join endpoints; reshape objects via an Effect command; combine paths; and split and cut paths. The chapter also includes three practice exercises.

The building blocks of a path

In Illustrator, all paths consist of anchor points connected by straight and/or curved segments. They can be open, with two endpoints, or closed, with no endpoints. Smooth anchor points have a pair of direction handles that move in tandem, whereas corner anchor points have no direction handles, one direction handle, or a pair of direction handles that move independently.**A** By dragging the end of a direction handle, you can change the shape of the curve it's connected to. The angle of a direction handle controls the slope of the curve that leads into the anchor point; the length of a direction handle controls the height of the curve.

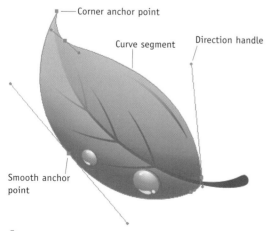

Corner anchor point

Curve segment

Direction handle

Smooth anchor point

A You can manipulate the basic components of a path manually by dragging, or by using a tool or command.

RESHAPE

12

Moving points and segments

If you move an anchor point, the segments that
are connected to it reshape, lengthen, or shorten
accordingly. If you move a straight segment, the
anchor points it's connected to move with it,
whereas if you move a curve segment, the curve
reshapes but the connecting anchor points remain
stationary.

Note: For the instructions in this chapter, make
sure **Highlight Anchors on Mouse Over** is checked
in Illustrator/Edit > Preferences > Selection &
Anchor Display. And while you're at it, you can also
choose preferences for the display of anchor points
and handles (see page 362).

To move an anchor point or a segment:

1. Choose the Direct Selection tool ▶ (A), and click
   a blank area of the document to deselect all.

2. Do any of the following: Drag an anchor
   point;**A** drag the middle of a segment;**B** or
   click an anchor point or segment, then press an
   arrow key. For the first two methods, you can
   use Smart Guides for positioning.

➤ Shift-drag a point or segment to constrain the
   movement to a multiple of 45°.

➤ You can move more than one point at a time,
   even if they're on different paths. To select
   them first, Shift-click them individually or drag
   a marquee around them.

Reshaping curves

In the preceding instructions, you learned that you
can drag an anchor point or a curve segment to
reshape a curve. Another—and more precise—way
to reshape a curve is to lengthen, shorten, or change
the angle of the direction handles on a curve point.

To reshape a curve segment:

1. Choose the Direct Selection tool ▶ (A).

2. Click an anchor point or a curve segment.**C**

3. Do either of the following:

   Drag the end of a direction handle toward or
   away from the anchor point.**D**

   Rotate the end of a direction handle around the
   anchor point. You can use Shift to constrain the
   angle, or use Smart Guides for positioning.

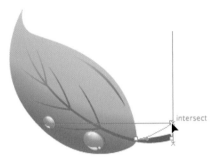

A An anchor point is moved, with the
help of Smart Guides for positioning.

B A segment is moved.

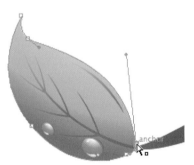

C An anchor point is selected on a shape.

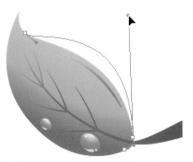

D The end of a direction handle is
dragged away from the anchor point.

Converting points

Corner anchor points either have no rabbit-ear direction handles, or they have direction handles that move independently of each other. The pair of direction handles on a smooth point always stays in a straight line and rotate in tandem (but they can be different lengths). With a click of a button, you can convert any corner point into a smooth one.

To convert a corner anchor point to a smooth anchor point:

1. In Illustrator/Edit > Preferences > Selection & Anchor Display, make sure **Highlight Anchors on Mouse Over** is checked.

2. Choose the Direct Selection tool ► (A).

3. Pass the pointer over a corner anchor point on a path, and when a point becomes highlighted (enlarged), click to select it.**A**

4. On the Control panel, click the **Convert Selected Anchor Points to Smooth** button.▐ **B–C** Direction handles will appear on the selected point.

5. *Optional:* To further modify the curve, with the Direct Selection tool, drag either of the direction handles.**D**

➤ You can also convert a corner point to a smooth point by using the Convert Anchor Point tool (Shift-C). Move the pointer over a corner point, and when it becomes highlighted (enlarged), drag away from it. Direction handles will appear as you drag.

➤ To round the corners on a path by using an editable and removable effect, choose Effect > Stylize > Round Corners.**E–F** (To straighten out the rounded corners, delete the effect listing from the Appearance panel; see page 187.)

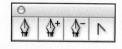

CREATING A TEAROFF TOOLBAR

To practice the techniques in this chapter, we recommend tearing off the toolbar for the Pen tool so the Pen and its cohorts are visible and easily accessible. (Later, once you memorize the shortcuts for accessing these tools, you won't need the toolbar.)A

Display the tearoff toolbar for the Pen tools.

A To convert a corner point to a smooth one, click it with the Direct Selection tool...

B ...then click the Convert Selected Anchor Points to Smooth button on the Control panel.

C Direction handles appear for the selected anchor point.

D You can drag either direction handle to modify the curve.

E This original object has some sharp corners.

F Effect > Stylize > Round Corners rounded off the corners.

To convert a smooth anchor point to a corner anchor point:

1. Choose the Direct Selection tool ➤ (A), and deselect all objects.

2. Pass the pointer over a smooth anchor point on a path, and when it becomes enlarged, click on it.**A**

3. On the Control panel, click the **Convert Selected Anchor Points to Corner** button.┬ **B** The direction handles will disappear from the anchor point.

➤ You can also convert a smooth point to a corner point by clicking it with the Convert Anchor Point tool ⌐ (Shift-C).

A Click a smooth anchor point, then click the Convert Selected Anchor Points to Corner button on the Control panel

B The smooth point is converted to a corner point.

In these instructions, you will convert direction handles that remain in a straight line into handles that can be rotated independently of each another.

To rotate direction handles independently:

1. Choose the Direct Selection tool ➤ (A).

2. Deselect all, click the edge of an object to display its anchor points, then click a smooth point.**C**

3. Choose the Convert Anchor Point tool ⌐ (Shift-C).

4. Drag one of the direction handles on the point. The curve segment will reshape as you drag.**D**

5. Choose the Direct Selection tool again (A), click the anchor point, then drag the other direction point for that anchor point.**E**

➤ To restore a corner point with direction handles that rotate independently to a smooth point, follow the instructions on the preceding page.

➤ When the Pen tool ⌐ (P) is selected, you can hold down Option/Alt to access a temporary Convert Anchor Point tool.

➤ To select all the direction handles on a selected object or objects, from the Select > Object submenu, choose Direction Handles.

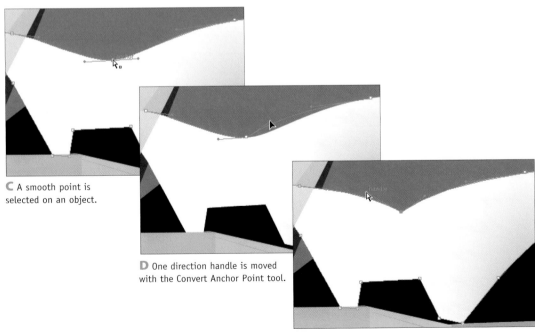

C A smooth point is selected on an object.

D One direction handle is moved with the Convert Anchor Point tool.

E Then the second direction handle is moved.

Adding points

Another way to reshape a path is by adding anchor points to it manually.

To add anchor points to a path manually:

1. Choose the Selection tool ⚊ (V), then select or isolate an object.

2. Do either of the following:

   Choose the **Add Anchor Point** tool ⚊ (+).

   Choose the **Pen** tool ⚊ (P), and make sure **Disable Auto Add/Delete** is unchecked in Illustrator/Edit > Preferences > General (yes, it's a confusing double negative).

3. Click the edge of the object. A new, selected anchor point appears. **A** Repeat, if desired, to add more points to the path.

   ➤ To locate the edge of a path, make sure Anchor/Path Labels ★ is checked in Preferences > Smart Guides, and turn on the Smart Guides feature (Cmd-U/Ctrl-U). As you move the pointer over the edge of an object, the word "path" or "anchor" appears.

   Logically, an anchor point that you add to a curve segment will be a smooth point with direction handles, whereas an anchor point that you add to a straight segment will be a corner point with no direction handles.

4. *Optional:* With the Direct Selection tool (A), move the new anchor point. **B** If it's a smooth point, you can also lengthen or rotate its direction handles.

   ➤ If you don't click precisely on a segment with the Add Anchor Point tool, an alert dialog may appear. Click OK, then try again.

   ➤ Hold down Option/Alt to use a temporary Delete Anchor Point tool when the Add Anchor Point tool is selected, and vice versa.

   ➤ You can also hold down Shift to disable the add and delete functions of the Pen tool. Release Shift before releasing the mouse button.

GETTING A GOOD CURVE

By paying attention to the placement of points, you can achieve smoother curves. When reshaping paths (and while drawing them, as in Chapter 21), place points at the ends of a curve instead of in the middle.

It's hard to draw a symmetrical curve if you place a point at the high point.

For a more symmetrical curve, place the points only at the ends instead.

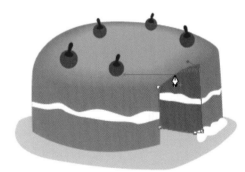

A A segment is clicked, to add a new point.

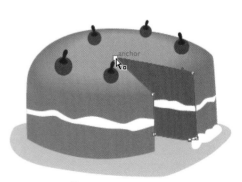

B The new point is moved.

The Add Anchor Points command inserts one point midway between each pair of existing anchor points in a selected object.

To add anchor points to a path via a command:

1. Choose the Selection tool ★ (V), then select the object(s) to which points are to be added.

2. Choose Object > Path > **Add Anchor Points**.**A–C** If desired, repeat to add yet more points.

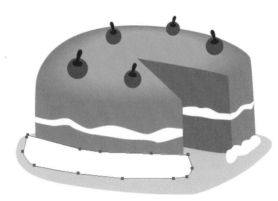

A A simple long, round-ended object is added to an illustration.

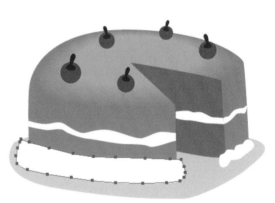

B We applied the Add Anchor Points command to the object.

SELECTING TOOLS FOR RESHAPING PATHS

Pen tool	P
Add Anchor Point tool	+
Delete Anchor Point tool	−
Convert Anchor Point tool	Shift-C
Pencil tool	N
Paintbrush tool	B
Scissors tool	C
Lasso tool	Q
Disable the Auto Add/Delete function of the Pen tool	Shift
When the Pen tool is selected, access the last-used selection tool	Cmd/Ctrl
Convert the Add Anchor Point tool to the Delete Anchor Point tool, or vice versa	Option/Alt

C We applied Effect > Distort & Transform > Roughen to alter the shape. Because points were added to the path, we were able to keep the Roughen settings low, which produced less overall distortion.

You can add segments to a path with the Pencil tool, regardless of which tool the path was drawn with, and whether or not the path has an applied brush stroke. If a path does have a brush stroke, another way to add to it is by using the Paintbrush tool.

To add to an open path with the Pencil or Paintbrush tool:

1. Choose the Selection tool ▶ (V), then select or isolate an open path.

2. Double-click the **Pencil** tool (N) to open the options dialog for that tool. Or if the path has a brush stroke, you may double-click the **Paintbrush** tool ✐ instead.

3. In the tool preferences dialog, make sure **Edit Selected Paths** is checked, then click OK.

4. Position the pointer directly over the path, then draw an addition to the path. **A–B**

➤ If you end up with a new, separate path instead of an addition to an existing path, delete the new one. On your next try, make sure the pointer is directly over the path before you start drawing. Or when using the Paintbrush tool, make sure the path you're adding to has a brush stroke.

To add to an open path with the Pen tool:

1. Choose the **Pen** tool ♦ (P).

2. Position the pointer over the endpoint of a path (the path doesn't have to be selected). A slash appears next to the Pen pointer when the tool is positioned correctly. **C**

3. Click the endpoint to make it a corner point, or drag from it to make it a smooth point. The point will become selected. **D**

4. Position the pointer where you want the next anchor point to appear, then click or drag.

5. If desired, continue to click to create more corner points or drag to create more smooth points. **E** Choose another tool when you're done adding to the path.

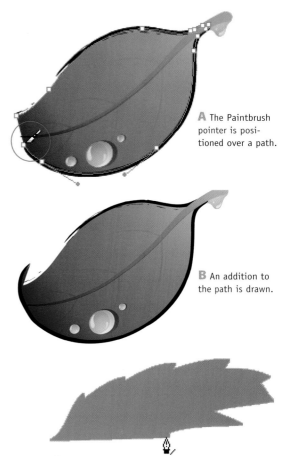

A The Paintbrush pointer is positioned over a path.

B An addition to the path is drawn.

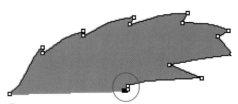

C The pointer is positioned over an endpoint (note the slash next to the Pen icon).

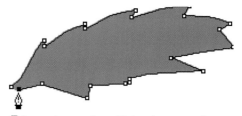

D After the endpoint is clicked, it becomes solid.

E More points are then added to the same path.

Deleting points

When you delete points from a closed path, it stays closed.

To delete anchor points from a path:

Method 1 (Pen tool)

1. Do either of the following:

   Choose the **Delete Anchor Point** tool (-).

   Choose the **Pen** tool (P), and make sure Disable Auto Add/Delete is unchecked in Illustrator/Edit > Preferences > General.

2. Cmd-click/Ctrl-click the edge of the object from which you want to delete anchor points.

3. Click an anchor point (don't press Delete!).**A** The point will be deleted.**B** Repeat to delete other anchor points, if desired.

➤ If you don't click precisely on an anchor point with the Delete Anchor Point tool, an alert dialog appears. Click OK and try again.

Method 2 (Control panel)

1. Choose the **Direct Selection** tool (A).

2. Deselect all, click the edge of an object to display its anchor points, then click a point (or Shift-click multiple points).

3. Click the **Anchors: Remove Selected Anchor Points** button on the Control panel.

A An anchor point is clicked with the Delete Anchor Point tool (or the Pen tool).

B The point is deleted.

Reshaping objects with the Pencil or Paintbrush tool

With the Pencil and Paintbrush tools, you can reshape a path by dragging along its edge.

To reshape a path with the Pencil or Paintbrush tool:

1. Do either of the following:

   To reshape a path that doesn't have an applied brush stroke, choose the **Pencil** tool ✎ (N).

   To reshape a path that does have a brush stroke, choose the **Pencil** tool ✎ (N) or the **Paintbrush** tool ✎ (B).

2. Cmd-click/Ctrl-click a path to select it.

3. Position the pointer directly over the edge of the path, then drag along it.**A** The path will reshape instantly.**B**

   Note: Be sure to position the pointer precisely on the edge of the path. If you don't, you will create a new path instead of reshaping the existing one.

➤ Caps Lock reverses the current Use Precise Cursors setting in Illustrator/Edit > Preferences > General. That is, it turns a tool icon pointer into crosshairs, or vice versa.

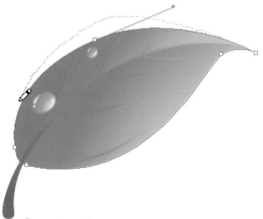

A A path is reshaped with the Pencil tool.

B The leaf shape is now wider.

Reshaping objects with the Blob Brush tool

In addition to being a great tool for producing "magic marker" drawings, as we showed you on pages 83–84, the Blob Brush tool can be used to reshape or smooth the edges of existing closed paths by drawing strokes. It can be used on ordinary paths, as well as on compound paths, masked objects within a clipping mask, or on the start or end object in a live blend.

To reshape an object with the Blob Brush tool: ★

1. Select or isolate an object that was created with any tool **A** (except a type or symbol tool), and make sure it has a stroke of None.◩ It can contain a solid fill color or a pattern, but not a graphic style.

2. Choose the **Blob Brush** tool 🖋 (Shift-B).

3. To add to the object, draw strokes around or across it. Your strokes will merge with the closed path.**B** Note: If your strokes produce a hole within the shape, the result will be a compound path (to learn about compound paths, see page 321).

   To smooth the edge of the object, hold down Option/Alt to access the Smooth tool temporarily, then drag along an edge of the object. The tool smooths an edge by reducing the number of anchor points.

➤ Press [or] to decrease or increase the diameter of the Blob Brush tool.

The versatile Blob Brush tool can also be used to merge multiple objects, but in a unique way—you draw strokes across them.

To combine objects using the Blob Brush tool: ★

1. Arrange two or more closed path objects relatively near or overlapping each other (no type objects). Make sure they have the same solid fill color or pattern and a stroke of None, but not a gradient or a graphic style. The objects must be on the same layer; see page 173. Select at least one of the objects.

2. Draw strokes across the objects. Note: If your strokes produce a hole within the shape, the result will be a compound path.

A To add shading to the cup, a basic polygon shape is used as a starting point, and is selected.

B The Blob Brush tool was used to reshape the object, to make it conform to the side of the cup.

EXERCISE: Draw and reshape objects in a freehand style ★

To master the art of drawing shapes by hand, use the Blob Brush tool to draw and add to a shape, **A–B** then erase unwanted parts of it with the Eraser tool. **C** Finally, use the Smooth tool to smooth out any rough edges. **D** By using this great trio of tools, you won't have to use the selection and pen tools in order to reshape a path, or fiddle with those nasty anchor points or direction handles.

A To create foam on the top of a glass, the Blob Brush tool was used to draw some simple shapes.

B The same tool was also used to fill in the shapes and to add "drips."

C The Eraser tool was used to reshape the edges of the drip shapes.

D Finally, the Smooth tool was used to smooth some of the edges.

Using the Reshape tool

The Reshape tool does a nice job of gently reshaping a path without distorting its shape. It's hard to describe what it does in words, so give it a try.

To use the Reshape tool:

1. Choose the Direct Selection tool ▶ (A), deselect all, then click the edge of a path. Only one point or segment should be selected.

2. Choose the **Reshape** tool ⛝ (it's on the Scale tool pop-out menu).

3. Do one of the following:

   Drag any visible **anchor point** on the path. A tiny square border will display around the point when you release the mouse.

   Drag any **segment** of the path. A new square border point is created.

   Shift-click or marquee **multiple anchor points** on the path (a square will display around each one), then drag one of the square points. The selected portion of the path will maintain its overall contour as it elongates or contracts, and the rest of the path will stay put.

EXERCISE: Draw a brush with the Reshape tool

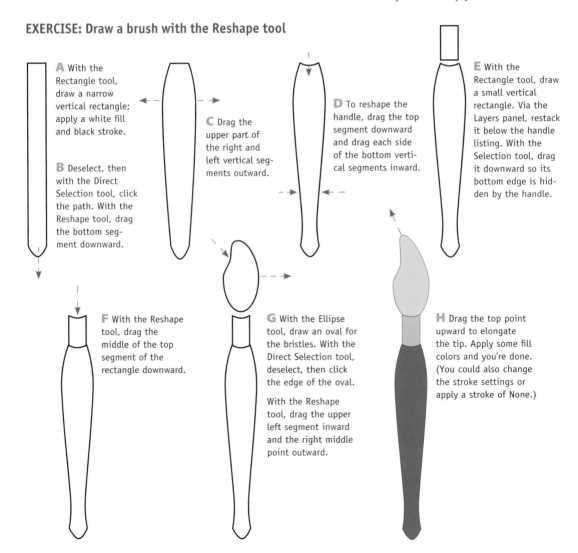

A With the Rectangle tool, draw a narrow vertical rectangle; apply a white fill and black stroke.

B Deselect, then with the Direct Selection tool, click the path. With the Reshape tool, drag the bottom segment downward.

C Drag the upper part of the right and left vertical segments outward.

D To reshape the handle, drag the top segment downward and drag each side of the bottom vertical segments inward.

E With the Rectangle tool, draw a small vertical rectangle. Via the Layers panel, restack it below the handle listing. With the Selection tool, drag it downward so its bottom edge is hidden by the handle.

F With the Reshape tool, drag the middle of the top segment of the rectangle downward.

G With the Ellipse tool, draw an oval for the bristles. With the Direct Selection tool, deselect, then click the edge of the oval.

With the Reshape tool, drag the upper left segment inward and the right middle point outward.

H Drag the top point upward to elongate the tip. Apply some fill colors and you're done. (You could also change the stroke settings or apply a stroke of None.)

Erasing sections of objects

The Eraser tool removes parts of objects that it passes over, and the remaining parts of the objects are reconnected automatically to form closed paths.

To erase parts of objects:

1. If you want to limit the effect of the Eraser tool to specific objects, select them first (say, if there are many objects close together in the artwork, and you want to erase only some of them). Otherwise, deselect all.**A**

   Note: The object can be a Live Paint object or a compound path, it can be in a clipping mask, and it may contain gradients or patterns. The Eraser tool doesn't work on symbol instances, type objects, objects in a blend, or objects within a distortion envelope.

2. Choose the **Eraser** tool 🧽 (Shift-E).

3. Do either of the following:

   Drag across parts of objects to be erased.**B–C** (Shift-drag to constrain your erasure strokes to an increment of 45°.)

   Option-drag/Alt-drag to create a marquee. Any parts of the artwork that fall within the marquee will be erased completely.

➤ Press [or] to decrease or increase the diameter of the Eraser tool. Double-click the tool icon to change the tool shape (see pages 298–299).

➤ If you drag with the Eraser tool on the inside of an object—without crossing over the edge—a compound path will be produced.

A This mountain range was drawn with the Pencil tool.

B With the Eraser tool, we erased sections of the object to create details on the mountains and lake.

USING THE PATH ERASER TOOL

To erase parts of a path without having to click points, choose the Path Eraser tool ✏ (the last tool on the Pencil tool pop-out menu). Select a path, then drag the eraser of the pencil pointer directly over the path.

C Additional erasures were made, but with a smaller diameter chosen for the Eraser tool. Finally, two colored rectangles were placed behind the mountain layer.

Aligning points

The Align buttons on the Control panel precisely realign selected endpoints or anchor points along the horizontal and/or vertical axis, and as a result, the paths those points belong to are reshaped.

To align points:

1. Choose the Lasso tool ⟨�⟩ (Q).

2. Drag to select two or more endpoints or anchor points **A** on one path or on different paths.

3. On the Control panel, do any of the following:

   To align the points by moving them along the horizontal (*x*) axis, click one of the **Horizontal Align** buttons.

   To align the points by moving them along the vertical (*y*) axis, click one of the **Vertical Align** buttons.

   To overlap the points along both the horizontal and vertical axes, click a **Horizontal Align** button, then a **Vertical Align** button. Use this method if you're planning to join the points into one point (see the instructions on the following page).

   If you click a Left, Right, Top **B**, or Bottom **C** Align button, points will align to the leftmost, rightmost, topmost, or bottommost selected point, respectively. If you click a Center Align button, **D** points will align to an equidistant location between the points.

➤ If you Shift-select points with the Direct Selection tool (instead of by dragging a selection marquee) before clicking an align button, points will align with and move toward the last selected point, regardless of which Horizontal or Vertical Align button you click.

➤ To align selected points via a command, Control-click/right-click and choose Average (Cmd-Option-J/Ctrl-Alt-J), then click Axis: Horizontal, Vertical, or Both in the dialog (fewer options are offered here than on the Control panel).

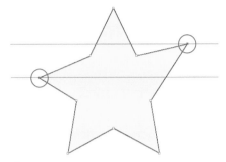

A Two anchor points are selected.

B The Vertical Align Top button is clicked.

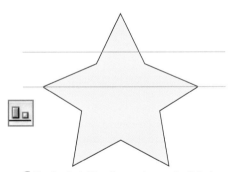

C The Vertical Align Bottom button is clicked.

D The Vertical Align Center button is clicked.

Joining endpoints

The Connect Selected End Points button connects two selected endpoints with a new straight segment or joins endpoints into one point. The endpoints you connect or join can be on separate open paths or on the same open path.

To connect two endpoints:

1. With the Direct Selection tool ⟨ (A) or the Lasso tool ⟨ (Q), select two endpoints. **A**

2. Click the **Connect Selected End Points** button ⟨ on the Control panel. A straight line segment now connects the points. **B**

To join two endpoints into one point:

1. With the Direct Selection tool ⟨ (A) or the Lasso tool ⟨ (Q), select two endpoints.

2. On the Control panel, click one of the three **Horizontal Align** buttons and one of the three **Vertical Align** buttons. The two selected endpoints are now right on top of each other.

3. Click the **Connect Selected End Points** button ⟨ on the Control panel or Control-click/right-click and choose Join. The Join dialog opens. **C**

4. Do one of the following:

   To join two corner points into one corner point with no direction handles, or to connect two smooth points into one smooth point with direction handles that move independently, click **Corner**.

   To connect two smooth points into a smooth point with direction handles that move in tandem, click **Smooth**.

   To join a corner point and a smooth point into a corner point with one direction handle, click **Corner** or **Smooth**.

5. Click OK. **D**

SHORTCUTS FOR AVERAGE AND JOIN

	Mac OS	Windows
Average endpoints (Average dialog)	Cmd-Option-J	Ctrl-Alt-J
Join endpoints	Cmd-J	Ctrl-J
Average and join endpoints	Cmd-Option-Shift-J	Ctrl-Alt-Shift-J

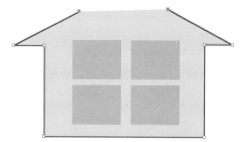

A Two endpoints are selected.

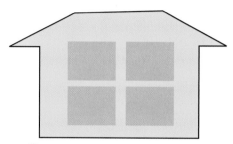

B The Connect Selected End Points button created a straight segment between them.

C If you click the Connect Selected End Points button when one selected endpoint is right on top of another, the Join dialog opens.

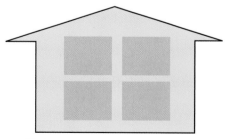

D This is the first figure on this page, after we clicked the Horizontal Align Center and Vertical Align Center buttons, clicked the Connect Selected End Points button, then clicked Corner in the Join dialog.

Reshaping objects using commands

Some of the commands on the Effect menu can be used to explode simple shapes into more complex ones, with practically no effort in your part. For example, the Zig Zag effect, used in the instructions below, adds anchor points to a path and then moves those points to produce waves or zigzags. Best of all, the Effect menu commands don't alter the actual path, so the results are editable and removable.

To apply the Zig Zag effect:

1. Select an object.

2. Choose Effect > Distort & Transform > **Zig Zag**. The Zig Zag dialog opens. **A** Check Preview.

3. Click Points: **Smooth** (at the bottom of the dialog) to create curvy waves, or **Corner** to create sharp-cornered zigzags.

4. Do either of the following:

   To move the added points by a percentage relative to the size of the object, click **Relative**, then move the Size slider.

   To move the added points by a specified distance, click **Absolute**, then choose or enter that distance via the **Size** slider or field.

5. Choose a number of **Ridges** per segment for the number of anchor points to be added between existing points. The greater the number of Ridges, the more complex the resulting object. If you enter a number, press Tab to preview it.

6. Click OK.**B–G**

   Note: To edit the results of the effect, click Zig Zag on the Appearance panel.

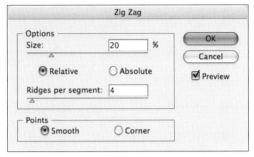

A Use the Preview option to preview settings for the Zig Zag effect.

B The original object is a star.

C The Zig Zag effect is applied (Relative, Size 20%, Ridges 4, Smooth).

D The original object is a circle.

E The Zig Zag effect is applied (Relative, Size 24%, Ridges 20, Corner).

F The original object is an ellipse.

G The Zig Zag effect is applied (Relative, Size 9%, Ridges 4, Smooth).

If you use one of the "easy" tools to create objects, such as the Rectangle, Ellipse, Star, Blob Brush, Pencil, or Paintbrush, followed by any of the simpler reshaping techniques that are covered in this chapter, you will be able create artwork that looks complex without having to painstakingly draw it with the Pen tool. One of the easiest ways to create illustrations is to combine objects via a command on the Pathfinder panel. For example, to combine whole objects, rather than joining points one pair at a time, you can simply click the Unite button on the Pathfinder panel, as in the instructions below. To learn more about this panel and about creating compound shapes, see Chapter 25.

To combine objects using a command:

1. Position two or more objects so they overlap one another at least partially.**A**

2. With any selection tool, marquee at least some portion of all the objects.

3. Display the **Pathfinder** panel ▣ (Cmd-Shift-F9/ Ctrl-Shift-F9).

4. Click the **Unite** (first) button ▣ on the panel. Voilà! The individual objects are now combined into one closed compound shape, to which the attributes of the formerly topmost object are applied.**B–F**

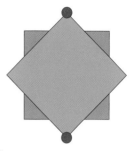

A Arrange two or more objects so they overlap before selecting them.

B We clicked the Unite button on the Pathfinder panel to combine the separate shapes into a single compound shape.

C The original objects consist of four objects.

D The Unite command is applied.

E The original objects consist of four objects.

F The Unite command is applied (Macintosh to Granny Smth!).

Slicing and dicing

The Scissors tool will open a closed path or split one open path into two. You can split a path either at an anchor point or in the middle of a segment.

To split a path with the Scissors tool:

1. Choose any selection tool, then click an object to display its points. Note: You can split a closed path that contains type (area type), but not an open path that contains type along or inside it.

2. Choose the **Scissors** tool ✂ (C).

3. Click the object's path: If you click once on a closed path, it will turn into a single, open path; if you click once on an open path, it will split into two paths.

   If you click a segment, two new endpoints will appear, one on top of the other.**A** If you click an anchor point, a new anchor point will appear on top of the existing one, and it will be selected.

4. To move the new endpoints apart, choose the Direct Selection tool ▶ (A), then drag the selected endpoint away from its mate or press an arrow key.**B**

To split a path via the Control panel:

1. Choose the Direct Selection tool ▶ (A).

2. Click a path to display its anchor points, then click an anchor point to select it.

3. Click the **Cut Path at Selected Anchor Points** button ⌇ on the Control panel. A new anchor point will appear on top of the existing one, and it will be selected.

4. To move the two new endpoints apart, drag the selected one.

A With the Scissors tool, click an anchor point or segment.

There is no segment, and therefore no stroke, between these endpoints.

B We moved the new endpoint on this newly opened path.

The Divide Objects Below command uses an object like a cookie cutter to cut the objects below it, then deletes the cutting object.

To cut objects via the Divide Objects Below command:

1. Create or select an object that contains a solid-color fill and/or stroke, to be used as a cutting shape (not a group or a Live Paint group).

   Optional: The Divide Objects Below command is going to delete the cutting object, so you may want to use Option-drag/Alt-drag to copy it first.

2. Place the cutting object on top of the object(s) to be cut.**A**

3. Make sure only the cutting object is selected.

4. Choose Object > Path > **Divide Objects Below**. The topmost shape (cutting object) is deleted and the underlying objects are cut into separate paths where they met the edge of the cutting object.**B–C**

5. Deselect. You can use the Selection tool to select or isolate any of the objects, then recolor or move them. Any objects that were in a group will remain so.

➤ To prevent an object below the cutting shape from being affected by the Divide Objects Below command, you can either lock it (see page 175) or hide it (see page 176).

DIVIDE VERSUS DIVIDE OBJECTS BELOW

The Divide Objects Below command (this page) deletes the cutting object and leaves the resulting objects ungrouped, whereas the Divide button on the Pathfinder panel (see page 318) preserves the paint attributes of all the objects, including the topmost object, and groups the resulting paths. Divide usually produces smaller pieces than Divide Objects Below.

A The white leaf shape (on top) is going to be the cutting object.

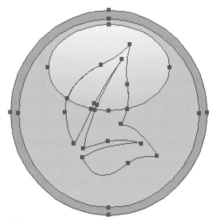

B The Divide Objects Below command used the leaf shape to cut through the underlying objects.

C We applied different fill colors to the resulting divided paths.

EXERCISE: Draw a glass of beer (or cream soda!)

1. With the Ellipse tool ⬭ (L), draw a vertical oval (approximately 3.5" wide by 5" high) and a smaller horizontal oval. With the Rectangle tool ▢ (M), draw a rectangle at the bottom of the vertical ellipse.

2. With the Selection tool ▶ (V), select all three shapes. Open the Art History > Impressionism swatch library panel, then apply a pale blue-gray fill and a black stroke. **A** On the Pathfinder panel, click the Unite button. ▢

3. With the Delete Anchor Point tool ✑ (-), click to delete the points shown in **B**.

4. With the Direct Selection tool ▶ (A), drag to select the bottom four points of the stem. Click the Convert Selected Anchor Points to Smooth button ⌐ on the Control panel. To reshape the stem, click then press arrow keys to move two points inward and two points outward, as shown in **C**. Adjust the bottom direction handles on the two lower points to reshape the bottom curve of the stem.

5. With the Ellipse tool, Option-drag/Alt-drag to create an oval the same width as the glass top, and fill it with a cream color. **D** With the Add Anchor Point tool ✑ (+), add five new points along the top of the oval. With the Direct Selection tool, select and drag each point separately, to make the oval look like foam. **E**

6. Use the Selection tool (V) to select the glass shape. With the Scale tool ▦ (S), start dragging, then hold down Option/Alt and drag diagonally inward to create a slightly smaller copy. Apply a light tan fill color and a stroke of None. With the Delete Anchor Point tool (–), click the bottom two points on the scaled copy. With the Direct Selection tool, move the top two corner points on the scaled copy closer to the top corners of the original glass shape. **F**

7. Deselect. Double-click the Blob Brush tool. ✎ Set the Size to 40 pt, the Angle to 40°, and the Roundness to 22%; click OK. Click a darker tan fill color, then drag vertically along the right edge of the glass to create shading. Double-click the tool again. Change the Angle value to –40°. then drag inside the left edge of the glass. **G**

8. Draw an oval for the base of the glass, and apply the same color attributes as the glass. Via the Layers panel, restack it below the glass object.

9. With the Blob Brush (Shift-B), create additional areas of shading and highlights on the glass and stem. Cheers! **H**

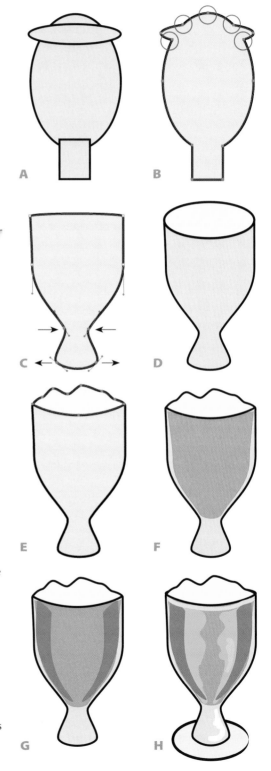

A   B

C   D

E   F

G   H

Until this point (unless you snuck ahead to this chapter!), you've been creating objects on a single, default layer that was created automatically when you created your document, and each new path was stacked above the last one automatically. In this chapter, you'll learn how to purposely change the stacking order of objects via the Layers panel 🐚 (F7). **A** You will use the panel to create top-level layers and sublayers; delete layers and objects; select layer listings; select objects; restack, duplicate, lock, unlock, hide, and show layers; collect objects onto a new layer; release objects to layers; and finally, merge and flatten layers.

Getting to know the Layers panel

With a document open, click the Layer 1 arrowhead on the Layers panel to expand the list of objects on that layer. Layer 1 is a top-level layer, meaning it's not nested within another layer.

Continued on the following page

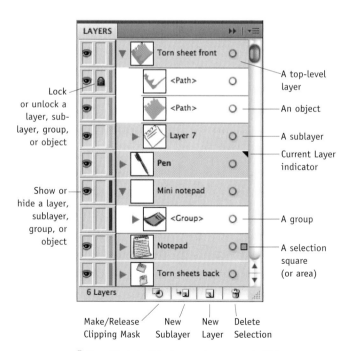

Lock or unlock a layer, sublayer, group, or object

A top-level layer

An object

A sublayer

Current Layer indicator

Show or hide a layer, sublayer, group, or object

A group

A selection square (or area)

Make/Release Clipping Mask

New Sublayer

New Layer

Delete Selection

A The objects in this document are nested within top-level layers and sublayers, at various stacking levels (the artwork is shown at the top of the page).

LAYERS

13

You can add as many layers as you like to a document, depending on available memory, and you can also create sublayers (nested layers) within any top-level layer. The actual objects that make up your artwork—paths, type, images, etc.—are nested within one or more top-level layers, or in groups or sublayers within top-level layers. When you create an object, it appears on the currently selected layer, but it can be moved to a different layer at any time, either individually or by restacking the whole layer or sublayer it resides in.

The Layers panel also has other important functions beyond restacking. You can use it to select, target (for appearance changes), show or hide, and lock or unlock any layer, sublayer, group, or individual object.

By default, each new vector object you create is listed as <Path> on the Layers panel; each placed raster image or rasterized object is listed as <Image> or by the name of the image file; each symbol is listed by the name of that symbol (e.g., "Blue Flower"); and each type object is listed by the first few characters in the object (e.g., "The planting season has begun" might be shortened to "The plan"). Similarly, object groups are listed by such names as Live Paint Group, Compound Path, etc. You may say "Whoa!" when you first see the number of listings on the Layers panel. Once you get used to working with it, though, you may become enamored of its clean, logical design, as we are, and enjoy how much easier it makes even simple tasks, such as selecting or locking objects.

➤ To rename a Layers panel listing, double-click the existing name.

You can choose different Layers panel options for each document.

To choose Layers panel options:

1. Choose **Panel Options** from the bottom of the Layers panel menu. The Layers Panel Options dialog opens.**A**

2. Keep **Show Layers Only** unchecked; otherwise the panel will list only top-level layers and sublayers, not individual objects.

3. For the size of the layer and object thumbnails, click a **Row Size** of Small (12 pixels), Medium (20 pixels), or Large (32 pixels), or click Other and enter a custom size (12–100 pixels).**B**

ONE CATCHALL NAME

In this book, we refer to paths, images, and text objects collectively as objects. If we need to refer to one of these categories individually for some reason, we will.

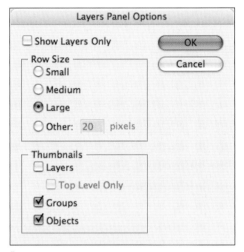

A Via the Layers Panel Options dialog, you can customize the Layers panel for each file.

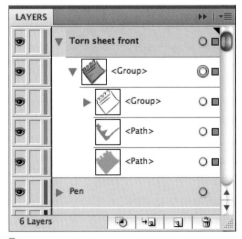

B For the Layers panel in our document, we chose the Large Row Size and turned Thumbnails off for Layers.

4. Check which **Thumbnails** you want the panel to display: Layers, Groups, or Objects. If you check Top Level Only for layers, thumbnails will display for top-level layers but not for sublayers.

5. Click OK.

Creating layers

In these instructions, you'll learn how to create the granddaddy of layers—top-level layers.

To create a new top-level layer:

Method 1 (quick, no options)

1. On the Layers panel 🖢 (F7), click the listing for the top-level layer above which the new layer is to appear.

2. Click the **New Layer** button 🔲 at the bottom of the panel. To the new layer, Illustrator will assign the next sequential number and the next available color, as listed on the Color menu in the Layer Options dialog.

Method 2 (choose options)

1. On the Layers panel (F7), click the listing for the top-level layer above which the new layer is to appear.

2. Option-click/Alt-click the **New Layer** button. 🔲 **A** The Layer Options dialog opens.

3. Do any of the following:

Change the layer **Name**.

Via the **Color** menu, choose a color to be used as a highlight color for selected objects on the layer and for the layer color on the Layers panel. Colors are assigned to new top-level layers based on their order on this menu.

► If the fill or stroke colors of objects on the layer are similar to the selection border color, you might want to choose a different selection color, for contrast.

Choose other layer options (see the sidebar on page 175).

4. Click OK. **B**

► Objects always reside in a top-level layer or sublayer (or in a group in either of the above)—they can't float around unassigned to any layer.

► Layers and sublayers are numbered in the order in which they're created, regardless of their position in the stacking order or their indent level.

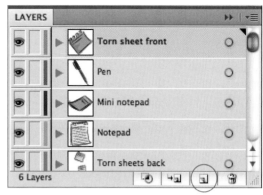

A Click a layer, then Option-click/Alt-click the New Layer button. In the Layer Options dialog, choose options for, or rename, the new layer.

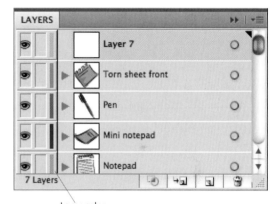

Layer color

B The new layer (Layer 7) appears above the "Torn sheet front" layer.

CREATING A TOP TOP-LEVEL LAYER QUICKLY

To create a new top-level layer in the topmost position on the panel, regardless of which layer listing is currently selected, Cmd-click/Ctrl-click the New Layer button on the Layers panel.

Once you become accustomed to adding and using top-level layers, you'll be ready to add another tier to the hierarchy: sublayers. Every sublayer is nested within (indented within) either a top-level layer or another sublayer. If you create a new object or group of objects when a sublayer is selected, the new object or group will be nested within that sublayer. You don't necessarily have to create or use sublayers, but you may find them to be helpful for keeping the panel organized, especially if your document contains a lot of objects.

By default, every sublayer has the same generic name: "Layer," but as with layers, you can rename them to make them easier to identify (e.g., "inner pieces" or "order form" or "tyrannosaurus").

To create a sublayer:

1. On the Layers panel 🕮 (F7), click the top-level layer (or sublayer) in which the new sublayer is to appear.

2. Do either of the following:

   To create a new sublayer without choosing options for it, click the **New Sublayer** button 🔲.A–B

   To choose options as you create a new sublayer, Option-click/Alt-click the New Sublayer button. In the Layer Options dialog, enter a Name, check or uncheck any of the options (see the sidebar on page 175), then click OK.

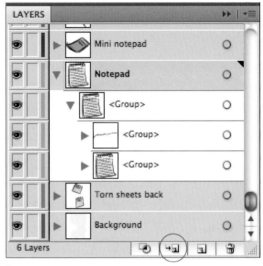

A Click a layer listing, then click the New Sublayer button.

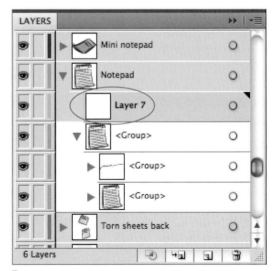

B A new sublayer listing (in this case, Layer 7) appears within our "Notepad" layer.

Deleting layers and objects

You know how to make 'em. Now you need to learn how to get rid of 'em.

Beware! If you delete a top-level layer or sublayer, all the objects on the layer are removed from the document.

To delete a layer, sublayer, group, or object:

1. On the Layers panel, 👁 click the layer, sublayer, group, or object to be deleted, or Cmd-click/Ctrl-click multiple listings. You can click multiple listings at the same indent level (e.g., all top-level layers), but not listings from different indent levels (e.g., not a top-level layer along with individual objects nested in a different top-level layer).

2. Do either of the following:

   Click the **Delete Selection** button 🗑 at the bottom of the Layers panel.**A–C** If the layer or sublayer that you're deleting contains any objects, an alert dialog will appear; click Yes.

   To bypass the prompt, drag the highlighted layers or objects over the Delete Selection button.🗑

➤ To retrieve a deleted layer and the objects it contained, use the Undo command immediately.

A This is the original artwork.

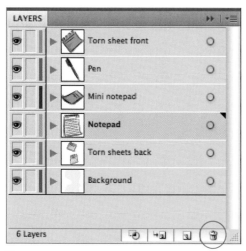

B Highlight a layer (or a sublayer, group, or object), then click the Delete Selection button.

C This is the artwork after we deleted the "Notepad" layer.

Selecting Layers panel listings

If you want to control where a new (or pasted) object will be stacked in a document, you need to click a top-level layer, sublayer, group, or object listing on the Layers panel before you paste or draw.

If you select an object, the listing for its top-level layer or sublayer becomes selected automatically, but the converse isn't true: simply clicking a top-level layer or sublayer listing won't cause objects to become selected in the document window. Selecting objects via the Layers panel is a separate task (see pages 170–172), and targeting items for appearance attributes serves yet another function (see the sidebar on page 170). Think of selecting layer listings as a layer management technique, and of selecting the objects themselves (making the anchor points, and possibly the bounding box, appear) as an essential first step in the editing process.

When creating a new object or placing an image into your artwork, bear the following in mind:

➤ If you click a top-level layer listing first (but not a sublayer or group), the new object will be listed at the top of the top-level layer.

➤ If you click a sublayer listing first (but no objects are selected), the new object will appear within that sublayer.

➤ If you select an object first, the new object will appear in the same layer or sublayer as the selected object, outside any group.

To select a layer, sublayer, group, or object listing:

Click a top-level layer, sublayer, group, or object name, or click the area just to the right of the name — not the circle or the selection area at the far right side of the panel. The Current Layer indicator (black triangle) **A** will move to the layer that the item you clicked resides in.

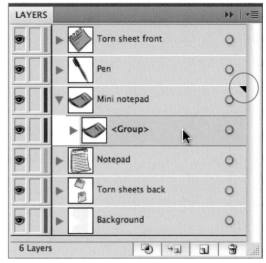

A When a group is clicked, the Current Layer indicator moves to the top-level layer the group resides in.

If multiple layer listings (layers, sublayers, groups, or objects) are selected, you can restack them on the panel at the same time or apply the same layer options to them. There are a few rules to remember here, too:

➤ You can select multiple sublayer listings within the same top-level layer, provided they're at the same nesting level, but you can't select multiple sublayer listings from different top-level layers.

➤ You can select multiple listings of the same category (e.g., multiple top-level layers) and nesting level, but you can't select multiple listings from different nesting levels (e.g., not both top-level layers and objects on another layer).

➤ You can select multiple object listings (such as a path and type) in the same top-level layer, but not from different top-level layers.

To select multiple layer listings:

1. On the Layers panel (F7), click a top-level layer, sublayer, or object.

2. Do either of the following:

   Shift-click the name of another layer, sublayer, or object. The items you clicked plus any items of a similar kind between them will become highlighted.

   Cmd-click/Ctrl-click other noncontiguous top-level layer, sublayer, or object names.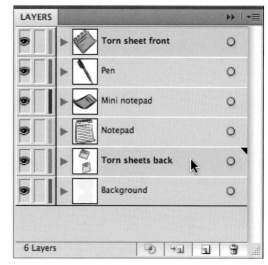

➤ Cmd-click/Ctrl-click to deselect any individual listings when multiple listings are selected.

➤ Although you can click multiple layers, only one top-level layer or sublayer will display a Current Layer indicator.

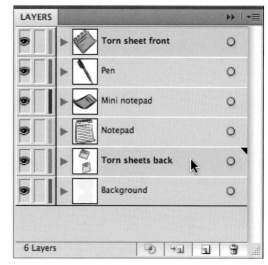

A Two noncontiguous top-level layer listings are selected.

Selecting objects via the Layers panel

In Chapter 8, you learned how to select objects by using a variety of selection tools and Select menu commands. You can also use the Layers panel to select paths or groups—that is, make the anchor points visible in the document window to ready them for editing or reshaping.

To select all the objects in a layer:

At the far right side of the Layers panel, click the **selection area A** for a top-level layer or sublayer. A colored selection square will appear for every sublayer, group, and object on that layer (if the layer list is expanded), and every object on the layer, regardless of its indent level, will become selected in the document window. The bounding box will also appear, if that feature is on.**B** In addition, unless the items are in a group, the target circle for each path and group will become selected.

➤ To deselect an individual object, expand the top-level layer or sublayer list for that object, then Shift-click the object's selection square.

To deselect all the objects in a layer:

Shift-click the selection square for the layer containing the objects to be deselected. All the objects in the layer will be deselected, including objects in any nested sublayers or groups.

THE CIRCLE OR THE SQUARE?

➤ If you click the target circle ⭕ on the right side of the Layers panel for a group or object, or click the selection area (to the right of the target circle), the object or group becomes selected and targeted and the item is listed on the Appearance panel. (See the next chapter.)

➤ If you click the selection area for a top-level layer, all the objects or groups on the layer become selected and targeted for appearance changes, and the item name (e.g., "Path" or "Mixed Objects") is listed on the Appearance panel. If you click the target circle for a top-level layer, all the objects on the layer become selected, but only the top-level layer is targeted; "Layer" becomes the current listing on the Appearance panel.

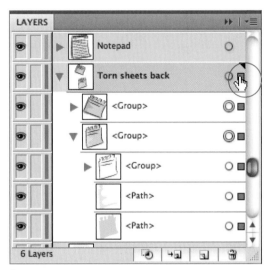

A Click the selection area for a layer to select all the paths and groups it contains. The selection squares appear (in the color that has been assigned to that layer).

B All the paths and path groups on the "Torn sheets back" layer became selected in the artwork.

To select an object via the Layers panel:

1. On the Layers panel, expand the top-level layer, sublayer, or group list for the object to be selected.

2. At the far right side of the panel, click the selection area or target circle for the object to be selected.

Using the Layers panel, you can select multiple groups or objects on different—even nonconsecutive—top-level layers or sublayers.

To select multiple objects on different layers:

On the Layers panel, make sure the listings for all the nested objects to be selected are visible (expand any layer or group lists, if necessary). Click the selection area or target circle for any object, then Shift-click any other individual groups or objects to add them to the selection. The items don't have to be listed consecutively.**A–B**

➤ To deselect any selected object individually, Shift-click its selection square or target circle.

A Objects from nonconsecutive stacking levels are selected (note the selection squares).

LOCATING A LISTING ON THE LAYERS PANEL

When the number of listings on the Layers panel grows long, it can be hard to locate a particular item. Organizing listings into sublayers can help, as does the Locate Object command. With the Selection tool, select the object in the document window whose listing you want to find, then choose Locate Object from the Layers panel menu. The list for the object's layer will expand and a selection square will appear for that item. (If "Locate Layer" appears on the panel menu instead of "Locate Object," choose Panel Options from the panel menu and uncheck Show Layers Only; the Locate Object command will become available.)

B Objects that we selected from different stacking levels are shown selected in the artwork.

On pages 90–91, you learned how to create, isolate, add a new object to, and ungroup a group. Here, you will select objects in a group by using the Layers panel.

To select a whole group via the Layers panel:

1. *Optional:* To put the group in isolation mode, double-click it with the Selection tool (V).**A** Note: If this doesn't work, make sure Double Click to Isolate is checked in Illustrator/Edit > Preferences > General.

2. To select all the objects in the group (including any groups nested inside it), click the selection area or target circle ⭕ for the group listing on the right side of the Layers panel.

➤ To select a whole group on the artboard in non-isolation mode, click an object in the group with the Selection tool (V). To select an object in a group (or individual anchor points or segments), use the Direct Selection tool (A). To make the bounding box around a selected group visible, choose View > Show Bounding Box.

To select two or more objects in a group:

1. Deselect all (Cmd-Shift-A/Ctrl-Shift-A).

2. Do either of the following:

   The group can be in isolation mode for this method, or not. Expand the group list on the Layers panel, then Shift-click the selection area or target circle ⭕ at the far right side of the panel for each object in the group to be selected.**B** (Shift-click it again to deselect any item.)

   With the group in isolation mode, choose the Selection tool, click an object, then Shift-click additional objects. (Shift-click any item again to deselect it.)

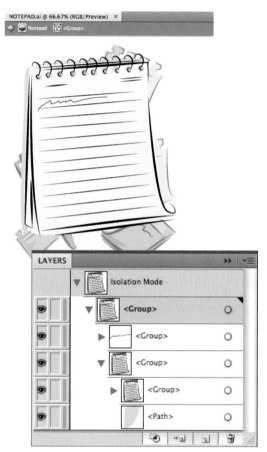

A When a group is in isolation mode, the Layers panel lists only that group and its objects. The artwork in the image shown above is in isolation mode.

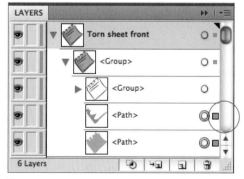

B To select some objects in a group, expand the group list, then Shift-click the selection area for the objects.

Restacking objects and layers

The order of objects (and layers) on the Layers panel matches the front-to-back order of objects (and layers) in the artwork. If you move a group, object, sublayer, or top-level layer upward or downward on the list, the artwork redraws accordingly. You can restack objects and layers by dragging (instructions below) or by using a command (next page).

To restack a layer, group, or object by dragging:

As you drag a top-level layer, sublayer, group, or object upward or downward on the Layers panel, do either of the following:

Keep the listing within the same indent level (say, to restack a group in its top-level layer).**A–C**

Move it to a different group or layer (release the mouse when the large black arrowheads point inward to the desired group or layer).

The document will redraw to reflect the new stacking position.**D**

➤ On page 91, you learned how to add an existing object to a group by using the Cut and Paste commands. If you want to move an existing object into (or out of) a group by using the Layers panel, follow the instructions on this page.

➤ If you move an object that's part of a group or clipping mask to a different top-level layer, the object will be released from that group or mask.

A This is the original artwork.

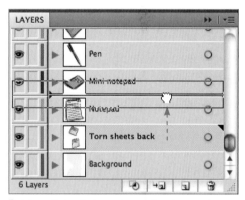

B A layer listing is dragged upward or downward to a new stacking position (the pointer becomes a hand icon).

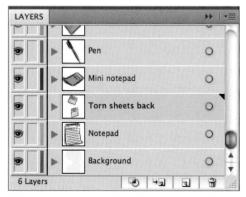

C The "Torn sheets back" layer is now in front of the Notepad layer.

D This is the result.

When the Layers panel contains many layers and a long list of objects, it can be cumbersome to expand and collapse layers when you need to restack an object. In that case, the Send to Current Layer command, discussed below, is faster.

To move an object to a layer via a command:

1. With the Selection tool ▶ (V), select one or more objects.

2. On the Layers panel, click the layer to which you want to move the selected object(s).

3. Right-click/Ctrl-click in the document window and choose Arrange > **Send to Current Layer** (or choose the command from the Object > Arrange submenu). Note: If the selected object was in a group, the whole group will be restacked.

➤ To reverse the current order of layers, groups, and objects on the Layers panel, Cmd-click/Ctrl-click noncontiguous items (or click then Shift-click a series of contiguous items), then choose Reverse Order from the Layers panel menu.

Duplicating layers and objects

Duplicate objects appear in the same *x/y* location as, and directly on top of, the objects they are duplicated from. If you duplicate a layer or sublayer, the word "copy" is added to the duplicate name.

To duplicate a layer, sublayer, group, or object:

Do one of the following:

On the Layers panel, click the layer, sublayer, group, or object to be duplicated, then choose **Duplicate** "[layer or object name]" from the Layers panel menu.

Drag a layer, sublayer, group, or object listing over the **New Layer** button ▣.**A–B**

Click the selection area for a sublayer, group, or object (expand the listing, if necessary), then Option-drag/Alt-drag the **selection square** upward or downward to the desired top-level layer or sublayer.**C–D** You can use this method to copy an object within a group or layer.

A To duplicate a layer (or a sublayer, group, or object), drag it over the New Layer button; note the plus sign in the pointer.

B A copy of the "Mini notepad" layer is made.

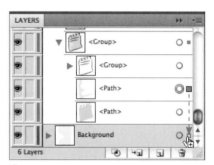

C To duplicate an object a different way, Option-drag/Alt-drag its selection square.

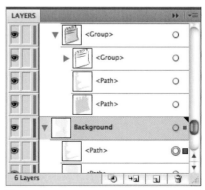

D A copy of the object appears in the "Background" layer.

Locking layers and objects

Locked objects can't be selected or modified, but they do remain visible. When a whole layer is locked, none of the objects it contains are editable. When you save, close, and reopen a file that contains locked objects, the objects remain locked.

Note: Remember, as an alternative, you can isolate an object or group without locking it, to make other objects temporarily uneditable.

To lock or unlock layers or objects:

Do one of the following:

On the Layers panel, click in the edit (second) column for a layer A, sublayer, group, or object. The padlock icon 🔒 appears. Click the icon to unlock the item.

To lock multiple layers, sublayers, groups, or objects, drag upward or downward in the edit column. Drag back over the padlock icons to unlock the items.

Option-click/Alt-click in the edit column for a top-level layer to lock or unlock all the other top-level layers except the one you click.

➤ If you lock an object and then lock its top-level layer, but later decide to unlock the object, you will have to unlock the top-level layer first.

➤ To lock layers via a command, select the layer listings to remain unlocked, then lock all the other layers by choosing Lock Others from the Layers panel menu.

➤ To make a layer unprintable, hide it by clicking the visibility icon; hidden layers can't be printed, exported, or edited. Another option is to double-click the layer and uncheck Print in the Layer Options dialog; the layer won't print, but it can be exported and edited, and it will remain visible.

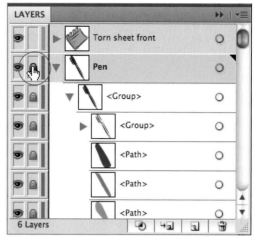

A When an entire layer is locked, none of the objects it contains can be selected or edited. Groups and individual objects can also be locked.

ONE-STOP SHOPPING FOR LAYER OPTIONS

➤ To open the Layer Options dialog, in which you can set multiple options, double-click a top-level layer or sublayer. You can change the Name; choose a different Color for selections on the layer (say, if the current selection color is too similar to colors in the artwork); and check or uncheck any options, such as Lock, Show, Print, or Preview (view). Options chosen for a top-level layer apply to all sublayers, groups, and objects it contains. Nonprinting layers are listed in italics on the Layers panel.

Note: The Template option, together with the Dim Images To option, makes a layer uneditable and dimmed, the first step in the process of tracing a placed image or object manually. For an even better method, live tracing, see Chapter 17.

➤ You can also double-click a group or object to access the Name, Lock, and Show options in a simpler Options dialog.

Hiding layers and objects

When you hide the objects you're not working on, you make your artwork look less complex, albeit temporarily, and allow the screen to redraw faster. You can hide a top-level layer (with all its nested layers), hide a group, or hide any individual object. Hidden objects don't print and are invisible in both Outline and Preview views. When you save, close, and reopen your file, hidden objects remain hidden.

To hide or show layers or objects:

Note: If you want to redisplay an object, but its top-level layer is hidden, you must show its top-level layer first.

Do one of the following:

Click the visibility icon for a top-level layer, sublayer, group, or object.**A–C** To redisplay what was hidden, click again.

Drag upward or downward in the visibility column to hide multiple, consecutive top-level layers, sublayers, groups, or objects. To redisplay what was hidden, drag again.

Display all layers, then Option-click/Alt-click in the visibility column to hide or show all the top-level layers except the one you click.

➤ To hide layers via a command, make sure all layers are visible (choose Show All Layers from the Layers panel menu if they're not), click the top-level layer or layers to remain visible, then choose Hide Others from the Layers panel menu.

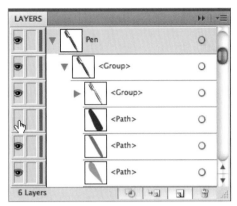

A You can hide or show an individual object or group...

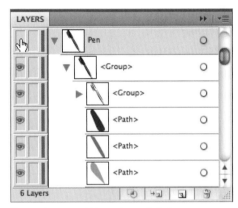

B ...and you can hide or show whole layers.

SHORTCUTS FOR CHANGING THE LAYER VIEW

When you choose a view for a top-level layer, all nested layers and objects within the layer display in that view.

Display layer in Outline view when the document is in Preview view	Cmd-click/Ctrl-click the visibility icon; Cmd-click/Ctrl-click the visibility icon again to redisplay the layer in Preview view
Display all layers in Preview view	Choose Preview All Layers from the Layers panel menu
Display all layers except one in Outline view	Cmd-Option-click/Ctrl-Alt-click the visibility icon for a top-level layer; repeat to redisplay all the layers in Preview view

C The "Pen" objects are now hidden.

Collecting objects into a new layer

The Collect in New Layer command collects all the currently highlighted top-level layers, sublayers, groups, or objects into a brand new layer.

To move multiple layers, sublayers, groups, or objects to a new layer:

1. Cmd-click/Ctrl-click the listings for the layers, groups, or objects to be gathered together.**A** They must all be at the same indent level (e.g., all objects from the same sublayer or on consecutive sublayers). Don't click the selection area.

2. From the Layers panel menu, choose **Collect in New Layer**. If you selected sublayers, groups, or objects in the previous step, they will now be on a new sublayer within the same top-level layer;**B** if you selected top-level layers, they will now be nested as sublayers within a new top-level layer.

   Quirky bug: To make the expand triangle appear for the new layer (for the first time), you have to click either its selection area or another layer.

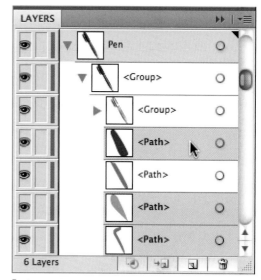

A Three path listings are selected.

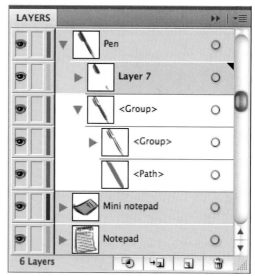

B The Collect in New Layer command gathered the three highlighted paths into a new sublayer (Layer 7).

Releasing objects to layers

The two Release to Layers commands are useful for preparing an Illustrator file for use as the contents of an object or frame animation. The commands disperse all objects or groups residing within the currently selected top-level layer onto new, separate layers within the same layer. In the animation program, you can then convert the layers from the placed file into separate objects or into a sequence.

Note: To export your artwork to Adobe Flash, see page 402.

Read step 2 carefully before deciding which command to use.

To move objects to new, separate layers:

1. On the Layers panel, click a top-level layer, sublayer, or group (not an object). **A** Ungroup any groups and expand any effects or blends.

2. Do either of the following:

   From the Layers panel menu, choose:

   Release to Layers (Sequence). B Each object within the selected layer or group listing will be nested in a separate new layer on the original layer; any former groups will be nested two levels deep. The original stacking order of the objects is preserved.

   If you're going to build a cumulative frame animation sequence in another program by adding objects in succession, choose **Release to Layers (Build). C** The bottommost layer will contain only the bottommost object; the next layer above that will contain the bottommost object plus the next object above it; the next layer above that will contain the two previous objects plus the next object above it, and so on.

➤ If you release a layer or sublayer that contains a clipping mask that was created via the Layers panel, the clipping mask remains in effect.

➤ If you release a layer or group that contains a Scatter brush, the brush object remains as a single <Path>. If you release just the object that contains the brush, each scatter unit in the brush is moved to a separate layer, and the original Scatter brush path is preserved.

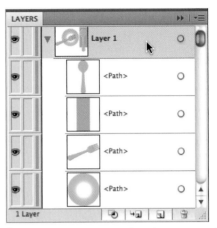

A A top-level layer is selected on the Layers panel.

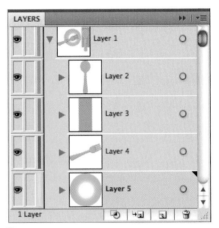

B We can choose the Release to Layers (Sequence) command...

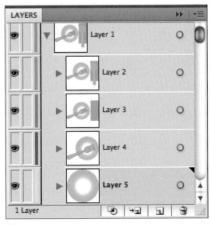

C ...or the Release to Layers (Build) command.

Merging layers and groups

If the number of layers and sublayers on the Layers panel gets unwieldly, you can consolidate them at any time by using the Merge Selected command. Unlike the Flatten Artwork command, which flattens an entire document (see the next page), the Merge Selected command merges just the multiple listings that you select.

In addition to merging layers (or sublayers) with one another, you can merge two or more groups, or merge a group with a sublayer, provided they both reside within the same top-level layer. In the latter case, the objects will be ungrouped and will be placed on the selected sublayer. You can't merge objects with each other.

To merge layers, sublayers, or groups:

1. *Optional:* Use File > Save As to preserve a copy of your file, with its layers intact.

2. As you Cmd-click/Ctrl-click the listings for two or more layers, sublayers, or groups, click last on the listing that the selected items are to be merged into. You can merge locked and/or hidden layers into other layers.

3. Choose **Merge Selected** from the Layers panel menu.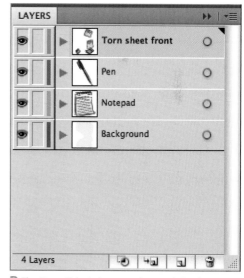

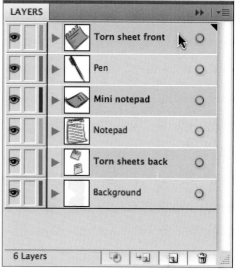

A Select the layers (or sublayers or groups) to be merged, clicking last on the layer the items are to be merged into.

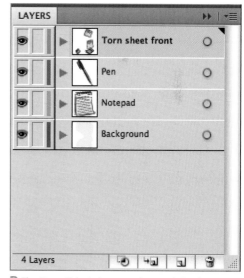

B The Merge Selected command merged the three selected layers into one.

Flattening artwork

The Flatten Artwork command reduces a document to one top-level layer, with sublayers and groups nested inside it. Objects remain fully editable. If your document contains any hidden top-level layers when you choose this command, you can opt via an alert dialog to keep the hidden artwork (by clicking No) or to allow the hidden layers to be discarded (by clicking Yes).

To flatten artwork:

1. *Optional:* Use File > Save As to preserve a copy of your file, with its layers intact.

2. Redisplay any hidden top-level layers and objects that you want to preserve.

3. By default, if no layers are selected, the Flatten Artwork command merges all the currently visible layers into whichever top-level layer has the Current Layer indicator. If you prefer to flatten the document into a layer of your choice, click it now.

4. Choose **Flatten Artwork** from the Layers panel menu. Note: If the document contains artwork on hidden layers, an alert dialog will appear.**A–C** Click Yes to discard the hidden artwork or click No to preserve it (it will become visible). Regardless of which button you click, the result will be a flattened file.

➤ The Flatten Artwork command can be undone.

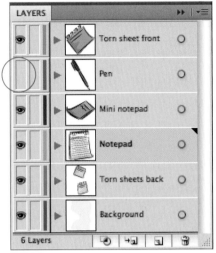

A One of the layers in this file is hidden and contains artwork, so an alert dialog will appear when we choose the Flatten Artwork command.

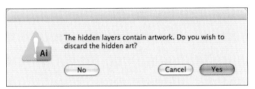

B It's always nice to get a second chance.

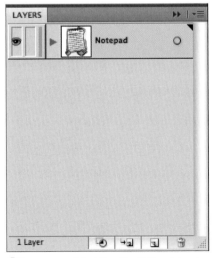

C Because we clicked Yes, the Flatten Artwork command flattened the artwork into the selected layer (Notepad) and discarded the hidden layer.

Appearance attributes are fill, stroke, effects, and transparency settings. In this chapter, you'll learn how to use the Appearance panel A–B to apply, edit, copy, and restack appearance attributes for a layer, sublayer, group, or object. The panel can be used to apply multiple fills and strokes to the same object, add effects and transparency settings, and in Illustrator CS4, to apply attributes quickly and easily via new in-panel links to Effect menu commands and to a temporary Stroke, Swatches, Transparency, and Color panel. ★ When an object is selected, its attributes are listed on the panel.

The best part about appearance attributes is that they change only how an object looks, not its actual underlying path. This means when you save, close, and reopen a document, the existing appearance attributes remain editable (and removable). Appearance attributes add speed and flexibility—as well as some complexity—to object editing. When you're finished with this chapter, be sure to continue with the next two chapters, which are closely related: Effects (Chapter 15) and Graphic Styles (Chapter 16).

14

A One of the circles is selected in this artwork.

Link to a temporary Color or Swatches panel

Stroke Weight

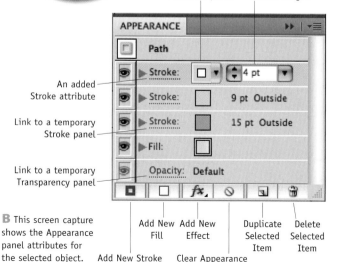

An added Stroke attribute

Link to a temporary Stroke panel

Link to a temporary Transparency panel

B This screen capture shows the Appearance panel attributes for the selected object.

Add New Fill

Add New Effect

Duplicate Selected Item

Delete Selected Item

Add New Stroke

Clear Appearance

Applying appearance attributes

You can either apply appearance attributes to individual objects one at a time, or you can target a whole top-level layer or group for appearance changes, in which case the attributes will apply to all the objects that are nested within the targeted layer or group. For example, if you target a layer and then change its opacity or blending mode, all the objects on that layer will adopt that opacity or blending mode. To edit an attribute at any time, you simply retarget the layer. When an object has more than just the basic fill and stroke attributes, its listing on the Layers panel has a gray target circle. **A** Appearance attributes can be modified or removed at any time, even after you save, close, and reopen the file.

A new feature in Illustrator CS4 is in-panel editing: If you click a link (blue underlined word), a related panel opens temporarily. One-stop editing.

To apply appearance attributes via in-panel editing links: ★

1. Do either of the following:

   In the document window, select an object.**B**

   On the Layers panel, ● click the target circle ○ for a layer, group, or object. A ring appears around the circle, signifying that it's now an active target. If you click the target circle for a layer, all the objects on the layer will become selected, and the word "Layer" will appear at the top of the Appearance panel.

2. Show the **Appearance** panel ● (Shift-F6).

3. For a targeted object, do any of the following:

   Click the **Stroke** and/or **Fill** color square, then click it once more to open a temporary Swatches panel or Shift-click it to open a temporary Color panel (**A**, next page). Choose a color.

   To change the stroke **Width**, click the **Stroke** color square, then click the up or down arrow or choose a preset value from the menu.

   To apply a **brush stroke**, click a **Stroke** listing, then choose from the Brush menu on the Control panel.

4. For a targeted object, group, or layer, do any of the following:

   Click the **Opacity** link (underlined word) to open a temporary Transparency panel, then

This layer is active but not targeted, and it doesn't contain appearance attributes.

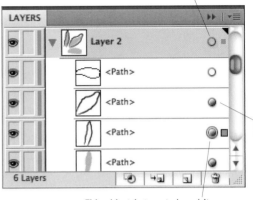

This object is targeted, and it contains appearance attributes.

This path object contains appearance attributes, but it isn't targeted.

A Learn to "read" the three different states of the target circles on the Layers panel.

B This is the original artwork.

choose a different blending mode from the menu in the upper left corner and/or change the Opacity value (click the arrowhead, then drag the slider).**B** To learn about the Transparency panel, see Chapter 27.

From the **Add New Effect** menu *fx.* at the bottom of the panel, ★ choose one of the Illustrator effects. For starters, try applying an effect on the Distort & Transform or Stylize submenu. Choose settings in the dialog, then click OK. The chosen command will be listed on the Appearance panel. (To learn about effects, see the next chapter.)

To untarget an object, group, or layer:

Shift-click the gray target circle ● or click a blank area of the artwork.

To choose default appearance settings for new objects:

If the **New Art Has Basic Appearance** command on the Appearance panel menu has a check mark, subsequently created objects will have just one fill and one stroke. If this option is unchecked, the appearance attributes currently displayed on the panel will apply automatically to any new objects you create.

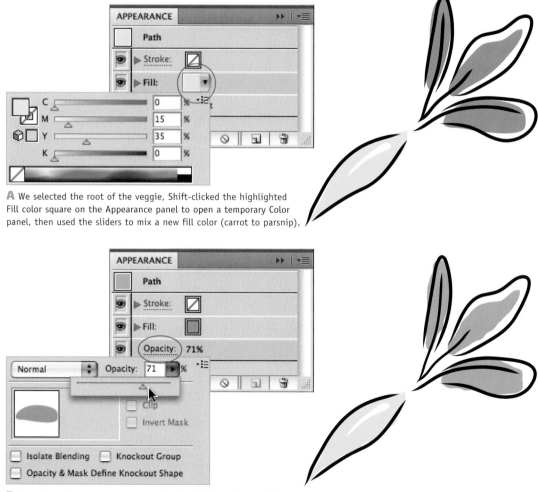

A We selected the root of the veggie, Shift-clicked the highlighted Fill color square on the Appearance panel to open a temporary Color panel, then used the sliders to mix a new fill color (carrot to parsnip).

B We selected the green area on one leaf, clicked the Opacity link on the Appearance panel, then lowered the opacity to 71%; we made the same change to the other leaves.

Deciphering the Appearance panel ★

Depending on what entity (object, group, or layer) is currently targeted and what attributes it has, one or more of these icons may display in the upper portion of the Appearance panel:

➤ For a layer or group (not an object), this icon ▣ signifies an added stroke and/or fill attribute, and this icon ▨ signifies transparency settings.

➤ Any entity may contain effects, which are signified by this icon: ***fx***.

The name for the currently targeted entity (e.g., Layer, Group, **A** or Path **B–C**) is listed in boldface at the top of the Appearance panel. Note that if the selected object happens to be type, the word "Type" will appear instead of the word "Path." The same holds true for an image ("Image"), a symbol ("Symbol"), or a compound shape ("Compound Shape")—you get the idea.

If you target an object that is nested within a layer and/or group to which appearance attributes have been applied, a "Layer" and/or "Group" listing will also appear above the "Path" listing at the top of the Appearance panel.

If you target a layer or group, a "Contents" listing also appears on the Appearance panel. Double-click a Contents listing to display Path attributes; click a Layer listing to display attributes that apply to the whole layer; or click a Group listing to display group attributes. (Yup, this can be confusing!)

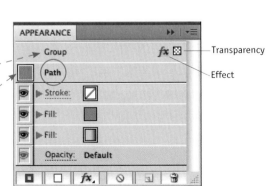

A When targeted, the group displays its own appearance attributes.

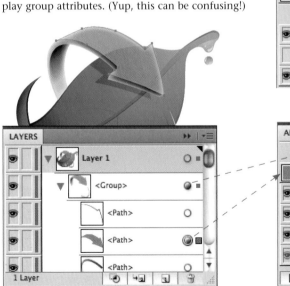

B The targeted path is nested in a group, which contains its own appearance attributes.

C The Appearance panel is listing the attributes for the currently targeted (and nested) path.

Transparency

Effect

To apply multiple stroke or fill attributes: ★

1. Target an object, group, or layer.A

2. Do either of the following:

   At the bottom of the Appearance panel, click the **Add New Stroke** button ◼ (Cmd-Option-/; Ctrl-Alt-/) **B** or the **Add New Fill** button ☐ (Cmd-/;Ctrl-/).

   Click a Stroke or Fill listing on the Appearance panel, then click the **Duplicate Selected Item** button at the bottom of the panel.

3. A second Stroke or Fill attribute appears on the panel. Click the new listing, then modify its attributes so it differs from the original one (or modify the original listing instead). Either way, make sure a narrower stroke is stacked above a wider one.**C–D** If the narrower stroke is left on the bottom, it will be hidden behind the other one. You can drag a listing upward or downward on the panel.

▶ If a targeted entity contains multiple fill attributes, and you want to change the opacity or blending mode for one of them, do so for the topmost fill listing.

▶ By changing the stacking position of a stroke or fill listing, you can change how the object looks. Remember to lower the opacity of the topmost Fill listing to reveal the attributes below it.

▶ When you select an object that contains multiple stroke attributes, an alert icon ⚠ may display next to its fill color on the Control panel. If you click the alert icon, the colors for the topmost Stroke and/or Fill listing will display on the Control and Color panels. ★

A The targeted object (the outer circle) has a gray fill and a green stroke.

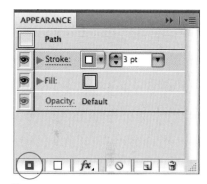

B The Add New Stroke button is clicked twice.

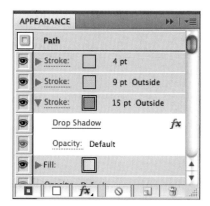

C The attributes were edited for all the stroke attributes. We made the bottommost stroke the widest of the three and applied a Drop Shadow effect to it.

D This is how the attributes (listed in the Appearance panel at left) look on the object.

Editing appearance attributes

In addition to listing appearance attributes and enabling you to apply them, the Appearance panel provides in-panel access to the Stroke, Color, Swatches, and Transparency panels—and the effect dialogs—for modifying existing appearance attributes.

To edit appearance attributes: ★

1. Do either of the following:

   In the document window, select an object that contains appearance attributes.

   On the Layers panel,◈ click the target circle for a layer, group,**A** or object.

2. On the Appearance panel,◉ click any existing appearance listing to open a related panel (or a dialog, for an effect).**B** If there are multiple Fill or Stroke listings, be careful to click the one you want to modify.

3. Make the desired edits **C** (see steps 3–4 on pages 182–183). For example, to modify a stroke, click the underlined Stroke link to open a temporary Stroke panel and choose options. To modify a brush stroke attribute, double-click the brush name on the Appearance panel to open the Stroke Options dialog; unfortunately, the preview option won't be available (see also page 303).

To add attributes to just a stroke or fill: ★

1. On the Layers panel,◈ click the target circle for a layer, group, or object.

2. On the Appearance panel,◉ click a **Stroke** or **Fill** listing, then click the expand arrow. Do any of the following:

   Click the **Opacity** link to open a temporary Transparency panel, then change the Opacity value and/or blending mode for that attribute.

   From the **Add New Effect** menu,*fx.* choose an effect for that attribute.

   The newly applied attributes will be nested within the currently expanded stroke or fill listing.

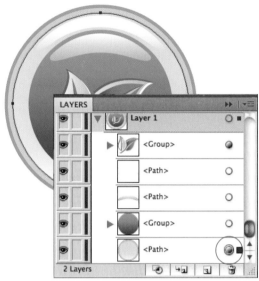

A A path is targeted via the Layers panel.

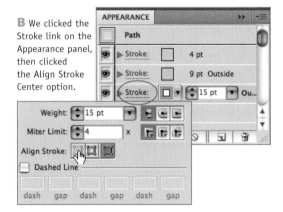

B We clicked the Stroke link on the Appearance panel, then clicked the Align Stroke Center option.

C The new stroke alignment option appears in the object.

Hiding and deleting appearance attributes

To hide an appearance attribute: ★

1. Target a layer, group,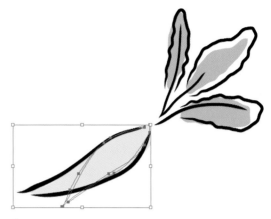 or object.
2. Click in the **visibility** column to make the icon and the targeted entity disappear **B–C** or reappear.

To delete an appearance attribute: ★

1. Target a layer, group, or object.
2. On the Appearance panel, click the attribute to be deleted, then click the **Delete Selected Item** button at the bottom of the panel.

➤ The sole remaining fill and stroke appearance attributes can't be removed. Clicking the Delete Selected Item button for either of these appearance attributes applies a color of None.

➤ To remove a brush stroke from a stroke attribute, see page 294.

Note: If you target a layer or group, the Clear Appearance and Reduce to Basic Appearance commands, discussed below, will remove only attributes that were applied to that layer or group, not attributes that were applied directly to nested paths within the layer or group. To remove attributes from a nested path, you must specifically target that path.

To delete all the appearance attributes from an item: ★

1. Target an object, layer, or group.
2. Do either of the following:

To remove all appearance attributes and apply a stroke and fill of None, click the **Clear Appearance** button at the bottom of the Appearance panel (for type, the fill color will become black).

To remove all the appearance attributes except the basic stroke and fill, choose **Reduce to Basic Appearance** from the Appearance panel menu.

A Target the group that contains the attribute to be hidden.

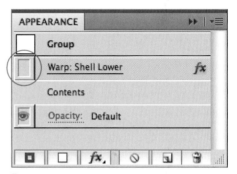

B On the Appearance panel, the visibility column for the Warp effect was clicked to hide that attribute.

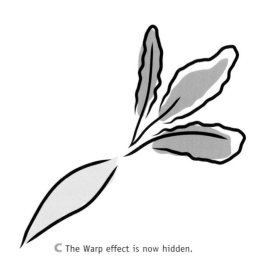

C The Warp effect is now hidden.

Copying appearance attributes

To copy appearance attributes from one object or layer to another:

Do either of the following:

Option-drag/Alt-drag the target circle on the Layers panel from the item whose attributes you want to copy onto the target circle for another layer, group, or object.**A**

Choose the Selection tool (V), click an object whose attributes you want to copy, then drag the square thumbnail from the uppermost left corner of the Appearance panel over an unselected object.**B**

➤ To remove the appearance attributes from one item and apply them to another, drag a target circle from one layer, group, or object to another one without holding down any modifier keys.

➤ To select objects in a document based on matching appearance attributes, select one of the objects, then choose Select > Same > Appearance.

Expanding appearance attributes

When you expand an object's appearance attributes, the paths that were used to create the attributes become (dozens of!) separate objects, and can be edited individually. Using this command may become a necessity when you need to export a file to a non-Adobe application that can't read appearance attributes per se.

To expand an object's appearance attributes:

1. Select an object that contains the appearance attributes (or graphic style) to be expanded.**C**

2. Choose Object > **Expand Appearance**.**D** On the Layers panel, you will now see a new <Group> (or a series of nested groups) containing the original object, the effects, and the appearance attributes, which will be listed either as individual paths or as images.

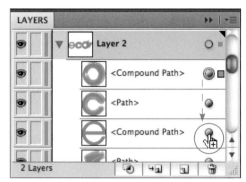

A To copy appearance attributes, either Option/Alt drag the target circle from one listing to another,...

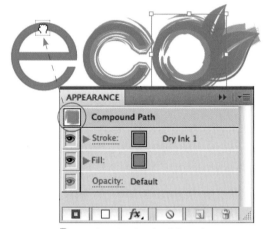

B ...or drag the thumbnail from the Appearance panel over an object.

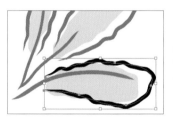

C An object containing appearance attributes is selected.

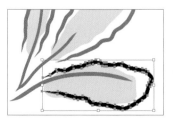

D The object's attributes are expanded.

Effects apply distortion, texture, artistic, shape, and stylistic changes to objects and imported images, with results ranging from subtle to marked. In this chapter, you will apply effects via the Appearance panel, the Effect menu, and the Effect Gallery, and explore a few effects in depth. (Effects can also be saved in and applied via graphic styles, which we show you how to do in the next chapter.)

The effect commands change only the appearance of an object—not its underlying path. Effects can be edited or deleted at any time without permanently affecting the object they're applied to, and without affecting other effects or appearance attributes on the same object. What's more, if you reshape the path of the underlying object, the effects adjust accordingly. In other words, effects are live.

Applying Illustrator effects

Users who are familiar with previous versions of Adobe Illustrator may notice that the program no longer has a Filter menu (no, you're not crazy). The Effect menu still contains Illustrator effects **A–B** and Photoshop effects. Most of the Illustrator effects, which are in the top section of the Effect menu, are

Continued on the following page

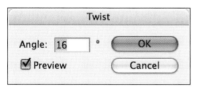

A Each Illustrator effect has its own dialog.

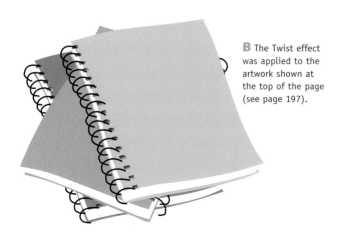

B The Twist effect was applied to the artwork shown at the top of the page (see page 197).

15

IN THIS CHAPTER

vector based, meaning they alter path shapes and output as vector objects.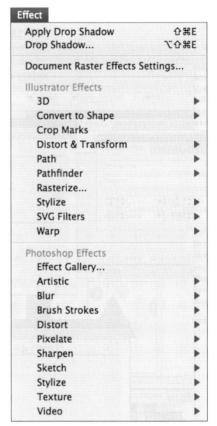 Exceptions are the Drop Shadow, Inner Glow, Outer Glow, and Feather commands on the Effect > Stylize submenu, which are rasterized (converted from vector to raster) upon output and when the object is expanded. All the Photoshop effects (on the bottom part of the Effect menu) are pixel based, which means they introduce painterly attributes, such as soft edges or transparency, and are rasterized upon output.

An individual dialog opens when you choose an Illustrator effect or when you choose a Photoshop effect from the Blur, Pixelate, Sharpen, or Video submenu. When you choose any of the other Photoshop effects or choose Effect > Effect Gallery, a large gallery dialog opens that contains most of the Photoshop effects and their options (see pages 199–200).

A few facts to remember about effects:

➤ Both Illustrator effects and Photoshop effects can be applied to one or more path objects; to an object's fill or stroke; to type, a group, a layer, or an embedded image; or to the embedded preview of a linked image (not to the linked image itself).

➤ If you apply an effect to a targeted layer or group, it affects all current and future objects on the layer or in the group.

➤ If an effect is applied to editable type, the type attributes remain editable.

➤ You can apply multiple effects to the same object. If you do so, you may notice that the effects preview more slowly in the dialog (a progress bar may display). Some effects are more memory-intensive than others.

The Illustrator effects can be applied via the Effect menu or via a new menu at the bottom of the Appearance panel. Regardless of which menu they were chosen from, applied effects are listed by name as appearance attributes on the Appearance panel.

To apply an Illlustrator effect: ★

1. Do either of the following:

   On the Layers panel ☙ (F7), click the **target** circle for a layer, group, or object.**B** The circle will now have a double border.

   To limit the effect to just a stroke or fill, select or isolate one or more ungrouped objects.

A The Effect menu has two sections: Illustrator Effects (mostly vector effects plus a few raster ones) in the top portion and Photoshop Effects (all raster effects) in the bottom portion.

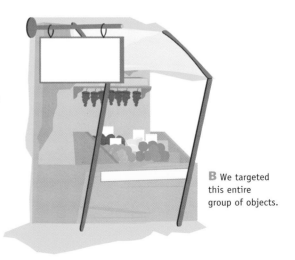

B We targeted this entire group of objects.

Display the Appearance panel ◉ (Shift-F6), then click the **Stroke** or **Fill** listing.**C**

2. From one of the submenus on the top portion of the **Add New Effect** menu *fx.* on the Appearance panel or from the **Effect** menu on the main menu bar, choose an Illustrator effect.

3. Check Preview (if available) to preview the effect as you choose options, then choose options.**A** After entering a value in a field, press Tab to update the preview.

4. Click OK.**B** The effect will be listed by name on the Appearance panel, either next to the object you applied it to or nested within the Stroke or Fill listing on the Appearance panel (click the expand arrowhead to display the listing).**D–E**

➤ To learn more about applying effects to type, see page 270.

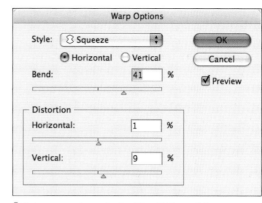

A Values were chosen in the Warp Options dialog.

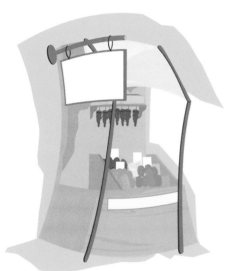

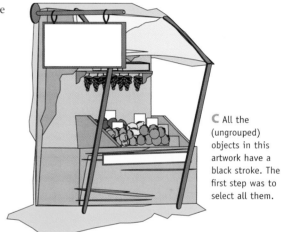

C All the (ungrouped) objects in this artwork have a black stroke. The first step was to select all them.

B This is the result of the Warp > Squeeze effect (it reminds us of the artist Chaim Soutine — minus the angst...)

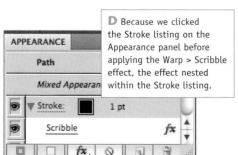

D Because we clicked the Stroke listing on the Appearance panel before applying the Warp > Scribble effect, the effect nested within the Stroke listing.

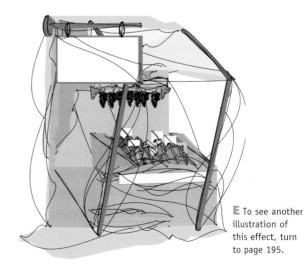

E To see another illustration of this effect, turn to page 195.

Editing an applied effect

To edit an applied effect: ★

1. Do either of the following:

   On the Layers panel (F7), target the layer, group, or object that the effect you want to edit is applied to.

   If you applied the effect to just an object's stroke or fill, select the object, then expand the Stroke or Fill listing on the Appearance panel.

2. Click the effect listing on the Appearance panel.**A** The effect dialog reopens.

3. Make the desired adjustments, then click OK.**B–C**

➤ When multiple effects are applied to the same object or attribute, you can restack an effect by dragging it upward or downward. Doing this will either enhance or block out other effects.

Deleting an applied effect

To remove an effect from an object, group, or layer: ★

1. On the Layers panel,👁 target the layer, group, or object that contains the effect to be removed.

2. On the Appearance panel,⊙ click to the right of the effect name, then click the **Delete Selected Item** button 🗑 on the panel.

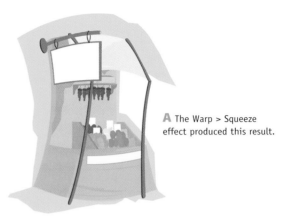

A The Warp > Squeeze effect produced this result.

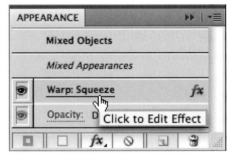

B After retargeting the group, we clicked the effect listing on the Appearance panel to reopen the dialog.

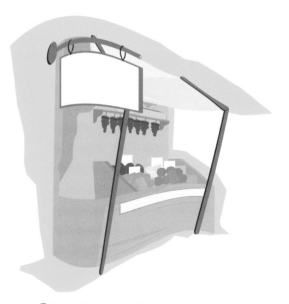

C In the Warp Options dialog, we changed the Style from Squeeze to Fish.

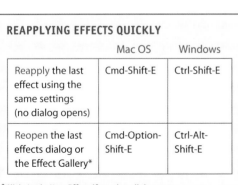

REAPPLYING EFFECTS QUICKLY		
	Mac OS	Windows
Reapply the last effect using the same settings (no dialog opens)	Cmd-Shift-E	Ctrl-Shift-E
Reopen the last effects dialog or the Effect Gallery*	Cmd-Option-Shift-E	Ctrl-Alt-Shift-E

*Click Apply New Effect if an alert dialog opens.

A few Illustrator effects up close

On this page and the next four pages, we illustrate a few Illustrator effects. In this first task, you will use a Convert to Shape effect to change an object's silhouette to a rectangle, rounded rectangle, or ellipse without altering the actual underlying path.

To apply a Convert to Shape effect:

1. On the Layers panel ● (F7), click the **target** circle for a layer, group, or object.**A** Or to limit the effect to a stroke or fill, select or isolate the object, then on the Appearance panel,● click the **Stroke** or **Fill** listing.

2. From the **Add New Effect** menu *fx.* on the Appearance panel ★ or from the **Effect** menu, under Illustrator Effects, choose Convert to Shape > **Rectangle**, **Rounded Rectangle**, or **Ellipse**. The Shape Options dialog opens.**B**

   ➤ You can also choose one of the three shapes from the Shape menu in the dialog.

3. Check Preview.

4. Do either of the following:

   Click **Absolute**, then enter the total desired Width and Height values for the shape's appearance.

   Click **Relative**, then enter the Extra Width or Extra Height if you want the shape to be larger or smaller than the actual path (enter a positive or negative value).

5. For the Rounded Rectangle shape, you can also change the **Corner Radius** value.

6. Click OK.**C–D**

➤ To simply round off sharp corners on an object without converting its shape, use Effects > Stylize > Round Corners.

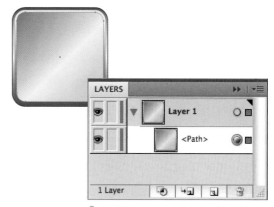

A An object is targeted (this object has a graphic style; see Chapter 16).

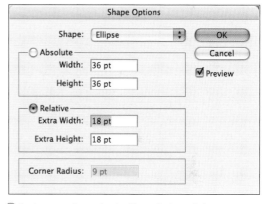

B Options are chosen in the Shape Options dialog.

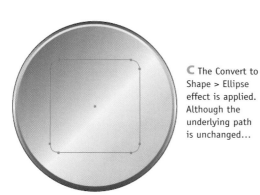

C The Convert to Shape > Ellipse effect is applied. Although the underlying path is unchanged...

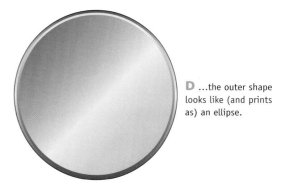

D ...the outer shape looks like (and prints as) an ellipse.

The Inner Glow effect spreads a color from the edge of an object inward; the Outer Glow effect spreads a color from the edge of an object outward.

To apply the Inner Glow or Outer Glow effect:

1. On the Layers panel ☙ (F7), click the **target** circle for a layer, group, **A** or object. Or to limit the effect to a stroke or fill, select or isolate the object, then on the Appearance panel, ◉ click the **Stroke** or **Fill** listing.

2. From the **Add New Effect** menu *fx.* on the Appearance panel ★ or from the **Effect** menu, under Illustrator Effects, choose Stylize > **Inner Glow** or **Outer Glow**.

3. In the Inner Glow **B** or Outer Glow dialog, check Preview, then do any of the following:

   Click the **color** square next to the Mode menu, then choose a different glow color (spot or process).

   Choose a blending **Mode** for the glow color.

   Choose an **Opacity** for the glow color.

   Click the **Blur** arrowhead, then move the slider in small increments to adjust how far the glow extends inward or outward. The higher the Blur value, the wider the glow area.

   For the Inner Glow effect, click **Center** to have the glow spread outward from the center of the object, or **Edge** to have it spread inward from the edge of the object toward the center.

4. Click OK. **C**

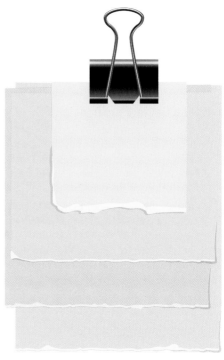

A We targeted the group of objects (the "papers").

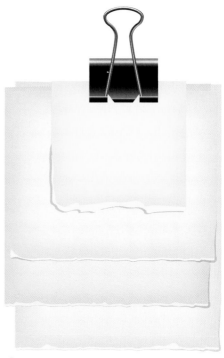

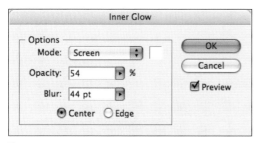

B Options were chosen in the Inner Glow dialog.

C This is the result of the Inner Glow effect.

The Scribble effect makes an object's fill and stroke look as though they were sketched with a felt-tip marker or pen.

To apply the Scribble effect:

1. On the Layers panel 🍃 (F7), click the **target** circle for a layer, group, **A** or object. Or to limit the effect to a stroke or fill, select or isolate the object, then on the Appearance panel, ⚫ click the **Stroke** or **Fill** listing.

2. From the **Add New Effect** menu *fx.* on the Appearance panel ★ or from the **Effect** menu, under Illustrator Effects, choose Stylize > **Scribble**. The Scribble Options dialog opens. **B**

3. Check Preview. Start by choosing a preset from the **Settings** menu. Follow the remaining steps if you want to choose custom settings for the preset; if not, click OK and you're done.

4. To change the angle of the sketch lines, enter an **Angle** value or rotate the dial.

5. Drag the **Path Overlap** slider toward Outside to allow the sketch lines to extend beyond the edge of the path (more fun), or toward Inside to confine them to the path. Choose a high **Variation** value to produce random variations in line lengths and a wilder, more haphazard look, or a low Variation for more uniform line lengths.

6. Under Line Options, do any of the following:

   Change the **Stroke Width** for the lines.

   Change the **Curviness** value to control whether the lines angle more sharply or loop more loosely when they change direction. The Variation slider controls the degree of random variation in the direction changes.

   Change the **Spacing** value to cluster sketch lines more tightly or to spread them further apart. The Variation slider controls the degree of random variation in the spacing.

7. Click OK. **C**

➤ If you change the settings in the Scribble Options dialog and then choose a preset from the Settings menu, the preset values will be restored to the sliders. Unfortunately, Scribble settings can't be saved as a preset.

A A group of bananas was targeted.

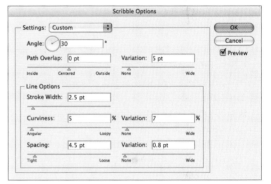

B Scribble options were chosen.

C The Scribble effect is applied, using the settings above.

The Drop Shadow effect creates soft, naturalistic shadows.

To apply the Drop Shadow effect:

1. On the Layers panel 🌐 (F7), click the **target** circle for a layer, group, or object.**A** Or to limit the effect to a stroke or fill, select or isolate the object, then on the Appearance panel,⊙ click the **Stroke** or **Fill** listing.

2. From the **Add New Effect** menu 𝑓𝑥, on the Appearance panel ★ or from the **Effect** menu, under Illustrator Effects, choose Stylize > **Drop Shadow**. The Drop Shadow dialog opens.**B** Check Preview.

3. To customize the drop shadow, do any of the following:

    Change the blending **Mode**.

    Change the **Opacity** value for the shadow.

    Enter an **X Offset** for the horizontal distance between the object and the shadow and a **Y Offset** for the vertical distance between the object and the shadow.

    Enter a **Blur** value (0–144 pt) for the width of the shadow.

    Click **Color**, click the color square, choose a different shadow color (spot or process) from the Color Picker, then click OK; or click **Darkness**, then enter a percentage of black to be added to the shadow.

4. Click OK.**C**

➤ The Drop Shadow command is no longer available as a filter.

A We targeted just the outer shape in this group of objects.

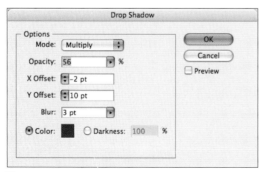

B Settings were chosen in the Drop Shadow dialog.

C This is the result of the Drop Shadow effect.

SPOT COLORS FOR EFFECTS

You can choose a spot color for the Drop Shadow, Inner Glow, and Outer Glow (Illustrator) effects. In the effect dialog, click the color square to open the Color Picker. Click the Color Swatches button, if necessary, to display a list of the swatches that are currently on the Swatches panel, and click the desired spot color (then click OK twice).

The Roughen effect adds anchor points and then moves them, resulting in an object that looks more irregular or hand drawn. It can be applied to whole objects or to just an object's stroke or fill.

To apply the Roughen effect:

1. On the Layers panel ◔ (F7), click the **target** circle for a layer, group, or object. Or to limit the effect to a stroke or fill, select or isolate the object, then on the Appearance panel,◉ click the **Stroke** or **Fill** listing.

   ► Choose View > Hide Edges (Cmd-H/Ctrl-H) to make the results easier to preview.

A We targeted the green tile objects in this original artwork.

2. From the **Add New Effect** menu 𝑓𝑥, on the Appearance panel ★ or from the **Effect** menu, under Illustrator Effects, choose Distort & Transform > **Roughen**. The Roughen dialog opens.**B** Check Preview.

3. Click **Relative** to move points by a percentage of the object's size, or **Absolute** to move points by a specific amount, then choose a **Size** amount (start with a low percentage) to specify how far the object's anchor points may move.

4. Choose a **Detail** amount for the number of points to be added to each inch of the path segments.

5. Click **Smooth** to produce curves, or click **Corner** to produce pointy angles.

6. Click OK.**C**

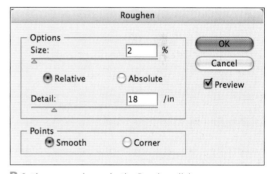
B Options were chosen in the Roughen dialog.

The Twist effect twists an object's overall shape. You can twist a single object or twist multiple objects together.

To apply the Twist effect:

1. Follow step 1 in the preceding set of instructions for one or more objects.

2. From the **Add New Effect** menu 𝑓𝑥, on the Appearance panel ★ or from the **Effect** menu, under Illustrator Effects, choose Distort & Transform > **Twist**. In the Twist dialog, check Preview.

3. Enter a positive **Angle** (press Tab) to twirl the path(s) clockwise or a negative value to twirl it counterclockwise (–360 to 360).

4. Click OK (see **A–B**, page 189).

C The Roughen effect is applied.

Rasterizing objects

The Rasterize command converts vector objects to bitmap images. Use the settings in the dialog to control, on a per-object basis, how an applied stroke, vector (Illustrator) effects, or bitmap (Photoshop) effects on the object are translated into pixels.

To rasterize a path object:

1. Select a path object or objects, or target them on the Layers panel.

2. Choose Object > **Rasterize.**

3. In the Rasterize dialog, choose a **Color Model** for the object. Depending on the current document color mode, you can choose CMYK for print output; RGB for video or onscreen output; Grayscale; or Bitmap for only black-and-white or black-and-transparent (no Photoshop effects will be available for this color model).

   Note: When we need to convert an image to grayscale, we prefer to do it in Adobe Photoshop before placing it in Illustrator. If you don't have access to Photoshop, choose the Grayscale color model in this dialog.

4. For **Resolution**, choose Screen for Web or video output, Medium for a desktop printer, or High for commercial printing; or enter a resolution in the Other field; or click Use Document Raster Effects Resolution to use the global resolution settings as specified in Effect > Document Raster Effects Settings (see page 393).

5. Click **Background**: White to make any transparent areas in the object opaque white, or Transparent to make the background trans-parent; we prefer the latter option (see the side-bar on this page).

6. Under **Options**:

   Choose **Anti-aliasing**: Art Optimized (Supersampling) to allow Illustrator to soften the edges of the rasterized shape, but keep in mind that this option could make type or thin lines look blurry. For type objects, Type Optimized (Hinted) is a better option. If you choose None, edges will be jagged.

   If you clicked Background: White and you want a white border to be added around the object, enter an **Add [   ] Around Object** value.

   Check Preserve Spot Colors (if available) to preserve spot colors in the object, if any.

7. Click OK.

➤ If the object contains a pattern fill and you want to preserve any transparency in the pattern, in the Rasterize dialog, click Background: Transparent and choose Anti-aliasing: Art Optimized.

➤ The Effect > Rasterize command ★ has all the same options as the command described at left except the Preserve Spot Colors option. When applied as an effect, the rasterization isn't permanent, and you can edit the settings at any time. However, an object to which this effect has been applied will be rasterized permanently (using the dialog settings) if: the Object > Expand Appearance command is applied; the file is saved in some formats, such as TIFF, GIF, or JPEG; or the file is exported to an application that doesn't read vector objects.

TRANSPARENT VS. CLIPPING MASK OPTIONS

Although both the Background: Transparent and Create Clipping Mask options in the Rasterize dialog remove an object's background, the results differ:

➤ The Transparent option creates an alpha channel in order to remove the background. The opacity and blending mode are restored to their default settings. The look of semitransparency is preserved, but not the look of a blending mode.

➤ The Create Clipping Mask option turns an object's path into a clipping path. Any existing transparency attributes are applied to the mask, transparency set-tings for the object revert to Normal mode and 100% opacity, and the look of transparency is lost. Any stroke or effects that extended beyond the object's path are clipped. If you click the Transparent option, there's no need to check Create Clipping Mask.

Using the Effect Gallery

The large Effect Gallery dialog provides access to most of the Photoshop effects and their settings. However, unlike the gallery in Illustrator CS3, this one lets you preview, apply, show, or hide only one individual effect at a time. If you want to apply multiple Photoshop effects, you have to make separate trips to the gallery. To work around this limitation, after applying multiple effects, click the visibility icon 👁 on the Appearance panel for any effects you want to hide or show. ★

To use the Effect Gallery:

1. Select a path object, an embedded image, **A** or editable or outline type.

2. From the **Add New Effect** menu *fx.* on the Appearance panel ★ or from the **Effect** menu (under Photoshop Effects), choose **Effect Gallery** or choose an individual Photoshop effect from any submenu except Pixelate, Blur, Sharpen, or Video.

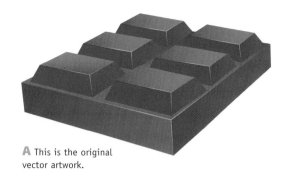

A This is the original vector artwork.

3. The resizable gallery dialog opens. **B** It contains a preview window, effect thumbnails, and settings for the current effect. If you want to switch to a different effect, expand a category in the middle panel of the dialog, then click a thumbnail, or choose an effect name from the menu on the right side of the dialog.

Continued on the following page

B The Effect Gallery has three panels.

Drag a magnified image in the preview window.

Click the arrowhead/chevron to hide the middle panel and expand the preview window to two panels wide; click it again to redisplay the middle panel.

Switch to a different effect by clicking a thumbnail in the middle panel or by choosing from this menu.

Choose settings for the current effect.

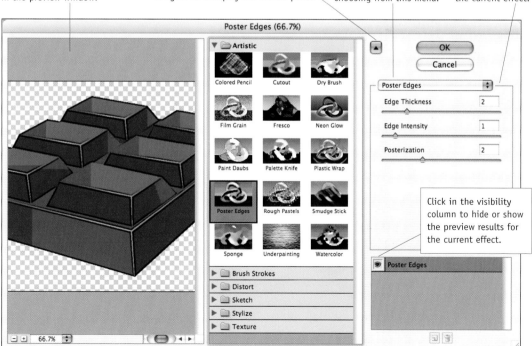

Click in the visibility column to hide or show the preview results for the current effect.

4. Choose settings for the chosen effect.

➤ You can change the zoom level for the preview via the zoom buttons or menu at the bottom of the dialog, and you can move a magnified preview in the window.

5. *Optional:* If you want to see the preview without the effect, click the visibility (eye) icon on the right side of the dialog; click it again to redisplay the effect. When you click OK, the effect will be applied to the selected object whether the visibility icon is present or not.

6. For some effects, such as Artistic > Rough Pastels and Underpainting, you can choose a texture type from the Texture menu. Move the Scaling slider to scale the pattern, and move the Relief slider, if there is one, to adjust the depth and prominence of the texture on the surface of the image.

7. Click OK.**A–E**

Note: All the Photoshop effects, along with the Stylize > Drop Shadow, Inner Glow, Outer Glow, and Feather effects, are rasterized upon output. To control which settings are used for this process, see page 393.

➤ In the Effect Gallery dialog, hold down Option/Alt and click Reset (the Cancel button becomes a Reset button) to restore the default settings to the first effect applied, or to restore the first effect applied, if you tried more than one.

➤ To intensify the results of a Photoshop effect on a vector object, apply an Illustrator effect such as Feather or Inner or Outer Glow first to add variation to the fill color.

➤ Strangely, the (vestigial?) buttons in the bottom right corner of the dialog aren't functional.

A The Artistic > Plastic Wrap effect is applied.

B The Sketch > Stamp effect is applied.

C The Distort > Diffuse Glow effect is applied.

D The Texture > Grain effect is applied.

E The Sketch > Charcoal effect is applied.

A graphic style is a saved collection of appearance attributes that can be applied to an object, group, or layer.

Any appearance attributes that can be applied to an object can be saved in a graphic style, such as fills and strokes, Stroke panel attributes, Transparency panel settings (opacity and blending mode), and effects.**A**

In this chapter, you will learn how to load graphic styles from a library panel to the Graphic Styles panel; apply, create, duplicate, edit, and delete graphic styles; save custom graphic style libraries; and break the link between an object and a graphic style, when needed.

To display the Graphic Styles panel,◻ **B** choose Window > Graphic Styles or press Shift-F5. You can also display a temporary Graphic Styles panel by clicking the graphic style thumbnail or arrowhead on the Control panel.

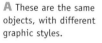

A These are the same objects, with different graphic styles.

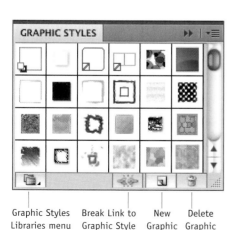

GRAPHIC STYLES

Graphic Styles Libraries menu · Break Link to Graphic Style · New Graphic Style · Delete Graphic Style

B The Graphic Styles panel

GRAPHIC STYLES

16

IN THIS CHAPTER

Graphic styles basics

When an object or group containing a graphic style is targeted, the name of the style and its attributes are listed on, and can be edited via, the Appearance panel.**A** The Graphic Styles and Appearance panels work hand in hand.

In case you're not already convinced that graphic styles are worth bothering with, here are some benefits to using them:

➤ By applying a graphic style, you can quickly apply many attributes at once.

➤ Like appearance attributes, graphic styles change the way an object looks without changing its underlying path.

➤ You can quickly link an object to a different graphic style at any time, or restore the default style of a 1-pt. black stroke and a solid white fill.

➤ If you edit a graphic style, the style updates instantly on any objects that it's linked to.

If you're wondering if graphic styles are like paragraph and character styles, you're right— except for one significant difference. If you modify an attribute directly on an object that a graphic style is linked to, that modification effectively breaks the link between the object and the style. In other words, if you subsequently edit the graphic style, it won't update on that particular object.

Graphic styles can be applied to layers, groups, or individual objects. When applied to a layer or group, a graphic style will be linked to all the objects in the layer or group, as well as to any objects that may subsequently be added to it.**B**

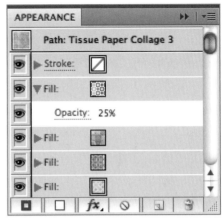

A When an object or group containing a graphic style is targeted, the style name and its attributes are listed on the Appearance panel.

The original objects

Jiggle Outline
(Type Effects library)

Shirofuchi 2
(Type Effects library)

Chisel
(Artistic Effects library)

Thick Orange Neon
(Neon Effects library)

Yellow Glow
(Image Effects library)

B We applied a few Illustrator graphic styles to these objects, just to give you an inkling of what styles can do.

Loading graphic styles from a library

The default Graphic Styles panel contains only six styles, but there are hundreds of other predefined graphic styles that you can load onto the panel.

To load graphic styles from a library:

1. From the **Graphic Styles Libraries** menu at the bottom of the Graphic Styles panel,⌐ choose a library name. A separate library panel opens.**A**

   Note: User libraries, which you will learn how to create on page 210, are opened from the User Defined submenu on the Graphic Styles Libraries menu.

2. Do one of the following:

   To add a style to the Graphic Styles panel by styling an object, select an object, then click a style thumbnail in the library. Or drag a style thumbnail from the library over any selected or unselected object. The chosen style will appear on the Graphic Styles panel.

   To add a style to the Graphic Styles panel without styling an object, deselect all, then click a style thumbnail in the library.

   To add multiple styles, click, then Shift-click consecutive styles or Cmd-click/Ctrl-click multiple styles on the library panel, then choose Add to Graphic Styles from the library panel menu.

3. To scroll through other predefined libraries in alphabetical order, click the **Load Previous Graphic Styles Library** button ◀ or **Load Next Graphic Styles Library** button ▶ on the library panel.

➤ If a graphic style that you apply contains a brush stroke, and the brush isn't already present on the document's Brushes panel, it will be added to the panel automatically.

➤ To change the view for the Graphic Styles panel, from the panel menu, choose Thumbnail View, Small List View, or Large List View. Two new display options on the panel menu are Use Square for Preview (the same thumbnail style as in previous versions of Illustrator) and Use Text for Preview (a "T" character displays in each thumbnail).★

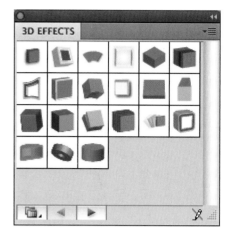

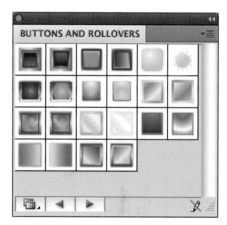

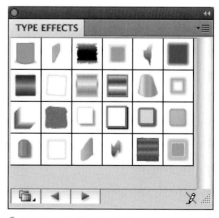

A Graphic style libraries display on a separate, free-floating panel. Click the Load Next or Load Previous button to cycle through the libraries.

Applying graphic styles

When you apply a graphic style to an object, the attributes in the style completely replace the existing attributes of the object. On the preceding page, you learned that a graphic style is applied to a selected object automatically if you click a style on a library panel. In these instructions, you will apply styles via the Graphic Styles panel. The link between the graphic style and object is preserved unless you break it deliberately (see page 210).

To apply a graphic style to an object:

1. Do either of the following:

   With the Selection tool (V), select one or more objects in the document window.

   On the Layers panel, click the target circle for an object, layer, or group. **A**

   Remember, for a top-level layer, selecting and targeting have different functions (see the sidebar on page 184).

2. Display the **Graphic Styles** panel, and load any styles onto it that you want to try out.

3. Click a style name or thumbnail on the panel. **B–C** The name of the graphic style that's linked to the currently selected object, group, or layer will be listed at the top of the Appearance panel.

   ➤ To view an enlarged thumbnail of a graphic style, Control-click/right-click and hold on any thumbnail on the panel. ★

➤ You can also apply a style by dragging from the Graphic Styles panel over any unselected object.

➤ If you apply a graphic style to a layer or group, **D** it will apply to all the current and subsequently created objects in that layer or group. You can also apply a different graphic style to individual objects nested within the layer or group (yes, this can lead to confusion!).

➤ Graphic styles can be applied to symbol instances by using the Symbol Styler tool (see page 349).

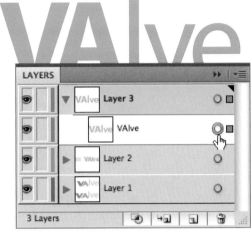

A Via the Layers panel, a text object is targeted for an appearance change.

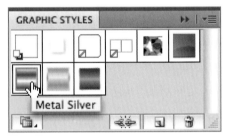

B A swatch is clicked on the Graphic Styles panel.

C The graphic style appears on the object (this is "Metal Silver," from the Type Effects library).

D A graphic style from the Buttons and Rollovers library was applied to this group of buttons.

To remove a graphic style that you have applied to an object, you can apply the Default Graphic Style, which is a solid white fill and a black stroke of 1 pt. (Note: If you prefer to break the link to a style without changing how the object looks, see page 210.)

To remove a graphic style from an object and apply the default style:

1. With the Selection tool (V), select the object to which you want to restore the default graphic style, or on the Layers panel, click the object's target circle.A

2. On the Graphic Styles panel, click the **Default Graphic Style** (the first thumbnail). B–C

If you apply a graphic style to a layer or group and then subsequently decide to remove it, you need to click a different button than for an object.

To remove a graphic style from a layer or group:

1. Target the layer or group from which you want to remove a graphic style.

2. At the bottom of the Appearance panel, click the **Clear Appearance** button.

If New Art Has Basic Appearance is checked on the Appearance panel menu, subsequently created objects will have one solid-color fill and one stroke attribute but no graphic styles or effects. If this option is unchecked, the appearance attributes currently displayed on the panel will apply automatically to future objects. If you want to specify the Default Graphic Style for an object you're about to create instead, follow these steps.

To establish the default style for future objects:

1. Deselect all.

2. On the Graphic Styles panel, click the **Default Graphic Style.**

A This object has a graphic style. We want to restore the default style to it.

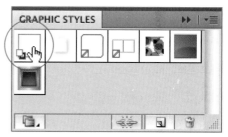

B The Default Graphic Style thumbnail is clicked on the Graphic Styles panel.

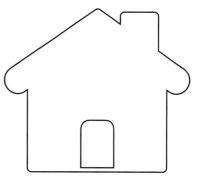

C The default graphic style consists of a white fill and a black 1-pt. stroke.

Instead of letting a graphic style wipe out all the existing attributes on an object, you can add the graphic style to the existing attributes. Styles from the Additive and Additive for Blob Brush libraries must be applied this way, but any other graphic style can also be applied as an additive style.

To add a graphic style to an object's existing attributes: ★

1. With the Selection tool (V), click an object that attributes or a graphic style have been applied to,**A** or target the object via the Layers panel.

2. If desired, open the **Additive** graphic style library or another library (see page 203).

3. On the Graphic Styles panel or a library panel, Option-click/Alt-click a style thumbnail.**B–D** The new style will be added to the existing attributes.

4. If you didn't get the results you expected, it's due to the stacking order of attributes on the Appearance panel. For example, a fully opaque fill attribute may be obscuring another fill attribute below it. To change the result, either change the opacity and/or blending mode of the upper attributes (see page 186) or restack them. To verify the effect of an attribute, hide and then show it by clicking in the visibility column.

A The Floating with Shadow style (from the Image Effects library) is applied to these objects.

B The Yellow Glow style (from the Image Effects library) is added to the existing style.

C The Outer Glow style (from the Additive library) is added to the original artwork.

The thumbnail for an additive style has a red slash. To apply it, you have to Option-click/Alt-click it.

D The Scribble 11 style (from the Scribble Effects library) is added to the original artwork.

Creating graphic styles

There are two ways to create a new graphic style: either from an existing object that contains the desired attributes or from a duplicate of an existing graphic style that you apply the desired attributes to. The first method will probably feel more natural and intuitive, especially if you want to experiment with various settings for the new style before creating it.

To create a graphic style from an object:

1. Target an object that has the attributes you want to save as a graphic style. If desired, use the Appearance panel to apply any additional attributes that you want the style to contain, such as effects or additional fills or strokes.**A**

2. Do either of the following:

   On the Graphic Styles panel, Option-click/Alt-click the **New Graphic Style** button, name the style in the Graphic Style Options dialog, then click OK.**B** The new style will appear as the last thumbnail or listing on the panel.**C**

   Drag the thumbnail from the uppermost left corner of the **Appearance** panel onto the Graphic Styles panel, or with the Selection tool, drag the object onto the Graphic Styles panel. Double-click the new style swatch, type a suitable name for it, then click OK.

To modify a duplicate graphic style:

1. On the Graphic Styles panel, click the style swatch or name to be duplicated, then click the New Graphic Style button. The numeral "1" will be appended to the style name (if this is the first duplicate of the style).

2. Double-click the duplicate style to open the Graphic Style Options dialog, name the style, then click OK.

3. If you click the duplicate graphic style swatch or name, the attributes it contains will be listed on the Appearance panel. Edit the style (see the instructions on the following page).

A Click the object that contains the attributes to be saved as a graphic style.

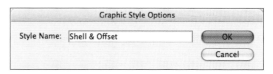

B Enter a Style Name for the new graphic style.

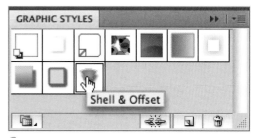

C The new style appears as the last swatch on the Graphic Styles panel.

Editing graphic styles

Beware! If you edit a graphic style, the changes will update on all the objects the style is currently linked to. If you don't want this to happen, duplicate the style first (see the instructions on the previous page), then edit the duplicate.

To edit a graphic style:

1. Apply the graphic style to be edited to an object, so you'll be able to preview your edits, and keep the object selected.**A–B**

2. Via the Appearance panel,◉ edit or restack the existing appearance attributes, add new attributes, or delete any unwanted attributes (see Chapter 14).**C–D** For example, you could apply a different solid-color, pattern, or gradient to an existing Fill attribute; create an additional Fill, Stroke, or effect attribute; edit the settings for an existing effect by clicking the effect name; or change the blending mode or opacity by clicking the Opacity link (see Chapter 27).

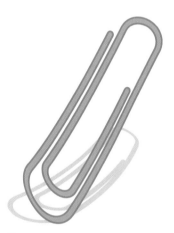

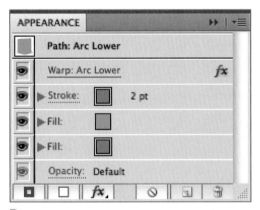

A Apply the graphic style that you want to edit to an object.

B The Appearance panel displays the attributes for the Arc Lower graphic style (note the topmost listing).

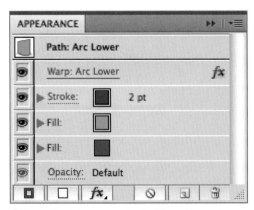

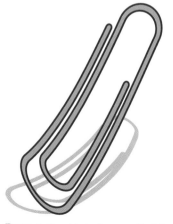

C We modified the settings for the Warp effect and changed the color for the Stroke and lower Fill attributes.

D This is the object after we edited the style attributes via the Appearance panel.

3. Do either of the following:

From the Appearance panel menu, choose **Redefine Graphic Style** "[style name]."

Option-drag/Alt-drag the square from the uppermost left corner of the Appearance panel over the original swatch on the Graphic Styles panel.

Regardless of which method you use, a progress bar may display temporarily, then the style swatch will update to reflect the modifications.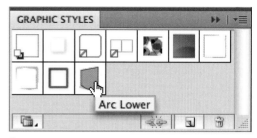 Any objects to which the style is linked will update automatically.**B**

➤ While editing a graphic style, be careful not to click other styled objects or graphic style swatches, or your current appearance settings will be lost.

Deleting graphic styles from the panel

If you delete a graphic style that's linked to any objects in your document, the attributes from the style will remain on the objects, minus the link.

To delete a style from the Graphic Styles panel:

1. On the Graphic Styles panel, click the style you want to remove, or Cmd-click/Ctrl-click multiple styles.

2. Click the **Delete Graphic Style** button on the panel.

3. Click Yes in the alert dialog. (Oops! Change your mind? Choose Undo.)

➤ To delete a selected graphic style without an alert dialog opening, Option-click/Alt-click the Delete Graphic Style button.

A The style updates on the Graphic Styles panel.

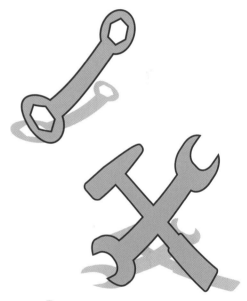

B The graphic style also updates automatically on any other objects that it's linked to.

Creating a custom graphic style library

If you save your favorite graphic styles to a custom library, you'll have access to the library for use in any document. You can organize and name your libraries in any logical way, such as by theme, client name, or project name.

To create a graphic styles library:

1. Make sure the Graphic Styles panel contains only the styles to be saved in a library.

2. *Optional:* To remove all the styles from the Graphic Styles panel that aren't currently being used in the document, choose Select All Unused from the Graphic Styles panel menu, click the Delete Graphic Style button 🗑 on the panel, then click Yes in the alert dialog.

3. From the **Graphic Styles Libraries** menu 🖳 at the bottom of the Graphic Styles panel, choose **Save Graphic Styles**. The Save Graphic Styles as Library dialog opens.

4. Type a name for the library in the Save As field. Keep the extension and the default location, which in the Mac OS is /Users/[user name]/Library/Application Support/Adobe/Adobe Illustrator CS4/en_US/Graphic Styles; and in Windows is C:\Documents and Settings\[user name]\Application Data\Adobe\Adobe Illustrator CS4 Settings\en_US\Graphic Styles. Click Save.

5. The new library will be listed on, and can be opened from, the **User Defined** submenu on the Graphic Styles Libraries menu.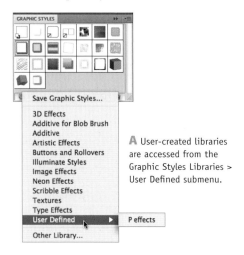

Breaking the link to a graphic style

If you break the link between an object and a graphic style and then subsequently edit the style, the style won't update on that object. You would want to do this prior to editing a graphic style if you didn't want those edits to appear on a particular object that the style is already applied to.

To break the link to a graphic style:

1. Do one of the following:

   With the Selection tool (V), select one or more objects in the document window.

   Click the target circle for an object on the Layers panel.

   If the style was applied to a group or layer, click the target circle for that layer, sublayer, or group on the Layers panel.

2. Do either of the following:

   Click the **Break Link to Graphic Style** button 🔗 at the bottom of the Graphic Styles panel.**B**

   Change any **appearance attributes** for the selected item or items (e.g., apply a different fill color, stroke setting, pattern, gradient, transparency setting, or effect). This effectively breaks the link.

   Note: The graphic style name is no longer listed at the top of the Appearance panel for the selected object(s).

A User-created libraries are accessed from the Graphic Styles Libraries > User Defined submenu.

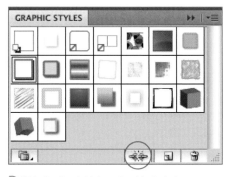

B Click the Break Link to Graphic Style button on the Graphic Styles panel.

If you have a digital photo or scanned graphic that you want to convert to editable vector art, this is the chapter for you. You will learn how to apply custom tracing settings before and after tracing, create and manage custom tracing presets, release a tracing, expand a tracing into separate paths, and convert a tracing to a Live Paint group.

The tracing features in Illustrator

The Live Trace command can detect and trace the color and shade areas in any raster image that you open or place into Illustrator, such as a Photoshop EPS, TIFF, JPEG, or PSD image, or scanned artwork, such as a logo. You can choose from a wide array of custom tracing options prior to tracing—and because traced objects are "live," you can also fine-tune the tracing results via the Tracing Options dialog before converting them into editable paths or a Live Paint group. You can use a built-in tracing preset (set of presaved settings) as a starting point, or create and save your own presets. Among the numerous settings that you can specify are the precision with which the image is traced, the stroke weight and length, the number of colors, and a color palette.

With such a wide range of tracing controls at your fingertips, you can produce everything from a close simulation of your original artwork to a loose rendering. Regardless of the type of imagery you trace, the end result will be editable paths with a specified number of fill and/or stroke colors. Although the Live Trace command doesn't have the natural editing power of the human eye and brain, it does a decent job, and you may find the results useful—provided you're willing to do a little cleanup work afterward. For creating complex, nongeometric artwork, it's much faster to start with a tracing than to draw a gazillion intricate shapes by hand. **A–C**

17

A A portion of the original photo

B The photo traced

C The tracing displayed as path outlines

Tracing a raster image

In these instructions, you'll trace a raster image using preset settings. In the instructions that begin on the next page, we'll show you how to choose custom settings for a tracing and apply custom settings to an existing tracing.

After tracing the image, you can either convert the results into editable paths via the Expand command or convert the artwork to a Live Paint group (see pages 217–218).

To trace a raster image:

1. Using File > **Open**,* open a raster image, such as a TIFF, JPG, or PSD file; or with an Illustrator document open, use File > **Place** to place a raster image. Note: If you open or place a PSD (Photoshop) file that contains layers with the Link option unchecked, the Photoshop Import Options dialog opens. Click Convert Layers to Objects to import the image as a series of objects on multiple layers, or click Flatten Layers to a Single Image to import the image as one flattened layer.

2. With the Selection tool, click the image object to be traced.

3. Do either of the following:

   To trace the object using preset settings, from the **Tracing Presets and Options** menu ▼ on the Control panel, choose a preset based on how detailed you want the end result to be. You can try out a few different presets.

   To trace the object using the last-used (or default) settings, click **Live Trace** on the Control panel. If an alert dialog appears, informing you that the tracing may proceed slowly, click OK. Some presets take longer to process than others.

   A progress bar may appear onscreen as Illustrator traces the object. New options will appear on the Control panel when the tracing is completed.

4. *Optional:* To customize the tracing, follow the instructions that begin on the next page.

A Place a raster image into an Illustrator document...

B ...then choose one of the tracing presets from the menu on the Control panel.

Custom
[Default]
Simple Trace
Color 6
Color 16
Photo Low Fidelity
Photo High Fidelity
Grayscale
Hand Drawn Sketch
Detailed Illustration
Comic Art
Technical Drawing
Black and White Logo
One Color Logo
Inked Drawing
Lettering
doggie
Tracing Options...

*To learn about the Open and Place commands, see pages 282–283.

C The Color 6 tracing preset produced this vector art. Yum.

Applying tracing options

By choosing settings in the Tracing Options dialog or from the Control panel, you can make your tracing conform closely to the original artwork or simplify it dramatically. And because tracings are live, you can choose these options before or after using the Live Trace command.

To apply tracing options:

1. *Optional:* To apply colors to the resulting vector art from a custom library, open that library via the Swatches Libraries menu. If you click the Load Previous or Load Next Swatch Library button, each library you display will be listed on the Palette menu in the Tracing Options dialog (see step 5).

2. Select a Live Trace object in your document.

3. Click the **Tracing Options Dialog** button ▦ on the Control panel. The Tracing Options dialog opens.**A** Check Preview (or to speed up processing, don't check it until step 6).

Note: You can choose whichever options in steps 4 through 8 seem appropriate for your tracing.

4. Choose a different **Preset** (the choices here are the same as on the Preset menu on the Control panel; see **A**, next page).

CHOOSE OPTIONS BEFORE TRACING

To choose custom options prior to tracing, click an image object in your Illustrator document. From the Tracing Presets and Options menu on the Control panel, choose Tracing Options, then follow steps 4–9, starting on this page.

5. Choose options in the **Adjustments** area to control how the image is prepped for retracing:

   From the **Mode** menu, choose Color, Grayscale, or Black and White, depending on how many colors you want the final tracing to contain.

   For Black and White mode only, choose a **Threshold** value (0–255; the default is 128). All pixels darker than this value will be converted to black; all pixels lighter than this value will be converted to white. You can also change the Threshold value on the Control panel.

   For Grayscale or Color mode, from the **Palette** menu, choose Automatic to have Illustrator use colors from the image in the tracing, or choose the name of any swatch library you opened in step 1 to have the final tracing contain colors just from that library (nifty feature!).

Continued on the following page

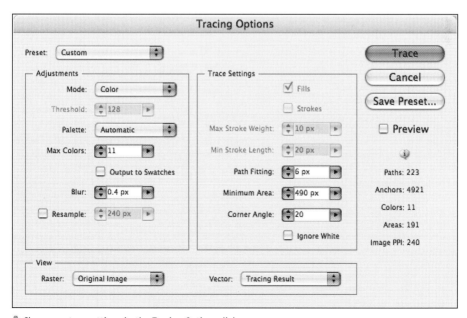

A Choose custom settings in the Tracing Options dialog.

For just Grayscale or Color mode and the Palette menu choice of Automatic, choose a Max Colors value for the maximum number of colors the final tracing may contain (2–256; the default is 6). For a hand-drawn look or a screen-printed look with fewer fill areas, keep this value low (say, 12 or less); this will also speed up the retracing. (You can also change the Max Colors value on the Control panel after exiting the dialog.)

Click **Output to Swatches** to save the colors in the resulting tracing as new global process color swatches on the Swatches panel.

Choose a **Blur** value (0–20 pixels) to reduce artifacts, noise, and extraneous marks. This simplifies the image for retracing by diminishing its sharpness.

Check **Resample** and change the resolution for the tracing. A lower resolution speeds up the retracing but also produces fewer image details and less precise outlines.

6. In the **View** area, make choices from the Raster and Vector menus to compare the source image to the tracing results (make sure Preview is checked when you do this):

The **Raster** options control how the underlying raster image displays: No Image hides the original image; Original Image shows the original image unchanged; Adjusted Image shows how the image will be preprocessed for tracing (e.g., by being resampled, or by having its colors or shades reduced); and Transparent Image dims the image so you can see the tracing results more clearly on top.

The **Vector** options control how the tracing results are displayed: No Tracing Result hides the tracing so you can view your original or adjusted image; Tracing Result displays the tracing based on the current dialog settings; Outlines shows the tracing paths only, without fills or strokes; and Outlines with Tracing displays the resulting paths on top

of a dimmed version of the resulting fills and strokes.

(These view settings can also be chosen via the Preview Different Views of Raster Image ▲ and Preview Different Views of Vector Result △ menus on the Control panel after exiting the dialog.**A**)

7. Choose **Trace Settings** options to control the resulting paths:

▶ As you choose Adjustments and Trace Settings, monitor the number of Paths, Anchors, Colors, and Areas in the resulting artwork via the readouts on the right side of the dialog.

For Black and White mode only, check **Fills** to create filled paths and/or **Strokes** to create stroked paths. If Strokes is checked, specify a Max Stroke Weight value (0–100 px; the default is 10). Areas this wide or narrower will become strokes; wider areas will become outlined areas. If Strokes is checked, specify a Min Stroke Length value (0–200 px; the default is 20). Areas this long or longer will be converted to strokes; areas that are shorter than this length will be ignored.

Specify a **Path Fitting** value to control how closely traced paths will follow the edges of shapes in the image (0–10 px; the default is 2). A low Path Fitting value produces a more accurate fit but also produces more anchor points.

Change the **Minimum Area** setting (default is 10 px) to minimize the number of extraneous small paths that are created. Specify the smallest area that you will permit the program to trace (0–3000 pixels square). For example, a 5 x 5-pixel object would occupy a 25-pixel area. For a medium-resolution image (200 ppi) using Grayscale or Color mode, a small Minimum Area value (10–60 px) produces a detailed, "photographic" tracing, whereas a larger area (144–300 px) produces a looser, more "hand-drawn" tracing. For a high-resolution image

| Preset: | Custom | ⊞ | Max Colors: 11 | Min Area: 490 px | ▲ | △ | Expand | Live Paint |

A These options are available on the Control panel when a tracing object is selected.

(300 ppi), a value of 600 px or greater would be needed to create a loose tracing. Adjust the Max Colors and Minimum Area settings to control the tightness or looseness of the tracing. (You can also change the Min Area value on the Control panel after exiting the dialog.)

Choose a **Corner Angle** for the minimum angle a path must have to be defined by a corner anchor point instead of a smooth point (0–180°; the default is 20°).

8. If you save your settings as a preset, you'll be able to apply them to any image and use them as a starting point when choosing custom settings. Click **Save Preset**, type a name for the preset in the Save Tracing Preset dialog, then click OK. (The Resample and View settings aren't saved.) Saved presets can be chosen from the Preset menu on the Control panel when a raster image or tracing object is selected, or from the Preset menu in the Tracing Options dialog.

9. Click **Trace. A–B** A progress bar will appear onscreen while Illustrator traces the image (be patient!), then a "Tracing" listing for the traced object (possibly nested) will appear on the Layers panel. If you're happy with the results, you can either expand the tracing into editable paths or convert it into a Live Paint group (see pages 217–218).

➤ If you choose the Black and White option from the Mode menu in the Tracing Options dialog and check Ignore White under Trace Settings, a fill of None will be applied to any white areas in the tracing (those areas will be transparent).

➤ You can also create a tracing preset by way of the Tracing Presets dialog; see the next page.

A After choosing the Detailed Drawing tracing preset, we changed the Threshold value to 135 and the Max Stroke Weight value to 2 px.

B We used custom options of Max Colors 171, Path Fitting 5 px, and Minimum Area 404 px for this tracing.

Managing tracing presets

Use the Tracing Presets dialog to create, edit, delete, import, or export custom tracing presets.

To create, delete, edit, import, or export a tracing preset:

1. Choose Edit > **Tracing Presets**. The Tracing Presets dialog opens.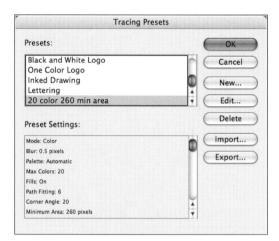

2. To create a new preset based on an existing one, click a preset on the Presets scroll list, or to create a new preset based on the default settings, click [Default]. Click **New**. The Tracing Options dialog opens. Enter a name, choose settings, then click Done.

   To edit an existing preset, click the preset on the Presets scroll list, then click **Edit**. The Tracing Options dialog opens. Choose settings, then click Done.

   To delete a preset, click the preset name, then click **Delete**.

   The Import and Export options enable you to share presets with other users. To import a user-saved preset, click **Import**; in the Import Presets File dialog, locate and click the desired preset file, then click Open. To export the current settings as a preset file, click **Export**; in the Export Presets File As dialog, keep the default location, then click Save.

3. Click OK.

Releasing a tracing

To restore a tracing object to its virgin bitmap state, you must use the Release command.

To release a tracing object:

1. Select the tracing object.

2. Choose Object > Live Trace > **Release**. The listing on the Layers panel will change from Tracing to Image, or to the file name of the original image.

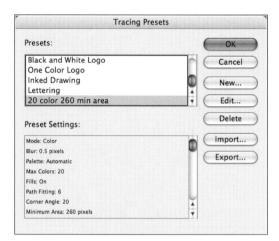

A Use the Tracing Presets dialog to create, edit, delete, import, or export tracing presets, which are collections of settings.

Converting a tracing to paths

The Expand command converts a tracing into standard paths, which can then be selected via the Layers panel and recolored, reshaped, or transformed, like any other paths. Once a tracing is expanded, it no longer has "live" properties, meaning its Tracing Options settings can't be altered.

To expand and recolor a live tracing:

1. Trace a placed image in your document, **A–B** and keep the Live Trace object selected.

2. On the Control panel, click **Expand**. On the Layers panel, you'll now see a group containing a gazillion paths (or possibly fewer, depending on the tracing settings used). If you turn on Smart Guides (with Object Highlighting) and pass the Selection tool over the former tracing, you'll see that each area in the artwork is now a separate path. **C**

3. Select the expanded group, then ungroup it (Cmd-G/Ctrl-G).

4. Select and recolor any of the resulting objects (**A–C**, next page).

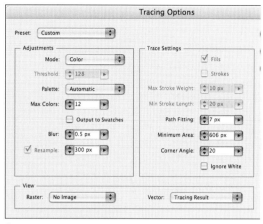

A These custom Tracing Options settings produced the tracing shown in the next figure.

B The low Max Colors value and high Minimum Area value (shown in **A**) produced these simplified shapes.

C The tracing is expanded (here, the objects are selected).

A After ungrouping the expanded tracing, we put a section of the building into isolation mode.

B We used the Scissors tool to cut the object in two. We selected the left object, then with the Eyedropper tool, clicked an area of sky to apply that color to it.

C This is the result.

An alternative to the Expand command is to convert a Live Trace object to a Live Paint group. This is a good route to take if your tracing is relatively simple and you want to utilize Live Paint features, such as the ability to hide or recolor edges or quickly recolor faces (fill areas). To learn about the Live Paint features, see the next chapter.

To convert a Live Trace object to a Live Paint group:

1. Select a Live Trace object.

2. On the Control panel, click **Live Paint**. Ta-da!

QUICK CLEANUP

The Eraser tool is handy for doing cleanup work after applying the Expand command to a tracing.

We want to differentiate the subject matter from the background in this expanded tracing.

An easy fix was to eliminate the entire background with the Eraser tool.

The Live Paint feature provides a novel way to fill paths. To create an "armature" for a Live Paint group, you can either create some open or closed paths with a drawing tool, such as the Pencil or Blob Brush tool, then convert the whole drawing into a Live Paint group, or you can convert a tracing into a Live Paint group and use Live Paint group features to recolor it.

With the Live Paint Bucket tool, you simply click or drag across any area that is formed by intersecting lines (called a face), and the current paint attributes are applied. Add to or reshape the Live Paint objects at any time, and the fill color flows into the new shape; that's what makes the whole process "live." Another unique feature of Live Paint groups is that you can recolor (or leave unpainted) individual line segments, called edges.**C** This method for recoloring sketches and tracings is flexible and fun.

In this chapter, you will learn how to convert ordinary objects to a Live Paint group, apply colors to faces and edges in the group, reshape parts of the group, add new faces and edges, and finally, expand or release the group into standard paths.

LIVE PAINT

18

IN THIS CHAPTER

A A pencil sketch was converted to a Live Paint group.

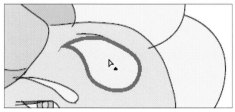

B A face in the group is selected.

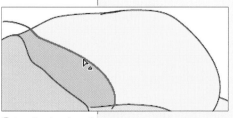

C An edge is selected.

Creating Live Paint groups

When drawing paths for a Live Paint group, the important requirement is that you allow your drawing lines to intersect. The Live Paint Bucket tool, which you'll use for coloring, detects and fills only faces (areas that are bounded by intersecting lines).

To create a Live Paint group from your artwork, you can either click the paths with the Live Paint Bucket tool or choose the Live Paint command. Both methods preserve only the basic fill and stroke settings. Other attributes, such as transparency settings, brush strokes, and live effects, are removed.

Note: Another way to create a Live Paint group, in addition to the two methods offered in step 3, is to trace an image via the Live Trace command (see the preceding chapter), then with the tracing object selected, click Live Paint on the Control panel.

To create a Live Paint group:

1. Draw some open or closed paths with any tool, such as the Pencil, Blob Brush, Pen, Arc, Line Segment, or Ellipse, and apply some stroke colors and weights. You may use the Paintbrush tool, but the Live Paint command will remove the brush stroke. As you create your sketch, you must let some or all of the segments intersect.

2. Select all the paths.

3. Do either of the following:

   Choose the **Live Paint Bucket** tool ⬚ (K), then click one of the selected objects. **B**

   Choose Object > Live Paint > **Make** (Cmd-Option-X/Ctrl-Alt-X).

   If a lavishly illustrated alert dialog appears, make sure your objects are still selected, then click again with the Paint Bucket tool. You may also get an alert about object features that may be discarded. On the Layers panel, the paths are now nested within a Live Paint group.

➤ To produce a Live Paint group from a symbol or blend, you must apply Object > Expand first; to use a clipping set in a Live Paint group, release the set first; or to create a Live Paint group from type, convert it to outlines via Type > Create Outlines first.

➤ Some Illustrator commands aren't available for Live Paint groups, such as the Clipping Mask, Pathfinder, and Select > Same commands.

A As you draw a picture, let your segments intersect. This portrait was drawn with the Pencil tool.

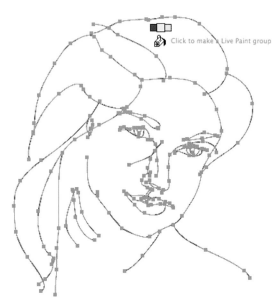

B Click one of the selected paths or enclosed areas with the Live Paint Bucket tool to convert them to a Live Paint group.

Using the Live Paint Bucket tool

On the next page, you'll learn how to use the Live Paint Bucket tool to recolor a Live Paint group. But before you do that, familiarize yourself with the Live Paint Bucket Options dialog so you can customize the tool.

To choose options for the Live Paint Bucket tool:

1. Do either of the following:

   Double-click the **Live Paint Bucket** tool.

   Select the Live Paint Bucket tool (K), then press Return/Enter.

2. The Live Paint Bucket Options dialog opens. **A** In the Options area:

   Click **Paint Fills** and/or **Paint Strokes**, depending on what you want the tool to paint. Note: If you're going to follow the instructions on the next page, check only Paint Fills.

   ► If you check just one of these options, you can Shift-click with the tool to switch its function between painting fills (faces) and applying stroke (edge) colors and weights. We actually find this to be the easiest method, because when the tool has only one function at a time, you can't inadvertently recolor a face when you intended to recolor an edge, or vice versa.

   Check **Cursor Swatch Preview** to display, in a tiny strip above the tool pointer, the current color (if you use the Color panel), or the color of the last chosen swatch on the Swatches panel and the two swatches adjacent to it. **B–C** We recommend keeping this option checked. The color strip is helpful and not too obtrusive.

3. *Optional:* If the current highlight color is too similar to colors in your artwork (or colors you're going to apply), check Highlight, then, from the Color menu, choose a preset color for the faces and edges the tool will pass over, or click the color swatch and choose a color from the Colors dialog. You can also change the Width for the highlight.

4. Click OK. Now you're ready to use the tool; turn the page.

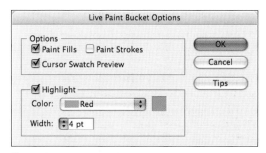

A Use the Live Paint Bucket Options dialog to specify default behavior for the tool.

B If the Cursor Swatch Preview option is on for the Live Paint Bucket tool and you mix a color via the Color panel, that color will display in the pointer.

C If the Cursor Swatch Preview option is on for the Live Paint Bucket tool and you click a swatch on the Swatches panel, that color and two adjacent swatches will display above the pointer.

When you apply fill or stroke attributes to a Live Paint group, faces or edges are recolored—not the actual paths. If you reshape a Live Paint group in any way, such as by editing the paths, colors in the group will reflow instantly into any newly created faces. In the steps below, you will recolor faces with the Live Paint Bucket tool. This technique reminds us of a drawing method we used as kids: we would draw a big swirly doodle on a piece of paper, then color in the shapes. It's so much faster in Illustrator!

Note: You can apply a solid color, pattern, or gradient to faces and edges in a Live Paint group. The term "color" in this chapter is a generic reference to all three kinds of swatches.

To recolor faces with the Live Paint Bucket tool:

1. Have a Live Paint group at the ready (you don't need to select it).**A** Double-click the **Live Paint Bucket** tool to open the Live Paint Bucket Options dialog. Check Paint Fills, uncheck Paint Strokes, then click OK.

2. Click the fill color square on the Tools or Color panel, then click a swatch or color group icon on the Swatches panel or choose a fill color via the Control panel. If the Cursor Swatch Preview option is checked in the tool options dialog, the currently selected swatch will display as the middle of the three colors above the pointer. You can press the left or right arrow key to select the previous or next swatch on the Swatches panel as your fill color. Keep pressing the key to move along the current row in the Swatches panel, or to cycle through the colors in the color group.

3. Do either of the following:

   Move the pointer over a face that you want to apply color to (an area where two or more paths intersect), and click within the highlighted face.**B**

   Drag across multiple faces.

➤ Hold down Option/Alt to turn the Live Paint Bucket tool into a temporary Eyedropper tool, and use it to sample a fill color from anywhere in the document window.

➤ The Arrange commands (Bring to Front, etc.) don't work on the parts of a Live Paint group.

A This Live Paint group was created from lines drawn with the Pencil tool.

B When the Live Paint Bucket tool is clicked on a face (an area where paths intersect) in a Live Paint group, the current fill color is applied (**B**, next page shows this face filled in).

FLOOD FILL

➤ Double-click a face with the Live Paint Bucket tool to fill adjacent faces across all edges that have a stroke of None.

➤ Triple-click a face to recolor all faces that already have the same color as the one you click, adjacent and not.

You can also use the Live Paint Bucket tool to apply stroke colors and/or stroke settings. Each edge can have a different color, weight, and other stroke attributes, or a stroke color of None. A unique feature of Live Paint groups is that only the edges you click are modified—not the whole path.

To modify edges with the Live Paint Bucket tool:

1. Double-click the **Live Paint Bucket** tool, ![icon] check Paint Strokes and uncheck Paint Fills in the Live Paint Bucket Options dialog, then click OK.

2. Click the stroke color square on the Tools or Color panel, then choose a stroke color. Also choose a stroke weight and other attributes via the Stroke panel, which you can access from the Control panel. Or if you want to remove colors from edges, choose a color of None.

3. Do one of the following:

   Move the pointer over an edge in a Live Paint group, then click. **A–C**

   Starting with the pointer positioned over an edge, drag across multiple edges.

   Note: Now that you know how to recolor faces and edges with the current Live Paint Bucket Options setting as just Paint Fills or Paint Strokes, you can hold down Shift to quickly toggle between the two functions.

➤ You can also recolor a Live Paint group by using the Recolor Artwork dialog (see Chapter 29).

➤ You can apply transparency settings, brush strokes, and effects to an entire Live Paint group, but not to individual faces or edges. For example, if you drag a brush from the Brushes panel over a Live Paint group, that brush will be applied to every edge in the group.

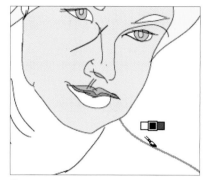

A Stroke attributes are being applied to an edge with the Live Paint Bucket tool.

B We drew additional paths on the neck, lips, and face to create more fillable faces.

C We used the Live Paint Bucket tool to fill the new faces and to apply a stroke of None to edges on the neck, cheeks, and forehead.A

FLOOD STROKE

➤ Double-click an edge with the Live Paint Bucket tool to apply the current stroke color and attributes to all edges that are connected to, and have the same stroke color and weight as, the one you click.

➤ Triple-click an edge to apply the current stroke color and attributes to all edges that have the same attributes as the one you click, contiguous and not.

Using the Live Paint Selection tool

The Live Paint Selection tool lets you select edges and/or faces in a Live Paint group. Choose options for the tool before using it.

To choose options for the Live Paint Selection tool:

1. Do either of the following:

   Double-click the **Live Paint Selection** tool.

   Click the Live Paint Selection tool (Shift-L), then press Return/Enter.

2. The Live Paint Selection Options dialog opens. 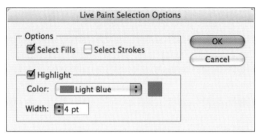 Check **Select Fills** and/or **Select Strokes** (and choose a different Highlight Color and/or Width for selections, if desired), then click OK.

➤ To avoid confusion, choose a different highlight color for the Live Paint Bucket tool than for the Live Paint Selection tool.

To select faces and/or edges with the Live Paint Selection tool:

1. Choose the **Live Paint Selection** tool (Shift-L), and choose options for the tool (instructions above). For example, if you want to select only faces in your Live Paint group, you could uncheck Select Strokes to prevent any strokes from becoming selected inadvertently.

2. Click an edge or face in a Live Paint group, then Shift-click additional edges or faces.  The selection can include both edges and faces. It displays as a gray pattern.

   ➤ Shift-click to deselect individual edges or faces.

3. Do any of the following:

   For the **faces**, click the fill color square on the Tools or Color panel, then choose a solid color,  gradient, or pattern. You can modify a gradient fill with the Gradient tool (see pages 308–309).

   For the **edges**, click the stroke color square on the Tools or Color panel, then choose a color. You can also change the stroke weight and other stroke attributes. Apply a stroke of None to any edges that you want to hide.

   To **delete** the currently selected edges or faces, press Delete/Backspace

4. When you're done making changes, click outside the Live Paint group to deselect it.

A Use the Live Paint Selection Options dialog to specify what the tool selects, and to choose a Highlight color for its selections.

B Three areas of the woman's hair are selected with the Live Paint Selection tool.

C A new fill color is applied to the selected faces.

COMPARING THE PENCIL AND BLOB BRUSH TOOLS FOR CREATING LIVE PAINT GROUPS ★

A When we used the Pencil tool to create a series of separate paths, we made sure the endpoints of every path overlapped another path in order to create closed areas.

B With the Live Paint Bucket tool, we applied fill colors to the faces and stroke colors to individual edges. The fact that we were able to apply a different stroke color to each separate former Pencil tool path proves that those paths became separate edges when they were converted to a Live Paint group.

C We used the Blob Brush tool to create a series of separate strokes, which we connected with other strokes in order to create closed areas. The result is one continuous closed path.

D With the Live Paint Bucket tool, we applied fill colors to the face areas, including one fill color to the entire former Blob Brush stroke outline. Since the Blob Brush drawing converted to just faces, we were able to apply stroke colors only to the entire perimeter of a face (orange to the outer edge of the stroke outline and yellow to the edge of the blue-green face).

➤ When drawing Pencil or Blob Brush artwork for a Live Paint group, try not to create overlapping shapes, which would produce extraneous face areas in the resulting group. For a Pencil drawing, although you could apply a stroke of None to hide overlapping edges in the group, that would be extra work; and for a Blob Brush drawing, you could erase the overlapping lines, but the erased areas would become separate, extraneous faces.

Reshaping Live Paint groups

With a Live Paint group in isolation mode, you can transform or move whole faces in the group or manipulate the anchor points on any individual edges. Colors will reflow into the modified areas. If you're comfortable editing objects in isolation mode, the steps below will feel like second nature. On the next page, you will learn how to add new faces to a Live Paint Group.

To reshape or move areas in a Live Paint group:

1. Choose the Selection tool ▶ (V), and make sure the Bounding Box feature is on (View menu).

2. To isolate a Live Paint group, double-click a face or edge in the group.

3. Do either of the following:

   With the **Selection** tool (V), either click a face that contains a fill color or click an edge. A bounding box with star-filled selection handles displays. Drag the face or edge to move it, or drag a handle on the edge to transform it.**A–B** You can also delete the current selection by pressing Delete/Backspace.

   With the **Direct Selection** tool (A), click an edge to display its anchor points and direction handles, then reshape it by manipulating the points or handles (see Chapter 12).

   Fill colors will reflow automatically into any areas you reshape or transform (see also the sidebar on the following page).

4. To exit isolation mode, click the gray isolation mode bar at the top of the document window or press Esc.

➤ To switch quickly between the Direct Selection tool for reshaping and the Live Paint Bucket tool for recoloring, press A for the former or K for the latter.

➤ You can use the Align buttons (on the Control or Align panel) to align selected anchor points.

A We selected an edge in a Live Paint group with the Selection tool, then lengthened it to intersect it with another edge. A new face was created.

B With the Live Paint Bucket tool, we applied a fill color to the new face.

Adding new faces and edges to a Live Paint group

Next, we'll show you two ways to add faces and edges to an existing Live Paint group.

To add new faces and edges to a Live Paint group:

Method 1 (Layers or Control panel)

1. Create a path on top of or next to a Live Paint group, or select an existing path.

2. Do either of the following:

   On the Layers panel, drag the new path listing into the **Live Paint Group** listing.

   Choose the Selection tool ▶ (V), marquee both the new paths and the Live Paint group, then click **Merge Live Paint** on the Control panel. Click OK if an alert dialog appears.

Method 2 (isolation mode)

1. Choose the Selection tool (V), then double-click the Live Paint group to put it in isolation mode.

2. With a drawing tool, such as the Pencil or Blob Brush, or a geometric tool, such as the Rectangle or Ellipse, draw the path to be added.**A–B** The new path will automatically be part of the Live Paint group.

3. To exit isolation mode, press Esc.

THE LIVE PAINT RULES — NOT

➤ Faces in a Live Paint group are recolored instantly when you reshape them or delete any of their edges. If you delete an edge that borders two faces, the fill color from the larger of the two faces is applied — usually.

➤ With a Live Paint group in isolation mode, if you create and then drag a new closed face over filled faces in the group, release the mouse, and then move the new face away from the group, any of the following may happen: some faces may adopt the fill color of another face in the group, some faces may adopt the color of the new face, or the new face may be filled with an existing color from the group. Go figure. If you don't like the results, undo.

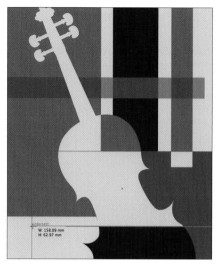

A With the Live Paint group in isolation mode, a rectangle is drawn across existing edges to create new faces.

B The Live Paint Bucket tool is used to apply fill colors to the new faces.

Choosing gap options for a Live Paint group

If you reshape an edge so as to create an opening (called a "gap") in a formerly closed area (face), any fill color in that face will disappear, because in the world of Live Paint, fills can't be applied to faces that have large gaps. Via the Gap Options dialog, you can specify a gap size to stop the fill colors from leaking. Each Live Paint group can have its own Gap Options settings.

To choose gap options for a Live Paint group:

1. Choose the Selection tool (V), then click a Live Paint group.

2. Click the **Gap Options** button 🔲 on the Control panel. The Gap Options dialog opens.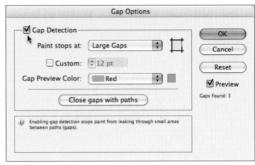

3. Check Preview, then do any of the following:

   Make sure **Gap Detection** is checked, then from the **Paint Stops At** menu, choose a gap size (say you want to close some existing gaps), or check Custom and enter a specific gap size (.01–72 pt). With our menu set to Large Gaps,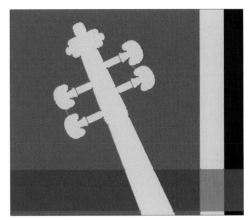 we are able to draw lines freely, as well as fill faces.

   From the **Gap Preview Color** menu, choose a preview color for the invisible (nonprinting) gap "lines" that stop paint leakage. You can also click the color swatch and choose a color from the Colors dialog. The gap lines display onscreen in a selected Live Paint group while the Gap Options dialog is open, or when View > Show Live Paint Gaps is on.

   Click the **Close Gaps with Paths** button to have Illustrator close up any existing gaps with edge segments (click Yes in the alert dialog). This may improve the processing time.

4. Click OK. If you increased the gap size, try using the Live Paint Bucket tool to fill areas that couldn't be filled before.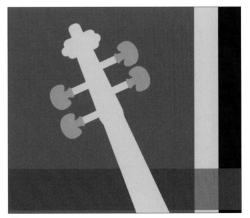 Colors will still leak from gaps that are larger than the gap size you specified.

MINIMIZE THE GAP

The more you allow lines to intersect in the original objects, the fewer gaps there will be when the objects are converted to a Live Paint group. You can delete or apply a stroke of None to any overhanging edges.

A Choose Gap Options to control color leakage in your Live Paint groups.

B The Paint Stops At: Large Gaps option is chosen. The gaps preview in the current Gap Preview Color.

C With the Large Gaps option chosen, we were able to fill the small- to medium-sized gaps in the open areas.

Expanding and releasing Live Paint groups

You can't apply appearances (such as brush strokes, transparency settings, or effects) selectively to individual parts of a Live Paint group; you have to expand or release it into ordinary Illustrator objects first. A Live Paint group may also need to be expanded or released before it can be exported to a non-Adobe application. Use these commands when you're done editing the group.

To expand or release a Live Paint group:

1. Using the Selection tool or the Layers panel, select a Live Paint group. *Optional:* Option-drag/Alt-drag the group to preserve a copy of it for future edits.

2. Do either of the following:

   On the Control panel, click **Expand** to convert the Live Paint group into an ordinary group containing two new groups.**A** The former faces will become filled paths in one group,**B** and the former edges will become paths with strokes in the other group.

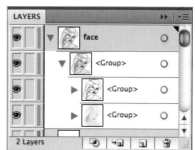

A The Expand command produced two nested groups.

Choose Object > Live Paint > **Release** to convert the Live Paint group to separate paths, each with a .5-pt. black stroke and a fill of None (not in a group). Use this option if, say, you want to start your sketch over with just linework, and you want to remove all the fill colors first.

➤ After applying the Expand command, you can apply stroke or fill attributes, such as a brush stroke or an effect, to the resulting paths.**C**

B We expanded the Live Paint group, then hid the <Group> layer that contains the stroked paths. Now only the filled paths are visible.

C Finally, we applied a .3-pt. brush stroke to the group of stroked paths to make the line work look more hand drawn.

EXPANDING A LIVE PAINT GROUP: FORMER PENCIL PATHS COMPARED WITH FORMER BLOB BRUSH STROKES ★

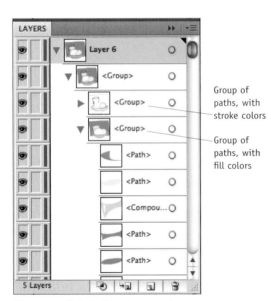

Group of paths, with stroke colors

Group of paths, with fill colors

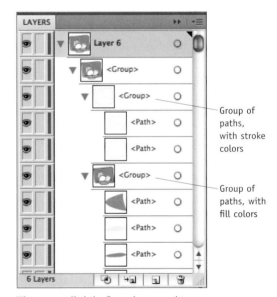

Group of paths, with stroke colors

Group of paths, with fill colors

When we applied the Expand command to a Live Paint group that was created with the Pencil tool, the result was two standard nested groups. The former edges became a group of stroked paths, and the former faces became a group of filled paths, as shown on the Layers panel.

When we applied the Expand command to a Live Paint group that was created with the Blob Brush tool, the result was also two nested groups. The former faces became a group of filled paths. We had applied color to only two edges in the Live Paint group, so only two stroked paths resulted when the group was expanded, as shown on the Layers panel.

The type controls in Illustrator are extensive, and worthy of the two chapters that we have devoted to them. You will create four kinds of type in this chapter: point type, type in a rectangle, area type (inside an object), and type along a path. You will also rotate type, import type from another application, thread type between objects, copy type and a type object, convert type into graphic outlines, and put type on a circle. In the next chapter, you will select type and change its attributes.

The type tools

There are three horizontal type tools: the Type tool, Area Type tool, and Type on a Path tool; and three vertical type tools: the Vertical Type tool, Vertical Area Type tool, and Vertical Type on a Path tool. With the exception of the versatile Type and Vertical Type tools, each tool has a specialized function.

➤ With the **Type** tool, T you can create a free-floating block of type that isn't associated with a path; **A** draw a rectangle with the tool and enter type inside the rectangle; enter type along the edge of an open path; or enter type inside a closed path.

➤ The **Area Type** tool T creates type inside an open or closed path. Lines of type that are created with this tool automatically wrap inside the path. **B**

➤ The **Type on a Path** tool ✎ creates a line of type along the outer edge of an open or closed path. **C**

➤ The **Vertical Type** tool ❘T has the same function as the Type tool, except that it creates vertical type.

➤ The **Vertical Area Type** tool ❘T creates vertical type inside an open or closed path.

➤ The **Vertical Type on a Path** tool ❘✎ creates vertical type along the outer edge of an open or closed path. **D**

CREATE TYPE

19

IN THIS CHAPTER

The type tools 231

Creating point type 232

Creating type in a rectangle. 233

Creating area type 234

Creating path type 235

Rotating type 237

Importing text. 238

Threading type 239

Copying and moving type 241

Creating type outlines. 242

Exercise: Put type on a circle 243

B Type created with the Area Type tool

The Area Type tool enters type into a path of any shape. The Area Type tool enters type into a path of any shape. The Area Type tool enters type into a path of any shape. The Area Type

The Type tool creates point type or type inside a rectangle.

A Type created with the Type tool

The Type on a Path tool enters type along a path.

C Type created with the Type on a Path tool

THE VERTICAL PATH TYPE

D Type created with the Vertical Type on a Path tool

Creating point type

Point type stands by itself—it's neither inside an object nor along a path. This kind of type is most suitable for small amounts of text that stand independently, such as headlines, titles, or labels for buttons.

To create point type:

1. Choose the **Type** tool **T** (T) or **Vertical Type** |**T** tool.

2. Click a blank area of an artboard where you want the type to start (don't click an object). A flashing insertion marker appears.

3. Enter type. Press Return/Enter each time you want to start a new line.

4. To complete the type object, do either of the following: **A**

   Click a selection tool on the Tools panel (don't use the keyboard shortcut to select it), then click outside the type block to deselect it.

   To keep the type tool selected so you can create another type object, either click the type tool or Cmd-click/Ctrl-click outside the type block to deselect it (a temporary selection tool).

➤ To align separate blocks of point type, use the align buttons on the Control panel or the Align panel (see pages 101–102).

➤ If you open a file (into Illustrator CS4) that contains text from a pre-CS version of Illustrator, an alert dialog appears, offering choices for updating the older, legacy text.

CHOOSE TYPE ATTRIBUTES BEFORE?

If you want to choose character and paragraph attributes for your type before creating it, you can do any of the following: choose from a variety of settings on the Character and Paragraph panels; choose font, point size, and paragraph alignment settings from the Control panel; or click a paragraph style on the Paragraph Styles panel. You'll learn about these panels in the next chapter.

Recolor after?

➤ When you enter type inside an object or along a path, a fill and stroke of None is applied to the object automatically. After entering type, if you want to apply fill and/or stroke colors to the type object, deselect it, click the edge of the object with the Direct Selection tool, then choose a color.

➤ To recolor the type itself, select it first with a type tool or a selection tool.

I don't know the key to success, but the
key to failure is trying to please everybody.

— *Bill Cosby*

A This point type was created with the Type tool.

Creating type in a rectangle

In the instructions below, you'll draw a rectangle, then enter type inside it. On the next page, you'll learn how to enter type inside an existing object of any shape.

To create type in a rectangle:

1. Choose the **Type** tool **T** (T) or **Vertical Type** ❗**T** tool.

2. Drag to create a rectangle (or Shift-drag to draw a square). When you release the mouse, a flashing insertion marker will appear.

3. Enter type.**A** The type will wrap automatically to fit into the rectangle. Press Return/Enter only when you need to create a new paragraph.

4. Do either of the following:

   Choose a selection tool on the Tools panel (don't use a keyboard shortcut to select the tool), then click outside the type block to deselect it.

   To keep the type tool selected so you can create another type object, either click the type tool or Cmd-click/Ctrl-click outside the type block to deselect it (a temporary selection tool).

   Note: If the overflow symbol ⊞ appears on the edge of the rectangle, it means the rectangle isn't large enough to display all the type. If you want to reveal the hidden type, click the object with the Selection tool, then drag a handle on its bounding box (View > Show Bounding Box). The type will reflow to fit the new shape. You can also reshape the object with the Direct Selection tool.**B** A third option is to thread the overflow type into another object; see page 239.

➤ If you drag to define an area with the Vertical Type tool, then enter type, the type will flow from top to bottom and from right to left.

➤ To create vertical type with the Type tool or horizontal type with the Vertical Type tool, hold down Shift, start dragging to create a rectangle, release Shift, then continue dragging to complete the rectangle; enter text.

'It spoils people's clothes to squeeze under a gate; the proper way to get in, is to climb down a pear tree.'

— *Beatrix Potter*

A Drag with the Type tool to create a rectangle, then enter type. To see the edges of the rectangle, choose Outline view or use Smart Guides with its Object Highlighting option.

'It spoils
    people's
      clothes to
        squeeze
          under a
            gate; the
              proper
                way to
                  get in,
                    is to climb
                      down a
                        pear tree.'

B This type rectangle was reshaped with the Direct Selection tool.

NO GOING BACK

➤ Once you place type inside or along a graphic object, it becomes a permanent type object; it can be converted back into a graphic object only via the Undo command. To preserve the original graphic object, Option-drag/Alt-drag it to copy it first.

➤ You can't enter type into a compound path, a mask object, a mesh object, or a blend, nor can you make a compound path from a type object.

➤ If you add type along a path that contains a brush stroke, the brush stroke is removed.

Creating area type

When you use the Area Type or Vertical Area Type tool to place type inside a path of any shape or inside an open path, the object is converted to a type object.

To enter type inside an object:

1. *Optional:* If you want to preserve the original object, drag-copy it.

2. To enter type in a closed path, choose the **Area Type** tool, [T] **Vertical Area Type** tool, [T] or either one of the **Type** tools (T or !T). Or to enter type inside an open path, choose either one of the Area Type tools.

3. Click precisely on the edge of the path. A flashing insertion marker appears, and any fill or stroke on the object is removed. The object is now listed as <Type> (not <Path>) on the Layers panel.

4. Enter type in the path, or copy and paste text from a text-editing application into the path. The text will stay inside the object and conform to its shape. **A–B** Vertical area type flows from top to bottom and from right to left.

   ► To make the type fit symmetrically within the object, choose a relatively small point size. On the Paragraph panel, check Hyphenate and click the Align Center button or one of the Justify alignment buttons.

5. Do either of the following:

   Choose a selection tool, then click outside the type object to deselect it.

   To keep the type tool selected (so as to enter type in another object), Cmd-click/Ctrl-click away from the type block to deselect it, release Cmd/Ctrl, then click the next type object; or click the tool that you used to enter the type.

   Note: To recolor the new type, see "Recolor After?" in the sidebar on page 232.

   ► The Area Type Options, which control the position of type inside a type object, are discussed on page 264.

SWITCHEROO

► To rotate vertical area type characters, select only the characters to be rotated. On the Control panel, click Character, then from the Character panel menu, choose Standard Vertical Roman Alignment to uncheck that option.

► To rotate horizontal or vertical type characters on a custom angle, see page 237.

This is text in a copy of a light bulb shape. You can use the Area Type tool to place type into any shape you can create. When fitting type into a round shape, place small words at the top and the bottom. This is text in a copy of a light bulb shape. You can use the Area Type tool to place type into any

A Area type

The kiss of memory made pictures of love and light against the wall. Here was peace. She pulled in her horizon like a great fish-net. Pulled it from around the waist of the world and draped it over her shoulder. So much of life in its meshes! She called in her soul to come and see.
ZORA NEALE HURSTON

B Type in a circle

Creating path type

Follow these instructions to place type along the inner or outer edge of a path. Type can't be placed on both sides of the same path, but it can be moved from one side of the path to the other after it's created.

To place type along an object's path:

1. Choose the **Type on a Path** ✎ or **Vertical Type on a Path** tool, ✎ then click the edge of a closed or open path.**A** Or choose the Type **T** or Vertical Type **!T** tool, then click an open path. The path can be selected, but it doesn't have to be.

2. When the flashing insertion marker appears, enter type. Don't press Return/Enter. The type will appear along the edge of the object, and the object will now have a fill and stroke of None.**B**

3. Do either of the following:

   Choose a selection tool (or hold down Cmd/Ctrl), then click outside the type object to deselect it.

   If you want to use the same type tool on another path, click the tool again.

➤ To adjust the spacing (kerning value) between letters, see page 252.

To reposition type on a path:

1. Choose the **Selection** tool ▶ (V) or **Direct Selection** ▶ tool (A).

2. Click on the type (not the path). Center, left, and right brackets will appear.**C**

3. As you do any of the following, be sure to drag the bracket (the vertical bar)—not the little square. If your tool switches to a type tool, choose a selection tool and try again.

   Drag the center bracket to the left or right to reposition the type block along the path.

   Drag the left bracket **D–E** to reposition the starting point of the type on the path. Or drag the right bracket back across the existing type (this will shorten the amount of type that's visible on the path and may produce a type overflow). For right-aligned type, do the opposite of the above.

   To flip the type to the opposite side of an open path, drag the center bracket perpendicularly across the path.

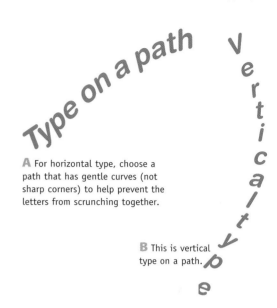

A For horizontal type, choose a path that has gentle curves (not sharp corners) to help prevent the letters from scrunching together.

B This is vertical type on a path.

The icons shown below appear next to the pointer when it's moved over a bracket on a selected type path.

C The left, center, or right brackets display for path type when it's selected with the Selection or Direct Selection tool.

D The left bracket is dragged to the right.

E The mouse is released.

Via the Type on a Path Options dialog, you can quickly change the shape, orientation, and alignment of type on a path. Moreover, the settings are editable and reversible.

To apply options to path type:

1. Choose the Selection tool, then click type on a path. The more curvy the path, the more obvious the option changes will be.

2. Choose Type > Type on a Path > **Type on a Path Options**. The dialog opens.

3. Check Preview.

4. Do any of the following:

   From the **Effect** pop-up menu, choose Rainbow, Skew, 3D Ribbon, Stair Step, or Gravity.**A**

   Choose **Align to Path**: Ascender, Descender, Center, or Baseline to specify which part of the text touches the path.**B** Baseline is the default setting.

   Check (or uncheck) **Flip**.

   Choose or enter a new letter **Spacing** value (–36 to 36). To avoid a text reflow, we recommend either leaving this option at the default value of 0 or changing it in very small increments.

5. Click OK. If you want to change or reverse any of the settings you've chosen, simply reselect the object and reopen the dialog.

➤ To adjust the spacing between characters, see page 252.

➤ The type effects can also be applied individually via the Type > Type on a Path submenu.

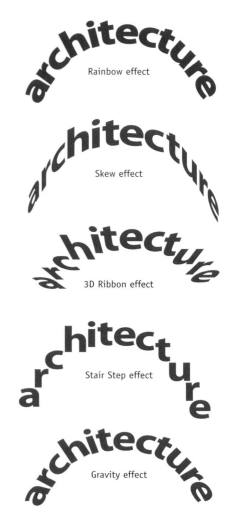

Rainbow effect

Skew effect

3D Ribbon effect

Stair Step effect

Gravity effect

A The Type on a Path effects change the shape and spacing of characters on a path.

Ascender

Center

Descender

Baseline

B Align to Path options

Rotating type

To rotate type characters at a custom angle:

1. Select a type object with the Selection tool, or select a type character or characters with a type tool.

2. Show the expanded Character panel **A** (Cmd-T/Ctrl-T); click the ✿ on the panel tab, if necessary. Choose or enter a positive or negative **Character Rotation** value.✿ **A**

➤ After rotating type, you may need to adjust the spacing between the characters (see page 252).

To make a whole horizontal type block vertical, or vice versa:

1. Choose the Selection tool,▶ then click a type object.

2. Choose Type > Type Orientation > **Horizontal** or **Vertical**.

A The orange letter was rotated 15°.

TRANSFORMING TYPE

To rotate type as in the numbers on the tickets shown below, use one of the tricks you learned in Chapter 11 (e.g., manipulate an object's bounding box or use the Free Transform tool).

➤ One way to create a "grunge" effect like this is by drawing strokes with the Paintbrush tool. For the tool, choose the Chalk Brush (in the Artistic_ChalkCharcoalPencil library) and a stroke color that's similar to the background.

➤ Use the Rainbow effect to produce curved type (see the preceding page).

➤ To carve the corners off a rectangle, place small circles in front of it, then use the Minus Front command on the Pathfinder panel (see page 316).

Importing text

The Place command lets you import text files in the following formats into an Illustrator document: plain text, ASCII (with the filename suffix .txt); Rich Text Format (.rtf); or Microsoft Word (.doc or .docx). The text will appear in a new rectangle.

Note: To enter text onto or into a custom path, first place it by following the instructions on this page, then copy and paste it onto or into the path (see "To move type from one object to another" on page 241).

To import text:

1. Choose File > **Place**.

2. In the Place dialog, locate and click the text file to be imported, then click Place.

3. If you selected a Microsoft Word or RTF file, the Microsoft Word Options dialog opens.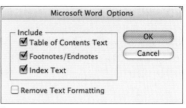 For a plain text format file, the Text Import Options dialog opens.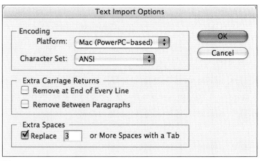 Decide which options you want included. For Microsoft Word or RTF text, if you want to preserve any text styling, be sure to leave Remove Text Formatting unchecked. The plain text format (called Text Only, in Microsoft Word) removes formatting and styling.

4. Click OK. The imported text will appear in a rectangle in the center of the current artboard.**C** To restyle it, see the next chapter. To thread overflow type, see the next page.

A For text in Microsoft Word or RTF format, choose settings in the Microsoft Word Options dialog.

B For text in the plain text format, choose settings in the Text Import Options dialog.

Let us spend one day as deliberately as Nature, and not be thrown off the track by every nutshell and mosquito's wing that falls on the rails. Let us rise early and fast, or break fast, gently and without perturbation; let company come and let company go, let the bells ring and the children cry,— determined to make a day of it. Why should we knock under and go with the stream? Let us not be upset and overwhelmed in that terrible rapid and whirlpool called a dinner, situated in the meridian shallows.

— *Henry David Thoreau*

C The placed text appears in a rectangle.

Threading type

Before you start threading (linking) your overflow text between text objects, consider this simple solution: If your type object is almost—but not quite—large enough to display all the type on or inside it, you can enlarge the object to reveal the hidden type by doing either of the following:

➤ Click the type block with the Selection tool (choose View > Show Bounding Box if the box isn't visible), then drag a handle on the bounding box.

➤ Deselect the type object, click the edge of the rectangle—not the type—with the Direct Selection tool (use Smart Guides with Object Highlighting to locate the rectangle), then Shift-drag a segment.

If your type overfloweth, you can spill, or thread, it into a different object or into a copy of the same object. Text can be threaded between different kinds of type objects, such as between path objects and area type objects.

To thread overflow type to another object:

1. Choose the Selection tool ▶ (V).

2. Select the original type object.

3. Click the **Out** port ⊞ on the selected object. The pointer becomes a Loaded Text pointer. **A**

4. Do either of the following:

   To create a new object to contain the overflow text, either click where you want a duplicate of the currently selected object to appear, or drag to create a rectangular type object. **B–C**

   Position the pointer over the edge of an existing object (the pointer changes to ▶⊞), then click the object's path. A fill and stroke of None will be applied to the path.

5. Overflow type flows from the first object into the second one. Deselect the objects.

➤ If you double-click an Out port with the Selection tool, a linked copy of the text object is created automatically.

NOT ALL IS COPIED

If you click to create a duplicate of a type object (step 4 on this page), only the object's shape is copied, not its fill and stroke attributes or area type options. To copy the fill and stroke attributes afterward, choose the Direct Selection tool, click the edge of the duplicate object, choose the Eyedropper tool (I), then click the background of the original text object. Before you click with the eyedropper, make sure the pointer doesn't have a little "t" in it.

In port

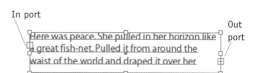

Out port

A To thread text, first click the Out port with the Selection tool...

Here was peace. She pulled in her horizon like a great fish-net. Pulled it from around the waist of the world and draped it over her

B ...then drag (or click) elsewhere with the Loaded Text pointer.

Here was peace. She pulled in her horizon like a great fish-net. Pulled it from around the waist of the world and draped it over her

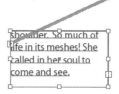

—*Zora Neale Hurston*

C The overflow type spills from the first object into the second, in the direction shown by the thread arrowheads.

Are you curious to see what's threaded to what? Display the text threads (the arrows that reveal the link from one text object to another).

To reveal the text threads:

Select a linked type object. If the thread lines aren't visible, choose View > **Show Text Threads** (Cmd-Shift-Y/Ctrl-Shift-Y). Note: The stacking order of type objects on the Layers panel has no effect on how text flows from one object to another.

When you unthread two objects, the chain is broken and the overflow text gets sucked back into the first object of the two. The path objects are preserved.

To unthread two type objects:

1. Choose the Selection tool ▶ (V), then click a threaded type object.

2. Do either of the following:

   Double-click the object's In port or Out port. **A–B**

   Click an In port or Out port, move the pointer slightly if you want to see the unthreading cursor, 🖑 then click the port a second time to cut the thread.

Follow these instructions if you want to keep the remaining links intact as you release just one object from a series of threaded obejcts. The type reflows into the remaining objects.

To release an object from a thread and preserve the remaining threads:

1. Choose the Selection tool (V), then click the type object to be released. **C**

2. Do either of the following:

   To unthread the object but preserve it, choose Type > Threaded Text > **Release Selection. D**

   To unthread the type object by deleting it, press Delete/Backspace.

➤ To disconnect all the objects from a text thread while keeping the type in its present objects, click one of the objects with the Selection tool, then choose Type > Threaded Text > Remove Threading.

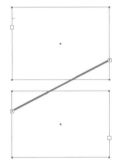

A When the Out port is double-clicked...

B ...that type object becomes unthreaded.

C The middle type object is selected...

D ...and then released from the thread.

Copying and moving type

One way to copy or move type, with or without its object, is by using the Clipboard, a temporary storage area in memory. The Clipboard commands are Cut, Copy, and Paste. You can copy type between Illustrator files, or from an Illustrator file to a Photoshop file. (For another way to copy a type object, see pages 98–99.)

To copy type and its object between files:

1. With the Selection tool ► (V), click the type object to be copied.

2. Choose Edit > **Copy** (Cmd-C/Ctrl-C).

3. Do either of the following:

   Click the tab for another Illustrator document, then choose Edit > **Paste** (Cmd-V/Ctrl-V). The type and its object appear.

   Launch Photoshop and click in a Photoshop document window, choose Edit > **Paste** (Cmd-V/Ctrl-V), click Smart Object in the Paste dialog, then click OK. The type and object will appear as imagery on a new Smart Object layer (see page 408).

➤ When a threaded text object is copied, only that single object and the text it contains are copied.

To move type from one object to another:

1. Choose the Type tool **T** (T) or Vertical Type **IT** tool.

2. Select (drag across) the type to be moved. Or to move all the text in a thread, click in one of the objects, then choose Select > All (Cmd-A/Ctrl-A).

3. Choose Edit > **Cut** (Cmd-X/Ctrl-X). **A** The object you cut the type from will remain a type object.

4. Do either of the following:

   Cmd-click/Ctrl-click the object the type is to be pasted into or onto, **B** then click the edge of the object. A blinking insertion marker appears. (Or to create path type, Option-click/Alt-click the object.)

   Cmd-click/Ctrl-click a blank area of the artwork, then drag to create a type rectangle.

5. Choose Edit > **Paste** (Cmd-V/Ctrl-V). **C**

Let us spend one day as deliberately as Nature. Let us spend one day as deliberately as Nature, and not be thrown off the track by every nutshell and mosquito's wing that falls on the rails.

A Type is selected, then Edit > Cut is chosen to put it onto the Clipboard.

B A path is clicked.

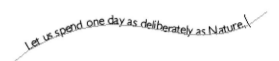

Let us spend one day as deliberately as Nature.

C Cmd-V/Ctrl-V is pressed, and the contents of the Clipboard appear on the path.

Creating type outlines

The Create Outlines command converts each character in a type object into a separate graphic object. As outlines, the paths can then be reshaped, used in a compound or as a mask, or filled with a gradient, like nontype objects.

To create type outlines:

1. Create type using any type tool. All the characters in the object or on the path will be converted, so enter only the text to be converted.

2. Once the type is converted into outlines, unless you undo the conversion immediately, you won't be able to change the font, apply other typographic attributes, or convert the outlines back to type, so we recommend duplicating the type object.

3. Choose the Selection tool (V), then click a character or the baseline. **A**

4. Do either of the following:

   Choose Type > **Create Outlines** (Cmd-Shift-O/Ctrl-Shift-O). **B–C**

   Control-click/right-click the object and choose **Create Outlines** from the context menu.

   The fill and stroke attributes and any appearances from the original characters will be applied to the outlines. If the type was formerly along or inside an object, the object will be preserved as a separate path—unless it formerly had a stroke and fill of None, in which case the object will be deleted.

   You can now reshape the points and segments on each path (see Chapter 12). If you converted multiple characters, double-click the group to put the resulting paths in isolation mode first.

➤ Each former type character becomes a separate compound path when converted to outlines. See the last tip on page 323.

A The original type object is selected.

B The type is converted to outlines.

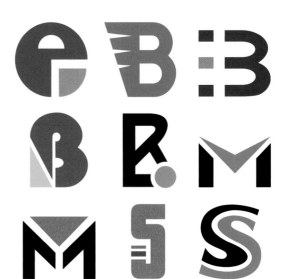

C Logos like these can be produced from type outlines.

LET THE CONVERTER BEWARE

The Create Outlines command is invaluable when you need to shape custom characters. Also, outlines can be printed from any application without printer fonts, which are required for printing "real" type. However, you should avoid creating outlines from small type, for several reasons: The command removes the hinting information that preserves character shapes for printing; second, outline shapes are slightly heavier than their nonoutline counterparts, which makes the characters less legible (especially if a stroke color is applied); and third, outlines increase the file size.

EXERCISE: Put type on a circle

Create the type

1. Deselect all, click Document Setup on the Control panel, choose Units: Inches, then click OK.

2. Using the Control panel, choose a fill color of None and a dark green stroke color.

3. Choose the Ellipse tool ⬭ (L), then click on an artboard to open the Ellipse dialog.

4. Enter "3" in the Width field, click the word Height, then click OK.**A**

5. Double-click the Scale tool.⬚ Enter "68" in the Uniform: Scale field, then click Copy. Deselect.

6. Choose the Type on a Path tool.↗

7. On the Control panel, click Character to open a temporary Character panel. Enter "28" in the Font Size field* and choose the Stencil font from the Font menu.

8. Click the top of the inner circle, then type the desired text (to copy our example, type "RECYCLED 100%"; press the Spacebar; to type an en dash in the Mac OS, press Option- – (hyphen), or in Windows, hold down Alt and enter 0150 on the number pad; then press the Spacebar again. Enter the same type and dash again without the last space).**B** Don't deselect.

9. With the Selection tool ▸ (V), drag the center bracket (it's near the bottom of the circle) along the outside of the small circle to reposition the type so that the dashes are on the top and bottom of the circle.**C** Note that the left and right

Continued on the following page

> ### DON'T SPACE OUT!
>
> ► If you press the Spacebar to access a temporary Hand tool when an insertion cursor is in a type block (a type tool is selected), you'll end up adding spaces to your text instead of moving the artwork in the window. Worse yet, if type is selected, you'll end up replacing your text with spaces. Instead, to acccess a temporary Hand tool, press Cmd/Ctrl, then add the Spacebar, release Cmd/Ctrl, then drag with the Spacebar still held down. Practice this until you get the hang of it.
>
> ► And another thing: When editing type, keep track of the pointer. If it's in a panel field, you will end up editing panel values instead of your type.

If you use the Stencil Std Bold font instead of the Stencil font, make the Font Size 24 pt.

A Create a circle.

B Create a smaller copy of the circle by using the Scale dialog, then add path type along the edge of the circle (the circle now has a stroke of None).

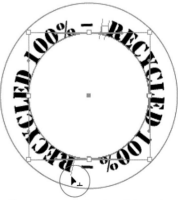

C Drag the center bracket of the path type to position the dashes at the top and bottom of the circle.

brackets are practically on top of each other near the starting point of the type. Don't move the left bracket over the right bracket or you may cause a text overflow.

Refine the type

1. Choose the Direct Selection tool ↖ (A). Click the large circle path. On the Appearance panel, click the Stroke listing, then click the up arrow to set the stroke to 5 pt.

2. Click the smaller circle path. Double-click the Stroke color square on the Appearance panel. On the temporary Swatches panel, choose the same dark green as on the large circle. Click the up arrow to set the stroke to 5 pt. 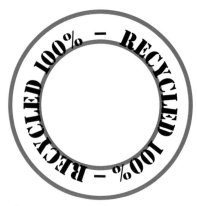**A**

3. Choose the Selection tool (V) and click on the type. Display the Character panel.**A** Increase the Baseline Shift value to center the type between the circles (we used a value of 7 pt.). If necessary, increase the Tracking value to space the type and the two dashes evenly.**B**

4. On the Color panel, click the fill square, then on the Swatches panel, apply the same dark green color to the type. (Don't apply a stroke color.)

5. Select both the circles by clicking on the large circle then Shift-clicking on the small circle. Choose Object > Group (Cmd-G/Ctrl-G).

6. *Optional:* To produce the artwork shown in **C** do the following:

   On the Layers panel,🌐 click the New Layer button to create a new layer.

   Display the Symbols panel.♣ From the Symbol Libraries menu at the bottom of the panel, choose Logo Elements. From the library panel, drag the Watercolor Leaf symbol into the middle of the circles. With the Selection tool, Shift-drag a corner handle of the symbol's bounding box to scale the symbol to fit within the small circle (choose View > Show Bounding Box if the box is hidden).

   On the Layers panel, click in the edit column for the symbol layer to lock the layer.

7. With no type selected, set both the Baseline Shift and the Tracking values on the Character panel back to the default value of 0 for any future type.

A Apply the same green color and the same stroke weight to the smaller circle.

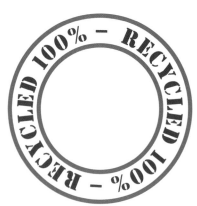

B Use the Baseline Shift and Tracking controls to adjust the type, and apply the same green.

C For the inner graphic, we dragged the Trees 1 symbol from the Nature library into the small circle and scaled it to fit.

In the preceding chapter, you learned how to create type; now you can reformat and refine it. The first step is to learn how to select type, the type object, or both. Once you've mastered those skills, you will use the Character and Control panels to change typographic attributes (such as the font and font size); the Glyphs and OpenType panels to insert special characters; the Paragraph panel to apply paragraph formats (such as alignment); the Paragraph Styles and Character Styles panels to apply collections of attributes quickly; and the Tabs panel to align columns of text. Finally, you will learn how to wrap type around an object; apply appearance attributes; and perform a few exercises.

Selecting type

Before type can be modified, it must be selected. On the next two pages, we'll show you how to select type with the following tools:

➤ The Selection tool selects both the type and the object that contains it.**A**

➤ The Direct Selection tool selects just the type object, or both the type object and the type.**B**

➤ The type tools select just the type, not the type object.**C**

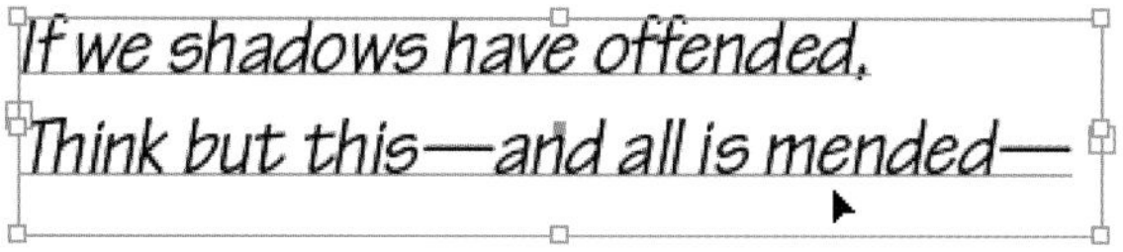

If we shadows have offended,
Think but this—and all is mended—

A Type and its object are selected with the Selection tool.

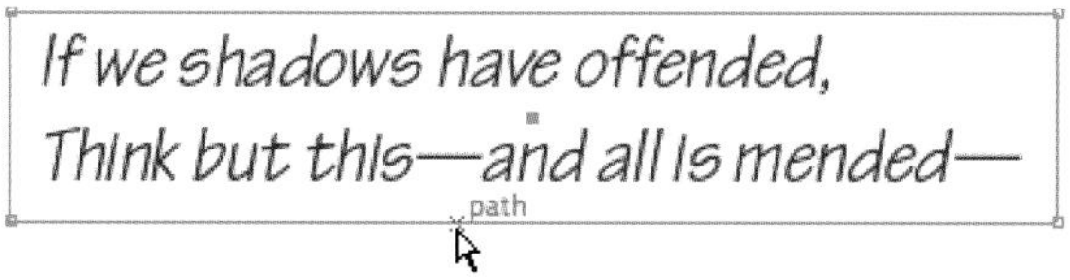

If we shadows have offended,
Think but this—and all is mended—
path

B A type object (but not the type) is selected with the Direct Selection tool.

If we shadows have offended,
Think but this—and all is mended—

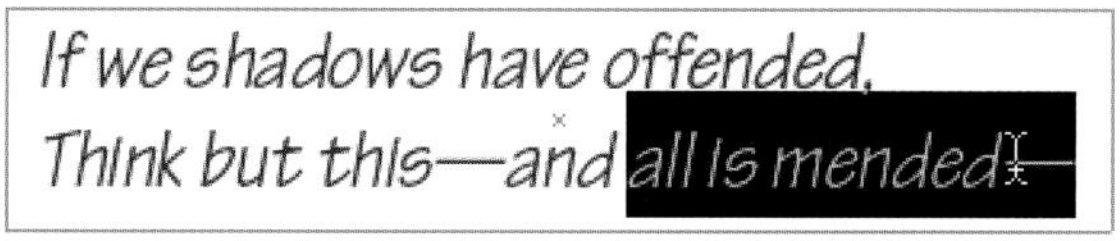

— *William Shakespeare*

C Type (but not the object) is selected with the Type tool.

20

Use the selection method described on this page if you're planning to move, transform, restyle, or recolor all the type in or on a type object. To reshape or recolor a type object (but not the type), use the first selection method on the next page instead. Or to edit, restyle, or recolor just some of the type in a block, use the second method on the next page.

To select type and its object:

1. Choose the **Selection** tool ▶ (V).

2. Turn on Smart Guides (Cmd-U/Ctrl-U), and make sure Object Highlighting is on in Illustrator/Edit > Preferences > Smart Guides.

3. For area type (inside an object):

   If the object contains a fill other than None, you can click anywhere on the object: the fill,* a character, the baseline, or the outer path. If the object doesn't contain a fill, click the type **A** or click the path of the type object (use Smart Guides to locate it).**B**

   For point or path type:

   Click on the type; **C** for path type, you can also click the path.

   If the bounding box feature is on (View > Show Bounding Box), a bounding box will surround the object.

QUICK-SELECT A TYPE TOOL

If you double-click a type character in a type object with the Selection or Direct Selection tool, the Type tool (or Vertical Type tool) becomes selected and an insertion point appears where you clicked.

APPLYING COLORS TO TYPE

When type is selected with the Selection tool or a Type tool, you can use the Color and Swatches panels to apply a fill and stroke color — simple. But to produce more creative display type, you need to work with the Appearance panel; see pages 270–272.

---

*If we shadows have offended,
Think but this—and all is mended—*

A To select type and its object, click right on the type...

*If we shadows have offended,
Think but this—and all is mended—*
path

B ...or click the path of the type object.

*If we shadows have offended,
Think but this—and all is mended—*

C Point type is selected.

---

*Provided Type Object Selection by Path Only is unchecked (the default setting) in Illustrator/Edit > Preferences > Type.

Use this selection method if you want to recolor or reshape just the type object.

To select a type object but not the type:

1. Choose the **Direct Selection** tool ▸ (A).
2. Click the edge of an area or path type object (use Smart Guides with Object Highlighting to locate it).**A** Any modifications you make now will affect only the type object—not the type.**B**

Use this selection method to select just the type—not the object—so you can edit the text, change its character or paragraph settings (Character or Paragraph panel), or change its fill, stroke, or opacity settings (Appearance panel).

To select type but not its object:

1. Choose any **type** tool.
2. Do any of the following:

   For horizontal type, drag horizontally with the I-beam cursor to select and highlight one or more words or a line of type.**C** For vertical type, drag vertically.

   For horizontal type, drag vertically to select whole lines of type. For vertical type, drag horizontally to select whole lines.

   Double-click to select a word.

   Triple-click to select a paragraph.

   Click in a text block or on a text path, then choose Select > All (Cmd-A/Ctrl-A) to select all the type in the block or path, plus any overflow type.

   Click to start a selection, then Shift-click where you want it to end. (Shift-click again, if desired, to extend the selection.)

3. Do either of the following:

   After modifying the type:

   If you want to do further editing, click in the type block to create a new insertion point.

   To deselect the type object, Cmd-click/Ctrl-click outside it.

➤ After recoloring type with text characters highlighted, to see how the new color looks, choose a selection tool.

INSERTING AND DELETING CHARACTERS

➤ To add characters to an existing type block, choose a type tool, click to create an insertion point, then start typing.

➤ To delete one character at a time, choose a type tool, click to the right of the character to be deleted, then press Delete/Backspace. Or to delete multiple characters, select them with a type tool, then press Delete/Backspace.

A The type object is selected; the type is not.

B The type object is reshaped and recolored.

C Two words are selected.

The Character, Paragraph, and Control panels

Next, we'll briefly introduce the Character, Paragraph, and Control panels, then show you how to use them to apply type attributes. Later in this chapter, we'll show you how to use the Character Styles and Paragraph Styles panels to apply collections of attributes quickly.

The **Character** panel A lets you modify the font, style, font size, kerning, leading, and tracking values for one or more selected text characters.A To access this panel quickly, press Cmd-T/Ctrl-T; or if a type object is selected, you can open it temporarily by clicking Character on the Control panel. To expand the panel to access horizontal scale, baseline shift, vertical scale, character rotation, underline, strike-through, and language options, choose Show Options from the panel menu or click the up/down arrow ⬍ on the panel tab.

The **Paragraph** panel ¶ lets you modify paragraph attributes, such as alignment and indentation.B To access this panel quickly, press Cmd-Option-T/Ctrl-Alt-T; or if a type object is selected, you can open it temporarily by clicking Paragraph on the Control panel. To expand the panel to access the Space Before Paragraph, Space After Paragraph, and Hyphenate options, choose Show Options from the panel menu or click the up/down arrow ⬍ on the panel tab.

In addition to providing access to temporary Character and Paragraph panels, the **Control** panel offers font, font size, and basic alignment controls for type.

➤ We find it convenient to store our Character and Paragraph panels as icons, so they're out of the way when we don't need them, yet readily accessible when we do.

A On the Character panel, as on other panels, you can use tool tips to identify features.

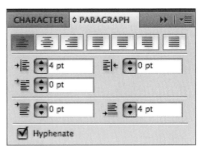

B Options on the Paragraph panel affect whole paragraphs.

PANEL SHORTCUTS

You can use the following shortcuts when entering values on the Character and Paragraph panels:

Apply a value and highlight the next field	Tab
Apply a value and highlight the previous field	Shift-Tab
Apply a value and exit the panel	Return/Enter
Display the Character panel and highlight the Font field	Cmd-Option-Shift-M/ Ctrl-Alt-Shift-M

Here is a quick summary of the basic methods for selecting type: to change the paragraph attributes of all the text in a type object or on a path, click the object or path with the Selection tool; or to change the attributes of one or more characters, words, or consecutive paragraphs, drag through them with a type tool.

Changing the font

For an easy but dramatic change to the appearance of your type, change its font and font style.

To change fonts:

1. Do either of the following:

   Choose any type tool, then select the type to be modified.

   Choose the Selection tool, then click a type object.

2. Do either of the following:

   Control-click/right-click the type and choose a font from either the **Font** submenu **A–B** or the **Recent Fonts** submenu on the context menu.

   On the **Character** panel **A C** or the **Control** panel, **D** choose a font from the **Font** menu and a style from the **Font Style** menu.

➤ To choose a font quickly, press Cmd-Option-Shift-M/Ctrl-Alt-Shift-M to highlight the Font field on the Character panel, then type the first few characters of the desired font name. The name with the closest spelling match appears in the field. Press Tab to proceed to the Font Style field, start typing the desired style name, then press Return/Enter to exit the panel.

➤ To have font families display in the actual typeface (WYSIWYG) on all the Font menus in Illustrator, go to Illustrator/Edit > Preferences > Type, check Font Preview, and choose Small, Medium, or Large for the display Size.

If you create mockups for Web pages, you might find the underline feature to be useful.

To apply underline or strikethrough styling:

1. Choose a type tool, then select some type.

2. On the **Character** panel (with its full options displaying), click the **Underline ⊥** button or the **Strikethrough ⊤** button. **E** (To remove the styling, click the same button again.)

A Select the type to be modified, then choose a font from the context menu.

B We changed the font and font style from Myriad Pro Regular to Gill Sans Bold.

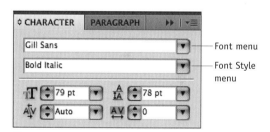

C The Character panel has two font controls.

D The Font and Font Style controls are also available on the Control panel.

You must learn to be <u>still</u> in the midst of activity and to be vibrantly ~~alive~~ in repose.

—*Indira Gandhi*

E You may find an occasional use for the Underline and Strikethrough options.

Changing the font size

You can change the font (point) size of individual characters or words, or of all the type in an object.

To change the font size:

1. Do either of the following:

   Choose any type tool, then select the type to be modified.

   Choose the Selection tool (V), then click the type object.

2. Do one of the following:

   On the **Character** panel **A** or the **Control** panel, enter the desired size in the **Font Size** field **A** (you don't need to reenter the unit of measure). You can also choose a preset size from the Font Size menu; or click the up or down arrow; or click in the Font Size field, then press the up or down arrow on the keyboard.

   ➤ If the selected type contains more than one font size, the Font Size field will be blank, but the new size you choose will apply to all of it. If you're using the Character or Control panel, you can press Return/Enter to apply the new value and exit the panel, or press Tab to apply the value and highlight the next field.

   Hold down Cmd-Shift/Ctrl-Shift and press > to enlarge the font size or < to reduce it.**B** The type will resize according to the current Size/Leading value in Preferences > Type; the default increment is 2 pt. To change the font size by five times the current Size/Leading value, hold down Cmd-Option-Shift/Ctrl-Alt-Shift and press > or <.

   Control-click/right-click the type and choose a preset size from the **Size** submenu on the context menu. (Choosing Other from the context menu highlights the Font Size field on the Character panel.)

   ➤ You can use the Horizontal Scale controls on the Character panel to make type wider (extend it) or narrower (condense it), or the Vertical Scale controls to make it taller or shorter. (Actually, it's better to use a typeface that has those characteristics by design, such as Helvetica Narrow and Gill Sans Condensed, which will have more balanced proportions.) If you do use the scale controls, to keep the distortion to a minimum, raise or lower the percentage by just a few points (e.g., 104% or 98%). (See also "Restoring the default scale values" at right.)

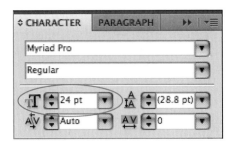

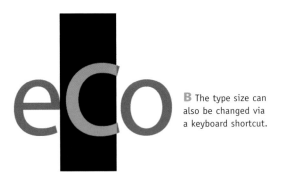

A Change the point size of type by using the Font Size controls on the Character or Control panel.

B The type size can also be changed via a keyboard shortcut.

RESTORING THE DEFAULT SCALE VALUES

To reset the Horizontal Scale and Vertical Scale to the default value of 100%, select the type or type object in question, then press Cmd-Shift-X/Ctrl-Shift-X.

SCALING TYPE INTERACTIVELY

To scale point or path type by dragging, select it first with the Selection tool, and make sure the bounding box is visible (if it's not, press Cmd-Shift-B/Ctrl-Shift-B). Drag a handle on the box, or Shift-drag it to scale the type proportionally. You can also scale a type object by using the Scale tool.

Changing the leading

Leading is the distance from baseline to baseline between lines of type, and is traditionally measured in points. Each line of type can have a different leading value. (To adjust the spacing between paragraphs, see page 259.)

Note: To change the vertical spacing in vertical type, change its horizontal tracking value (see the next page). In vertical type, leading controls the horizontal spacing between vertical columns.

To change the leading of horizontal type:

1. Do one of the following:

   To change the leading of an entire block of type, click it with the Selection tool.

   To change the leading of all the lines in a paragraph, select it with a type tool (triple-click in the paragraph).

   To change the leading of an entire line of type, drag across it with a type tool, making sure to include any spaces at the end of the line.

2. Do either of the following:

   On the **Character** panel,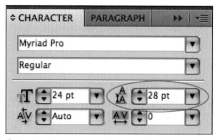 enter a **Leading** value;**A–C** or choose a preset leading value from the Leading menu; or click the up or down arrow.

   Hold down Option/Alt and press the up arrow on the keyboard to decrease the leading or the down arrow to increase it, according to the Size/Leading increment, which is set in Illustrator/Edit > Preferences > Type (the default is 2 pt.). To change the leading by five times the current Size/Leading increment, hold down Cmd-Option/Ctrl-Alt as you press an arrow.

➤ With Auto chosen on the Leading menu, the leading will be calculated as a percentage of the largest font size on each line. The default Auto Leading percentage of 120% can be changed in the Justification dialog, which opens from the Paragraph panel menu.

A On the Character panel, enter a Leading value, or click the up or down arrow, or choose a preset value from the menu.

> How can one conceive of a one-party system in a country that has over 200 varieties of cheese?

B This 12-pt. type has loose, 18-pt. leading.

> How can one conceive of a one-party system in a country that has over 200 varieties of cheese?
>
> — *Charles de Gaulle*

C This 12-pt. type has tight, 13-pt. leading.

Applying kerning and tracking

Kerning is the addition or removal of space between pairs of adjacent characters. Kerning values for specific character pairs (e.g., an uppercase "T" next to a lowercase "a") are built into all fonts. The built-in kerning values are usually suitable for small text, such as body type (see the sidebar on this page), but not for large type, such as headlines and logos. You can remedy any awkward spacing in large type by applying manual kerning values. To kern a pair of characters, you will insert the cursor between them first.

Tracking is the adjustment of spacing between three or more selected characters. On occasion, you might apply tracking to a whole line of type, or on a very rare occasion, to a whole paragraph or block.

To apply manual kerning or tracking:

1. Do either of the following:

    Zoom in on the type to which kerning or tracking is to be applied. Choose a type tool, then either click to create an insertion point between two characters for kerning, or highlight a range of text for tracking.

    To track (not kern) all the type in an object, choose the Selection tool, then click the object.

2. Do either of the following:

    In the **Kerning** or **Tracking** area on the Character panel, A A enter a positive value to add space between the characters or a negative value to remove space; B–D or choose a preset value from the menu; or click the up or down arrow.

    Hold down Option/Alt and press the right arrow on the keyboard to add space between letters or the left arrow to remove space, based on the current Tracking value in Illustrator/Edit > Preferences > Type. To kern or track by a larger increment, hold down Cmd-Option/Ctrl-Alt as you press an arrow.

➤ Tracking/kerning changes the vertical spacing of characters in vertical type.

➤ To undo manual kerning for selected characters (or with your cursor between a pair of characters), reset the Kerning value in the Character panel to 0 (zero).

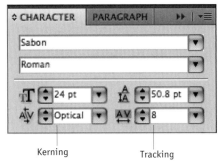

Kerning   Tracking

A Use the kerning and tracking controls to refine the letter spacing.

Simone

B The original type contains no manual kerning or tracking.

Simone

C We tightened the spacing between the first two characters in this word via kerning,...

Simone

D ...then tightened the spacing between the last five characters via tracking.

THE AUTO KERNING OPTIONS

Illustrator offers a choice of three kinds of automatic (nonmanual) kerning on the Kerning menu on the Character panel:

➤ Auto (or "metrics" kerning), the default method, is applied to new or imported text based on the information for character pairs (such as To, Ta, We, Wo, and Yo) that is built into each font.

➤ Metrics-Roman only ★ uses the same built-in kerning data as Auto, but applies it only to text that is set in Roman (e.g., non-Asian) language fonts.

➤ Optical is a good choice for text set in a font that has inadequate or no built-in kerning, or that contains multiple typefaces or font sizes. Illustrator will adjust the spacing between adjacent characters as it sees fit.

The Fit Headline command uses tracking values to quickly fit a one-line paragraph of horizontal or vertical area type to the edges of its object.

To fit type to its container:

1. Choose any type tool.

2. Select or click in a single-line paragraph of area type (not a line within a larger paragraph). **A**

3. Choose Type > **Fit Headline**. **B**

➤ If you scale a type object that the Fit Headline command was applied to, you will need to reapply the Fit Headline command afterward.

FIT HEADLINE

A The cursor is inserted into a line of type.

FIT HEADLINE

B The Fit Headline command added space between the characters to fit the line of type to the full width of the object.

WORD AND LETTER SPACING SETTINGS

To change the horizontal word or letter spacing for justified paragraphs, choose Justification from the Paragraph panel menu, then in the Justification dialog, change the Minimum, Desired, and Maximum values for Word Spacing or Letter Spacing. The Desired setting also affects nonjustified paragraphs. (Tip: Try reducing the word spacing for large type.) Glyph Scaling (50%–200%) affects the width of all characters.

Ocean
Body more immaculate than a wave,
salt washing away its own line,
and the brilliant bird
flying without ground roots.

Normal word and letter spacing

	Minimum	Desired	Maximum
Word Spacing:	80%	100%	133%
Letter Spacing:	0%	0%	0%

Ocean
Body more immaculate than a wave,
salt washing away its own line,
and the brilliant bird
flying without ground roots.

Loose letter spacing

	Minimum	Desired	Maximum
Word Spacing:	80%	100%	133%
Letter Spacing:	5%	10%	20%

Ocean
Body more immaculate than a wave,
salt washing away its own line,
and the brilliant bird
flying without ground roots.

Tight word spacing

	Minimum	Desired	Maximum
Word Spacing:	70%	70%	100%
Letter Spacing:	0%	0%	0%

Using smart punctuation

The Smart Punctuation command converts applicable text (listed under "What to type" in the sidebar at right) to professional typesetting characters, when available in the current font. You can apply the command to just selected text or, even better, to the entire document. If you want to set yourself apart from the amateurs, use this feature and typographers quotes (discussed next)! Notes: To set ligatures and expert fractions in an OpenType font, use the OpenType panel (see page 256). The Smart Quotes option in the Smart Punctuation dialog overrides the current Double Quotes and Single Quotes settings in the Document Setup dialog.

To create smart punctuation:

1. To change all the type in your document, don't select anything; **A** or with a type tool, select the text to be smart punctuated.

2. Choose Type > **Smart Punctuation**.

3. Check the desired **Replace Punctuation** options, **B** and click Replace In: **Selected Text Only** (see step 1) or **Entire Document**.

4. *Optional:* Check Report Results to have a list of your changes appear onscreen after you click OK.

5. Click OK. **C**

To specify quotation marks for future type:

1. Deselect, then click **Document Setup** on the Control panel (Cmd-Option-P/Ctrl-Alt-P).

2. Under Type Options, check **Use Typographers Quotes** and choose the **Language** the text is going to be typeset in. The standard Double Quotes and Single Quotes marks for that language will display on the two menus.

3. Click OK.

THE SMART PUNCTUATION OPTIONS

Option in the Smart Punctuation dialog	What to type	The result
ff, fi, ffi Ligatures	ff, fi, ffi	ff, fi, ffi
ff, fl, ffl Ligatures	ff, fl, ffl	ff, fl, ffl
Smart Quotes	' "	' " " '
Smart Spaces (one space after a period)	. T	. T
En (dashes)	--	–
Em Dashes	---	—
Ellipses	...	…

> "We are living in a world today where lemonade is made from artificial flavors and furniture polish is made from real lemons."
>
> -- *Alfred E. Newman*

A Dumb punctuation: Straight quotation marks, double hyphens instead of dashes, and no ligatures. Bad, bad, bad.

B Check the desired Replace Punctuation options in the Smart Punctuation dialog.

> "We are living in a world today where lemonade is made from artificial flavors and furniture polish is made from real lemons."
>
> — *Alfred E. Newman*

C Smart punctuation: Smart quotation marks, a single dash, and ligatures (the "fi" in "artificial" and the "fl" in "flavors"). To hang punctuation, see page 266.

Inserting alternate glyphs

The OpenType font format was developed jointly by Adobe and Microsoft to help prevent font substitution and text reflow problems when transferring files between platforms. Fonts names that include the word "Pro" have an expanded character set.**A** The OpenType format also allows for a wide range of stylistic variations, called glyphs, for any given character in a specific font (sounds like something in *The Hobbit*!). For each individual character in an OpenType font, you can choose from an assortment of alternate glyphs, such as ligatures, swashes, titling characters, stylistic alternates, ordinals, and fractions. You can insert alternate glyphs manually by using the Glyphs panel (instructions below) or automatically by using the OpenType panel (see the next page). The Glyphs panel isn't just used for OpenType fonts, though—you can also use it to locate and insert characters in non-OpenType fonts.

To replace or insert a glyph using the Glyphs panel:

1. Choose a type tool, then select a character or click in the text to insert the text cursor.

2. Display the **Glyphs** panel **Aa** (choose Glyphs from the Type menu or from the Window > Type submenu). If you selected a character in the previous step, it will be highlighted on the panel.

3. From the **Show** menu,**B** choose a category of glyphs to be displayed on the panel: Alternates for Current Selection,**C** Entire Font, Access All Alternates, or a specific category. The category choices will vary depending on the current font and whether you selected a character or merely created an insertion point.

4. Double-click a glyph to insert or to use as a replacement for the selected character; or if the square containing the currently highlighted glyph has a mini arrowhead in the lower right corner, click the arrowhead and choose a glyph from the menu. The chosen glyph will appear in your text.

➤ To change the display size of the glyphs on the Glyphs panel, click the Zoom Out or Zoom In button in the lower right corner.

➤ A different font and font style can be chosen from the menus at the bottom of the panel.

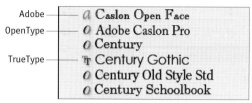

A With Font Preview checked in Preferences > Type, a unique symbol displays for each font type on the Font menu on the Character panel.

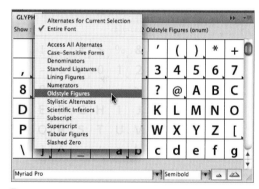

B Choose from the Show menu on the Glyphs panel to control which categories of glyphs are displayed.

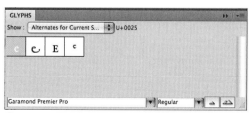

C In this Glyphs panel, the letter "e" is clicked for our chosen font and Alternates for Current Selection is chosen on the Show menu.

By using the OpenType panel, you can control whether alternate glyphs in an OpenType font will be substituted for standard characters automatically, where applicable. For example, you can choose to have a glyph for a properly formatted fraction be inserted automatically whenever you type fraction characters, such as ½ for 1/2 or ¾ for 3/4. Other options include ligature glyphs for specific letter pairs (such as ff, ffl, and st) and swash, titling, and other special characters.

To specify or insert alternate glyphs for OpenType characters:

1. Display the **OpenType** panel 𝒪 (Cmd-Option-Shift-T/Ctrl-Alt-Shift-T).**A**

2. Do either of the following:

   To change all applicable occurrences in existing text, either select a type object with the Selection tool or highlight one or more characters with a type tool.

   To specify alternate glyph options for future text to be entered in an OpenType font, choose a type tool, then choose from the font menu on the Control or Character panel. The Pro fonts offer the widest assortment of glyph options.

3. Click any of the available buttons on the panel.**B–C** The choices will vary depending on the glyph set of the current font.

➤ The Figure menu on the OpenType panel controls the style and spacing of numerals. The Tabular options, which insert an equal amount of spacing between numerals, are designed to properly align columns of numerals in a table. The Proportional options allow for variable spacing based on the actual width of each numeral character, and improve the appearance of nontabular numerals. Oldstyle numerals are beautiful, but have variable heights, so they're appropriate only in special design settings.

➤ If a chosen font lacks a true superscript, superior, subscript, or inferior glyph, or doesn't contain nonstandard fractions (such as 5/25), you can use options on the Position menu on the OpenType panel to produce the desired "faux" glyph: ⁵⁄₂₅.

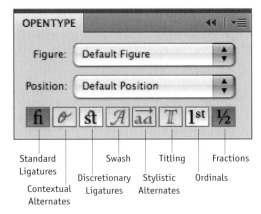

A The OpenType panel lets you control which categories of alternate glyphs will replace standard characters in current or future text.

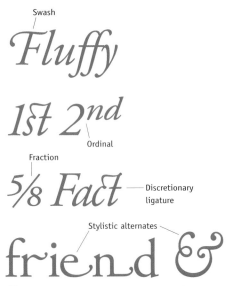

B The OpenType panel inserts alternate characters like these.

1ˢᵗ	Available
1ˢᵗ	Selected
1ˢᵗ	Not available

C The buttons on the OpenType panel have three states.

Applying hyphenation

The auto Hyphenate option affects only currently selected or subsequently created text.

To hyphenate text and choose hyphenation options:

1. *Optional:* To hyphenate or change the hyphenation settings for existing text, select it with a type tool or the Selection tool.

2. On the **Paragraph** panel,¶ with its full set of options showing, check **Hyphenate**.

3. If you want to choose hyphenation options, choose **Hyphenation** from the Paragraph panel menu. In the Hyphenation dialog,**A** check Preview.

4. In the **Words Longer Than [ ] Letters** field, enter the minimum number of characters a word must contain in order to be hyphenated (3–25). We usually enter a value of 6 or 7.

   In the **After First [ ] Letters** field, enter the minimum allowable number of characters to precede a hyphen (we use a value of 3 or 4).

   In the **Before Last [ ] Letters** field, enter the minimum allowable number of characters that can be carried over to the next line following a hyphen (we use a value of 3 here, too).

   In the **Hyphen Limit** field, enter the maximum allowable number of hyphens in a row (0–25). When there are more than two hyphens in a row, the text can be hard to read—and it looks ugly, too.**B**

   Or for a less calculated approach to achieving the desired number of line breaks (try this on existing text), simply move the **Hyphenation Zone** slider toward Better Spacing or Fewer Hyphens.

   Finally, decide whether you want Illustrator to **Hyphenate Capitalized Words** (preferably not).

5. Click OK.

➤ In Preferences > Hyphenation, you can confirm the default language for hyphenation, enter hyphenation exceptions, and even specify how particular words are to be hyphenated.

OUR FAVORITE COMPOSER

On the Paragraph panel menu, you have a choice of two line-composer options for selected type, or for future type when no type is selected:

➤ Adobe Every-line Composer (the option we strongly prefer) examines all the lines within a paragraph and adjusts line lengths and endings to optimize the overall appearance of the paragraph.

➤ Adobe Single-line Composer adjusts line breaks and hyphenation of each line, without regard to other lines or the overall paragraph.

Always examine your hyphenated text, and if necessary, correct any awkward breaks manually.

GIMME NO BREAK

To prevent a particular word from breaking at the end of a line, such as a compound word (e.g., "Single-line"), to reunite an awkwardly hyphenated word (e.g., "sex-tuplet"), or to keep related words together (e.g., "New York City"), select the word or words, then from the Character panel menu, choose No Break.

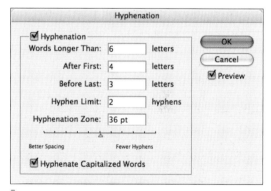

A Set parameters for hyphenation in the Hyphenation dialog.

AN
OVER-
ABUN-
DANCE
OF HY-
PHENS
MAKES
FOR TIR-
ING
READ-
ING.

B Granted, this is an extreme example, but it makes the point.

Changing paragraph alignment

Before learning how to apply alignment, indentation values, and other paragraph formats, you need to know what a paragraph is, at least as far as Illustrator is concerned. To start a new paragraph as you enter a block of text (or to create a paragraph break where your cursor is inserted in existing text), press Return/Enter. Every paragraph ends with one of these hard returns.

➤ To reveal the nonprinting symbols for paragraph endings, ¶ soft returns, ↵ spaces, ▪ and tabs, ➡ choose Type > Show Hidden Characters (Cmd-Option-I/Ctrl-Alt-I).

Note: To create a soft return (line break) within a paragraph in nontabular text in order to bring text down to the next line, press Shift-Return.

To change paragraph alignment:

1. Do either of the following:

   Choose a type tool, then click in a paragraph or drag through a series of paragraphs.

   Choose a selection tool, then click a type object.

2. Do either of the following:

   Display the **Paragraph** panel ¶ (Cmd-Option-T/Ctrl-Alt-T, or click **Paragraph** on the **Control** panel), then click an **alignment** button. **A–B** The first three alignment options (Left, Center, and Right) are also available as buttons on the Control panel.

   Use one of the keyboard shortcuts listed in the sidebar on this page.

➤ Don't bother applying any of the justify alignment options to point type (type that's not inside an object), because it doesn't have outer edges for the type to justify to.

SHORTCUTS FOR PARAGRAPH ALIGNMENT

	Mac OS	Windows
Left	Cmd-Shift-L	Ctrl-Shift-L
Center	Cmd-Shift-C	Ctrl-Shift-C
Right	Cmd-Shift-R	Ctrl-Shift-R
Justify Last Left	Cmd-Shift-J	Ctrl-Shift-J
Justify All (including the last line)	Cmd-Shift-F	Ctrl-Shift-F

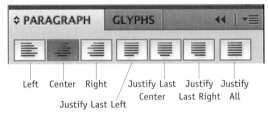

Left   Center   Right   / Justify Last   Justify   Justify
                          Center   Last Right   All
         Justify Last Left

A Click a paragraph alignment button on the Paragraph panel.

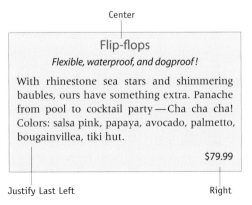

B A few of the paragraph alignment options are shown above.

Changing paragraph indentation

You can apply left and first-line indentation values to area type and point type, and also apply a right indentation value to area type.

To change paragraph indentation:

1. Do either of the following:

   Choose a type tool, then select the paragraph(s) to be modified or click to create an insertion point in a single paragraph.

   Choose a selection tool, then click a type object.

2. On the **Paragraph** panel,¶ do either of the following:

   Change the **Left Indent** and/or **Right Indent** value, then press Return/Enter or Tab;**A–B** or click the up or down arrow; or click in the field, then press the up or down arrow on the keypad. Note: These values also affect any lines that follow a soft return, which always belong to the preceding paragraph.

   To indent only the first line of each paragraph, enter a positive **First-Line Left Indent** value.

Changing inter-paragraph spacing

Use the Space Before Paragraph field or the Space After Paragraph field on the Paragraph panel to add or subtract space between paragraphs. (To adjust the spacing between lines of type within a paragraph, use leading, which is discussed on page 251.)

To adjust the spacing between paragraphs:

1. Select the type to be modified: To modify the space before only one paragraph in a type block, select the paragraph with a type tool; or to change all the type in an object, click the object with the Selection tool.

2. In the **Space Before Paragraph** or **Space After Paragraph** field on the extended **Paragraph** panel,¶ **A** enter a positive value to move paragraphs farther apart or a negative value to bring them closer together (press Return/Enter or Tab to apply),**C** or click the up or down arrow.

➤ Keep in mind that the Space Before Paragraph value combines with the Space After Paragraph value from the paragraph above, so you could wind up with more space between paragraphs than you intend. The simplest approach, when adding space between paragraphs, is to enter a positive value for one of the two features and leave the other value at zero.

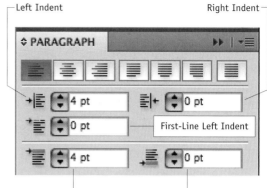

Left Indent · Right Indent

First-Line Left Indent

Space Before Paragraph · Space After Paragraph

A The Paragraph panel has many indent and spacing options.

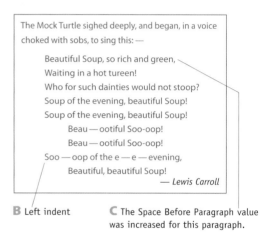

The Mock Turtle sighed deeply, and began, in a voice choked with sobs, to sing this: —

Beautiful Soup, so rich and green,
Waiting in a hot tureen!
Who for such dainties would not stoop?
Soup of the evening, beautiful Soup!
Soup of the evening, beautiful Soup!
Beau — ootiful Soo-oop!
Beau — ootiful Soo-oop!
Soo — oop of the e — e — evening,
Beautiful, beautiful Soup!
— *Lewis Carroll*

B Left indent   **C** The Space Before Paragraph value was increased for this paragraph.

CREATING A HANGING INDENT

To create a hanging indent, enter a positive Left Indent value and a negative First-Line Left Indent value. Press Tab to align the second column of text.

Bene.:	Pray thee, sweet Mistress Margaret, deserve well at my hands by helping me to the speech of Beatrice.
Marg.:	Will you then write me a sonnet in praise of my beauty?
Bene.:	In so high a style, Margaret, that no man living shall come over it; for, in most comely truth, thou deservest it.
Marg.:	To have no man come over me? Why, shall I always keep below stairs?
Bene.:	Thy wit is as quick as the greyhound's mouth; it catches.

— *William Shakespeare*

Using paragraph and character styles

Now that you know how to style type manually by using the Paragraph and Character panels, you're ready to learn how to format type by using character and paragraph styles, which allow you to achieve the same goal with much less sweat. If you use a word processing or layout program, you may already be familiar with the general concept. In addition to making typesetting easier, type styles also help ensure consistent formatting across multiple artboards or even related documents.

A paragraph style is a collection of paragraph formats, such as leading and indentation, plus character attributes, such as the font and font size. When you click a paragraph style, all currently selected paragraphs are reformatted with the attributes in that style.**A**

A character style contains only character attributes, and is normally used to accentuate or reformat select characters or words within a paragraph (such as bullets, or boldfaced or italicized words), not whole paragraphs. Character styles are applied in addition to paragraph styles—they're the icing on the cake.

To create, modify, and apply type styles, you will use the Paragraph Styles and Character Styles panels.

To create a paragraph or character style:

1. Display the **Paragraph Styles** or **Character Styles** panel (Window > Type submenu).**B** If this is your first foray into styles, we recommend working with paragraph styles first.

2. This is the easy way: Apply the attributes to be saved in the style to some text. With a type tool, click in the type, then Option-click/Alt-click the **New Style** button at the bottom of the Paragraph Styles or Character Styles panel.

3. An options dialog opens. Change the default **Style Name** to a descriptive one that will help you remember the style's function (such as "Subheads" or "Body Indent").

4. Click OK. To apply styles, see the next page.

➤ To create a variation on an existing style, drag the existing one to the Create Style button, then for the duplicate style that you have just created, follow the instructions on page 262. The two Normal styles can't be duplicated.

There is something that comes home to one now and perpetually ▲ It is not what is printed or preached or discussed.... ▲ It eludes discussion and print. ▲ It is not to be put in a book.... ▲ It is not in this book ▲ It is for you whoever you are ▲ It is no farther from you than your hearing and sight are from you ▲ It is hinted by nearest and commonest and readiest.... ▲ It is not them, though it is endlessly provoked by them.... ▲ What is there ready and near you now?

—Walt Whitman

A paragraph style   A character style

A Use paragraph styles to format the main text (body, headers, subheads, etc.) and character styles to format special characters or words within a paragraph.

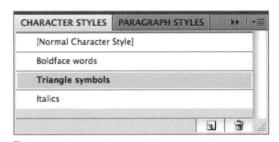

B Open the Character Styles and Paragraph Styles panel group.

To apply a type style:

1. For paragraph styling, click in or select a type object, or drag through some paragraphs in a type object.

   For character styling, select one or more type characters (not a whole object).

2. Click a style name on the **Paragraph Styles** or **Character Styles** panel. How easy was that?

   Note: If the text doesn't adopt all the attributes of the style sheet, see the next instructions.

▶ To choose a style for text before creating it, deselect all, click a style name on the Paragraph panel, then create your text.

A + (plus) sign after a style name on the Paragraph Styles or Character Styles panel signifies that the selected text contains attributes (overrides) that are not in the style definition. This will occur, for example, if you style some text manually after applying a style. If you want to force the text to match the exact attributes as defined in the applied style, you have to clear the overrides, as described below.

To remove overrides from styled text:

1. Select the characters or paragraphs that contain overrides to be removed. **A** Or to "fix" the whole object, select it with the Selection tool.

2. Hold down **Option/Alt** and click a name on the **Paragraph Styles** or **Character Styles** panel. **B** The manually applied attributes in your text will disappear, and the + sign will disappear from the style name on the panel. Note: See also the sidebar on this page.

There are two ways to edit a type style: by restyling a word or paragraph and then using it to redefine the style (this page), or by using the Paragraph or Character Style Options dialog (next page).

To edit a type style by redefining it:

1. Select a word or paragraph that has been assigned the style to be edited (the style name will become selected on the panel), and change any of its paragraph and/or character attributes manually by using the Paragraph, Character, Control, or Tabs panel.

2. Choose **Redefine Paragraph Style** from the **Paragraph Styles** panel menu or **Redefine Character Style** from the **Character Styles** panel menu. The style will update to reflect the custom styling in the selected text.

GEORGES BRAQUE (1882–1963)

There is only one **valuable** thing in art: the thing you cannot explain (as reported in *Saturday Review*, May 28, 1966).

A paragraph style   A character style

A The boldfacing for the word "valuable" was applied manually, so Illustrator considers it an override.

GEORGES BRAQUE (1882–1963)

There is only one valuable thing in art: the thing you cannot explain (as reported in *Saturday Review*, May 28, 1966).

B We selected the main paragraph, then Option/Alt clicked the paragraph style on the Paragraph Styles panel. This removed the boldfacing override, but not the character styling (for "Saturday Review").

WHAT IF...

If you unintentionally apply a character style to a whole type object and then apply a paragraph style, only the formats from the paragraph style will be applied, not the character attributes, and the override symbol [+] won't display next to the paragraph style name. To force a paragraph style to override a character style completely, select the type object, then click [Normal Character Style] on the Character Styles panel.

TWO KINDS OF OVERRIDES

When you Option-click/Alt-click a paragraph style to remove manual overrides, remember that to remove overrides from a character style, you'll have to Option-click/Alt-click that style, too.

To edit a type style via an options dialog:

1. Deselect all, then double-click a style name on the **Character Styles** or **Paragraph Styles** panel.

2. The Character Style Options or Paragraph Style Options dialog opens. **A** It contains multiple option sets, which are accessed by clicking in the list on the left side. Check Preview to preview the changes in your document as you edit the style definition:

   Click **Basic Character Formats** to choose basic character attributes, such as the font, font style, size, kerning, leading, and tracking.

   Click **Advanced Character Formats** to choose horizontal and vertical scaling, baseline shift, or rotation values.

   In the Paragraph Style Options dialog, you also have access to the **Indents and Spacing**, **Tabs**, **Composition** (composer and hanging punctuation options), **Hyphenation**, and **Justification** option sets.

   Click **Character Color**, click the fill (or stroke) square, then choose a fill (or stroke) color for

the type. Colors from the Swatches panel will be listed here. For a spot color, you can choose a Tint percentage. For the stroke, you can also choose a Weight.

Click **OpenType Features** to choose options to be applied if the style uses an OpenType font (see page 256).

➤ Click General at any time to display a combined, expandable list of all the settings in the style.

3. Click OK. All the type in your document to which the style is currently applied will update automatically.

➤ You can click Reset Panel in either style options dialog to clear all the settings in the current option set. A few nonnumeric options (such as Kerning) can be reset to a blank state (no value) by choosing "(Ignore)" from the menu.

➤ A dash/green background in a check box means that option won't override any attributes that were applied manually to text in the document.

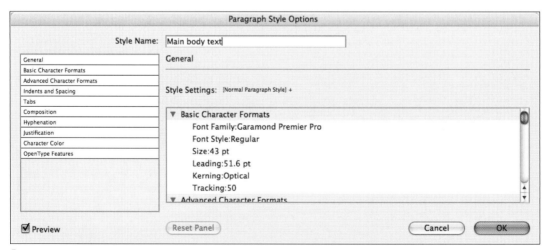

A The General option set of the Paragraph Style Options dialog merely lists all the attributes in the current style. Use the other option sets to edit the style.

When you delete a paragraph or character style, the text attributes don't change in the document—the text merely ceases to be associated with the style.

To delete a character or paragraph style:

1. Deselect all.

2. Do either of the following:

   Click a style name (or Cmd-click/Ctrl-click multiple style names) on the **Character Styles** or **Paragraph Styles** panel, then click the **Delete Selected Styles** button.

   Drag a style name over the **Delete Selected Styles** button.

3. If the style is being used in your document, an alert dialog appears; click Yes. You can't undo the deletion!

➤ You can't delete the Normal Paragraph Style or Normal Character Style.

➤ To delete all unused styles (styles that aren't assigned to any text in your document), choose Select All Unused from the panel menu before clicking the Delete Selected Styles button.

You can load paragraph and character styles from one file to another. If you're working on a series of documents for the same client, this is a good way to keep your type styling consistent.

To load type styles from another Illustrator document:

1. From the **Character Styles** or **Paragraph Styles** panel menu, choose one of the following:

   Load Character Styles.

   Load Paragraph Styles.

   Load All Styles to load both character and paragraph styles.

2. In the Select a File to Import dialog, locate and double-click the desired Illustrator document name; or click the document name, then click Open. Note: If an incoming style bears the same name as a style in the current document, it won't load.

Changing the offset values

By using the Area Type Options dialog, you can change the inset spacing between area type and the edge of its type object, or reposition the first line of type in a type object.

To change the offset values:

1. Select an area type object with a selection tool or type tool. **A**

2. Choose Type > **Area Type Options**.

3. In the Area Type Options dialog, **B** check Preview.

4. In the Offset area, choose an **Inset Spacing** value for the area between the type and the type object. **C**

5. To control the distance between the first line of type and the current inset, choose a **First Baseline** option. We usually use Ascent, Cap Height, or Fixed:

   Ascent to have the top of the tallest characters touch the top of the object.

   Cap Height to have uppercase letters touch the top of the object.

Leading to make the distance between the first baseline of text and the top of the object equal to the leading value.

x Height to have the top of the "x" character in the current font touch the top of the object.

Em Box Height to have the top of the em box in an Asian font touch the top of the object.

Fixed, then enter a Min value for the location of the baseline of the first line of text.

Legacy to use the method from previous versions of Illustrator.

Optional: Change the minimum baseline offset value in the Min field. Illustrator will use either this value or the First Baseline option value, whichever is greater.

6. Click OK.

➤ If you select an area type object and then reopen the Area Type Options dialog, the current settings for that type object will display, and can be edited.

The human race has one really effective weapon, and that is laughter.

— *Mark Twain*

A The type touches the edges of the object.

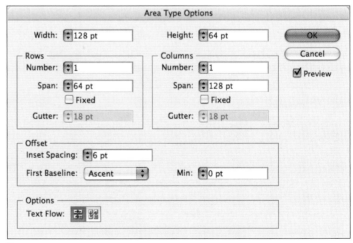

B You can use the Offset controls in the Area Type Options dialog to reposition type within an object.

The human race has one really effective weapon, and that is laughter.

— *Mark Twain*

C The Inset Spacing is changed to 6 pt.

Changing the baseline shift value

By using the Baseline Shift feature, you can shift characters upward or downward from their baseline or, for path type, from a path. Note: To shift whole lines of type, adjust the leading instead.

To shift type from its baseline:

1. Select the type characters to be shifted.**A**

2. Do either of the following:

   On the **Character** panel 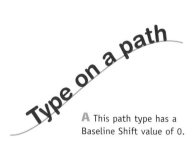 (with its full options displaying), enter a positive **Baseline Shift** value to shift characters upward or a negative value to shift them downward;**B–E** or choose a preset value from the menu; or click the up or down arrow.

   Hold down Option-Shift/Alt-Shift and press the up arrow on the keyboard to shift the characters upward or the down arrow to shift them downward, using the current Baseline Shift increment in Illustrator/Edit > Preferences > Type (2 pt is the default). Or use Cmd-Option-Shift/Ctrl-Alt-Shift with an arrow to shift the type by five times that increment.

➤ To access superscript and subscript characters in an OpenType font, use the OpenType panel.

➤ To change the Baseline Shift value quickly, click in the field, then press the up or down arrow on the keyboard.

A This path type has a Baseline Shift value of 0.

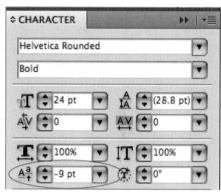

B The Baseline Shift feature shifts selected characters upward or downward.

C Now the type has a Baseline Shift value of –9 pt.

D The original artwork contains some type on a path.

E To move the type toward the inner circle, we shifted it downward by –7 pt.

Hanging punctuation

The Roman Hanging Punctuation command adds a professional typesetter's touch to your document by forcing punctuation marks that fall at the beginning and/or end of a line of area type to hang partially or fully outside the type block. This feature affects single and double quotation marks, hyphens, periods, commas, asterisks, ellipses, en dashes, em dashes, colons, semicolons, and tildes.

To hang punctuation:

1. With a type tool, select a paragraph in an area type object; or with a selection tool, select the whole object. Or to enable the feature for future type objects, deselect all.

2. From the **Paragraph** panel menu, choose **Roman Hanging Punctuation.A**

➤ For a more visually pleasing alignment of letters (not punctuation) at the beginning and/or end of lines in a type object, such as the letters "W," "O," or "A," select the object, then choose Type > Optical Margin Alignment. Some characters may shift slightly outside the block, but they will still print.

Setting tabs

The only way to align columns of text or numerals properly is by setting tabs—not by pressing the Spacebar. The default tab stops are half an inch apart. After inserting tabs in your text by following the instructions below, use the Tabs panel to change the alignment type or location of the tab markers, or to add an optional leader character (such as a repeating period in a table of contents).

To insert tabs into text:

1. Do either of the following:

    Press **Tab** once as you input copy, before typing each new column. The cursor will jump to the nearest default tab stop.**B**

    To insert a tab into existing text, click just to the left of the text that is to start a new column, then press **Tab** (just once!). The text will move to the nearest default tab stop.

2. To customize the tab settings, follow the instructions on the next page.

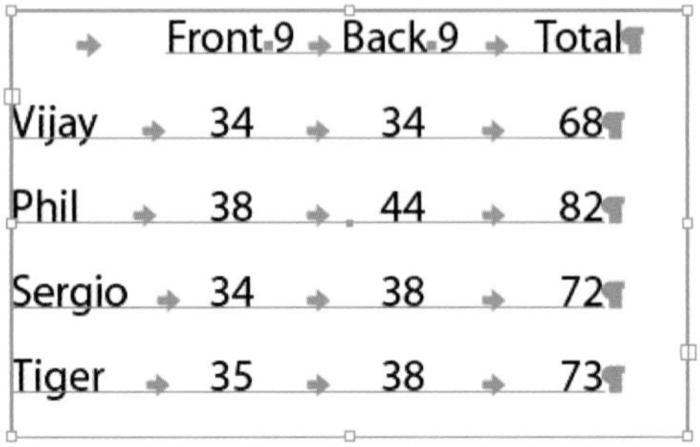

"Dining is and always was a great artistic opportunity."

— *Frank Lloyd Wright*

A Let it hang out, with Roman Hanging Punctuation.

→	Front·9 →	Back·9 →	Total¶
Vijay →	34 →	34 →	68¶
Phil →	38 →	44 →	82¶
Sergio →	34 →	38 →	72¶
Tiger →	35 →	38 →	73¶

B This text is aligned using tab stops. The nonprinting tab characters display when Type > Show Hidden Characters (Cmd-Option-I/Ctrl-Alt-I) is chosen.

To set or modify custom tab stops:

1. After following the preceding set of instructions, do either of the following:

   Choose the Selection tool, then click a text object.

   Choose a type tool and select some text.

2. Display the **Tabs** panel 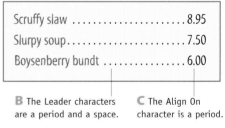 (Window > Type > Tabs or Cmd-Shift-T/Ctrl-Shift-T).**A**

3. If the panel is floating (not docked), you can click the **Position Panel Above Text** button to align the ruler with the left and right margins of the selected text for horizontal type, or the top and bottom margins for vertical type.

4. Do any of the following:

   To **insert** a new marker, click just above the ruler (the selected text will align to that stop), then with the marker still selected, click an alignment button in the upper left corner of the panel. Repeat to add more markers.

   ► Option-click/Alt-click a selected marker to cycle through the alignment types.

   To **delete** a marker, drag it off the ruler. Or to delete a marker and all markers to its right, Cmd-drag/Ctrl-drag it off the ruler.

   To **move** a tab marker, drag it to the left or right, or enter an exact location in the X field for horizontal type, or the Y field for vertical type. Cmd-drag/Ctrl-drag a marker to move that marker and all the markers to its right by the same distance.

5. *Optional:* Click a tab marker in the ruler, then in the Leader field, enter a character (or up to eight characters), such as a period, to be repeated between the tab and the succeeding text.**B**

   ► To change the attributes of the leader characters in your text, use a character style.

6. *Optional:* For the Decimal-Justified tab alignment option, in the Align On field, you can enter a character for the numerals to align to.**C** Unlike the Leader option, you must actually type the Align On characters in your text.

► To create a sequence of tab stops that are equidistant from one another, click one marker, then choose Repeat Tab from the panel menu. Beware! This command deletes all existing markers to the right of the one you clicked and inserts the new ones.

► The Tabs panel ruler units display in the increment specified in the Document Setup dialog.

► Choose Snap to Unit from the Tabs panel menu to have tab markers snap to the nearest ruler tick mark as you insert or move them. Or Shift-drag a marker to invoke the opposite behavior of the current Snap to Unit setting.

Scruffy slaw 8.95
Slurpy soup 7.50
Boysenberry bundt 6.00

B The Leader characters are a period and a space.

C The Align On character is a period.

Left-, Center-, Right-, and Decimal-Justified alignment buttons for horizontal type (or Top-, Center-, Bottom-, and Decimal-Justified buttons for vertical type)

Numeric location of the currently selected marker

Optional Leader character

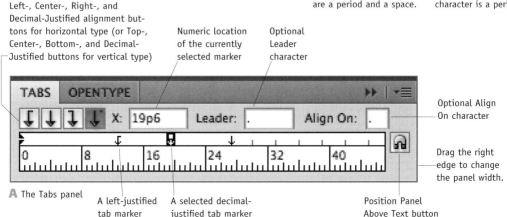

Optional Align On character

Drag the right edge to change the panel width.

A The Tabs panel

A left-justified tab marker

A selected decimal-justified tab marker

Position Panel Above Text button

Creating special effects with type

Type can wrap around an Illustrator path, an Illustrator type object, or a placed bitmap image.

To wrap type around an object:

1. Create area type (type inside an object). For the cleanest wrap, choose one of the justify alignment options for the type.

2. Follow this instruction carefully, or the wrap won't work: Make sure the object that the type is going to wrap around (we'll call it the "wrap object") is in front of the type to wrap around it, on the same top-level layer, sublayer, or group. You can use the Layers panel to restack the wrap object, if necessary. It can be a vector object, or a bitmap (placed) image that is surrounded by transparency.

3. Select the wrap object. **A**

4. Choose Object > Text Wrap > **Make**. If an alert dialog appears, click OK.

5. Choose Object > Text Wrap > **Text Wrap Options**. In the dialog, **B** click Preview, then enter or choose an **Offset** value for the distance between the wrap object and any type that wraps around it (start with just a few points). If the wrap object is a placed image, the type will wrap around opaque or partially opaque pixels in the image.

6. Click OK. **C** Try moving the wrap object slightly; the text will rewrap around it.

➤ To prevent a text object from being affected by the wrap object, via the Layers panel, restack it above the wrap object or to a different top-level layer.

➤ To change the Offset for an existing wrap object, select it, then choose Object > Text Wrap > Text Wrap Options to reopen the dialog. (In case you're wondering, the Invert Wrap option forces the text to wrap inside the path instead of outside it.)

To release a text wrap:

1. Select the wrap object (not the type).

2. Choose Object > Text Wrap > **Release**.

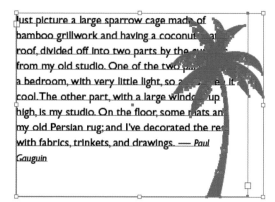

Just picture a large sparrow cage made of bamboo grillwork and having a coconut thatch roof, divided off into two parts by the curtains from my old studio. One of the two parts makes a bedroom, with very little light, so as to keep it cool. The other part, with a large window up high, is my studio. On the floor, some mats and my old Persian rug; and I've decorated the rest with fabrics, trinkets, and drawings. — *Paul Gauguin*

A Select the object that the area type is going to wrap around.

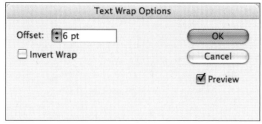

(Text Wrap Options dialog showing Offset: 6 pt, Invert Wrap unchecked, Preview checked, OK and Cancel buttons)

B In the Text Wrap Options dialog, enter an Offset value and check Preview to gauge the effect.

Just picture a large sparrow cage made of bamboo grillwork and having a coconut-thatch roof, divided off into two parts by the curtains from my old studio. One of the two parts makes a bedroom, with very little light, so as to keep it cool. The other part, with a large window up high, is my studio. On the floor, some mats and my old Persian rug; and I've decorated the rest with fabrics, trinkets, and drawings. — *Paul Gauguin*

C Now the type is wrapping around the palm tree.

EXERCISE: Create a shadow for point type

A drop shadow that you create using the following method (unlike the Effect > Drop Shadow command) will be an independent vector object, and can be modified with effects, the transform tools, and other techniques.

1. Create some large point type.

2. *Optional:* Select the type, then apply some positive tracking (Option-right arrow/Alt-right arrow).

3. With the Selection tool, select the type.

4. Apply a dark fill color and a stroke of None.

5. Option-drag/Alt-drag the type block slightly to the right and downward.

6. With the copy of the type block still selected, choose a lighter shade of the same color.

7. On the Layers panel, ▲ drag the copy of the type below the original, A and make sure it still has a selection square.

8. From the Add New Effect menu *fx.* on the Appearance panel, choose Ilustrator Effect > Stylize > Feather. Check Preview, choose a Radius value (try a low value of around 1–3 pt), then click OK. Next, click the Opacity link to open a temporary Transparency panel, and lower the opacity slightly. B

Slant the shadow

1. Make sure the shadow object is still selected.

2. Double-click the Shear tool ⬚ (on the Scale tool pop-out menu).

3. Enter "45" in the Shear Angle field, click Axis: Horizontal, then click OK.

4. Press arrow keys to align the baseline of the shadow text with the baseline of the original text. C

Reflect the shadow

1. Select the shadow type.

2. Double-click the Reflect tool ⬚ (on the Rotate tool pop-out menu), click Axis: Horizontal, then click OK.

3. With the Selection tool, drag the shadow type so its baseline meets the baseline of the original type. D

A Create a shadow, then stack it below the original type via the Layers panel.

B Apply the Feather effect and lower the opacity.

C Slant the shadow using the Shear tool.

D Reflect the shadow using the Reflect tool.

A DIFFERENT SLANT

After following steps 1–8 at left, use the Layers panel to select the shadow object, choose the Free Transform tool, then vertically scale the object by dragging its top center handle, or Cmd/Ctrl the handle to shear it. Or to reflect the shadow block with the same tool, drag the top center handle downward all the way across the object.

Applying appearance attributes to type

When applying attributes (e.g., an added fill, stroke, or effects) to editable type, it's important to understand the difference between selecting the type object and selecting the type characters. This is made clear by viewing the Appearance panel.

► When a type object is selected with the Selection tool, the word **Type** is listed in boldface at the top of the Appearance panel. For newly created and colored type, no Stroke or Fill listings will display.**A** Effects apply to the whole type object (both the fill and stroke) and are listed on the panel when the type object is selected.**B**

► If you highlight text characters with a type tool or double-click the word **Characters** on the Appearance panel, only the original Stroke, Fill, and Opacity attributes for those characters are listed on the panel.**C** (If you want to redisplay the attributes that apply specifically to the type object, click the word "Type" at the top.)

If you find this confusing, just remember that if the listing next to the color square at the top of the panel says "Characters," your edits will affect just the selected characters, whereas if it says "Type," your edits will affect all the type in the object.

► To apply transparency settings to the fill or stroke on type, see page 333.

A When type is selected with the Selection tool, "Type" is listed next to the color square on the Appearance panel.

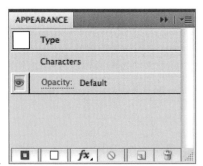

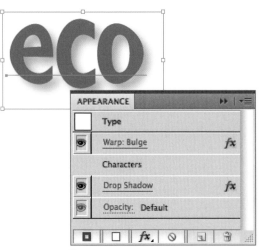

B Effects can be applied to a type object (not to type characters). The top listing on the Appearance panel is "Type."

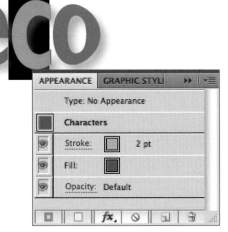

C When type is selected with a Type tool, "Characters" is listed next to the color square on the Appearance panel, and the Stroke and Fill colors (not the effect listing) display.

Next, we'll show you two ways to embellish type, to build on the skills you learned in Chapter 14.

EXERCISE: Add multiple strokes to a character

1. Create a type character in a bold font of your choice, approximately 230 pt. in size. Set the Horizontal Scale to 108%.

2. Click the type object with the Selection tool (V). **A** From the Swatches Libraries menu on the Swatches panel,⊞ choose Gradients > Metals.

3. On the Appearance panel,◉ click the Add New Fill button,☐ then in the Metals library, click the Gold (first) swatch. On the Gradients panel,▧ enter an Angle value of –90°.

4. On the Appearance panel, click the Stroke color square, then Shift-click it to open a temporary

Color panel. Enter C18, M25, Y94, and K0. Click the up arrow to change the weight to 12 pt.**B–C**

5. Continuing on the Appearance panel, click the Add New Stroke button.◻ Apply a color of C0 M7, Y51, and K8, and a weight of 8 pt.

6. Click the Add New Stroke button once more. Apply a color of C20, M40, Y96, and K8, and a weight of 2 pt.

7. From the Add New Effect menu,*fx*, choose Illustrator Effects > Stylize > Drop Shadow. Check Preview, choose settings, then click OK.**D–E**

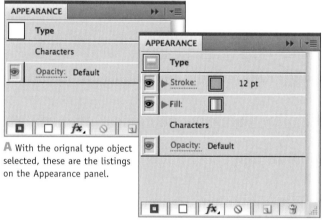

A With the original type object selected, these are the listings on the Appearance panel.

B A new fill and stroke were added to the type object.

C This is the type object after the Gold gradient fill and a 12-pt. tan stroke were applied.

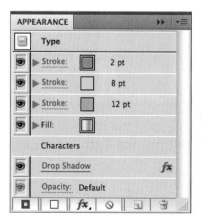

D The Appearance panel lists the two new strokes and the effect that were applied to the type object.

E This is the final result.

EXERCISE: Use the Free Distort effect on type

1. Create a type character in an extra or ultra bold font,* approximately 230 pt. in size. Choose the Selection tool (V).

2. On the bottom of the the the Appearance panel, click the Add New Fill button.

3. Click the Fill color square and choose a light brown color, or Shift-click the Fill color square to mix a color via a temporary Color panel.

4. Double-click the Stroke color square and click a dark brown swatch. Click the up arrow to change the weight to 7 pt.**A**

5. Double-click the Characters appearance listing, then set both the Stroke and Fill listings to a color of None.

6. Click the Type appearance listing to view the appearance attributes for the type object. Click the Fill listing, then from the Add New Effect menu,***fx,*** choose Distort & Transform > Free Distort.**B** In the Free Distort dialog, move the top left and right points downward and to the left to slant the fill. Click OK.**C**

➤ To edit the Free Distort settings, expand the Fill listing, then click Free Distort.

A We used the Appearance panel to add a new fill and stroke appearance to a type object.

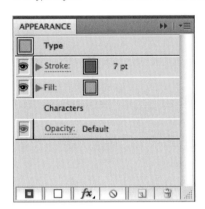

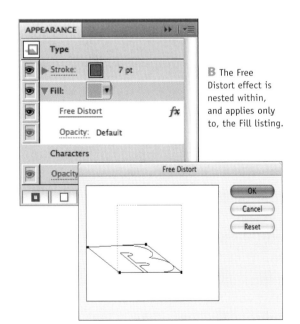

B The Free Distort effect is nested within, and applies only to, the Fill listing.

C The Fill attribute for the type is distorted. (The point type on the bottom has a stroke color and a fill of None.)

*If you don't have such a font, choose a bold font, then on the Character panel, increase the Horizontal Scale to around 140%.

Mastering the Pen tool—Illustrator's most difficult tool—takes patience and practice. Once you become comfortable using it, refer to Chapter 12 to learn how to reshape the resulting paths. If you find the Pen tool to be too difficult to use, remember that you can create shapes using other methods. For example, you can draw simple geometric shapes (Chapter 6) and then combine them (Chapter 25), or draw in a freehand manner with the Blob Brush or Pencil tool (Chapter 7).

Drawing with the Pen tool

The Pen tool creates precise curved and straight segments that are connected by anchor points. Click with the tool to create corner points and straight segments without direction handles, **A** or drag with the tool to create smooth points and curve segments with direction handles. **B** The shape of the resulting curve segments is determined by the distance and direction in which the mouse is dragged. You can also use the Pen tool to create corner points that join nonsmooth curves. **C**

In the instructions on the following pages, you'll learn how to draw straight segments, smooth curves, and nonsmooth curves. Once you master all three techniques, you'll naturally combine them without really thinking about it as you draw shapes: Drag-drag-click, drag, click-click-drag…

21

A This corner point joins two straight segments, and has no direction handles.

B A smooth point has a pair of direction handles that move in tandem. This is a smooth curve.

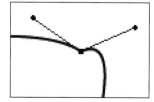

C This corner point has direction handles that move independently. This is a nonsmooth curve.

Before you tackle the challenge of drawing curves with the Pen tool, practice the easier task of clicking with the tool to create an open or closed polygon.

To draw a polygon with the Pen tool:

1. If the current fill choice is a solid color, gradient, or pattern (not None), your Pen path will be filled when you create the first three points. If you prefer to have the segments appear as lines only, choose a stroke color and a fill of None.

2. Choose the **Pen** tool ✒ (P).

3. Turn on **Smart Guides** (Cmd-U/Ctrl-U), and in Illustrator/Edit > Preferences > **Smart Guides**, check all the Display Options boxes.

4. Click to create the first anchor point, then click to create a second one. A straight segment will connect the two points.

5. Click to create additional anchor points. They will be connected by straight segments. Use Smart Guides (Alignment Guides option) if you want to position points and segments precisely as you draw them.**A**

6. To complete the shape as an **open** path, do either of the following:

    Click the Pen tool or any other tool on the Tools panel (the polygon will remain selected).

    Cmd-click/Ctrl-click outside the new shape or press Cmd-Shift-A/Ctrl-Shift-A to deselect it.

    Or to complete the shape as a **closed** path, position the Pen pointer over the starting point (a tiny circle appears next to the pointer, as well as the "anchor" label), then click the point.**B–D**

➤ If the artboard starts to fill up with extraneous points as a result of "false starts," use the Object > Path > Clean Up command (check just the Delete: Stray Points option).

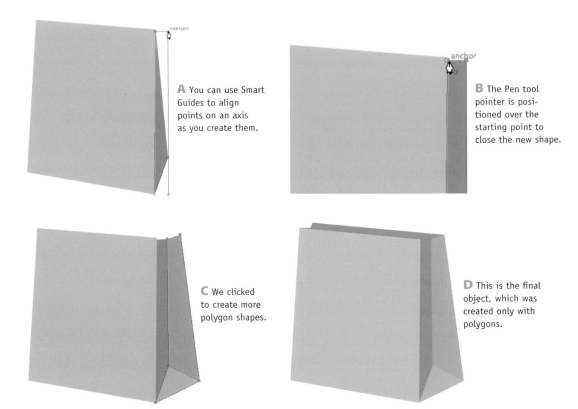

A You can use Smart Guides to align points on an axis as you create them.

B The Pen tool pointer is positioned over the starting point to close the new shape.

C We clicked to create more polygon shapes.

D This is the final object, which was created only with polygons.

Follow these instructions to create smooth curves with the Pen tool. Smooth anchor points that connect curve segments always have a pair of direction handles that move in tandem; the longer the direction handles, the steeper or wider the curve.

To draw curves with the Pen tool:

1. Choose the **Pen** tool 🖋 (P).

2. Turn on **Smart Guides** (Cmd-U/Ctrl-U), and in Illustrator/Edit > Preferences > Smart Guides, check all the Display Options boxes.

3. Drag (don't click) to create the first anchor point.**A** The angle of the direction handles on the point will mimic the direction you drag.

4. To create a second anchor point, release the mouse, move it away from the last anchor point, then drag a short distance in the direction you want the curve to follow.**B** A curve segment will connect the first and second anchor points, and the next pair of direction handles will appear.

   ➤ To produce smooth, symmetrical curves, place the points at the beginning and end of each arc rather than at the middle. You can use Smart Guides to align new points to existing paths.

5. Drag to create more anchor points and direction handles.**C–E** The points will be connected by curve segments.

6. To complete the object as an **open** path, do either of the following:

   Click the Pen tool or any other tool (the path will remain selected).

   Cmd-click/Ctrl-click outside the new shape or press Cmd-Shift-A/Ctrl-Shift-A (for the Deselect command).

   Or to complete the object as a **closed** path, position the Pen pointer over the starting point (a tiny circle appears next to the pointer, as well as an "anchor" label). Drag from the point, then release the mouse.

➤ To prevent the curves from looking bumpy and irregular, use just the minimum number of anchor points necessary to define them. Also try to produce relatively short direction handles by dragging a short distance—you can always lengthen them later.

➤ You can practice drawing curves by converting a curved object to a guide (see page 104) and then tracing the guide lines.

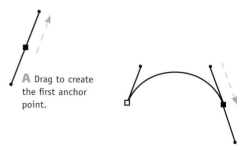

A Drag to create the first anchor point.

B Release and reposition the mouse, then drag in the direction you want the curve to follow.

C Continue to reposition and drag the mouse.

D Continue to reposition and drag.

E A smooth curved shape is used as a clipping mask for the background of this illustration.

USING SMART GUIDES WHILE DRAWING A PATH

You can use Smart Guides to align new anchor points with existing selected or unselected points.

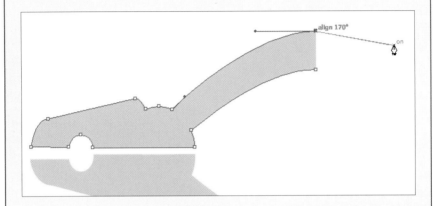

ADJUSTING POINTS WHILE DRAWING A PATH

➤ To reposition a point as you create it, keep the mouse button down, hold down the Spacebar, then drag the point, or to move a smooth point, drag the direction handle. Release the Spacebar and reposition the mouse, then continue to draw. Practice this; you sort of have to think ahead.

➤ If the last point you created was a corner point and you want to add a direction handle to it, position the Pen tool pointer over it, then drag; a direction handle appears. Release and reposition the mouse, then continue to draw.

➤ If the last anchor point you created was a smooth point (two direction handles) and you want to convert it to a corner point (one direction handle), click it with the Pen tool, release and reposition the mouse, then continue to draw. (See the following page.)

YOU'RE A GENIUS

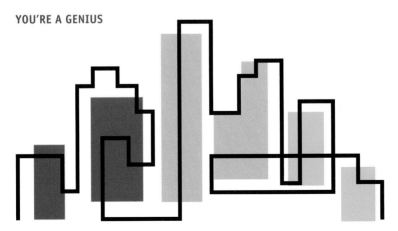

If you get fed up with the Pen tool, create a cityscape like this and maybe you'll feel better. Draw some rectangles with the Rectangle tool, and then with the Pen tool, click, click, click to create the black lines (black stroke, fill of None).

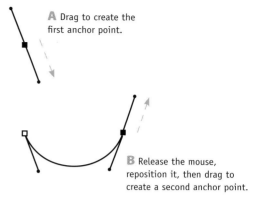

Converting anchor points on paths

Yet another use for the Pen tool is to create corner points that join nonsmooth curves. The latter are segments that curve on the same side of an anchor point (unlike the segments that can curve on both sides of a smooth anchor point).

If you move one of the direction handles that are connected to a corner point, the contour of the curve changes on just that side of the point. Smooth points and corner points can be combined in the same path, of course. You can convert smooth points into corner points (or vice versa) as you draw them (instructions on this page) or after you draw them (instructions on the next page).

To convert smooth points into corner points as you draw them:

1. Choose the **Pen** tool ✎ (P).

2. Drag to create the first anchor point. **A**

3. Release the mouse, move it away from the last anchor point, then drag a short distance to create a second anchor point. **B** A curve segment will connect the first and second anchor points, and a second pair of direction handles will appear. The shape of the curve segment will be determined by the distance and direction in which you drag.

4. Do either of the following:

   Position the pointer over the last anchor point, Option-drag/Alt-drag from that point to drag one direction handle independently, release Option/Alt and the mouse, reposition the mouse, then drag the next point in the direction you want the curve to follow. **C** (So many words to describe a process that will become intuitive with practice!)

   Click the last anchor point to remove one of the direction handles from that point.

5. Repeat the last two steps to draw more anchor points and curves.

6. To close the shape, do either of the following: **D–E**

   Drag on the starting point to keep it as a smooth point.

   Click the starting point to convert it to a corner point with one direction handle.

A Drag to create the first anchor point.

B Release the mouse, reposition it, then drag to create a second anchor point.

C Option-drag/Alt-drag from the last anchor point in the direction you want the new curve to follow. Both direction handles are now on the same side of the curve segment.

D Drag to create another anchor point, and so on.

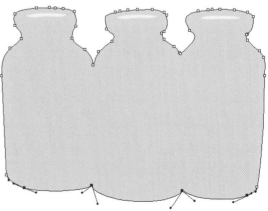

E Nonsmooth curves are defining the bottom edges of these bottle shapes.

To convert points on an existing path:

Method 1 (Control panel buttons)

1. Choose the **Direct Selection** tool (A), then click a path.

2. Click a point to be converted.

3. On the Control panel, click the **Convert Selected Anchor Points to Corner** button or the **Convert Selected Anchor Points to Smooth** button.

   ➤ Read about the Selection & Anchor Point Display Preferences on page 362. To make it easier to locate anchor points, check Highlight Anchors on Mouse Over.

Method 2 (Convert Anchor Point tool)

1. Choose the **Direct Selection** tool (A), then click a path.

2. Choose the **Convert Anchor Point** tool (Shift-C).

3. To help you locate the anchor points easily, turn on **Smart Guides** (Cmd-U/Ctrl-U) and in Illustrator/Edit > Preferences > Smart Guides, check **Anchor/Path Labels**.

4. Do any of the following:

   Drag new direction handles from a corner point to convert it to a smooth point. **A**

   To convert a smooth point to a corner point with a nonsmooth curve, rotate a direction handle from the point so it forms a V shape with the other direction handle. **B**

   Click a smooth point to convert it to a corner point with no direction handles. **C–D**

   ➤ To turn the Pen tool into a temporary Convert Anchor Point tool, hold down Option/Alt. To turn the Pen tool temporarily into the last-used selection tool, hold down Cmd/Ctrl.

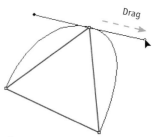

Drag

A A corner point is converted to a smooth point.

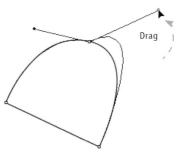

Drag

B A smooth point is converted to a corner point, producing a nonsmooth curve.

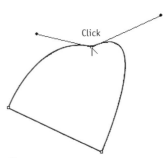

Click

C A nonsmooth curve is converted to a corner point.

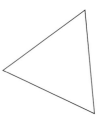

D Then back to the original triangle (no direction handles).

EXERCISE: Draw a knife with the Pen tool

Draw the knife blade

1. Create a long horizontal artboard. Choose the Pen tool ✑ (P). Choose a light blue-gray solid fill color and a stroke of None.

2. Drag downward and to the right to create the first anchor point. Reposition the pointer to the right and click, move the mouse upward, then click again to create a straight vertical edge. **A–B**

3. Complete the shape by clicking back on the starting point. **C** If necessary, choose the Direct Selection tool ⬈ (A) and drag the handle at the tip of the blade to reshape the blade. Cmd-click/Ctrl-click to deselect.

4. On the Color panel, choose white as the fill color, then add a touch of Cyan or Blue to it.

5. To create the narrow cutting edge of the blade, with the Pen tool, click the tip of the blade. Reposition the pointer over the curve of the

blade, drag to create a curve that mimics the blade shape, **D** click twice to create a short, straight vertical edge, **E** drag to create a matching curve for the top of the edge of the blade, then click back on the starting point. **F** Reshape the new object, if necessary (as described in step 3).

Draw the knife handle

1. Deselect. Choose a black as the fill color. With the Pen tool (P), drag over the top right edge of the blade. Working from left to right, drag to create four smooth curve points for the top and end of the handle. **G**

2. Wending your way back to the left, drag to create four smooth curve points for the bottom of the handle. **H** Finally, click near the bottom of the blade, then click the starting point for the handle shape (**A**, next page).

Continued on the following page

A For the blade of the knife, drag to create the first point, then click to create the next one.

B Click to create a straight edge.

C Click the starting point to close the shape.

D For the edge of the blade, click to create a point, then drag to create a curve.

E Click twice to create a straight edge.

F Drag to create a matching curve, then click the starting point to close the shape.

G Drag to create four smooth curve points for the top and end of the knife handle.

H Drag to create four smooth curve points to define the bottom of the handle.

Create a shadow for both parts of the knife

1. Choose the Selection tool ▶ (V). Option-drag/ Alt-drag the blade object slightly downward and to the left. **B** On the Layers panel, drag the listing for the blade copy to the bottom of the layer.

2. Drag the bottom center handle of the bounding box on the blade copy upward slightly to make it more squat. Fill the shadow with a medium-dark color. **C**

3. Option-drag/Alt-drag the handle object slightly downward and to the left. **D** On the Layers panel, drag the listing for the copy to the bottom of the layer.

4. Fill the handle copy with the same shadow color that you used in step 2.

5. Deselect. With the Direct Selection tool ▶ (A), move the bottom left corner point of the handle copy to smooth the contour between one shadow shape and the other (it may help to isolate and/or zoom in on the object). **E**

6. Create a new layer, and stack it below the existing ones. With the Rectangle tool ▢ (M) draw a rectangle behind all the objects, and fill it with a lighter version of the color you chose for the shadows. Time to cook dinner!

A Click to complete the bottom part of the handle, then click the starting point to close the path.

B Option-drag/Alt-drag the blade object downward to copy it. Restack the copy to the bottom of the layer.

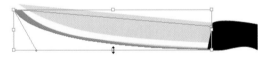

C To scale the shadow, drag the center handle on the bounding box of the copy upward, and fill the path with a medium-dark color.

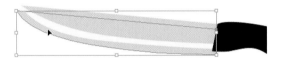

D Option-drag/Alt-drag the handle object downward to copy it (shown tinted above, for clarity). Restack the copy to the bottom of the layer.

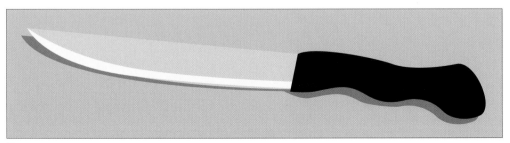

E Fill the shadow for the knife handle with the same color that you used for the blade shadow. If necessary, with the Direct Selection tool, adjust the corner points on the shadow shapes to smooth the transition between them.

If you want to incorporate a photo into your Illustrator design (say, layer type over a photo for a book jacket, poster, or product label) or you need to import an image for tracing, now you will learn how. You will import images and graphics into an Illustrator document via the Open and Place commands; work with the Links and Control panels to edit, replace, locate, update, relink, and convert your linked images; and drag and drop images between applications.

How images are acquired

Methods for acquiring images from other applications include the Open command, the Place command, and drag-and-drop. Your chosen method will depend on what file formats are available for saving the file in its original application and how you plan to use the imagery in Illustrator.

When you open a document from another drawing (vector) application via the Open command, a new Illustrator file is created, and the acquired objects can be manipulated using Illustrator tools and commands. When you open a bitmap image by using the Open command, the image isn't converted into separate vector objects, but rather is embedded in a new file as an object in its own box.

Via the Place command, you have a choice of linking or embedding an image into an existing Illustrator file. For print output, the recommended formats for linked images—EPS, TIFF, and PDF—preserve the color, detail, and resolution of the original image. If you place a layered Photoshop (PSD) file into Illustrator, you can choose via a dialog to have it appear as a single flattened object or as separate objects on separate layers.

You can also acquire images by using the drag-and-drop method: simply drag an image from one Illustrator window into another or from a document window in another application, such as Photoshop, into your Illustrator document, and a duplicate image appears in the target file automatically.

A bitmap image that you acquire in Illustrator via the Open, Place, or drag-and-drop method can be moved, placed on a different layer, masked, modified using any transformation tool, or modified using the Photoshop effects. All three methods preserve the resolution of the original image.

(The Clipboard commands—Cut, Copy, and Paste—can also be used to acquire images; see page 99.)

ACQUIRE IMAGES

22

IN THIS CHAPTER

To produce the artwork shown above, we used editable type as a clipping path to partially mask a placed image (to learn about clipping masks, see Chapter 26). We also added a second type object and an object with a solid white fill.

Using the Open command

The Open command opens your chosen file as a separate Illustrator document. A list of some of the file formats that you can open in Illustrator appears in the sidebar at right.

Note: To preserve the editability of appearances and text in an Adobe PDF file, use the Open command (this page) instead of the Place command (next page).

To import a file by using the Open command:

1. Do either of the following:

   In Bridge, click a thumbnail, then choose File > Open With > **Adobe Illustrator CS4**.

   In Illustrator, choose File > **Open** (Cmd-O/ Ctrl-O). The Open dialog opens. In the Mac OS, choose Enable: All Readable Documents to dim files in formats that Illustrator can't read. In Windows, you can filter out files via the Files of Type menu, or choose All Formats (the default setting) to display files in all formats. Double-click a file name; or locate and click a file name, then click Open.

2. If you chose a multipage PDF file, the Open PDF dialog appears.**A** Check Preview, click an arrow to locate the desired page (or enter the desired page number in the field), then click OK. Respond to any alert dialogs that appear (see the sidebar on the following page).

   If you chose a Photoshop PSD file that contains layers or layer comps, the Photoshop Import Options dialog opens. See pages 284–285.

   Other formats may cause a different dialog to open. Choose options, then click OK.

IMPORTABLE FILE FORMATS

You can open or place the following file formats into Illustrator CS4:

➤ Raster (bitmap) formats: BMP, GIF, JPEG, JPEG2000, PCX, PDF, PIXAR, PNG, PSD, TGA, and TIFF.

➤ Graphics (vector) formats: CGM, CorelDRAW (versions 5 through 10), DWG (AutoCAD drawing and export), EMF, FreeHand (up to version 11), PDF, PICT, SVG, SVGZ, and WMF. Illustrator can't open Macromedia Flash SWF files.

➤ Text formats: Plain text (TXT), RTF, and MS Word (up to version 2008 in Macintosh and version 2007 in Windows).

To open native Illustrator files into Illustrator, see Chapter 5.

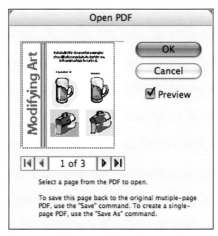

A For a multipage PDF file, navigate to the page to be opened.

Using the Place command

When you use the Place command, the chosen file appears in an existing Illustrator document. You can reposition it on the artboard, restack it via the Layers panel, use it in a mask, transform it, apply effects to it, or change its opacity or blending mode. For a list of "Place-able" file formats, see the sidebar on the preceding page. When using the Place command in Illustrator, you can choose whether or not to link or embed the file into your document (you will learn how to manage linked files later in this chapter).

To import a file by using the Place command:

1. Open an Illustrator file, and click a layer for the image to appear on.

2. Do either of the following:

   In Illustrator, choose File > **Place**, then click a file to be placed. Check **Link** to place only a screen version of the image into your Illustrator document, with a link to the original image file. The original image file won't be affected by your edits in Illustrator, but in order for it to print properly, it must be available on your hard disk. Illustrator won't color-manage the linked image. Or uncheck Link to embed a copy of the actual image into the Illustrator file and allow Illustrator to color-manage the image. The embedded image will increase the storage size of your Illustrator file. Click **Place**.

   In Bridge, click a thumbnail, then choose File > Place > **In Illustrator**. The image will be linked automatically.

   An options dialog may open. For example, if you place a Photoshop PSD file that contains layers (with the Link option unchecked), or a Photoshop PSD file that contains layer comps (with the Link option checked or unchecked), the Photoshop Import Options dialog opens. See the next page.

➤ When selected, a linked image will have an X on top of it, in the selection color of the current layer.**A**

DECIPHERING THE ALERT DIALOGS

When opening or placing an image into Illustrator, any of these alert dialogs may crop up:

➤ The Illustrator PDF: Warnings alert lists missing fonts and/or objects that have been reinterpreted. Click OK to accept the substitutions (or click Cancel).

➤ The Embedded Profile Mismatch, Paste Profile Mismatch, and Missing Profile alerts let you decide how to color-manage an imported image that either contains or lacks an embedded color profile.

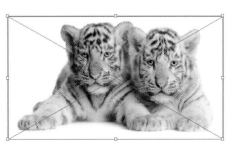

A A linked image is selected in an Illustrator document.

Choosing Photoshop import options

Importing a single-layer image

If you import a single-layer Photoshop PSD image via the Open or Place command, it will be listed on the Layers panel by its file name on the currently active layer, and no dialog will open (if any alerts appear, see the sidebar on the preceding page). No clipping mask will be generated by Illustrator, but any Photoshop clipping path will remain in effect and will be listed by the name that was assigned to it in Photoshop.

Importing a multilayer image

If you place a Photoshop PSD file that contains layers with the Link option unchecked, place a Photoshop PSD file that contains layer comps with or without the Link option unchecked, or open a Photoshop PSD file that contains layers or layer comps, the Photoshop Import Options dialog opens. Check **Show Preview** to display a thumbnail preview of the image. The other options are described below.

A We used the Place command with the Link option unchecked to import a Photoshop PSD file containing layers, and this Photoshop Import Options dialog opened.

Importing layer comps

Choose from the **Layer Comp** menu to import a layer comp, if the file contains any. Any comments entered in Photoshop for the chosen comp will display in the Comments window. If you need to import additional layer comps from the same Photoshop image, you'll have to use the Place command separately for each one.

If the image contains layer comps and you checked Link in the Place dialog, you can choose When Updating Link: **Keep Layer Visibility Overrides** to preserve the layer visibility (hide or show) state the layers were in when you originally placed the image and have any subsequent visibility changes made in Photoshop be ignored; or choose **Use Photoshop's Layer Visibility** to apply any subsequent layer visibility changes made in Photoshop.

Importing Photoshop layers

If you unchecked the Link option in the Place dialog, you now have the option to keep or flatten the layers. If you click **Convert Layers to Objects**, each object will be nested within an image group on the current layer.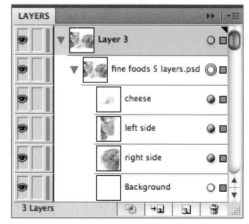 Transparency levels, blending modes, layer masks, and vector masks will be preserved, will be listed as editable appearances (see page 186), and will be targeted to the appropriate converted object in Illustrator. Layer groups will

B With Convert Layers to Objects checked, each Photoshop layer became a separate Illustrator object, nested within a group.

be preserved, and any layer or vector masks will remain in effect. A vector mask will be listed as a clipping path on the Layers panel, whereas a layer mask will become an opacity mask and will display on the Transparency panel. Plain type will remain editable, if possible (see the second to last paragraph on this page). Each converted layer from the Photoshop file will be listed separately on the Links panel, but any imagery outside the original canvas area will be trimmed.

If you click **Flatten Layers to a Single Image** instead, a flattened version of the image will be nested within the current layer. All transparency levels, blending modes, and layer mask effects will be applied to the flattened image but won't be listed as editable appearances in Illustrator.

Check **Import Hidden Layers** and/or **Import Slices**, if available (and if desired), to import those elements with the file.

Linked files are flattened automatically (that is, the Convert Layers to Objects option is dimmed).

When you click Convert Layers to Objects in the Photoshop Import Options dialog, the Background from the Photoshop file will become one of the nested objects within Illustrator, and will be opaque. You can change its opacity, hide it, or delete it via the Layers panel in Illustrator.

TIFF IMPORT OPTIONS

When you place a layered TIFF file into Illustrator, the TIFF Import Options dialog opens, offering the same options as in the Photoshop Import Options dialog. When saving a file in the Photoshop (PSD) format isn't an option for some reason, the TIFF format is an acceptable alternative.

Other Photoshop issues

In Photoshop, the position of adjustment layers in the layer stack affects how image layers are converted into objects when the file is placed and embedded (not linked) into Illustrator. Any layers above an adjustment layer in the Photoshop file will be converted to separate objects in Illustrator. Any layers below an adjustment layer in the Photoshop file will be flattened, along with the adjustment layer, into one object in Illustrator, allowing the appearance of the adjustment to be preserved. You can delete or hide adjustment layers in Photoshop before placing an image into Illustrator. Hidden adjustment layers aren't imported.

When placing or opening a Photoshop EPS file, any Photoshop shape layers will become clipping masks in Illustrator, editable text will become a compound path, and all other Photoshop layers will be flattened into one object below the shape layer(s). In contrast, each layer from a Photoshop PSD file is converted to a separate object layer.

If you place a Photoshop file that contains editable type into Illustrator (with the Link option unchecked) and click Convert Layers to Objects, the type objects will remain editable, provided the type layer in Photoshop was neither warped nor had any effects applied to it. If you want to import a type layer as vector outlines instead, in Photoshop, use Layer > Type > Convert to Shape, save the file, then open the file in Illustrator via the Open or Place command.

If the current layer in a Photoshop file contains pixels that extend outside the live canvas area, those pixels will be dropped when you import it into Illustrator, no matter which method you use —drag-and-drop, place, or open. Before acquiring an image from Photoshop, make sure the pixels that you want to import are visible within the live canvas area in the original file.

Managing linked images

To keep your Illustrator files from becoming too large, you can link the images you import instead of embedding them. A screen version of each image serves as a placeholder in your document, but the actual image remains separate from the Illustrator file. To link a file, use the File > Place command with the Link option checked.

The Links panel A lists all the linked and embedded files in your Illustrator document, and to help you and your output service provider keep track of those files, offers a number of useful controls. It lets you monitor the status of linked images, relink a missing image, open a linked image in its original application, update a modified image, and convert a linked image to an embedded one.

Some Links panel commands are also available on the Control panel when a linked image is selected in your document. B–D In fact, you can open a temporary Links panel by clicking either Linked File or Image on the Control panel.

To edit a linked image in its original application:

1. Do either of the following:

   On the **Links** panel, click the image name, then click the **Edit Original** button.

   Click the image in the document window, then click **Edit Original** on the Control panel.

   The application in which the linked image was created will launch, if it isn't already running, and the image will open.

2. Make your edits, resave the file, then return to Illustrator. If an alert dialog appears, E click Yes. The linked image will update in your document.

   Note: In Illustrator/Edit > Preferences > File Handling & Clipboard, under Files, you can choose preferences for linked images. For example, via the Update Links menu, you can specify whether linked images will update automatically when modified in their original application (see page 371).

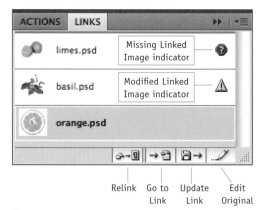

Relink Go to Update Edit
        Link   Link   Original

A The Links panel lets you keep track of, replace, and embed your linked files.

B When a linked image is selected in your document, you can click Linked File on the Control panel to open a temporary Links panel, or click the image name to access Links panel commands.

C When an embedded TIFF or JPEG image is selected in your document, you can click Image on the Control panel to open a temporary Links panel, or click the image name to access Links panel commands.

D When any other type of embedded image is selected in your document, you can click Embedded on the Control panel to access Links panel commands.

E This prompt appears if you edit a linked file in its original application via the Edit Original button.

If you replace one placed image with another, any transformations, effects, or transparency that you applied to the image in Illustrator, such as scaling or rotation, will be applied automatically to the replacement.

To replace a linked or embedded image:

1. Do either of the following:

   On the Links panel, click the name of the file to be replaced, then click the **Relink** button. 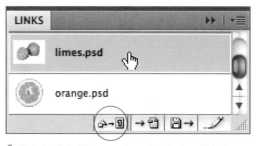 **A**

   Click the image in the document window, then on the Control panel, click the image name or the Embedded link (not the Embed button) and choose **Relink** from the menu.

2. In the Place dialog, locate the desired replacement file, then click Place. **B**

➤ Another way to replace a placed image is to select it in the document window, choose File > Place, locate the replacement image, check Replace, then click Place.

Via the Placement Options dialog, you can control how a replacement image fits within its bounding box.

To choose placement options for a replacement linked image:

1. Do either of the following:

   Click a replacement linked image in the document window, then on the Control panel, click the image name and choose **Placement Options**.

   On the Links panel, click a replacement linked image, then choose **Placement Options** from the panel menu.

2. In the Placement Options dialog, choose a Preserve option, then study the thumbnails and read the description to learn how the image will be affected.

3. *Optional:* For any option other than Transforms or Bounds, you can click a point on the Alignment icon. The artwork will be aligned to that point on the bounding box. To prevent the artwork from extending beyond the bounding box, you can check Clip to Bounding Box.

4. Click OK.

LINKING VERSUS EMBEDDING IMAGES

➤ A linked image will be listed on the Layers panel as <Linked File> (or, for a PSD or TIFF file, as the file name) within the currently active layer. Any clipping path in the original file will be applied, but won't be listed separately on the Layers panel.

➤ An embedded JPEG image will be listed on the Layers panel as an image object on the current layer; a file in another format will be nested within a group. If a clipping path is included, it will remain in effect and will be listed on the Layers panel as such, above the image object.

➤ Photoshop effects on the Effect menu can be applied to both linked and embedded images and will remain editable.

➤ You can apply Transparency panel settings to, or transform (move, rotate, shear, or reflect), both linked and embedded images.

A Click the linked image to be replaced, then click the Relink button.

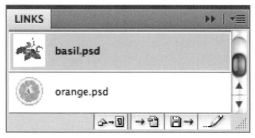

B The "limes.psd" image is replaced with "basil.psd."

The simple Go To Link command locates a placed image for you, then selects it on its artboard within the document window. It may come in handy if your document contains a lot of linked images.

To go to a linked or embedded image:

On the Links panel, click an image name, then click the **Go to Link** button.➔🖼

➤ If you click an image name on the Links panel, then choose Reveal in Bridge from the panel menu, the thumbnail for that image will be selected in the Bridge window.

➤ When you shrink (scale down) a linked or embedded image in Illustrator, its resolution increases accordingly; enlarge it and its resolution decreases.

If this icon ⚠ appears on the Links panel, it means the original file has been modified and the link is now outdated. Follow the instructions below to update the link. This will also be necessary if you edit the original file (via the Edit Original button) and Manually is the current setting on the Update Links menu in Illustrator/Edit > Preferences > File Handling & Clipboard. (If the setting is Automatically, the image will update automatically; or if the setting is Ask When Modified, an alert will appear, offering you the option to update the file.)

To update a modified linked image:

1. On the Links panel, click the name of the modified image.⚠

2. Do either of the following:

   Click the **Update Link** button 💾➔ at the bottom of the Links panel.

   Click the image in the document window, then click the image name on the Control panel and choose **Update Link** from the menu.

To locate or replace images upon opening a file:

An alert dialog will appear if you move an image file from its original location, or rename it, after it has been linked to an Illustrator file, and then reopen the Illustrator file.**A** Do one of the following:

To locate the missing image, click **Repair**, locate the file, then click Replace.

To substitute another file for the missing one, click **Replace**, locate a replacement file, then click Replace.

If you click **Ignore**, the linked image won't display, but a question mark icon will display for that file on the Links panel and its bounding box will be visible in the Illustrator file if Smart Guides are on and you pass the cursor over it. To completely break the link and prevent an alert prompt from appearing for that image in the future, delete the bounding box and resave the file.

Optional: Check Apply to All to have whichever button you click apply to any other missing images.

To locate or replace a missing linked image in an open file:

1. Do either of the following:

   On the Links panel, click the name of the missing image,❓ then click the **Relink** button.➔🗑

   Click the image in the document window, then on the Control panel, click the image name or the Embedded link (not the Embed button) and choose **Relink** from the menu.

2. In the Place dialog, locate the missing file, then click Place.

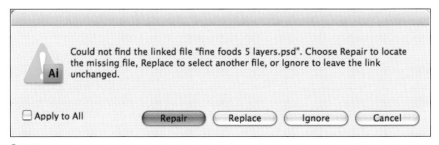

A If Illustrator detects that a linked file is missing when a document is opened, this alert will appear.

To view information about a file:

1. Do either of the following:

On the Links panel, double-click the listing for a linked or embedded file.

Click the image in the document window, then click the image name on the Control panel and choose **Link Information**.

2. A dialog appears, listing data about the image, such as its file name, location, size, format, date modified, and transform settings. Click OK.

➤ To view metadata about a linked file, such as keywords, copyright info, and IPTC contact, info, click the file on the Links panel, then choose Link File Info from the panel menu.

The Embed Image command changes a file's status from linked to embedded. Be aware that this will increase the file size.

To change a file's status from linked to embedded:

Do either of the following:

On the Links panel, click the name of a linked image,A then choose **Embed Image** from the Links panel menu.B

Click a linked image in the document window, then click **Embed** on the Control panel.

When you embed a multilayer Photoshop image, the Photoshop Import Options dialog opens. See pages 284–285.

➤ You can't convert an embedded image to a linked one, but you can relink to the original image by clicking the file name on the Links panel, then clicking the Relink button.

CHOOSING LINKS PANEL DISPLAY OPTIONS

➤ To change the size of the image thumbnails on the Links panel, choose Panel Options from the panel menu, click the preferred size, then click OK.

➤ To change the sorting order of the listings, from the panel menu, choose Sort by Name (alphabetical order), Sort by Kind (file format), or Sort by Status (missing, then modified, then embedded, then fully linked). To sort only selected links, Cmd-click/Ctrl-click the file names first.

➤ To control which categories of links display on the panel, choose Show All, Show Missing, Show Modified, or Show Embedded from the panel menu.

A Click an image name on the Links panel, then choose Embed Image from the panel menu.

Embedded files have this icon

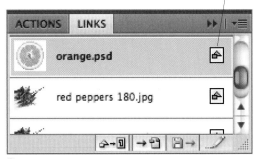

B Note that the file name is listed for embedded TIFF, GIF, JPEG, and flattened PSD files, but not for embedded files in other formats.

Dragging and dropping images into Illustrator

Drag-and-drop is a quick method for duplicating imagery between applications or files; the copy is made automatically. You can drag and drop objects between Illustrator documents, as we showed you in Chapter 9, or between Illustrator and Adobe Dreamweaver, Adobe InDesign, or any other drag-aware application. You can also drag and drop a pixel selection or layer from Photoshop to Illustrator, as in the instructions below.

Note: When we need to acquire a Photoshop image for an Illustrator document that will be output to print, instead of using drag-and-drop, we convert the image to CMYK Color mode in Photoshop, save it in the Photoshop PSD format, then acquire it via File > Place in Illustrator.

To drag and drop a selection or layer from Photoshop to Illustrator:

1. In Photoshop, click a pixel layer. *Optional:* Create a selection on the layer.

2. Open an Illustrator file. Arrange the Illustrator and Photoshop Application frames so both document windows are visible.

3. In Photoshop, choose the **Move** tool (V), then drag the selection or layer into the Illustrator document window; a copy of the image appears.

   The selection or layer will be embedded at the resolution of the original image. In the Mac OS, the image will be nested within a new <Group> in the currently active layer; in Windows, it will be listed as <Image>.

➤ The drag-and-drop method doesn't use the Clipboard.

➤ The opacity of a "dropped" Photoshop selection or layer will become 100%, regardless of its original opacity (it may appear lighter if its original opacity was below 100%). You can lower the transparency in Illustrator, if desired. Photoshop blending modes are ignored.

➤ Layer masks and vector masks from Photoshop will be applied to the "dropped" image (meaning the image will be clipped), and then will be discarded. Any clipping paths in the Photoshop file will be ignored. In the Mac OS, a generic clipping path (based on the dimensions of the Photoshop selection or layer) will appear within the image group, but can be deleted without changing how the image looks. You can create a clipping mask in Illustrator to mask the image.

➤ If you drag and drop a selection or pixel layer (even editable type or a shape layer) from Photoshop with the Move tool, it will become rasterized, if it isn't already. Any transparent pixels will become opaque white. If you drag and drop a selected path (or vector mask) from Photoshop to Illustrator with the Path Selection tool, it will become a compound path in Illustrator and won't be rasterized. Another option is to copy a path from Photoshop and paste it into Illustrator, in which case the Paste Options dialog opens. Click Paste As: Compound Shape (fully editable) or Compound Path (faster); the Compound Shape option is recommended for multiple or overlapping paths.

To drag and drop an image into Illustrator from Bridge:

1. Open or create an Illustrator document.

2. In Bridge, click an image thumbnail.

3. Do either of the following:

   To **link** the image, drag the thumbnail into an Illustrator document window.

   To **embed** the image, Shift-drag the thumbnail into an Illustrator document window.

   Now that was easy.

You can embellish plain vanilla path edges with a brush stroke that looks like ink, paint, or chalk, or that contains a pattern or multiple vector objects. The four flavors of brushes—Calligraphic, Scatter, Art, and Pattern*—are stored on and accessed from the Brushes panel ✿ (F5).**A** The default Brushes panel contains only a small handful of the available brushes; of course we'll show you how to add more.

Not only do Illustrator brushes have all the advantages of vector graphics (small file sizes, resizability, and crisp output), they're also live: If you edit a brush that's being used in your document, you'll be given the option via an alert dialog to update the paths in which the brush is being used. And of course if you reshape a path (see Chapter 12) or increase the stroke width, the brush stroke reconforms automatically to the new contour.

In this chapter, you will embellish existing path edges with brushes; remove and expand brush strokes; create and edit custom Calligraphic, Scatter, and Art brushes; modify existing brush strokes; create and load brush libraries; and add, duplicate, and delete brushes from the Brushes panel.

There are two ways to produce brush strokes: You can choose the Paintbrush tool and a brush and draw a shape with a brush stroke built into it right off the bat, which we showed you how to do on page 81, or you can apply a brush stroke to an existing path of any kind, which is shown on the following page.

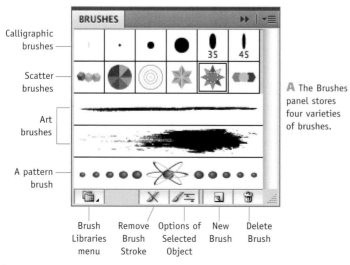

Calligraphic brushes

Scatter brushes

Art brushes

A pattern brush

Brush Libraries menu

Remove Brush Stroke

Options of Selected Object

New Brush

Delete Brush

A The Brushes panel stores four varieties of brushes.

To learn about Pattern brushes, see Illustrator Help.

Applying brushes to existing paths

On page 81, you learned how to draw paths with the Paintbrush tool, and in those instructions, you chose a brush for the tool before using it. In these instructions, you will apply a brush stroke to an existing path. It doesn't matter which tool the path was created with (e.g., Type, Star, Polygon, Ellipse, Pencil, Blob Brush, Line Segment, or Pen tool).

To apply a brush to an existing path:

1. Display the **Brushes** panel 🖌 or click the Brush thumbnail or arrowhead on the Control panel.

2. Do either of the following:

   Click a path of any kind with any selection tool,**A** then click a brush on the Brushes panel.**B–D**

   Drag a brush from the Brushes panel onto a path or type (the object doesn't have to be selected). Release the mouse when the pointer is over the object.

3. *Optional:* Change the stroke width or color (a color change won't show up on a Pattern brush).

> **SCALE STROKES?**
>
> If you scale an object that has a brush stroke and Scale Strokes & Effects is checked in the Scale dialog (double-click the Scale tool) or in Illustrator/Edit> Preferences (Cmd-K/Ctrl-K) > General, the brush stroke will also scale. With this option unchecked, a brush stroke will stay the same size when an object is scaled.

➤ What's the difference between a Pattern **E** and a Scatter brush? **F** For a Scatter brush, you can specify a degree of randomness for the size, spacing, and scatter variables; not so for a Pattern brush. Also, pattern brushes are made from up to five tiles (Side, Outer Corner, Inner Corner, Start, and End), which enable the strokes to fit tightly on a path. Unlike Scatter brushes, Pattern brushes are used for creating borders or frames.

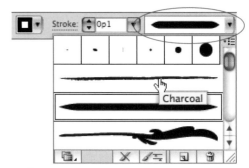

B ...then click a brush on the Brushes panel (here, it is being accessed from the Control panel).

A Select a path...

C The Art brush we chose appears on the path.

D This is an Art brush stroke.

E And this is a Pattern brush stroke.

F This is a Scatter brush stroke.

Using the Brushes panel

After opening a brush library, you can either apply a brush from the library directly to any path in your document or add brushes from the library to the Brushes panel. Brushes on the panel save with the current document.

Furthermore, you can use any brush from a library as the starting point for creating a custom brush. After adding it to your document's Brushes panel, you can duplicate it, if desired (see page 301), and then customize it to your liking.

To load brushes from a library:

1. From a submenu on the **Brush Libraries** menu 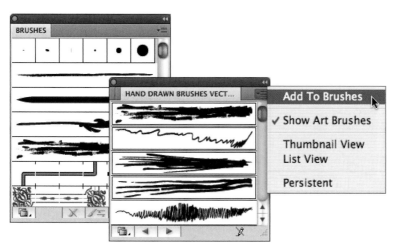. at the bottom of the Brushes panel, choose a library name.

2. Deselect all the objects in your document (Cmd-Shift-A/Ctrl-Shift-A).

3. Do one of the following:

   Click a brush in the library; it will appear on the Brushes panel.

   Click, then Shift-click, a consecutive series of brushes in the library, then choose **Add to Brushes** from the library menu.**A**

   Drag a brush directly from the library onto any object in the document window (the object doesn't have to be selected). The brush stroke will appear on the object and the chosen brush will also appear on the Brushes panel.

➤ Once a library panel is open, you can cycle through other libraries by clicking the ▶ or ◀ button at the bottom of the library panel.

➤ To close a whole library panel, click its close button; to close a single library on the panel, Control-click/right-click its tab and choose Close from the context menu.

A To append multiple brushes to the Brushes panel for the current document, click, then Shift-click to select them, then choose Add to Brushes from the library panel menu.

To choose display options for the Brushes panel:

From the Brushes panel menu:

Choose **List View** to have a small thumbnail, the brush name, and an icon for the brush type (Calligraphic, Scatter, Art, or Pattern) display for each brush on the panel;**A** or choose **Thumbnail View** to display larger thumbnails without the name and icon.

To control which brush types (categories) display on the panel, choose **Show** [brush type] to check or uncheck that option.

➤ You can drag any brush upward or downward on the panel to a different location within its own category. To move a series of brushes, click, then Shift-click them first.

Removing brush strokes

When you remove a brush stroke from a path, you're left with a plain vanilla path. It will have the same color and width as the former brush stroke.

To remove a brush stroke from an object, group, or layer:

1. Do either of the following:

   Select one or more objects that a brush stroke is applied to.**B**

   Target a layer or group that a brush stroke is applied to.

2. On the Brushes panel 🖌 (F5), click the **Remove Brush Stroke** button.✖ **C**

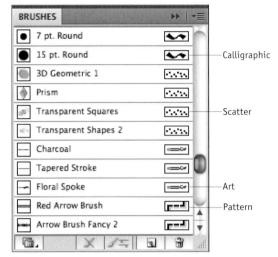

A When the Brushes panel is in List view, icons for the four brush categories display on the right side.

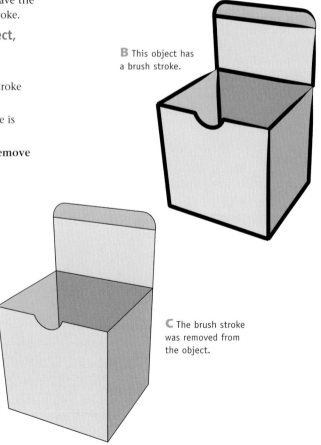

B This object has a brush stroke.

C The brush stroke was removed from the object.

Expanding brush strokes

When a brush stroke is expanded, it is converted into ordinary editable outlined paths (objects in the shape of the former brush strokes). The stroke will no longer be live, though, so you won't be able to replace it via the Brushes panel or edit it by editing the brush.

To expand a brush stroke into paths:

1. Select an object that has a brush stroke.

2. Choose Object > **Expand Appearance**. Each brush stroke (and fill, if any) is now a separate object or objects, nested (or double- or triple-nested) in a group sublayer on the Layers panel.**A–B**

➤ To select all of the objects in your document that contain a brush stroke, from the Select > Object submenu, choose Brush Strokes.

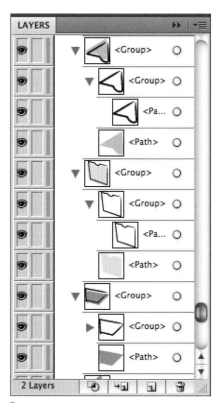

A The Expand Appearance command converted the brush strokes and fills to separate objects, unconnected to the original path.

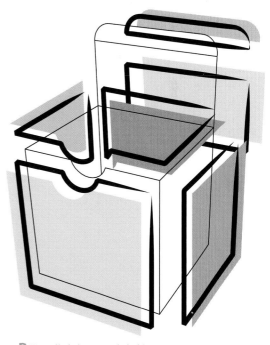

B We pulled the expanded objects apart.

Next, we'll show you how to create and modify Scatter, Calligraphic, and Art brushes.

Creating and editing Scatter brushes

Objects in a Scatter brush are placed evenly or randomly along the contour of a path. You can create a Scatter brush from an open or closed path, or from a type character, type outline, blend, or compound path, but not from a gradient, bitmap image (placed or rasterized), mesh, or clipping mask.

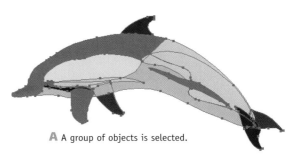

A A group of objects is selected.

To create or edit a Scatter brush:

1. Skip this step if you're going to edit an existing brush. To create a new brush, select one or more objects,**A** then click the **New Brush** button on the Brushes panel. In the New Brush dialog,**B** click **New Scatter Brush**, then click OK. The Scatter Brush Options dialog opens. Enter a name, click OK, then apply the new brush to any path.**C** (Note: You will reopen the options dialog in the next step; when you do, you can take advantage of the Preview option, which is available only for brushes that are in use.)

2. Deselect all, then on the Brushes panel, double-click the Scatter brush to be edited. The Scatter Brush Options dialog opens.**D**

3. Check **Preview** to view the changes on paths where the brush is in use.

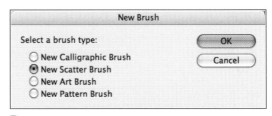

B New Scatter Brush is clicked in the New Brush dialog.

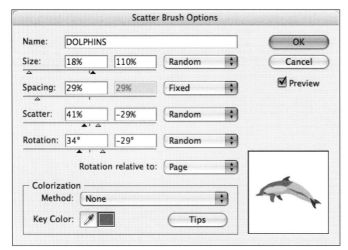

C The new brush is applied to a path.

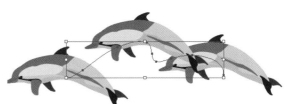

D Use the Scatter Brush Options dialog to adjust the settings for a new or existing brush. These settings produced the results shown on the next page.

CREATING BRUSH VARIATIONS

To create a variation of an existing brush of any type, duplicate it first by following the instructions on page 301. To create a variation of a brush in a library, add the brush to the Brushes panel, then duplicate it.

4. For **Size**, **Spacing**, **Scatter**, and **Rotation**, choose one of the following variations from the menu:

Fixed to use a single fixed value.

Random, then move the sliders to define a range within which that property can vary.

If you have a graphics tablet hooked up, choose **Pressure**, **Stylus Wheel**, **Tilt**, **Bearing**, or **Rotation**. Move the sliders (or enter different values in the two fields) to define a range within which that property can respond to stylus pressure. Light pressure uses the minimum property value from the left field; heavy pressure uses the maximum property value from the right field.

The following is a description of the properties:

Size controls the size of the scatter objects.

Spacing controls the spacing between the scatter objects.

Scatter controls the distance between the objects and the path. When Fixed is chosen as the Scatter setting, a positive value places all the objects on one side of the path, whereas a negative value places all the objects on the opposite side of the path. The further the Scatter value is from 0%, the less closely the objects will adhere to the path.

Rotation controls how much the scatter objects can rotate relative to the page or the path. From the **Rotation Relative To** menu, choose **Page** or **Path** for the axis of rotation.

5. For the **Colorization** options, see the sidebar on page 301.

6. Click OK. If the brush is in use in the document, an alert dialog will appear. **A** Click **Apply to Strokes** to update those objects with the revised brush, **B** or click **Leave Strokes** to leave the existing objects unchanged.

➤ Shift-drag a slider in the Scatter Brush Options dialog to also move its counterpart in the same direction. Option-drag/Alt-drag a slider to simultaneously move the slider and its counterpart toward or away from each other.

➤ To orient scatter objects uniformly along a path, set Scatter and Rotation to Fixed, set Scatter to 0°, and choose Rotation Relative To: Path.

➤ To edit a Scatter brush on a path manually, see page 302.

A This alert dialog appears if you modify a brush that's currently in use on objects in the document.

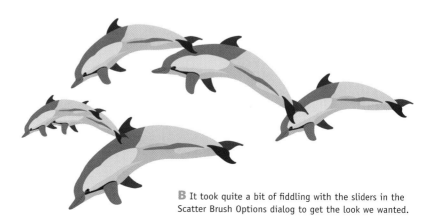

B It took quite a bit of fiddling with the sliders in the Scatter Brush Options dialog to get the look we wanted.

Creating and editing Calligraphic brushes

Calligraphic brush strokes vary in thickness as you draw, as in traditional calligraphy.

To create or edit a Calligraphic brush:

1. Skip this step if you're going to edit an existing brush. To create a new brush, click the **New Brush** button ⬚ on the Brushes panel. In the New Brush dialog, click **New Calligraphic Brush**, then click OK. The Calligraphic Brush Options dialog opens. Enter a Name, click OK, then apply the new brush to any path. (See the Note in step 1 on page 296.)

2. Deselect all, then on the Brushes panel, double-click the Calligraphic brush to be edited. **A–B** The Calligraphic Brush Options dialog opens. **C** If you're creating a new brush, enter a new name; or to edit an existing brush, leave the name as is.

3. Check **Preview** to view the changes on paths where the brush is in use (this option is available only for brushes that are in use). The brush shape will also preview in the dialog.

4. For **Angle**, **Roundness**, and **Diameter**, choose one of the following variations from the menu:

   Fixed to keep the value constant.

   Random, then move the Variation slider to define a range within which that brush attribute can vary. A stroke can range between the value

A The brush we're going to edit is in use on these objects.

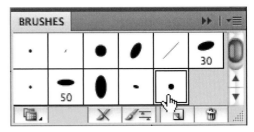

B We double-click the Calligraphic brush on the Brushes panel.

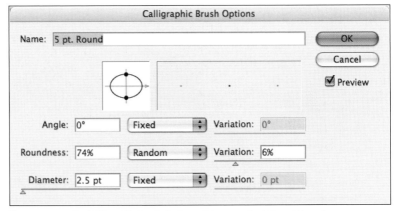

C You can use the Calligraphic Brush Options dialog to adjust the settings for a new or existing brush. These settings produced the results shown on the next page.

specified for Angle, Roundness, or Diameter, plus or minus the Variation value. For example, a 50° angle with a Random Variation value of 10 could have an angle anywhere between 40° and 60°.

If you're using a graphics tablet, choose **Pressure**, **Stylus Wheel**, **Tilt**, **Bearing**, or **Rotation**. Move the Variation slider to define a range within which the brush attribute can respond to pressure from a stylus. Light pressure produces a brush attribute based on the Angle, Roundness, or Diameter value minus the Variation value, whereas heavy pressure produces a brush attribute based on the specified value plus the Variation value.

5. Enter an **Angle** (–180˚ to 180˚) or drag the gray arrowhead on the circle. A 0° angle produces a stroke that is thin when drawn horizontally and thick when drawn vertically; a 90° angle produces the opposite result.

6. Enter a **Roundness** value (0–100%), or reshape the tip by dragging either of the two black dots inward or outward on the ellipse.

7. For the brush size, enter a **Diameter** value (0–1296 pt.) or drag the slider.

8. Click OK. If the brush is already in use in the document, an alert dialog will appear.**A** Click **Apply to Strokes** to update the existing strokes with the revised brush,**B** or click **Leave Strokes** to leave the existing strokes unchanged.

A This alert dialog appears if you modify a brush that's currently in use.

B We clicked Apply to Strokes in the alert dialog to allow the brush strokes to update on these objects.

Creating and editing Art brushes

An Art brush can be made from one or more paths (even a Blob Brush object or a compound path), but not from a gradient, mask, mesh, editable type, or bitmap image. When applied to a path, an Art brush stroke will conform to the path. If you reshape the path, the Art brush stroke will stretch or bend to fit the new path contour (fun!). If you browse through the predefined Art brushes, you'll see that some are simulated art media brushes and some are recognizable objects, such as arrows, banners, and ribbons.

To create or edit an Art brush:

1. Skip this step if you're going to edit an existing brush. To create a new brush, select one or more objects,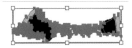 then click the **New Brush** button on the Brushes panel. In the New Brush dialog, click **New Art Brush**, then click OK. The Art Brush Options dialog opens. Enter a Name, click OK, then apply the new brush to any path. (See the Note in step 1 on page 296.)

2. Deselect all, then on the Brushes panel, double-click the Art brush to be edited. The Art Brush Options dialog opens.**B** If you're creating a new brush, enter a new name; to edit an existing brush, leave the name as is.

3. Check **Preview** to view the changes on paths where the brush is in use (this option is available only for brushes that are in use).

4. Do any of the following:

   Click a **Direction** button to control the orientation of the object on the path. The object will be drawn in the direction the arrow is pointing. The direction will be more obvious for objects that have a distinct or recognizable orientation (e.g., type outlines, a tree, a building).

   Enter a **Width** to scale the brush, and check **Proportional** if you want to preserve the proportions of the original object as you scale it. Press Tab to preview.

   Check **Flip Along** to reverse the object on the path (from left to right) and/or check **Flip Across** to reverse the object across the path (up to down).

5. Choose a **Colorization** option (see the sidebar on the following page).

6. Click OK.**C–D**

➤ To edit an Art brush manually on a path, see page 302.

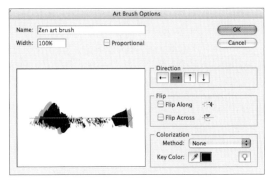

A To create an Art brush, select one or more objects.

B Use the Art Brush Options dialog to choose settings for a new or existing brush.

C Our new Art brush is applied to two paths, which were drawn with the Paintbrush tool.

D We chose brown as the stroke color, then double-clicked the new brush on the Brushes panel to reopen the Art Brush Options dialog. There, we increased the brush Width and chose the Tints Colorization Method.

Duplicating brushes

Using the Duplicate Brush command as a starting point, you can create a variation of an existing brush—a slimmer or fatter version, for example.

To duplicate a brush:

1. Deselect all objects.

➤ To duplicate a brush in a library, you must add it to the Brushes panel first.

2. Do either of the following:

Click the brush to be duplicated, then choose **Duplicate Brush** from the panel menu.

Drag the brush to be duplicated to the **New Brush** button 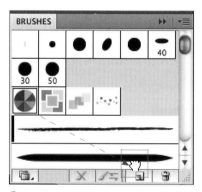.**A**

The word "copy" will be appended to the brush name.**B** To modify the brush, follow the instructions for that brush type in this chapter.

A Drag the brush to be duplicated over the New Brush button.

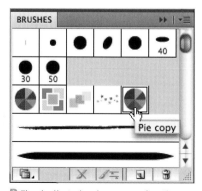

B The duplicate brush appears after the last brush icon in its own category.

THE COLORIZATION OPTIONS

To change the way a brush applies color, from the Colorization Method menu in the Brush Options dialog for an Art or Scatter brush, choose one of the options listed below. To recolor an existing brush stroke via the same menu, see page 303.

➤ None to leave the original brush colors unchanged.

➤ Tints to change black areas in the brush stroke to the current stroke color at 100% and non-black areas to tints of the current stroke color. White areas stay white. Use for grayscale or spot colors.

➤ Tints and Shades to change colors in the brush stroke to tints of the current stroke color. Black and white areas stay the same.

➤ Hue Shift to apply the current stroke color to the main color (the "key" color) in a multicolor brush and to change other colors in the brush to related colors. To change the key color, with the Hue Shift option chosen, click the Key Color eyedropper, then click a color in the preview area of the dialog (not in the artwork). The changes won't display until you exit the dialog. (The Key Color eyedropper isn't available for the Options of Selected Object feature, which is discussed on page 303.)

To open the informative Colorization Tips dialog (shown below), click the Tips icon.

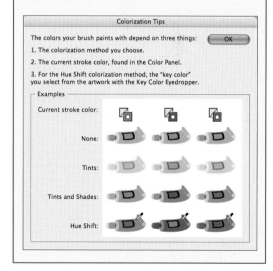

Editing brushes manually

On the previous page you learned how to edit a brush via its options dialog. In these instructions, you will edit a brush manually in a document.

To edit a Scatter or Art brush manually:

1. Deselect all objects (Cmd-Shift-A/Ctrl-Shift-A), then drag a brush from the Brushes panel 🖌 onto a blank area of the artboard. **A–B**

2. Edit the brush objects. To recolor or transform the entire brush, select it (Selection tool) or isolate it. To recolor or transform individual objects in the brush, select them by using the Direct Selection tool or the Layers panel.

   ► You can recolor the brush objects by using the Recolor Artwork dialog. See Chapter 29.

3. Choose the Selection tool (V).

4. Do either of the following:

   To replace the existing brush with the edited one, Option-drag/Alt-drag the modified brush object or objects into the Brushes panel, and release the mouse when the pointer is over the original brush icon and the icon has a highlight border. **C**

   To make the object(s) into a new, separate brush, drag it (or them) onto the panel without holding down Option/Alt. The New Brush dialog opens. Click New Scatter Brush or New Art Brush, then click OK.

5. The Scatter Brush Options or Art Brush Options dialog opens. Enter a name, then click OK.

6. If you decided to replace the existing brush, and it is currently in use in the document, an alert dialog appears. Click **Apply to Strokes** to update the paths with the revised brush, **D** or click **Leave Strokes** to leave them be.

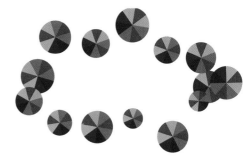

A The Scatter brush is applied to a path.

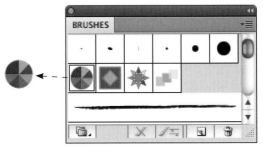

B The brush is dragged from the panel to an artboard.

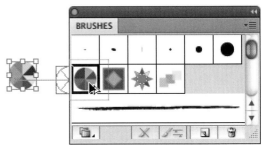

C After recoloring the objects via the Recolor Artwork dialog, we Option-drag/Alt-drag them over the original brush on the Brushes panel.

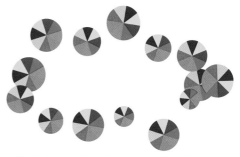

D The brush updates instantly on the path.

Editing brush strokes on objects

If you edit a brush, either manually or via the options dialog, all objects in which that brush is being used will update to reflect your changes. If you prefer to edit a brush stroke on an individual object or objects—without editing the actual brush—follow these instructions (the same controls are used).

To change the stroke options for an individual object:

1. Select one or more objects to which the same brush is currently applied.

2. If you want to recolor the brush stroke via the Colorization menu (step 7), choose a stroke color now.

3. Click the **Options of Selected Object** button on the Brushes panel. The Stroke Options dialog opens.

4. Check Preview.

5. For a Scatter brush stroke, follow step 4 on page 297, for a Calligraphic brush stroke, follow steps 4–7 on pages 298–299; or for an Art brush stroke, follow steps 4–5 on page 300.**A**

6. Click OK.**B** Your edits will affect only the selected object or objects, not the brush on the Brushes panel.

7. *Optional:* For a Calligraphic or Art brush stroke set to any Colorization method except None, you can also change the stroke color manually via the usual controls (e.g., Color, Color Guide, or Swatches panel).**C**

➤ If you edit the actual brush after using the Options of Selected Object feature, your custom options will be removed.

➤ To restore the original brush stroke to the object, select the object, then click the original brush.

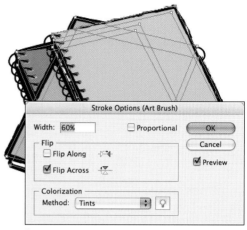

A We selected some objects containing brush strokes, clicked the Options of Selected Object button, then changed the Width of the brush.

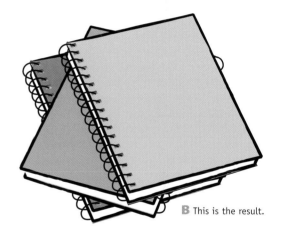

B This is the result.

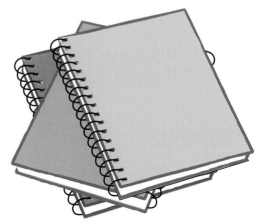

C After exiting the options dialog, we changed the stroke colors via the Swatches panel.

Deleting brushes

When you delete a brush that's being used in your document, you will be given an option via an alert dialog to expand or remove the brush strokes.

To delete a brush from the Brushes panel:

1. Deselect all objects in your document.

2. Do either of the following:

   On the Brushes panel, click the brush to be deleted.

   To delete all the brushes that aren't being used in the document, choose **Select All Unused** from the Brushes panel menu.

3. Click the **Delete Brush** button 🗑 on the Brushes panel.

4. An alert dialog appears. If the brush is not currently in use in the document, click Yes.**A** If the brush is in use in the document,**B** click **Expand Strokes** to expand the brush strokes (they'll be converted into standard paths and will no longer be live), or click **Remove Strokes** to remove them from the objects. If the brush contains a graphic style, yet another alert dialog will appear.**C**

➤ To restore a deleted brush to the Brushes panel, choose Undo immediately. Or if the brush is in a library, you can add it again to the Brushes panel (see page 293).

Creating brush libraries

By saving your brushes in a library, you'll be able to find them easily and load them into any file.

To create a brush library:

1. Set up your Brushes panel so it contains only the brushes to be saved in a library. You can create new brushes or add them from a library panel; delete any brushes you don't want saved in the library.

2. From the **Brush Libraries** menu 📖. at the bottom of the Brushes panel, choose **Save Brushes**.

3. In the Save Brushes as Library dialog, enter a name for the library. Keep the default location. In the Mac OS, that location is Users/ [user name]/Library/Application Support/Adobe Illustrator CS4/en_US/Brushes; in Windows, it's C:\Documents and Settings\[user name]\ Application Data\Adobe\Adobe Illustrator CS4 Settings\en_US\Brushes.

4. Click Save. The library will now be listed on, and can be opened from, the **User Defined** submenu on the **Brush Libraries** menu.

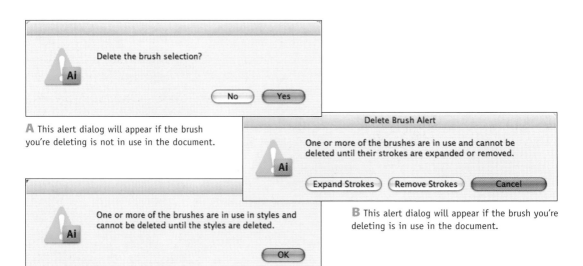

A This alert dialog will appear if the brush you're deleting is not in use in the document.

B This alert dialog will appear if the brush you're deleting is in use in the document.

C This alert dialog will appear if the brush you're deleting is part of an applied graphic style.

A gradient fill is a soft, gradual blend between two or more solid colors. Gradients can be used to add shading or volume for a touch of realism, or to add depth to abstract shapes. In this chapter, you will load gradients from a library; fill one or more objects with a gradient; create a simple two-color gradient; add, delete, recolor, and change the opacity of colors in a gradient; save a gradient to the Swatches panel; change a gradient's position, length, shape, and angle; spread a gradient across multiple objects; and expand a gradient into paths.

Illustrator CS4 introduces several significant enhancements, such as the ability to edit a gradient interactively by using on-object controls (referred to collectively as the "annotator"), access a temporary coloring panel from the annotator or the Gradient panel, change the opacity of individual gradient colors, and compress a radial gradient from a circular shape to an elliptical one, and vice versa.

Applying a gradient

A gradient can be composed of two solid colors (a starting and an ending color) or multiple colors; it can spread from one side of an object to another (linear) or outward from the center of an object (radial);**A** and it can be applied to individual objects, or across multiple objects in one full sweep.

Continued on the following page

A This artwork contains one radial gradient (the sun) and two linear gradients (the sky and water).

IN THIS CHAPTER

The first step is to load some predefined Illustrator gradients onto your document's Swatches panel.

To load gradients onto the Swatches panel:

1. Display the Swatches panel.■ From the **Show Swatch Kinds** menu at the bottom of the panel, choose **Show Gradient Swatches**, and from the panel menu, choose **Large Thumbnail View**.

2. Click the **Swatch Libraries** menu ■, at the bottom of the Swatches panel, and from the **Gradients** submenu, choose a library.

3. A separate library panel opens.**A** Do either of the following:

   Click a gradient on the panel; it will appear on the Swatches panel.

   Cmd-click/Ctrl-click (or click, then Shift-click) to select multiple gradients, then choose **Add to Swatches** from the panel menu.

➤ To view the other gradient libraries, click the Load Next Swatch Library ■ or Load Previous Swatch Library ◀ button on the library panel.

Now you're ready to apply a gradient to an object.

To fill an object with a gradient: ★

Do one of the following:

Select one or more objects, then click a gradient swatch on the Swatches panel ■ (it can be accessed quickly via the Control panel) or on an open gradient library panel.

Select one or more objects,**B** and display the Gradient panel.■ Click the arrowhead next to the Gradient Fill square ▮ to open the gradient menu,**C** then click a gradient (the gradients currently residing on the Swatches panel are listed on this menu).**D**

Drag a gradient swatch from the Swatches panel, from any open gradient library panel, or from the Gradient Fill square on the Gradient panel over any selected or unselected object.

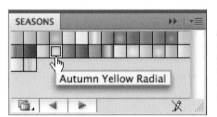

A The gradient library opens as a floating panel (the Brights, Foliage, and Simple Radial libraries also contain some simple gradients).

B A plain vanilla rectangle is selected.

Gradient menu

Gradient Fill square

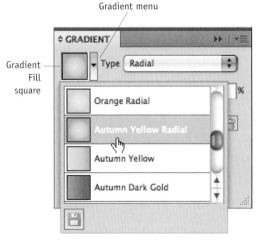

C Click a gradient on the gradient menu on the Gradient panel.

D The object is filled with a soft radial gradient.

Creating a two-color gradient

A custom gradient can contain all CMYK colors, all RGB process colors, tints of the same spot color, or multiple spot colors. In these instructions, you'll create a simple, two-color gradient. On the next two pages, you'll add more complexity.

To create and save a two-color gradient: ★

1. *Optional:* Select one or more objects.

2. Display the Gradient panel ■ (Cmd-F9/Ctrl-F9). Open the gradient menu,▐ then click the black-and-white **Linear Gradient**. Note: If that gradient isn't listed on the menu, simply make sure there are just two color stops below the gradient slider (you can drag any intermediate stop downward off the slider to remove it).

3. On the panel, double-click the right color stop below the gradient slider **A** to display a temporary coloring panel. You can click the ✿ to switch to an abridged Color panel or the ▦ to display an abridged Swatches panel.**B** Click a swatch or mix a color, then click outside the temporary panel to close it.

4. Repeat the previous step for the left color stop.

5. From the Type menu, choose **Radial** or **Linear**.

6. *Optional:* Move the midpoint diamond to the right to produce more of the starting color than the ending color, or to the left to do the opposite (the results will be evident if you selected an object in step 1).**C**

7. If you select another object or swatch now, the new gradient will be lost—unless you save it by doing either of the following, and then save your document:

   At the bottom of the gradient menu ▐ on the Gradient panel, click the **Save to Swatches Library** button.▐

   To name the gradient as you save it, click the **New Swatch** button ▣ on the Swatches panel, enter a name, then click OK.

➤ To swap the starting and ending colors (or any other two colors) in a gradient, Option-drag/Alt-drag one stop on top of the other. To reverse the order of all the colors in a gradient, use the Reverse Gradient button.▐

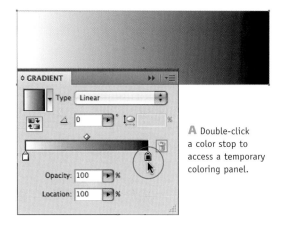

A Double-click a color stop to access a temporary coloring panel.

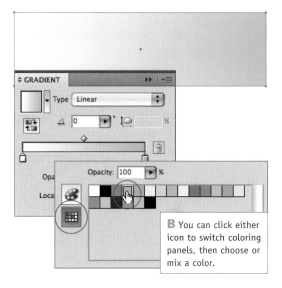

B You can click either icon to switch coloring panels, then choose or mix a color.

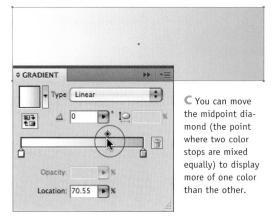

C You can move the midpoint diamond (the point where two color stops are mixed equally) to display more of one color than the other.

Editing gradient colors via on-object controls

Sometimes it's hard to predict how a gradient is going to look on a particular object. The new inter-active on-object controls solve this dilemma by letting you recolor, add, move, remove, or change the opacity or spread of any color in a gradient. For other controls, see pages 311–312.

To edit the colors in a gradient via on-object controls: ★

1. Display the full Gradient panel ▦ (double-click the panel tab, if necessary).

2. Apply a gradient to an object, and keep the object selected.

3. Choose the **Gradient** tool ▦ (G). The gradient annotator bar should display over the object. If not, choose View > **Show Gradient Annotator** (Cmd-Option-G/Ctrl-Alt-G).

4. Position the pointer over the annotator to expand it; color stops will display below the annotator.**A** To **recolor** an existing stop, double-click it; a temporary coloring panel appears.**B** You can click the 🖌 icon to switch to an abridged Color panel or the ▦ icon to display an abridged Swatches panel. Click a swatch or mix a color, then click outside the panel to close it.

5. To **add** a color to the gradient, click below the annotator; a new color stop appears.**C** Recolor the new stop as in the preceding step.

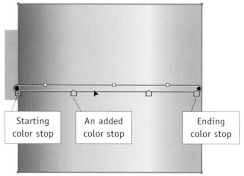

Starting color stop | An added color stop | Ending color stop

A To display the annotator, select an object that contains a gradient fill and select the Gradient tool.

B Double-click a color stop on the annotator to open a temporary coloring panel. We clicked the Color panel button so we could mix a color.

C Click below the annotator to add a new color stop at that location.

APPLYING A GRADIENT TO TYPE

To apply a gradient to type, select it with the Selection tool, click the Add New Fill button □ on the Appearance panel (Cmd-/; Ctrl-/) to create a new fill attribute, then apply a gradient.

6. On the annotator, do any of the following:

To change how abruptly a color **spreads** into adjacent colors, move the stop to the left or right.**A**

To adjust how colors are **distributed**, move one of the midpoint diamonds (located above the annotator) to the left or right. The diamond marks the location at which two adjacent colors are mixed equally (50% each).

To **duplicate** a color stop, Option-drag/Alt-drag it to the left or right.

To **remove** a color stop, drag it downward off the annotator.**B**

To change the **opacity** of a color stop, double-click the stop, then change the Opacity value via the temporary coloring panel.**C**

Note: Edits made via on-object controls also appear on the Gradient panel. To learn about the panel, including three controls for which there are no equivalent features on the annotator, see page 313.

➤ To save your edits to the original swatch or as a new swatch, follow the steps on the next page.

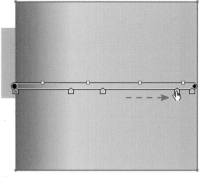

A Move a color stop toward or away from an adjacent stop to control how abruptly that color spreads into the adjacent one.

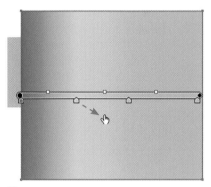

B To remove a color stop, drag it downward off the annotator bar.

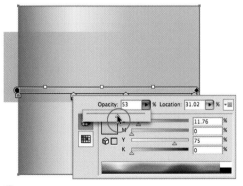

C To adjust the opacity for a color stop, double-click the stop, then use the Opacity control on the temporary panel. Underlying objects will be visible below any partially or fully transparent areas in the gradient.

Saving a gradient as a swatch

To save an edited gradient as a swatch:

1. Edit a gradient by following the instructions on the preceding two pages or in the sidebar on page 313.

2. Read the two methods below before performing either one:

    To update the **existing swatch** with your edits, Option-drag/Alt-drag the Gradient Fill square on the Gradient panel over the swatch on the Swatches panel. **A–B** Beware! If you do this, the gradient will update in all objects in which it is being used, whether those objects are selected or not.

    To save the modified gradient as a **new** swatch, from the bottom of the gradient menu ▯ on the Gradient panel, click the **Save to Swatches Library** button. 🖫 ★ **C** Alternatively, you can drag the Gradient Fill square from the Gradient panel to the Swatches panel. The gradient won't update in any unselected objects.

➤ To save gradient swatches as a library, see page 123. User-defined libraries are listed on, and can be chosen from, the User Defined submenu on the Swatch Libraries menu. 🗐.

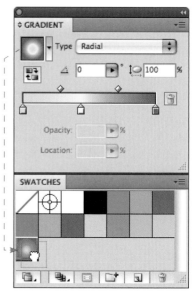

A To replace an existing swatch with your edited one, Option-drag/Alt-drag the Gradient Fill square over a swatch on the Swatches panel.

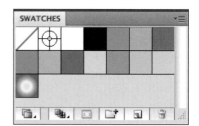

B The new swatch replaces the old.

REAPPLYING THE LAST-USED GRADIENT

To apply the last-used gradient to any selected object, do one of the following:

➤ Click the Gradient Fill square on the Gradient panel

➤ Press . (period)

➤ Click the Gradient button on the Tools panel

APPLYING A GRADIENT TO A "STROKE"

Normally, you can't fill a stroke with a gradient, but Illustrator has provided a workaround. Make the stroke fairly wide, then apply Object > Path > Outline Stroke to convert it into a closed object. Deselect, select the new object with the Direct Selection tool, then apply a gradient (see page 320).

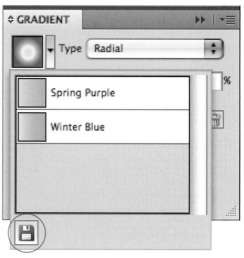

C To save the current gradient as a new swatch, click the Save to Swatches Library button on the Gradient menu.

Changing the position, length, or angle of a gradient in an object

In these instructions, and in the instructions on the next page, you will use on-object controls to change the origin, length, or angle of a linear gradient fill on a selected object.

To change the position, length, or angle of a linear gradient in an object: ★

1. Select an object that contains a linear gradient fill.

2. Choose the Gradient tool ▣ (G). The annotator should display on the object.* A

3. On the annotator, do any of the following:

   To reposition the **origin** (starting color) of the gradient, drag the round endpoint. The annotator for a linear gradient always crosses through the center of the object.

   To **lengthen** or **shorten** the gradient, drag the diamond-shaped endpoint outward or inward. B Shorten the annotator bar to make the transitions between colors more abrupt, or lengthen it to make the transitions more gradual.

   ➤ You can position the round or diamond-shaped endpoints outside the object, in which case colors at the beginning or end of the gradient won't display in the object.

   To change the gradient **angle**, position the pointer just outside the diamond-shaped endpoint, then when the rotation pointer appears, ⟳ drag in any direction. C

   To change the **length** and **angle** of the gradient simultaneously, hold down Option/Alt and drag the diamond-shaped endpoint.

➤ If you change the position, length, or angle of the annotator on an object and then apply a different gradient fill of the same type (radial or linear) to the object, the current position, length, and angle will be applied to your new gradient choice.

A To display the annotator, select an object that contains a gradient fill and choose the Gradient tool.

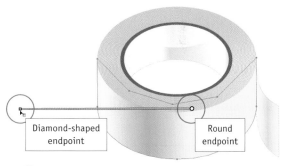

Diamond-shaped endpoint | Round endpoint

B We moved the round endpoint to reposition the starting color in the gradient, and dragged the diamond-shaped endpoint to lengthen the overall fill. Color transitions are now more gradual, and the gradient extends beyond the object (although it displays only within the object).

C To change the gradient angle, rotate the diamond-shaped endpoint.

*To show the annotator if it's hidden, choose View > Show Gradient Annotator (Cmd-Option-G/Ctrl-Alt-G).

To change the position, length, shape, or angle of a radial gradient in an object: ★

1. Select an object that contains a radial gradient fill.

2. Choose the Gradient tool ▦ (G).**A** The annotator should display on the object.*

3. On the annotator, do any of the following:

   To reposition the **center** of the gradient, drag the larger of the two round endpoints.**B** The annotator for a radial gradient doesn't have to remain centered on the object.

   To lengthen or shorten the **radius** of the gradient (and thereby scale the ellipse), drag the diamond-shaped endpoint. Or to preview the results as you scale the ellipse, drag the smaller circle (located on the edge of the ellipse) inward or outward.**C** The shorter the radius, the more abrupt the color transitions, and vice versa.

➤ You can position the round or diamond-shaped endpoints outside the object, in which case colors at the beginning or end of the gradient won't display in the object.

To change the **aspect ratio** of the ellipse to make the gradient more oval (or more round), drag the larger circle (located at the edge of the ellipse) inward or outward.**D**

To change the **gradient angle**, position the pointer on edge of the ellipse, then when you see the rotation pointer,⟲ drag in any direction. (An angle change in a radial gradient will be visible only if the gradient is oval-shaped.)

➤ To move the center of the radial gradient fill away from the center of the gradient ellipse, drag the smaller round endpoint on the slider away from the larger one.

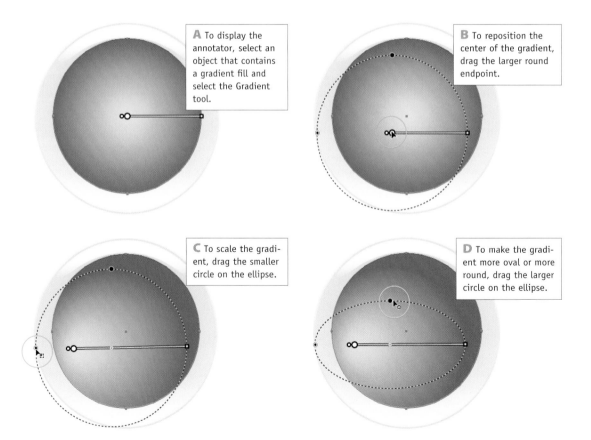

A To display the annotator, select an object that contains a gradient fill and select the Gradient tool.

B To reposition the center of the gradient, drag the larger round endpoint.

C To scale the gradient, drag the smaller circle on the ellipse.

D To make the gradient more oval or more round, drag the larger circle on the ellipse.

*To show the annotator if it's hidden, choose View > Show Gradient Annotator (Cmd-Option-G/Ctrl-Alt-G).

Spreading a single gradient across multiple objects

Normally, when you fill multiple selected objects with a gradient, the gradient starts anew in each object. With the Gradient tool, you can spread an existing gradient so it sweeps across all the objects.

To spread a gradient across multiple objects: ★

1. Select several objects. Click a gradient swatch to fill all of them with the same gradient.**A** Keep them selected.

2. Choose the Gradient tool ▦ (G).

3. Drag across all the objects in one pass.**B** (Or Shift-drag to constrain the angle to a multiple of the current Constrain Angle setting in Illustrator/Edit > Preferences > General.)

4. While the objects are still selected, use the **Group** command (Cmd-G/Ctrl-G).

   Note: To edit the gradient, select the group, then use the Gradient panel to modify the colors, angle, etc. (see below).

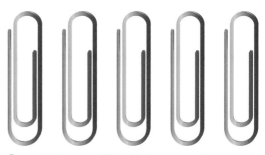

A Several objects are filled with the same gradient.

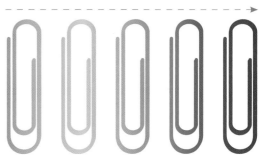

B We dragged across all the objects using the Gradient tool (in the direction shown by the arrow). Now the gradient extends from the first object to the last one.

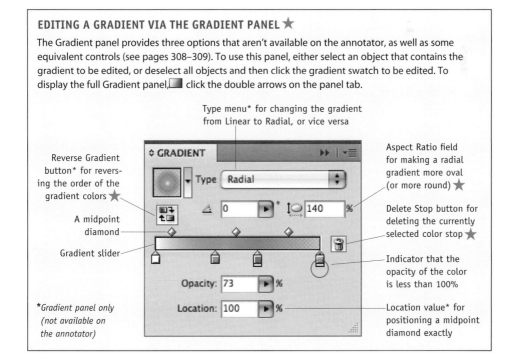

EDITING A GRADIENT VIA THE GRADIENT PANEL ★

The Gradient panel provides three options that aren't available on the annotator, as well as some equivalent controls (see pages 308–309). To use this panel, either select an object that contains the gradient to be edited, or deselect all objects and then click the gradient swatch to be edited. To display the full Gradient panel,▦ click the double arrows on the panel tab.

Type menu* for changing the gradient from Linear to Radial, or vice versa

Reverse Gradient button* for reversing the order of the gradient colors ★

A midpoint diamond

Gradient slider

*Gradient panel only (not available on the annotator)

Aspect Ratio field for making a radial gradient more oval (or more round) ★

Delete Stop button for deleting the currently selected color stop ★

Indicator that the opacity of the color is less than 100%

Location value* for positioning a midpoint diamond exactly

Expanding a gradient into paths

The Expand command lets you expand the colors in a gradient fill into a collection of individual paths. One practical reason for doing this might be if a gradient is causing a printing error and must be simplified.

To expand a standard gradient into separate objects:

1. Select an object that contains a gradient fill. **A**

2. Choose Object > **Expand**. The Expand dialog opens.

3. Click Expand Gradient to: **Specify**, then enter the desired number of objects to be created. **B** To print the expanded gradient successfully, this number must be high enough to produce smooth color transitions (say, over 100). Or if you want to expand it intentionally into obvious bands of color, enter a value below 20.

4. Click OK. **C** Note: If the original gradient contained too few colors, the resulting number of objects may not match the number of objects specified in the dialog.

➤ To expand a gradient using the current Specify [ ] Objects setting without opening the dialog, hold down Option/Alt while choosing Object > Expand.

➤ To learn about color-separating a gradient, see the sidebar on page 381.

A The original object contains a linear gradient fill.

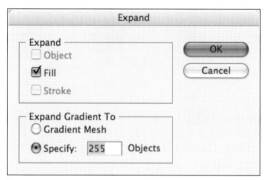

B In the Expand dialog, specify the number of objects to be produced from the gradient.

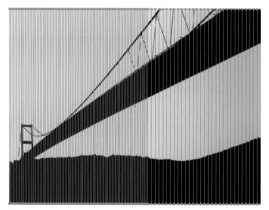

C The Expand command converted the gradient into a series of separate rectangles in different shades, grouped together with a clipping mask.

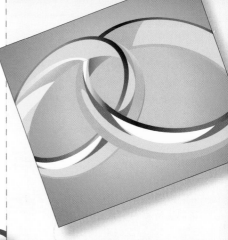

All the commands discussed in this chapter enable you to combine two or more objects into a new shape. You will learn about the Shape Mode commands, which create one or more standard paths or an editable compound shape from multiple objects; the Pathfinder commands and effects, which produce either a flattened, closed object or a compound path; and the Compound Path command, which joins two or more objects into one object, creating a "hole" where the original objects overlapped. In addition, you will learn how to add objects to, reverse an object's fill in, and release a compound path.

Applying the Shape Mode commands

Depending on how they are applied, the Shape Mode commands on the Pathfinder panel ◪ combine selected, overlapping objects into one or more standard paths or into a compound shape. The former result is permanent, whereas the latter result is editable and reversible.

If you choose the compound shape option, the resulting objects will be nested individually within a Compound Shape listing on the Layers panel. If you move or reshape an individual object within the compound shape, the overall shape adjusts accordingly. And if you release the compound shape, the original, precompound attributes are restored to the objects.

Here are few guidelines to bear in mind as you use the Shape Mode commands:

➤ They can be applied to multiple standard paths, compound paths, or outline type. An editable type object or a blend can be combined with other objects into a compound shape, but neither the type nor the blend can be positioned as the topmost object.

➤ The Shape Mode commands can't be applied to placed images, rasterized images, or mesh objects.

➤ The Unite, Intersect, and Exclude commands apply the color attributes and any effects from the topmost object to the resulting path or shape and remove all other color attributes, whereas the Minus Front command applies the color attributes and any effects from just the backmost object. Remember to put the objects in the desired stacking position before applying the command.

Continued on the following page

COMBINE PATHS

25

IN THIS CHAPTER

OTHER WAYS TO WORK WITH INTERSECTING SHAPES

➤ You can hide or recolor intersecting faces or edges in a Live Paint group (see Chapter 18). The result will look similar to some of the Pathfinder commands, but will be easier to edit.

➤ On page 152, we showed you how to combine objects by using the Blob Brush tool.

To combine objects into a path by using a Shape Mode command: ★

1. *Optional:* Duplicate the objects to be combined to preserve a copy.

2. Select two or more overlapping objects.

3. On the Pathfinder panel,⬚ click one of the **Shape Mode** buttons: **A**

   Unite joins the perimeter of the selection into one path, deletes the segments where the paths intersect, and closes any open paths (see also page 159).**B**

   Minus Front subtracts the objects in front from the backmost object, preserving the color attributes of only the backmost object. The result is one path or multiple nonoverlapping paths.**C**

   Intersect preserves the areas where objects overlap and deletes the nonoverlapping areas. The result is one path.**D** Note: If you get an alert prompt, make sure every object overlaps all the other objects.

   Exclude deletes the areas where the objects overlap, preserving only the nonoverlapping areas. The result is multiple nonoverlappping paths, nested in a group layer.**E**

➤ You can apply new color attributes to the newly combined path.

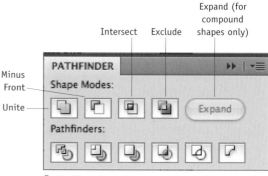

A The Shape Mode buttons on the Pathfinder panel combine two or more selected objects into a path or a compound shape.

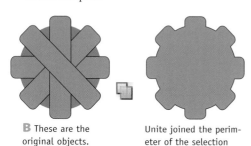

B These are the original objects.

Unite joined the perimeter of the selection to produce one path.

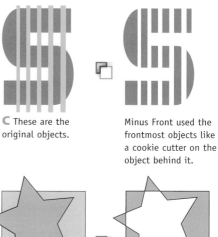

C These are the original objects.

Minus Front used the frontmost objects like a cookie cutter on the object behind it.

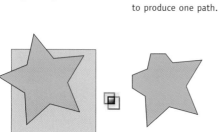

D These are the two original objects.

Intersect preserved only the area where the original objects overlapped.

E These are the two original objects.

Exclude removed the areas from where the original objects overlapped.

When you Option-click/Alt-click a Shape Mode button, a compound shape is produced. Unlike the result that simply clicking the button produces (previous page), in this case, all of the original objects are preserved. (You won't see all the original color attributes or effect settings, however, unless you release the compound shape.)

To combine objects into a compound shape by using a Shape Mode command: ★

1. Select two or more overlapping objects.

2. On the Pathfinder panel, ⬚ Option-click/Alt-click a **Shape Mode** button (**A**, previous page):

   Unite joins the perimeter of the selection into one compound shape, applies the color attributes of the frontmost object to the result (including to any open paths), and hides the object edges in the interior of the shape.**A–B**

   Minus Front subtracts the objects in front from the backmost object, preserving the color attributes of only the backmost object. The subtracted objects are hidden.

   Intersect applies the color attributes of the frontmost object only to the areas where all the selected objects overlap and hides all nonoverlapping areas.

   Exclude turns areas where objects overlap into transparent cutouts, through which any underlying objects will be visible.

3. *Optional:* Double-click the compound shape to isolate it, then change its color attributes, or move or transform individual objects within it to alter its contour.**C**

If you expand a compound shape that contains interior cutouts or more than one path shape, the result is a compound path, whereas a single shape without cutouts expands to a single path. Compare these results with those of the Release Compound Shape command.

To expand a compound shape:

1. Select the compound shape.

2. Click **Expand** on the Pathfinder panel.

The Release Compound Shape command restores the original objects and their color attributes.

To release a compound shape:

1. Select the compound shape.

2. Choose **Release Compound Shape** from the Pathfinder panel menu.**D**

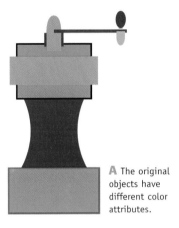

A The original objects have different color attributes.

B We Option/Alt clicked the Unite button to create a compound shape.

C In isolation mode, we used the Selection tool to reshape an object in the compound shape.

D The Release Compound Shape command restored the original object colors.

Applying the Pathfinder commands

Next, you will use the Pathfinder commands on the Pathfinder panel to divide, trim, merge, crop, outline, or subtract areas from selected overlapping paths. The result will be separate, nonoverlapping closed paths or lines, nested within a group. (To learn how the Pathfinder effects on the Effect menu differ from these commands, see page 324.)

Keep the following guidelines in mind as you use the Pathfinder commands:

➤ The original objects can't be restored after the command is applied (except by choosing Undo immediately), so be sure to duplicate the objects first.

➤ Illustrator may take the liberty of closing any open paths for you as it performs the command, so we also recommend closing all open paths first. See our instructions for converting a stroke or an open path into a filled object on page 320.

➤ Transparency settings are preserved.

➤ For the Trim, Merge, and Crop commands, preexisting stroke colors are deleted, unless the object contained an effect or a brush stroke.

➤ The objects that you apply the command to may contain patterns, gradients, brush strokes, or effects.

➤ Editable type must be converted to outlines first.

To apply a Pathfinder command:

1. Select two or more overlapping objects.

2. Click one of the **Pathfinder** buttons on the Pathfinder panel: 🔳 A

   Divide turns each overlapping area into a separate, nonoverlapping object. **B–C** (Read about the setting for Divide and Outline in the sidebar at right.)

   ➤ After applying the Divide command, double-click the group to isolate it. You can apply new fill colors or effects; apply a fill of None; lower an object's transparency; or remove an object to create a cutout effect. You can also move any indivdual object with the Selection tool.

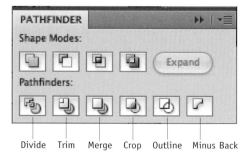

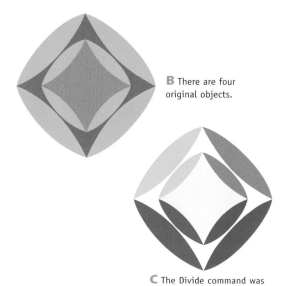

A The Pathfinder buttons on the Pathfinder panel produce separate closed paths or lines.

B There are four original objects.

C The Divide command was applied, and then the resulting shapes were recolored.

CHOOSING PATHFINDER OPTIONS

To open the Pathfinder Options dialog, from which you can choose the following preferences for the Pathfinder commands, choose Pathfinder Options from the Pathfinder panel menu:

➤ The higher the Precision value (.001–100 pt), the more precisely the commands are applied, and the longer they take to process.

➤ With Remove Redundant Points checked, duplicate anchor points in the same x/y location will be deleted.

➤ With Divide and Outline Will Remove Unpainted Artwork checked, the Divide and Outline commands will delete any overlapping areas of selected paths that have a fill of None.

Trim preserves the frontmost object shape but deletes sections of objects that are behind and overlap it.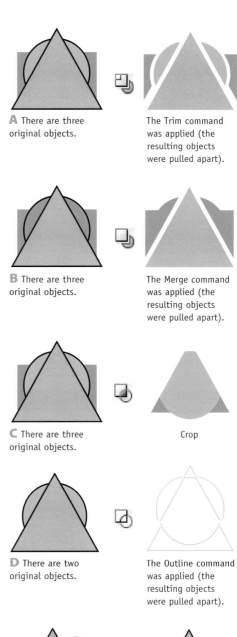 Adjacent or overlapping objects of the same color or shade remain separate (the opposite of the behavior of the Merge command). Stroke colors are deleted, unless the object contains an effect or a brush stroke.

Merge unites only adjacent or overlapping objects that contain the same fill attributes into one object or into nonoverlapping objects (the original objects can contain the same or different stroke attributes).

Crop crops away areas of objects that extend beyond the edges of the frontmost object, and removes the fill and stroke from the frontmost object. Crop works like a clipping mask, except that you can't restore the original objects (unless you choose Undo immediately).

Outline converts all the objects into 0-pt. stroke segments and converts the fill colors to stroke colors. The resulting strokes can be transformed, reshaped, and recolored individually. (Read about the setting for Divide and Outline in the sidebar on the preceding page.)

Minus Back subtracts the objects in back from the frontmost object, leaving only portions of the frontmost object. The color attributes and appearances of the frontmost object are applied to the resulting path. The objects must overlap at least partially for this command to produce a result.

3. To edit the resulting paths, put the group into isolation mode by double-clicking it with the Selection tool.

➤ To apply the last-used Pathfinder command to any selected objects, press Cmd-4/Ctrl-4.

A There are three original objects.

The Trim command was applied (the resulting objects were pulled apart).

B There are three original objects.

The Merge command was applied (the resulting objects were pulled apart).

C There are three original objects.

Crop

D There are two original objects.

The Outline command was applied (the resulting objects were pulled apart).

E There are three original objects.

The Minus Back command was applied (the objects in back cut through the topmost one).

Instead of letting a Pathfinder command close open paths for you, you can use the Outline Stroke command to turn the stroke on a path into a filled object first. This command can also be used to convert a line or a stroke into a closed path so it can then be filled with a gradient, or to prepare it for trapping.

To convert a stroke or an open path to a filled object:

1. Select an object that contains a stroke in the desired weight.**A**

2. Choose Object > Path > **Outline Stroke**. The new object will be the same width as the original stroke, and the original fill color, if any, will be preserved as a separate object.**B–C**

A Select an object that contains a stroke in the desired weight.

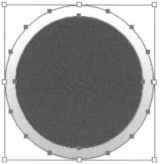

B The Outline Stroke command converted the stroke to a compound path, to which we applied a gradient fill.

C In the final art, the compound path has a stroke color of black.

HOW COMPOUND SHAPES...	...DIFFER FROM COMPOUND PATHS	AND HOW THEY'RE ALIKE
Subpaths are nested as separate objects within a Compound Shape listing on the Layers panel.	Subpaths become part of one Compound Path object and listing. The original objects are no longer listed separately.	Select or transform a whole compound shape or whole compound path with the Selection tool.
Option-click/Alt-click a Shape Mode button to produce a compound shape; each button produces a different result.	There is only one kind of compound path: Overlapping areas are subtracted from the backmost object, period.	Double-click with the Selection tool to isolate a compound path or compound shape, then click to select and edit a whole subpath within it.
The Release Compound Shape command restores the original objects and their appearances.	Released objects adopt the appearances of the compound path, not their original appearances.	A stroke applied to a compound shape or compound path will appear on the outer edge of the overall shape and on any interior cutout shapes.

Using the Compound Path command

The Make Compound Path command joins two or more objects into one object. A transparent hole is created where the objects originally overlapped, through which underlying shapes or patterns are revealed. Regardless of their original color attributes, all the objects in a compound path are painted with the attributes of the backmost object, and form one unit. A compound path can be released at any time, at which point the original object shapes (but not their color attributes) are restored.

To create a compound path:

1. Arrange the objects to be made "see-through" in front of a larger shape.**A**

2. Select all the objects.

3. Do either of the following:

   Choose Object > **Compound Path** > **Make** (Cmd-8/Ctrl-8).

   Provided the objects aren't in a group, you can Control-click/right-click on the artboard and choose **Make Compound Path** from the context menu.

   The frontmost objects will cut through the backmost object like cookie cutters.**B–C** A Compound Path listing appears on the Layers panel; the original objects are no longer listed individually. (Compound shapes, by contrast, are preserved as individual objects within a Compound Shape listing on the Layers panel.)

   The fill and stroke attributes of the backmost object (including any brush stroke) are applied to sections of all the selected objects.

   If the see-through holes don't result, follow the second set of instructions on the next page.

➤ When combined into a compound path, all the objects are moved to the layer of the frontmost object.

➤ To help prevent a printing error, avoid creating a compound path from very complex shapes, and also avoid creating multiple compound paths in the same file.

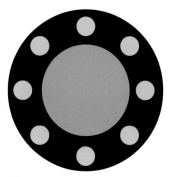

A Place smaller objects on top of a larger one, select all the objects, then Control-click/right-click and choose Make Compound Path.

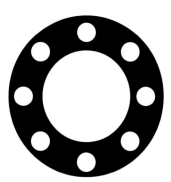

B The objects are converted to a compound path.

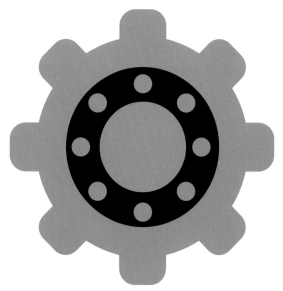

C An object was placed behind the compound path.

Working with compound paths

To add an object to a compound path:

1. Move the object to be added in front of the compound path. (If it's in back, its attributes will be applied to the compound path.) You can restack it by dragging its selection square upward on the Layers panel.

2. Select both the compound path and the object to be added to it.

3. Choose Object > **Compound Path** > **Make** (Cmd-8/Ctrl-8).

By flipping the Reverse Path Direction switch on the Attributes panel, you can remove the fill color of any shape in a compound path, and thereby make that object transparent (or vice versa).

To reverse an object's fill in a compound path:

1. Deselect the compound path.

2. Choose the Direct Selection tool (A).

3. Click the edge of the object in the compound path whose color you want to reverse.**A** Only that path should be selected.

4. Show the **Attributes** panel 🖾 (Cmd-F11/ Ctrl-F11).

5. Click the **Reverse Path Direction Off** button 🖅 or the **Reverse Path Direction On** button 🖅 (the one that isn't currently highlighted).**B–C**

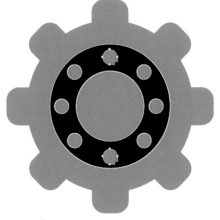

A Two objects are selected in the original compound path.

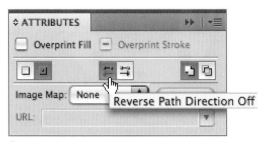

B We clicked the Reverse Path Direction Off button on the Attributes panel.

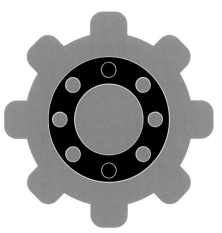

C The color of the two selected holes is reversed.

You can release a compound path back to the original individual objects at any time.

To release a compound path:

1. Select a compound path.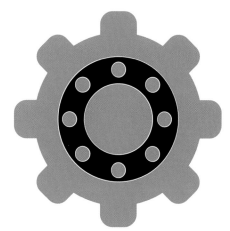A

2. Do either of the following:

   Control-click/right-click the artboard and choose **Release Compound Path** from the context menu.

   Choose Object > **Compound Path** > **Release** (Cmd-Option-Shift-8/Ctrl-Alt-Shift-8).

   All the objects will be selected and will now contain the attributes, effects, and appearances from the compound path—not their original, precompound appearances.B You can use Smart Guides (with Object Highlighting on) to figure out which shape is which.

➤ All the released objects will be nested within the top-level layer that the former compound path resided in.

➤ The Type > Create Outlines command always produces a compound path. If the former character had a counter (an interior shape, such as in the letters P, A, O, R, or D) and you release the compound path, the counter will be a separate path and will have the same color attributes and appearances as the outer part of the letterform.C–D

A Click a compound path.

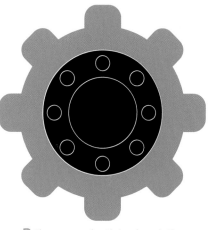

B The compound path is released; the holes are no longer transparent.

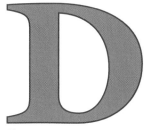

C All type outlines are compound paths.

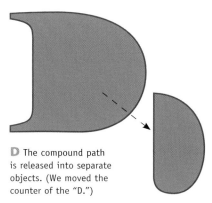

D The compound path is released into separate objects. (We moved the counter of the "D.")

Applying the Pathfinder effects

The Pathfinder effects function like the commands on the Pathfinder panel, except for the following important differences:

► Like other Illustrator effects, the Pathfinder effects modify an object's appearance but not its actual paths—until the file is flattened for output. For example, the Divide, Trim, and Merge effects don't break up overlapping areas into separate objects (as the commands on the Pathfinder panel do) until the file is flattened.

► The effects don't create compound shapes or compound paths.

► You can easily delete the effect at any time, because it is listed on the Appearance panel as an attribute (see page 187).

To apply a Pathfinder effect: ★

1. Collect two or more objects into a layer or group, then target the layer or group (we do mean target—not select). If you don't do this, an alert dialog may appear when you choose the effect.**A** We suggest you delete any applied Stylize or Photoshop effects from the objects.

2. Display the **Appearance** panel ◉ (Shift-F6), then choose an effect from the **Pathfinder** submenu on the **Add New Effect** menu.*fx*. **B–C**

► To move an object into or out of a group that a Pathfinder effect is applied to, move the object's selection square upward or downard on the Layers panel.

► To learn more about effects, see Chapter 15. Like other effects, a Pathfinder effect can be included in a graphic style (see Chapter 16).

► If you expand an object to which a Pathfinder effect has been applied (by choosing Object > Expand Appearance), the result will be one path or a group of paths.

To replace a Pathfinder effect: ★

1. Target the layer or group that the Pathfinder effect is applied to.

2. On the Appearance panel, click the Pathfinder effect listing. The Pathfinder Options dialog opens. Check Preview.

3. From the **Operation** menu, choose a different **Pathfinder** option, then click OK.

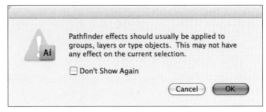

A This alert dialog may appear if you don't target a layer or group before applying a Pathfinder effect.

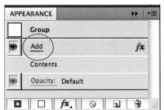

B We applied the Add Pathfinder effect (via the Appearance panel) to unite the objects in this group.

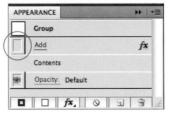

C When we hid the effect on the Appearance panel, the individual object paths redisplayed.

When objects are put in a clipping set, the topmost object (called the "clipping path") crops objects or images below it, like a picture frame or mat. Parts of objects that extend outside the clipping path object aren't visible and don't print. This mechanism allows you to fit multiple objects within the confines of a shape without having to spend time cropping and reshaping them. The clipping path and the masked objects are referred to collectively as a "clipping set." The masked objects can be moved, reshaped, or recolored, and can be restacked within the set. A clipping set can be released at any time.

Creating a clipping set

You can create a clipping set from all the objects on a given layer, in which case it is called a "layer-level" set, or from multiple selected objects on one or more layers, in which case it is called an "object-level" set. The methods for creating these two types of clipping sets differ, as do the methods used to select objects within them, but in all other respects they function the same way.

Before creating a clipping set, review these general guidelines:

► If you need to restack an object before creating a clipping set, drag its listing upward or downward on the Layers panel.

► The clipping path object (the one that works like a frame) can be an open or closed path, editable type, a compound shape, or a closed object produced by the Unite command (Pathfinder panel).

► To help prevent a printing error, avoid using very complex objects in a clipping set.

► When you create a clipping set, the clipping path is assigned a stroke and fill of None, and all the objects remain selected. The underlined words "<Clipping Path>" appear on the Layers panel (unless editable type is used as the clipping path, in which case the type characters are listed instead). When you create an object-level clipping set, the objects are moved automatically into a new group.

Continued on the following page

CLIPPING MASKS

26

When you use the Make Clipping Mask command, the objects to be put into a clipping set can be on any layer. The command moves the objects into a new group listing on the layer in which the clipping path resides.

To create an object-level clipping set:

1. Arrange the object or objects to be masked.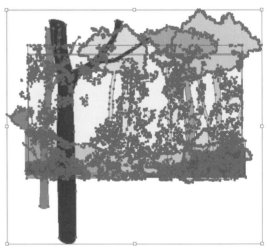 They can be grouped, or not. Stack the clipping path object so it's in front of the objects to be masked.

2. With the Selection tool (V), select the clipping path and the objects to be masked.

3. Do either of the following:

   Control-click/right-click and choose **Make Clipping Mask**.

   Choose Object > **Clipping Mask** > **Make** (Cmd-7/Ctrl-7).**B**

   The clipping path and masked objects will be moved into a new group on the top-level layer in which the clipping path resides.

The Make/Release Clipping Mask button on the Layers panel clips all the objects and groups on the currently active layer (whether the objects are selected or not) and uses the topmost object of the layer or group as the clipping path.

To create a layer-level clipping set:

1. Collect only the objects to be put in a clipping set on the same layer, and make sure the object to be used as the clipping path is the topmost listing on that layer. Keep the layer selected.

2. Click the **Make/Release Clipping Mask** button on the Layers panel.

A A rectangle is positioned in front of the objects to be clipped, and all the objects are selected.

B The Object > Clipping Mask > Make command is applied. Sections of objects that extend beyond the bounds of the rectangle (the clipping path) are hidden.

Selecting objects in a clipping set

Only the sections of masked objects located within the confines of a clipping path are visible, whether the set is selected or not.

Follow the instructions below to select a whole clipping set, which includes the clipping path and the masked objects. The bounding box for a clipping set surrounds the clipping path, not the outermost masked objects (this is also new to CS4).

To select a whole clipping set: ★

Do either of the following:

On the Layers panel 🐟 (F7), click the selection area for the clipping set (group or layer).

For an object-level clipping set (group), choose the Selection tool (V), then click a visible part of any masked object in the document window.

The procedure for selecting individual objects in a clipping set differs depending on whether the set is object-level or layer-level. (To select objects in a layer-level clipping set, see the following page.)

To select objects in an object-level clipping set: ★

Method 1: Isolation mode

1. Choose the Selection tool (V). In the document window, double-click a visible part of one of the masked objects to put the group into isolation mode.

2. Use the Selection tool to move, transform, or recolor any object in the clipping set, **A** or the Direct Selection tool (A) for reshaping. (When you're ready to exit isolation mode, press Esc.)

Method 2: Control panel buttons

1. Choose the Selection (V).

2. To select all the masked objects and not the clipping path (say you want to move or transform all the masked objects in unison), click any visible object within the set, then click the **Edit Contents** button 🔘 on the Control panel. **B–C**

To select just the clipping path, click any object within the clipping set, then click the **Edit Clipping Path** button 🔲 on the Control panel.

➤ You can also select the clipping path or a masked object in an object-level clipping set by clicking its selection area on the Layers panel.

A With the clipping set in isolation mode, you can edit individual objects as you would objects in an ordinary group.

B We clicked the Edit Contents button on the Control panel to select the masked objects, in order to move them.

C The masked objects were moved downward within the "frame" of the clipping path.

To select objects in a layer-level clipping set: ★

1. Choose the Selection tool (V), then click an object in the clipping set (a clipped object or the clipping path). You can use Smart Guides (with Object Highlighting on in Illustrator/ Edit > Preferences > Smart Guides) to locate it.

2. Use the Selection tool to move or transform any object in the clipping set, the Direct Selection tool (A) to reshape a selected object, or the Color or Appearance panel to recolor it. To isolate an individual object, double-click it.

➤ You can also select the clipping path or a masked object in a layer-level clipping set by clicking its selection area on the Layers panel.

RECOLORING A CLIPPING PATH

To apply a fill or stroke color to a clipping path, click its selection area on the Layers panel first. The stroke color will be visible no matter what, whereas the fill color will be visible only if there are gaps between the masked objects.

This is the original clipping set.

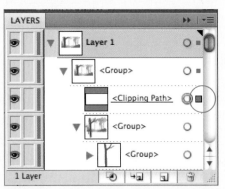

The clipping path is selected via its selection square on the Layers panel.

We added a stroke color (dark green) and a fill color (midnight blue).

Adding to and deleting from a clipping set

To add an object to a clipping set:

1. Choose the Selection tool (V).

2. In the document window, drag the object to be added over the clipping set. **A**

3. On the Layers panel, expand the list for the clipping set group or layer.

4. Drag the listing for the object to be added to the set upward or downward into the group or layer, below the Clipping Path listing. **B–C**

To copy an object in a clipping set:

1. On the Layers panel, expand the group or layer that contains the clipping set, then click the selection area for the object to be copied.

2. Option-drag/Alt-drag the selection square upward or downward, and release it somewhere within the same clipping set group or layer, below the Clipping Path listing.

3. The copy will be in the same *x/y* location as the original object, so you'll need to reposition either object with the Selection tool.

➤ By clicking in the edit column on the Layers panel, you can lock or unlock any object within a clipping set or lock or unlock a whole set.

➤ To restack an object in a clipping set, on the Layers panel (F7), drag the object name upward or downward to a new position within its group or layer.

To take an object out of a clipping set, all you have to do is drag it outside its group or top-level layer on the Layers panel.

To take an object out of a clipping set:

1. Expand the clipping set list on the Layers panel.

2. On the Layers panel, drag the listing for the nested object upward or downward out of the group or layer.

➤ To take an object out of a clipping set and also delete it from the document, select it, then press Delete/Backspace. Adios.

A An new circle is moved over the clipping set.

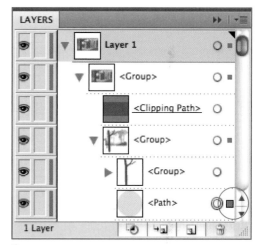

B We moved the new path to the desired stacking position within the clipping set group.

C Once in a blue moon?

Releasing a clipping set

When you release a clipping set, the masked objects are restored to their preclipped state. The former clipping path is listed again as a standard path on the Layers panel, but it will have a stroke and fill of None (not its former attributes)—unless you applied a color to it while it was a clipping path. The steps for releasing a clipping set differ depending on how it was created (whether it is object-level or layer-level).

To release an object-level clipping set: ★

1. Do either of the following:

    With the Selection tool (V), click any visible part of the clipping set.

    On the Layers panel, click the selection area for the group that contains the clipping set.

2. Do either of the following:

    Control-click/right-click in the document window and choose **Release Clipping Mask**.

    Choose Object > **Clipping Mask** > **Release** (Cmd-Option-7/Ctrl-Alt-7).

    The group listing for the clipping set disappears from the Layers panel.

To release a layer-level clipping set: ★

1. On the Layers panel (F7), click the layer that contains the clipping set to be released.

2. Click the **Make/Release Clipping Mask** button ◔ at the bottom of the Layers panel.

A This is the result after we released the clipping set shown in **C** on the preceding page. The large blue rectangle was formerly a clipping path; now it's an ordinary object.

Objects have different densities depending on the type of material they're made of, and may look different depending on how much light is filtering through or reflecting off them. Study an object on your desk for a minute, such as a lamp or a beverage in a glass. You might say "The shade is white" when you describe it simply, but on closer inspection, you may notice that rather than being a dense, uniform color, it contains various permutations of white. And if the lamp is on and light is projecting through it, the shade will look semitransparent rather than opaque.

By using Illustrator's transparency controls, you can add a touch of realism to your drawings. If you draw a window, for example, you can add a tinted, semisheer, diaphanous curtain on top of it. Draw some autumn leaves, and you could lower their opacity to make them look semitransparent. Even abstract designs can be enhanced by opacity changes.

Changing an object's opacity or blending mode

You can change the opacity of any kind of object, even editable type. You can also choose a blending mode for any object to control how its colors blend with the colors in the objects below it. Objects that you add to a group or layer adopt the transparency settings of that group or layer. Illustrator's opacity and blending mode controls are available on the Transparency panel, which can be accessed via the Window menu, the Control panel, and the Appearance panel.

The fine print: To export a file that contains nondefault transparency or blending mode settings to another application, either keep it in the Adobe Illustrator (.ai) format, if the target application supports that format, or save a copy of it in the PDF format (see pages 398–401).

Continued on the following page

TRANSPARENCY

27

IN THIS CHAPTER

To change the opacity or blending mode of an object, group, or layer: ★

1. Do one of the following:

On the Layers panel ◉ (F7), select (or click the target circle for) the object or image to which you want to apply opacity or blending mode settings.**A–B**

To edit the appearance of all the objects on a group or layer, click the target circle for the group or layer.

Select or isolate an object or objects in the document window.

Select some type characters with a type tool, or select a whole type object with the Selection tool.

(To change the opacity of just the fill or stroke on type, see the second task on the next page.)

2. Do either of the following:

To change just the opacity, enter or choose an **Opacity** percentage (0–100%) on the Control panel.

To change the opacity and/or blending mode, click the **Opacity** link on the Control or Appearance ★ panel to open a temporary Transparency panel (or press Cmd-Shift-F10/Ctrl-Shift-F10 to open the Transparency panel ◉). A thumbnail for the selected or targeted layer, group, or object displays on the panel. Choose a different **blending mode** from the menu and/or move the **Opacity** slider.**C–D**

A This is the artwork we started with.

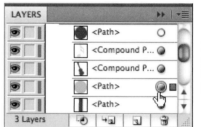

B On the Layers panel, click the target circle for an object, group, or layer.

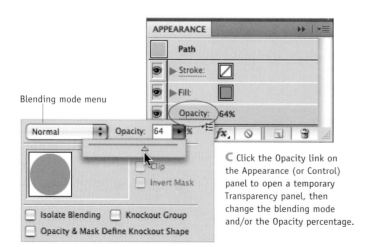

Blending mode menu

C Click the Opacity link on the Appearance (or Control) panel to open a temporary Transparency panel, then change the blending mode and/or the Opacity percentage.

D The opacity and blending modes were changed for some of the objects.

To change the opacity or blending mode of an object's fill or stroke: ★

1. On the Layers panel, click the target circle for an object.**A** (For a type object, follow the next set of instructions instead.)

2. On the Appearance panel ◉ (Shift-F6), expand the Fill or Stroke listing, then click Opacity to open a temporary Transparency panel. Move the **Opacity** slider **B** or choose a **blending mode**. When you click back in the Appearance panel, you will see your new transparency settings listed there.

If you want to change the opacity of the stroke on a type object separately from the fill, or vice versa, and you also want to keep the type editable, follow these instructions.

To change the opacity or blending mode separately of the fill and stroke in type: ★

1. Select a type object using the Selection tool or the Layers panel.**C** You're going to add an extra fill and stroke attribute, so make sure the type is large enough for both of those attributes to be visible.

2. At the bottom of the Appearance panel, click the **Add New Fill** button □ (Cmd-/;Ctrl-/). A new fill attribute and stroke attribute are created.

3. Click the **Fill** color square and choose a fill color. Double-click the **Stroke** color square and choose a stroke color; also use the controls on the panel to change the stroke weight.

4. Double-click **Characters** on the Appearance panel. All the characters in the object will become selected.

5. Click the Fill listing on the Appearance panel, then click the **Delete Selected Item** button 🗑 on the panel; do the same for the Stroke listing. None is now the fill and stroke setting for Characters.

6. Click the **Type** listing at the top of the Appearance panel.

7. Expand the new Fill or Stroke listing, click **Opacity**, then change the **Opacity** percentage **D** and/or the **blending mode**.

➤ If you don't need to keep the type editable, you can change the stroke or fill opacity by converting the type to outlines, then follow step 2 in the first task on this page.

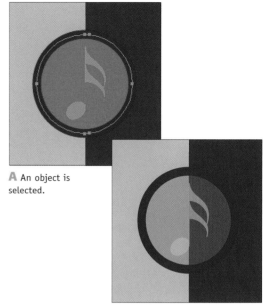

A An object is selected.

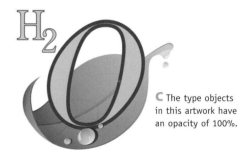

B The opacity is lowered for the object's fill, but not for its stroke.

C The type objects in this artwork have an opacity of 100%.

D The fill opacity of the "0" was reduced to 30%, but the stroke opacity was left at 100%.

Controlling which objects the transparency settings affect

If you apply a blending mode to multiple selected objects, that mode becomes an appearance for each object. In other words, the objects blend with one another and with any underlying objects below them. By using the Isolate Blending option, used in the instructions below, you can seal a collection of objects so they blend with one another but not with the objects below them.

Note that the Isolate Blending option has no effect on opacity settings. In other words, whether this option is on or off, underlying objects will still show through any objects that aren't fully opaque.

To restrict a blending mode to specific objects:

1. On the Layers panel ☁ (F7), click the target circle for a group or layer that contains nested objects to which a blending mode or modes other than Normal have been applied.**A**

2. On the Transparency panel,☁ check **Isolate Blending**.**B** (If this option isn't visible, click the double arrowhead on the panel tab.) Nested objects within the targeted group or layer will blend with one another, but not with any underlying objects below it.

    Note: To reverse the effect, retarget the group or layer, then uncheck Isolate Blending.

➤ If Isolate Blending is checked for objects that are nested within a group or layer and you export the Illustrator file to Photoshop (via File > Export, with the Photoshop .psd format chosen and the Write Layers option clicked), the group will be preserved as separate layers within a layer group, and each nested layer will keep the blending mode setting that it was assigned in Illustrator.

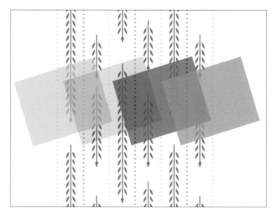

A The original objects consist of a pattern and a group of rectangles. The blending mode and opacity for each rectangle interacts with all the underlying layers.

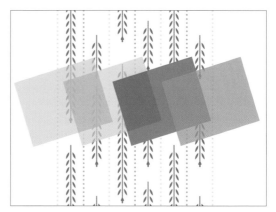

B With Isolate Blending on for the group of rectangles, the blending modes affect only objects within the group. (Note that where objects in the group don't overlap one another, you can still see through to the pattern below.)

The Knockout Group option on the Transparency panel controls whether objects within a group or layer will show through (knock out) one another in the areas where they overlap. This option affects only objects within the same targeted group or layer.

To knock out objects:

1. Nest objects in the same group or layer and arrange them so they partially overlap one another. In order to see how the Knockout Group option works, to some or all of the nested objects, apply opacity values below 100% and/ or apply different blending modes (other than Normal mode).

2. On the Layers panel ☜ (F7), target the group or layer that the objects are nested within.**A**

3. On the Transparency panel,☻ click the **Knockout Group** box once or twice, until a check mark displays.**B** With this option checked, objects nested in the group won't show through one another, but you will still be able to see through any semitransparent objects in the group to underlying objects.

   Note: To turn off the Knockout Group option at any time, target the group or layer that the option is applied to, then click the Knockout Group box until the check mark disappears.

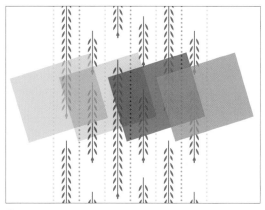

A The Knockout Group option is off for the group of rectangles (Isolate Blending is also off, in this case).

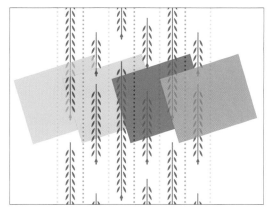

B With the Knockout Group option on, the rectangles are no longer transparent to one another or blend with one another (but they still blend with the underlying pattern).

Using the transparency grid

Once you start changing the opacity settings for objects, you may find it hard to distinguish among objects that have a light but solid tint and those that are semitransparent (have an opacity below 100%). With the transparency grid on, you will be able to see the gray-and-white checkerboard through semitransparent objects.

To show or hide the transparency grid:

Choose View > **Show Transparency Grid** (Cmd-Shift-D/Ctrl-Shift-D).**A** Repeat to hide the grid.

You can change the colors or size of the transparency grid to make it contrast better with the colors in your artwork.

To choose preferences for the transparency grid: ★

1. Deselect all, then click **Document Setup** on the Control panel.

2. In the **Transparency** area, do the following: **B**

   Choose a **Grid Size** of Small, Medium, or Large.

   From the **Grid Colors** menu, choose Light, Medium, or Dark for a grayscale grid, or choose a preset color combo. (Or to choose custom grid colors, click the top color swatch, choose a color in the Colors dialog, then click OK. Repeat for the second swatch.)

3. *Optional:* Check Simulate Colored Paper if you want objects and placed images in your document to look as though they're printed on colored paper. The object color will blend with the "colored paper," which displays on all the artboards. The top color swatch is used as the paper color. You will need to hide the transparency grid to view the effect of this option.

4. Click OK.

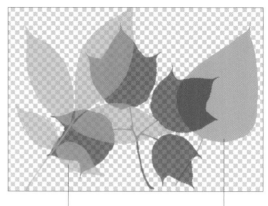

A semitransparent object   A light-colored, opaque object

A With the transparency grid showing, it's easy to see which objects are fully opaque and which are not.

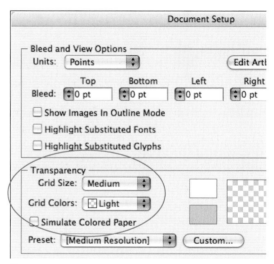

B Choose Transparency options in the Document Setup dialog.

Objects that are stored on the Symbols panel can be placed singly or in multiples into any document, enabling you to create complex art quickly and easily. Any object that can be created in Illustrator can be stored on the Symbols panel ♣ (Cmd-Shift-F11/Ctrl-Shift-F11).**A** Illustrator supplies you with hundreds of symbols, and you can also create your own.

To place a single instance of a symbol onto the artboard, you drag it out of the panel or click the Place Symbol Instance button. To place multiple instances of a symbol (into what is called a symbol set), you either drag with the Symbol Sprayer tool or hold the tool down in one spot. To create a flowering forest meadow, for example, you could create a few tree symbols and flower symbols by dragging and a set or two of grass symbols by spraying.

In this chapter, in addition to learning how to create symbol instances and sets, you will learn how to replace, create, delete, and edit symbols, as well as expand symbol instances. And by using the Symbol Shifter, Scruncher, Sizer, Spinner, Stainer, Screener, and Styler tools (that's a tongue-twister!), you will change the stacking order, position, size, rotation angle, color tint, transparency, and style, respectively, of multiple symbol instances in a selected symbol set. These tools alter the way the instances look without breaking the link to the original symbol.

Continued on the following page

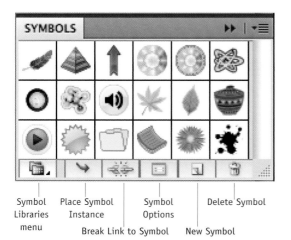

A Use the Symbols panel to store, duplicate, replace, and delete symbols, and to place symbol instances into your artwork.

SYMBOLS

28

IN THIS CHAPTER

The reverse is also true: If you edit the original symbol that some instances are linked to, your changes will appear instantly in all those instances.

Another advantage of using symbols is efficient storage. For example, say you were to spray multiple instances of a tree symbol. Even though you visually see a dozen tree shapes in your document, Illustrator defines the object only once in the document code. This helps reduce the file size and speeds up printing or downloading. File size is especially critical when outputting to the Web in SVG (Scalable Vector Graphics) and Flash (swf) formats. Because each symbol is defined only once in the exported SVG image or Flash animation, the size of the export file is kept relatively small and the download time is minimized.

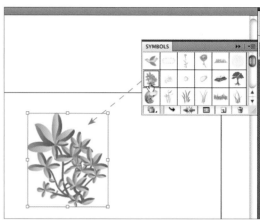

A Drag a symbol from the Symbols panel onto an artboard.

Creating individual symbol instances

In the following instructions, you will create individual symbol instances. Later in this chapter, you will place multiple instances of a symbol quickly by using the Symbol Sprayer tool.

The default assortment of symbols on the panel is limited. On the next page, you will learn how to access other libraries of predefined symbols, and on page 341, you will learn how to create and save your own libraries.

To create individual symbol instances:

1. Display the **Symbols** panel.

2. Do either of the following:

    Drag a symbol from the Symbols panel onto an artboard.**A**

    Click a symbol on the Symbols panel, then click the **Place Symbol Instance** button on the panel. The instance will appear in the center of the document window.

3. Repeat the preceding step if you want to add more instances.**B** To demonstrate the fact that each instance is linked to the original symbol, select an instance on the artboard, then look at the Symbols panel; the symbol thumbnail becomes selected on the panel automatically. Later in this chapter, you will learn how to preserve or break this link.

➤ To duplicate an instance, Option-drag/Alt-drag it in your artwork. The duplicate instance will also be linked to the symbol on the panel.

➤ You can transform a symbol instance or set by manipulating its bounding box (Selection tool).

B This graphic was created from symbols in the Nature library, which is shown on the next page.

Accessing the symbol libraries

Next, you will learn how to access the Adobe symbol libraries.

To access symbols from other libraries:

1. From the **Symbol Libraries** menu 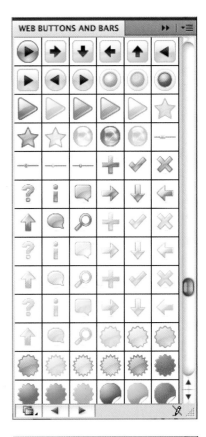 at the bottom of the Symbols panel, choose a library. (Once you create your own libraries, you'll be able to choose them from the User Defined submenu on the Symbol Libraries menu.) A separate library panel opens.**A**

2. Do either of the following:

   Click a symbol on the library panel; it appears on the Symbols panel.

   To add multiple symbols from a library, click, then Shift-click a series of consecutive symbols or Cmd-click/Ctrl-click nonconsecutive ones, then choose **Add to Symbols** from the library panel menu.

   Drag a symbol from a library panel into your document; the symbol will appear on the Symbols panel automatically.

3. To browse through other libraries, click the **Load Next Symbol Library** button ▶ or **Load Previous Symbol Library** button ◀ at the bottom of the library panel.

➤ To change the Symbols panel display, from the Symbols panel menu, choose Thumbnail, Small List View, or Large List View. In Thumbnail view, you can identify the symbol names by using tool tips.

➤ Choose Sort by Name from the panel menu to sort the symbols alphabetically by name. You can also rearrange the symbols on the panel by dragging.

➤ Symbols on the panel save with the current file.

A These are just two of the many predefined symbol libraries available in Adobe Illustrator.

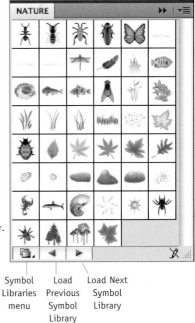

Symbol Libraries menu   Load Previous Symbol Library   Load Next Symbol Library

Replacing symbols

When you replace a symbol in a solo instance or in a symbol set with a different symbol, any transformations, transparency settings, or symbolism tool changes (e.g., from using the Symbol Shifter tool) that were applied to the original instance or set will appear automatically in the replacements.

To replace one symbol with another in an instance:

1. With the Selection tool (V), click a symbol instance in your document.**A**

2. On the Control panel, click the **Replace** thumbnail or arrowhead; a temporary Symbols panel opens. Click a replacement symbol.**B–C**

When you apply a replacement symbol to a set, all the instances in the set are replaced with the new one, even if they originated from different symbols (to create a symbol set, see page 342).

To replace the symbols in a symbol set:

1. With the Selection tool (V), click a symbol set in your document.

2. Click a replacement symbol on the Symbols panel, then choose **Replace Symbol** on the panel menu.

Creating symbols

Now that you're acquainted with the Symbols panel, you're ready to create your own symbols. Any Illustrator object (or group of objects) can be made into a symbol: a standard path, compound path, embedded raster image, type—even another symbol. Well…within reason. If you're planning to spray your new symbol densely all over a document, you should probably try to keep it simple.

Note: Although the object that you create a symbol from can contain a brush stroke, blend, effect, graphic style, or even other symbols, those elements won't be editable in the symbol instances. You can, however, apply a graphic style to instances via the Symbol Styler tool (see page 349).

To create a symbol from an object in your artwork:

1. Create one or more objects or a group. Color it and scale it to the desired size. We also recommend that you duplicate it, because it won't be editable as a standard object once a symbol

A Click an instance in your document.

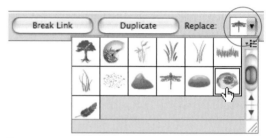

B Click the Replace thumbnail or arrowhead on the Control panel, then click a replacement symbol on the temporary Symbols panel.

C The dragonfly turns into a fish.

is created from it. Keep the object(s) or group selected. **A**

2. Choose the Selection tool (V), then click the **New Symbol** button ▣ at the bottom of the panel. The Symbol Options dialog opens. **B**

3. Enter a name for the new symbol, click **Graphic**, then click OK. **C**

Saving symbol libraries

If you save the symbols currently on the Symbols panel as a library, you'll be able to access them quickly at any time via the Symbol Libraries menu.

To save a symbol library:

1. Make sure the Symbols panel contains only the symbols to be saved in a library, then from the Symbol Libraries menu ▣ at the bottom of the Symbols panel, choose **Save Symbols**. The Save Symbols as Library dialog opens.

2. Type a name for the library in the Save As field, keep the default location (the Symbols folder), then click Save.

3. The new library (or any other user-saved library) can now be opened from the **User Defined** submenu on the Symbol Libraries menu. It will open as a separate panel.

Deleting symbols from the panel

If you try to delete a symbol from the Symbols panel that's being used in your document, you will be given a choice via an alert dialog to expand or delete the instances that were created from it.

To delete symbols from the Symbols panel:

1. Click a symbol on the Symbols panel, then click the **Delete Symbol** button 🗑 at the bottom of the panel.

2. If there are no instances of the deleted symbol in your document, click **Yes** in the alert dialog.

   If the document does contain instances of the symbol, a different alert dialog appears. Click **Expand Instances** to expand the linked instances into nonsymbol objects, or click **Delete Instances** to delete the linked instances (or click Cancel to call the whole thing off).

A Select an object or group in a document.

B In the Symbol Options dialog, enter a name for the new symbol and click Graphic.

C The new symbol appears on the panel.

RENAMING SYMBOLS AND INSTANCES

► To rename a symbol, click the symbol on the panel, click the Symbol Options button ▣ at the bottom of the panel, then change the name in the dialog.

► If you're going to export your symbol artwork to the Flash (swf) format, you can assign names to individual instances. Click an instance, then enter a new name in the Instance Name field on the Control panel.

For the remaining instructions in this chapter, we recommend opening the tearoff toolbar for the symbolism tools, to keep them readily accessible. **A**

Creating symbol sets with the Symbol Sprayer tool

The Symbol Sprayer tool sprays multiple instances of a symbol into a symbol set, and can also be used to delete instances from a set. It's easy and fun to use. You can choose from a slew of options for the tool, but first use it to do a little spraying.

To create instances with the Symbol Sprayer tool:

1. Choose the **Symbol Sprayer** tool (Shift-S).

2. On the Symbols panel, ♣ click a symbol.

3. Click to create one instance per click, or click and hold or drag to create multiple instances quickly. **B** The instances will appear in a set (within one bounding box).

4. *Optional:* To create another set, Cmd-click/Ctrl-click outside the bounding box for the current set to deselect it, then click, or click and hold or drag to create instances.

To add symbols to an existing set, you must use the Symbol Sprayer tool (not the Place Symbol Instance button).

To add instances to a symbol set:

1. Select a symbol set with the Selection tool or the Layers panel.

2. Click a symbol on the Symbols panel. It can be a different symbol than those already in the set.

3. Use the **Symbol Sprayer** tool. **C**

To delete instances from a symbol set:

1. Select a symbol set with the Selection tool or the Layers panel.

2. If the set contains instances from more than one symbol, do either of the following:

   To restrict the deletion to instances of only one symbol, click that symbol on the Symbols panel.

   To allow instances of more than one symbol to be deleted, click a blank area of the Symbols panel to deselect all the symbols.

3. Choose the **Symbol Sprayer** tool.

4. Option-click/Alt-click or Option-drag/Alt-drag within the set.

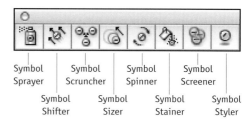

Symbol Sprayer   Symbol Scruncher   Symbol Spinner   Symbol Screener
Symbol Shifter   Symbol Sizer   Symbol Stainer   Symbol Styler

A The Symbol Sprayer tool creates symbol instances, whereas the other symbolism tools modify symbol instances in various ways.

B Create a symbol set with the Symbol Sprayer tool.

C To add instances of a different symbol to a set, select the set, choose the Symbol Sprayer tool, click a new symbol on the Symbols panel, then drag within the set.

Choosing options for the symbolism tools

In the Symbolism Tools Options dialog, you can choose global settings that apply to all the symbolism tools as well as settings that apply just to individual tools. The global settings and the settings that apply to just the Symbol Sprayer are discussed below; settings that are unique to other symbolism tools are mentioned on pages 346–349.

To choose options for the symbolism tools:

1. *Optional:* If you want to change the density for an existing set or sets in your document, select them now.

2. Double-click any symbolism tool. The Symbolism Tools Options dialog opens.**A**

3. To specify a default size for all the symbolism tools, choose or enter a **Diameter** value.

4. The current choice on the **Method** pop-up menu in the Symbolism Tool Options dialog applies to all the symbolism tools except the Symbol Sprayer and Symbol Shifter.

5. To adjust the rate at which the tools produce changes or the sprayer creates instances, choose an **Intensity** value (1–10). The higher the Intensity, the more rapid the changes. Or if you're going to use a stylus and you want it to control the intensity instead, choose any option from the menu except Fixed.

   ➤ The Diameter and Intensity values can also be adjusted on the fly. See the sidebar on page 345.

6. To specify how tightly the instances will be packed within each set when the Symbol Sprayer tool is used, choose a **Symbol Set Density** value (1–10). Changes to this value will also affect any currently selected sets.

7. Check **Show Brush Size and Intensity** to have a change to the current Diameter setting be reflected as a ring around the tool icon, and a change to the Intensity setting be expressed as a shade on that ring (black for high intensity, gray for medium intensity, and light gray for low intensity). With this option off, you'll see just a tool icon onscreen without the ring.

8. Click OK.

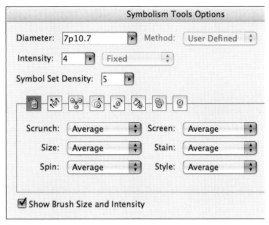

A Use the Symbolism Tools Options dialog to choose global and individual properties for the eight symbolism tools. The pop-up menus in the lower portion of the dialog appear only when the Symbol Sprayer tool icon is selected.

USER DEFINED DEFINED (FOR THE SPRAYER)

For each property of the Symbol Sprayer tool (Scrunch, Size, Spin, Screen, Stain, and Style), you can choose either Average or User Defined:

With Average chosen, the tool adds each new instance based on an average sampling of neighboring instances already in the set, within the diameter of the brush cursor.

With User Defined chosen, the properties will be based on the following values:

➤ Scrunch (density) uses the original symbol density, not modified densities in a set; Size uses the original symbol size, not modified sizes in a set.

➤ Spin is based on the direction in which the mouse is moved.

➤ Screen applies the instance at 100% opacity, not the modified opacity values in a set.

➤ Stain is based on the current fill color at a 100% tint.

➤ Style is based on whichever graphic style is currently selected on the Graphic Styles panel.

Note: The settings chosen from the six individual tool menus are unrelated to the Method setting, which applies to the other symbolism tools.

Editing symbols

In these instructions, you will edit the actual symbol in the panel. When you do so (beware!), the edits will be applied to any and all instances in the document that it is linked to.

To edit a symbol:

1. Do either of the following:

   Double-click a symbol on the Symbols panel. A temporary instance of the symbol appears in your document, in isolation mode.**A**

   Click a symbol instance in your document, click **Edit Symbol** on the Control panel, then click OK if an alert dialog appears. The instance is now in isolation mode.

2. Select and modify the object(s).**B**

3. Exit isolation mode by clicking the gray bar at the top of the document window. The edits will be applied to the original symbol on the Symbols panel,**C** and any instances that are currently linked to that symbol will update automatically. Any transformations that were applied to those instances before the symbol was edited will be preserved.

When you break the link between an instance or set and the original symbol, the instance is converted to a normal object or objects.

To break the link between instances and a symbol:

1. Select a symbol instance or set in your document.

2. Do either of the following:

   Click the **Break Link to Symbol** button ⚛ at the bottom of the Symbols panel. This method must be used when breaking the link for a whole symbol set.

   Click **Break Link** on the Control panel.

➤ To select all the instances of a particular symbol in your document, click the symbol on the Symbols panel, then choose Select All Instances from the panel menu.

➤ To create a variation of an existing symbol, break the link first by following the instructions above. Edit the object(s) or group, then drag it into the Symbols panel. In the Symbol Options dialog, enter a name, click Type: Graphic, then click OK.

A A temporary instance of the symbol appears in the document window, in isolation mode.

B Edit the temporary instance.

C When you exit isolation mode, the symbol updates on the Symbols panel.

REDEFINING A SYMBOL

To replace an existing symbol with a new object or objects, Option-drag/Alt-drag the nonsymbol object over the symbol on the Symbols panel to be replaced (or select the object, click the symbol to be replaced on the panel, then choose Redefine Symbol from the panel menu). Any instances that are linked to that symbol will update accordingly.

Using the Symbol Shifter, Scruncher, Sizer, Spinner, Stainer, Screener, and Styler tools

The tools discussed here can be used to modify attributes of individual instances or instances in a set, such as their stacking position, location, size, orientation, color, transparency, or graphic style, without breaking the link to the original symbol.

To use the Symbol Shifter, Scruncher, Sizer, Spinner, Stainer, Screener, or Styler tool:

1. Select a symbol set or instance in your document.

2. Choose the **Symbol Shifter, Scruncher, Sizer, Spinner, Stainer, Screener,** or **Styler** tool. 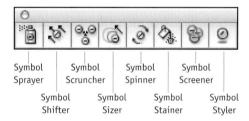A

3. *Optional:* Choose settings via the Symbolism Tool Options dialog (see page 343) or via any of the shortcuts listed at right.

4. Do any of the following:

   Click an instance.

   Drag within a symbol set.

   Hold the mouse button down within a set.

   ➤ Although the symbolism tools affect all the instances in a set, by choosing a small brush diameter and by positioning your pointer carefully, you can control where the tool has the most impact. The effect is strongest in the center of the brush and diminishes gradually toward its perimeter.

The tools are discussed and illustrated individually on the next four pages. Special shortcuts for the tools are also included.

➤ If a selected set contains instances from more than one symbol and one of those symbols is selected on the Symbols panel, modifications made by a symbolism tool will be limited to only the instances of that symbol. To remove this restriction so you can modify instances of different symbols, deselect all symbols first by clicking a blank area of the Symbols panel.

➤ When using a symbolism tool (such as the Symbol Shifter, Scruncher, or Sizer) to modify a set, keep these two seemingly conflicting tendencies in mind: The tool will shift or scale the instances while also trying to maintain the existing set density. Yin and yang.

Continued on the following page

SHORTCUTS FOR QUICK DIAMETER OR INTENSITY CHANGES

When you use a symbolism tool, you can quickly change the tool Diameter or Intensity without opening the Symbolism Tool Options dialog:

Increase the brush Diameter	Press or hold down] (right bracket)
Shrink the brush Diameter	Press or hold down [(left bracket)
Increase the brush Intensity	Press or hold down Shift-]
Decrease the brush Intensity	Press or hold down Shift-[

Symbol Sprayer   Symbol Scruncher   Symbol Spinner   Symbol Screener

Symbol Shifter   Symbol Sizer   Symbol Stainer   Symbol Styler

A All the symbolism tools except the Sprayer are used for modifying existing symbol instances.

The Symbol Shifter tool 🌀

The Symbol Shifter tool has two functions. It either shifts instances in a set sideways, based on the direction in which the mouse is dragged, or changes their stacking (front-to-back) order. Having the ability to bring instances forward or behind other instances would be useful, say, in a set in which trees are obscuring some figures: You could move the trees closer together to create a forest, then bring the figures forward, in front of the trees.

➤ Shift-click with this tool to bring an instance in front of adjacent instances, or Option-Shift-click/ Alt-Shift-click within a symbol set to send an instance behind adjacent instances.**A–B**

The Symbol Scruncher tool 🌀

The Symbol Scruncher tool either pulls symbol instances closer together or spreads them apart. A symbol set of clouds or fish, for example, could be contracted (scrunched) to bring the instances closer together or expanded to spread them apart.

➤ You can drag with the tool; or hold the mouse button down in one spot; or Option-drag/ Alt-drag to spread the instances apart.**C–D**

A With the Symbol Shifter tool, drag in the direction in which you want the instances to shift. The tool tries to preserve the current density and arrangement of instances as it performs its job. Here, it is being used with Option-Shift held down on a symbol set...

B ...to shift the green leaves behind the red ones.

C Option/Alt drag across a symbol set with the Symbol Scruncher tool...

D ...to spread the instances apart. The leaves are "unscrunched."

The Symbol Sizer tool 🔘

Because the Symbol Sprayer tool can't create instances of variable sizes, the Symbol Sizer is useful for applying scale variations to existing instances.

➤ Click on or drag across instances to enlarge them,**A** or Option-click/Alt-click or Option-drag/Alt-drag to shrink them. Instances closest to the center of the cursor will scale the most.

The Method options for this tool are as follows: User Defined sizes the instances based on how you use the mouse, Average gradually makes variably sized instances more uniform in size, and Random adds variability to the scale changes.

There are two extra features for this tool in the options dialog. Proportional Resizing prevents instances from being distorted as they are resized. Resizing Affects Density allows instances to either move apart when they're enlarged or move closer together when they're scaled down; with this option unchecked, the Sizer tries to preserve the existing set density.

The Symbol Spinner tool 🔘

The Symbol Spinner tool rotates instances (changes their orientation).

The Method options for this tool are as follows: User Defined rotates symbol instances in the direction in which the mouse is dragged,**B–C** Average gradually makes the orientation of all rotated instances within the brush diameter more uniform, and Random varies their orientation.

As you use this tool, temporary arrows appear in the direction the instances are rotating. If the arrows are hard to see against the artwork, change the selection color for the layer the set resides in to a more contrasting color.

A Instances are scaled — some enlarged, some shrunk — with the Symbol Sizer tool (Method: Random).

B The Symbol Spinner tool is dragged in the direction shown by the arrows (Method: User Defined).

C Some of the leaves were rotated.

The Symbol Stainer tool

The Symbol Stainer tool colorizes solid-color fills, patterns, and gradients in symbol instances with variable tints of the current fill color. This is a useful tool because you can't recolor instances via the usual Illustrator color controls. You could use the Stainer to vary the shades of green in foliage, the shades of brown in buildings, etc.

➤ Before using this tool, choose a fill color to be used for staining. Click or drag on an instance or within a set to apply a tint of the current fill color; continue clicking or dragging to increase the amount of colorization, up to the maximum amount.**A** Option-click/Alt-click or Option-drag/ Alt-drag to decrease the amount of colorization and restore more of the original symbol color. Shift-click or Shift-drag to restain only instances that have already been stained. You can apply more than one color to a set.

The Method options for this tool are as follows: User Defined gradually stains instances with the current fill color; Average evens out the amount of any existing staining without applying a new stain; and Random varies the colorization, for a more naturalistic effect (we've gotten good results with this setting).

Note: The Symbol Stainer results increase the file size and diminish performance, so don't use this tool if you're going to export your file in the Flash (SWF) format or if system memory is a concern.

The Symbol Screener tool

The Symbol Screener tool increases or decreases the opacity of instances within the brush diameter. Use this tool to fade instances and make them more transparent, either randomly or uniformly.

➤ Click and hold on or drag across instances to make them more transparent.**B** Option-click/ Alt-click on or Option-drag/Alt-drag across instances to restore their opacity.

The Method options for this tool are as follows: User Defined gradually increases or decreases the transparency, Average makes nonuniform transparency more uniform, and Random varies the transparency. If this tool doesn't produce any results, choose the User Defined or Random option for it.

A We chose a dark red as the fill color and the Random method before using the Symbol Stainer tool on this set.

B The Symbol Screener tool is clicked on some instances.

The Symbol Styler tool

The Symbol Styler tool applies the graphic style that's currently selected on the Graphic Styles panel to symbol instances. By selecting different styles on the Graphic Styles panel, you can apply multiple styles to a symbol set. The tool can also be used to remove styling.

➤ Click a symbol instance or set and the Symbol Styler tool before clicking a graphic style on the Graphic Styles panel (you can access it via the Control panel).

➤ Click and hold on or drag across an instance or instances to apply the current graphic style.A–B The longer you hold the mouse down, the more completely the style settings are applied. Pause for the screen to redraw. This can take some time, even on a fast machine.

➤ Shift-click or Shift-drag to gradually apply the currently selected graphic style only to instances that are already styled, without applying it to any unstyled instances.

➤ Option-click/Alt-click or Option-drag/Alt-drag to remove any existing styling.

The Method options for this tool are as follows: User Defined gradually increases or decreases the amount of styling; Average evens out the amount of styling already applied to instances, without applying any new styling; and Random doesn't seem to make any difference, at least in our testing.

A This is the original symbol set.

B And this is the set after the Symbol Styler tool was used to apply a few different graphic styles.

Expanding symbol instances

When applied to a symbol set, the Expand command breaks the set apart into individual instances without breaking the link to the original symbol, and nests the resulting instances within a group on the Layers panel. When the command is applied to an individual symbol instance, its link to the original symbol is broken, and the resulting paths are nested within a group on the Layers panel.

To expand a symbol instance or set:

1. Select a symbol instance, multiple instances, or symbol set.**A**

2. Choose Object > **Expand** (or choose Object > **Expand Appearance** if you applied an effect or graphic style to the symbol instance or set).

3. In the Expand dialog,**B** check **Object** and **Fill**, then click OK.

4. If you expanded a symbol **set**,**C** you can now use the Direct Selection tool to move the individual instances apart, if desired, or double-click the group with the Selection tool to isolate it, then modify the instances. In either case, they will remain linked to the original symbol.

    If you expanded an individual **instance**,**D** it will now be a group of paths, unlinked from the original symbol.**E** You can edit it in isolation mode.

➤ If you use the Symbol Stainer tool on a symbol set and then expand the set, the instances that were modified by the tool will now have a numeric listing on the Layers panel.

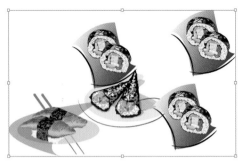

A A symbol set is selected.

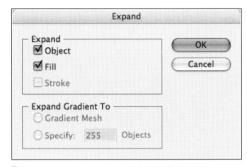

B Object and Fill are checked in the Expand dialog.

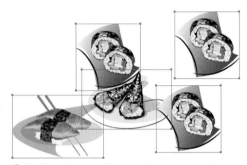

C The Expand command was applied to the symbol set; the result is individual instances.

D An individual symbol instance is selected.

E The Expand command was applied to an individual symbol instance. (We moved the resulting paths apart.)

Now that you're comfortable using the basic color controls in Illustrator, you're ready to explore the Recolor Artwork dialog.* This complex and impressive dialog lets you edit colors in an active group or in selected artwork, generate color schemes based on harmony rules and variation types, save the resulting colors as a group to the Swatches panel and, should the need arise, reduce the number of colors in your artwork. You might find this feature useful if you want to apply a set of coordinated colors quickly, if your projects require you to work with an approved group of colors, or if you simply want to see how your artwork might look in a new range of hues, tints, or saturation values.

Creating color groups via the Recolor Artwork dialog

There are so many features in the Recolor Artwork dialog, we've decided to break our instructions down into four manageable tasks. In this first task, you will save the existing colors in your artwork as a group, for safekeeping, and then create new color groups based on those colors.

To create a color group via the Recolor Artwork dialog:

1. Select the objects to be recolored. **A**

2. Do either of the following:

   Click the **Edit or Apply Colors** button ♻ at the bottom of the Color Guide panel.▣ The current color group on the panel is applied instantly to the objects in the preview.

   Click the **Recolor Artwork** button ♻ on the Control panel. The colors in the selected objects are unchanged in the preview, at least initially.

Continued on the following page

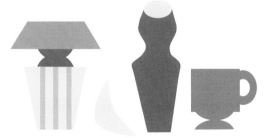

A These are the original objects.

This dialog was called "Live Color" in Illustrator CS3.

LIVE COLOR

29

3. In the Recolor Artwork dialog,**A** click the **Edit** tab. Check **Recolor Art** (bottom of the dialog).

4. If the list of Color Groups isn't displaying on the right side of the dialog, click the **Show Color Group Storage** button.

5. To create a color group from the selected objects, click the **Get Colors from Selected Art** button ⊞ at the top of the dialog, and enter a descriptive name in the adjacent field. Click the **New Color Group** button.⊞ The new group appears on the list of Color Groups (and also on the Swatches panel). You can click this group to restore the original object colors at any time.

6. To try out some new colors on the selected objects, start by choosing a rule from the **Harmony Rules** menu at the top of the dialog. You may recognize these rules from the Color Guide panel.

7. To adjust all the colors in the selected objects, do either or both of the following:

Use the tool tip to find out whether the slider below the color wheel says "**Adjust brightness**" or "**Adjust saturation**." Click the button above it if you want to switch modes, then move the slider to adjust the lightness or color purity.

From the Color Mode menu, choose **Global Adjust**, then move the **Saturation**, **Brightness**, **Temperature**, and **Luminosity** sliders to adjust the colors.

8. Click the **New Color Group** button ⊞ to save the active color group to the list of Color Groups (and to the Swatches panel).

9. Continue to create as many new groups as you like by repeating steps 6–8, and recolor your artwork at any time by clicking a different group on the Color Groups list.**B**

10. If you want the edits to be applied to the artwork, keep Recolor Art checked, or uncheck it if you don't, then click OK.

➤ To delete a color group, click the group, then click the Delete Color Group button.🗑

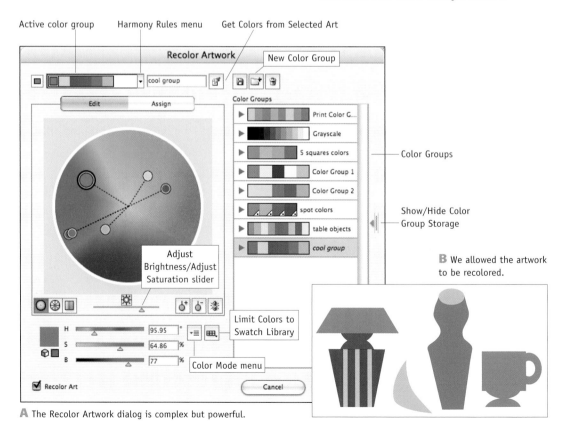

A The Recolor Artwork dialog is complex but powerful.

Using the color wheel in the Recolor Artwork dialog

Next you will use the color wheel in the Recolor Artwork dialog to adjust the hue, saturation, and brightness of process colors in your artwork.

To use the color wheel in the Recolor Artwork dialog:

1. Select the objects to be recolored.**A**

2. On the Control panel, click the **Recolor Artwork** button.

3. In the Recolor Artwork dialog, check **Recolor Art**, then click the **Edit** tab.

4. If you don't see a color wheel, click the **Display Smooth Color Wheel** button.

5. Edits to the color wheel affect the active color group. To choose that group, either click the **Get Colors from Selected Art** button at the top of the dialog or click a group on the **Color Groups** list. In addition, you may choose a new rule from the **Harmony Rules** menu.

   Each round marker on the color wheel represents a color in the current group; the largest marker represents the current base color.**B** The arrangement of markers reflects either the colors in the selected artwork or colors that are based on the current harmony rule relationships.

6. When the dialog is first opened (or if the Get Colors from Selected Art button is clicked), the lines connecting the markers to the hub are dashed and the color markers can be moved independently from one another. If you click a color group or choose a harmony rule, the connecting lines become solid and the color relationships are preserved, as the color markers can be moved only as a unit. Depending on how you want to edit the artwork colors in the next step, click the **Unlink Harmony Colors** button to unlink the markers, or click the **Link Harmony Colors** button to link them.

7. From the **Color Mode** menu, choose **HSB**. To edit the current color group, do any of the following:

   Drag a color marker around the wheel to shift it to a different **hue C** (and **A**, next page). The Hue (H) slider moves accordingly.

Continued on the following page

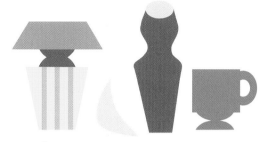

A This is the original artwork.

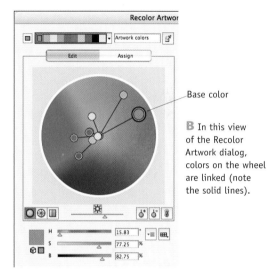

Base color

B In this view of the Recolor Artwork dialog, colors on the wheel are linked (note the solid lines).

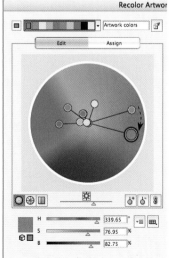

C To shift all the hues, the base color marker is dragged in a circular direction.

Drag a color marker inward or outward to adjust the **saturation** or **brightness**, depending on the current status of the **Show Saturation/Brightness and Hue** button. ☀ ❋ B

➤ If colors are linked (connected by solid lines) when you move the base color marker, all the markers will move.

Hold down **Shift** as you drag a marker inward, outward, or around the wheel to constrain the change to just the saturation, brightness, or hue.

To add a new color (and marker) to the group, click the **Add Color** tool, ⌀⁺ then click in the wheel.

To remove a color from the group, Control-click/right-click the marker to be removed and choose **Remove Color**. ★

To choose a **replacement color**, double-click a color marker to open the Color Picker, or Control-click/right-click a marker and choose **Select Shade** or **Color Picker**. ★ C–D (In the picker, click Color Models to display the process color controls, or click Color Swatches to view the colors that are currently on the Swatches panel.)

8. Although you could click the Save Changes to Color Group button 💾 to save your changes to the existing group, that step can't be undone, so a better way to save your edited colors is to modify the group name, then click the **New Color Group** button. ⬚⁺ The new group displays on the list, and your original group colors are preserved.

9. Do either of the following:

To save any new color groups to the Swatches panel and **recolor** the selected objects, click OK.

To save any new color groups to the Swatches panel **without recoloring** the selected objects, uncheck **Recolor Art**, then click OK.

A The hues are changed.

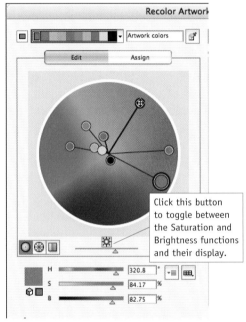

Click this button to toggle between the Saturation and Brightness functions and their display.

B Drag a color marker inward or outward to adjust either the brightness or the saturation.

C These are the results after we increased the saturation for the yellow marker and replaced the base color (with green).

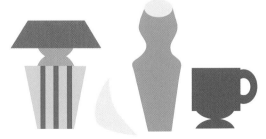

D And this is after we clicked the Unlink Harmonies button and then moved some of the markers individually.

Assigning colors to artwork via the Recolor Artwork dialog

By using the Assign tab of the Recolor Artwork dialog, you can control which colors in a group will replace specific colors in your artwork. The features in this tab can be confusing, so don't worry if it takes a few tries to get accustomed to using them. We will cover just the main features.

To assign colors to artwork via the Recolor Artwork dialog:

1. Select the objects to be recolored.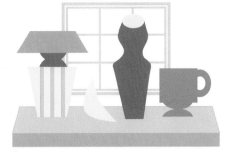

2. On the Control panel, click the **Recolor Artwork** button. In the Recolor Artwork dialog, check **Recolor Art**.

3. Click the **Assign** tab. Colors from the currently selected objects display in the Current Colors column, and colors from the active color group display in the New column.

4. To change the active color group, click a group on the **Color Groups** list on the right side of

A This is the original artwork.

the dialog C and/or choose a new rule from the **Harmony Rules** menu at the top of the dialog.

5. If the new active color group contains fewer colors than the current colors, the current colors that are close in hue, shade, or tint to one another will be grouped in the same row and will be assigned the same new color, thereby reducing the number of colors. The solid colors and tints to be assigned to a row will display in the New column. **D**

Continued on the following page

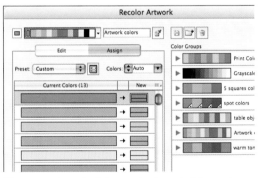

B In the Assign tab of the Recolor Artwork dialog, colors from the selected artwork display in the Current Colors column, and replacement colors are shown in the New column.

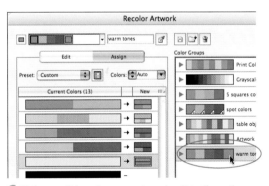

C Click one of the color groups to assign it to the active color group. Because the group we clicked contains just five colors, Illustrator combined similar colors into four multi-color rows in the Current Colors column.

D A new color group is assigned to the artwork.

RESTORING THE ORIGINAL COLORS

To restore the original colors to your artwork, click the Get Colors from Selected Art button at the top of the Recolor Artwork dialog.

Click a color in the **New** column (a white border displays around it, and the row becomes selected). To edit the color, move the sliders below the columns; or double-click the color, then use the Color Picker; or click Color Swatches in the picker to choose from the colors that are currently on the Swatches panel.

6. Do any of the following:

To reassign a color to a different New color, drag a block from the **Current Colors** column into a different row. **A–B**

To reassign a whole multicolor row to a different New color, drag the **selector bar** (which is located at the left edge of the row) into a different row. **C**

To reassign a New color to a different Current Colors row, drag it upward or downward in the **New** column.

➤ To prevent a row of Current Colors from being reassigned to a New color, click the arrow between the two columns. **D–E** (To permit the colors to be assigned, click between the two columns again.)

7. *Optional:* Click the New Color Group button to save the active color group to the Color Groups list (and to the Swatches panel).

8. Click OK.

➤ To locate one of the Current Colors in your artwork, click the "Click colors above to find in artwork" button, then click a color in the Current Colors column. Just that color will display fully; other current colors will be dimmed. Or to locate all of the colors in a multicolor row, click the selector bar. Click the button you activated to turn the feature off.

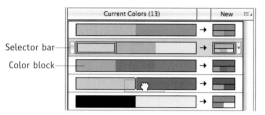

Selector bar
Color block

A Drag a Current Color block into another row to reassign it to a different New color.

B The tabletop and window are now blue-green.

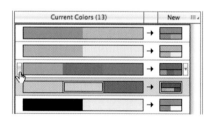

C You can drag the selector bar to relocate a whole row.

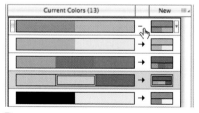

D Click between two columns to remove the arrow, and thereby prevent colors in that row from being reassigned.

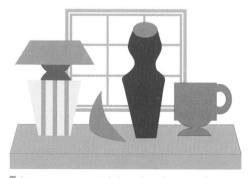

E Because we prevented the reds and oranges from being reassigned, the original cup color was preserved.

Reducing colors via the Recolor Artwork dialog

Yet another use for the Recolor Artwork dialog is to reduce the number of colors in your artwork. This is helpful, say, if you're planning to print your artwork using one, two, or three spot colors instead of the usual four process colors.

To reduce colors in artwork via the Recolor Artwork dialog:

1. *Optional:* If you're going to reduce the colors in your artwork to specific process or spot colors, make sure the desired colors are on your document's Swatches panel. Deselect your artwork, select the desired colors, then on the Swatches panel, click the New Color Group button 🖺 to put them in a group.

2. Use File > Save As (Cmd-Shift-S/Ctrl-Shift-S) to copy your file.

3. Select the objects for color reduction. **A**

4. On the Control panel, click the **Recolor Artwork** button. 🌑

5. In the Recolor Artwork dialog, click the **Assign** tab. Check **Recolor Art** to preview changes in your artwork (and to allow your changes to apply to the artwork when you exit the dialog).

6. Do either of the following:

   From the **Colors** menu, choose the desired number of colors. **B–C** That number of colors from the active color group will be applied to your artwork, starting from the first color, in order. If you created a color group (step 1, above), you can click that group now. If you didn't create a specific color group, you may click a different color group or choose a new harmony rule.

Continued on the following page

A The original artwork contains 13 colors.

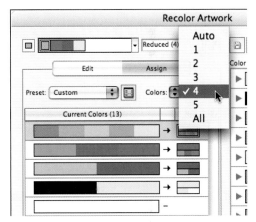

B When you select a value from the Colors menu, the Current Colors are reduced to that number.

C The number of Current Colors in this artwork was reduced to the first four colors in its original color group.

LIMITING COLORS ON THE WHEEL

To limit the colors on color wheel and the Harmony Rules menu to colors in a library, from the Limit Color Group to Swatch Library menu, 🎛️ choose a library name (e.g., Color Books > PANTONE Solid Coated). The chosen library name will be listed above the menu button. (To remove the current restriction, choose None from the same menu.)

From the **Preset** menu, choose **1-**, **2-**, or **3 Color Job.**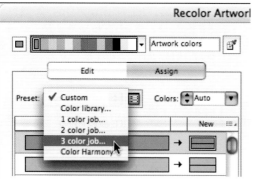 When the dialog opens, from the Library menu,⊞, choose a matching system library or choose None, then click OK. If you chose a library, the active color group will now be limited to colors in that library.**B–C**

➤ To reset the artwork colors to the active color group at any time, choose Auto on the Colors menu or choose Color Harmony on the Preset menu. Or to restore the original colors to your artwork, click the Get Colors from Selected Art button.

7. Follow steps 5–7 on pages 355–356 to reassign and edit the New colors.

8. *Optional:* Click the New Color Group button to add the reduced color group (now the active color group) to the Swatches panel.

9. Click OK.

➤ To control whether black is recolored in your artwork or preserved, click the Color Reduction Options button next to the Preset menu. In the Recolor Options dialog,**D** check or uncheck Preserve: Black. This dialog contains the same Preset and Colors menus as the Recolor Artwork dialog, plus Colorize Method options. To learn more about these options, see "Color > Working with color groups (harmonies) > Reduce colors in your artwork" in Illustrator Help.

A You can also reduce the number of Current Colors by choosing a Color Job option from the Preset menu.

B Here, the same artwork is reduced to three colors by way of the 3 Color Job preset.

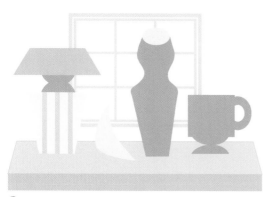

C The 1 Color Job preset is applied, with an even more minimal result. (We changed the sole color in the New column to green.)

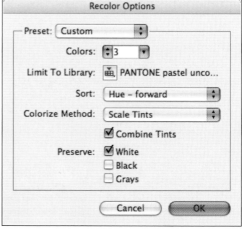

D In the Recolor Options dialog, you can specify whether black in the artwork is recolored or preserved.

The preferences are settings for various Illustrator features that apply to the current and future documents. Use this chapter as a reference guide to options in the 12 panels of the Preferences dialog. To open this dialog, press Cmd-K/Ctrl-K; or deselect all, then click Preferences on the Control panel; ★ or choose from the Illustrator/Edit > Preferences submenu. To switch panels once the dialog is open, choose from the menu at the top of the dialog or click Next or Previous.

General Preferences

Keyboard Increment
This value is the distance (0–1296 pt) a selected object moves when an arrow key is pressed on the keyboard. To move a selected object by 10 times the current Keyboard Increment, press Shift-arrow.

Constrain Angle
This is the angle (–360 to 360°) for the x and y axes. The default setting is 0° (parallel to the edges of the document window). Tool functions, transformations,

Continued on the following page

WHAT THE CONSTRAIN ANGLE AFFECTS

► Type objects

► Rectangle, Ellipse, and Graph tools

► Some transformation tool dialogs (Scale, Reflect, and Shear, but not Rotate or Blend)

► Gradient tool and Pen tool (with Shift key down)

► Objects moved with Shift down or via an arrow key

► Grid

► Smart Guides (Construction Guides and Transform Tools options)

► Info panel readouts

Note: To establish a Constrain Angle based on an object that was rotated by using the Rotate tool, select the object, then enter the Angle readout ⌂ from the Info panel as the new Constrain Angle.

As an object is drawn, it conforms to our current Constrain Angle of 25°.

PREFERENCES

30

IN THIS CHAPTER

dialog measurements, the construction of new objects, Smart Guides, the grid, etc. are calculated relative to the current Constrain Angle.

Corner Radius

This value controls the degree of curvature in the corners of objects drawn with the Rounded Rectangle tool (0–1296 pt.; 12 pt is the default). 0 produces a right angle. This value can also be established in the Rounded Rectangle dialog.

Disable Auto Add/Delete

Checking this option disables the ability of the Pen tool to change to a temporary Add Anchor Point tool when it is moved over a path segment on a selected path, or to a temporary Delete Anchor Point tool when it is moved over an anchor point.

Use Precise Cursors

When this option is checked, the drawing and editing tool pointers display as crosshairs instead of as the tool's icon. To turn this option on temporarily when the preference is off, press Caps Lock.

Show Tool Tips

When this option is checked and you rest the pointer on an application feature, such as a panel button, tool, swatch, or icon, a short description of that feature pops up onscreen. For some features, such as tools, the shortcut is also listed. We recommend keeping this option on, as helpful reminders.

Anti-aliased Artwork

When this option is checked, edges of existing and future vector objects (not placed images) look smoother onscreen. It doesn't affect print output.

Select Same Tint %

When this option is checked, the Select > Same > Fill Color and Stroke Color commands select only objects containing the same spot (not process) color and tint percentage as the currently selected object. When this option is off, the tint percentage is ignored as a criterion.

Append [Converted] Upon Opening Legacy Files

With this option checked, when opening a file that was created in Illustrator 10 or earlier into a CS version of the application, Illustrator appends the word "[Converted]" to the file name.

Double Click to Isolate

If this option is checked and you double-click an object or group, the object or group is put into isolation mode and other objects become temporarily uneditable. To exit isolation mode, click the gray bar at the top of the document window or press Esc. We recommend keeping this option checked. To put an object (or group) into isolation mode when this option is off, select the object, then click the Isolate Selected Object button ⌗ on the Control panel.

Use Japanese Crop Marks

Check this box to use Japanese-style crop marks when outputting color separations.

Transform Pattern Tiles

With this option checked, if you use a transformation tool (such as the Scale tool) on an object that contains a pattern, the pattern also transforms. This setting can also be turned on or off in the Move dialog, on the Transform panel menu, and in the dialogs for the individual transformation tools.

Scale Strokes & Effects

Check this box to allow an object's stroke weight and effects to be scaled when you scale an object by using its bounding box, the Scale tool, or the Free Transform tool. This option can also be turned on or off in the Scale dialog and on the Transform panel menu.

Use Preview Bounds

If this option is checked, an object's stroke weight and any effects are included as part of an object's height and width dimensions. It affects the Align commands, the Transform panel calculations, and the dimensions of the bounding box. (If you were to select an object, apply a command on the Effect > Distort & Transform submenu, and then turn this feature on and off, you would see a change in the size of the bounding box.)

Reset All Warning Dialogs

Click this button to allow warnings in which you checked "Don't Show Again" to redisplay when editing operations cause them to appear.

RESETTING THE PREFERENCES

To restore all the default Illustrator preferences, quit/exit Illustrator, then relaunch the program while holding down Cmd-Option-Shift/Ctrl-Alt-Shift.

Preferences

General

Keyboard Increment: 1 pt

Constrain Angle: 0 °

Corner Radius: 12 pt

OK

Cancel

Previous

Next

☐ Disable Auto Add/Delete
☑ Use Precise Cursors
☑ Show Tool Tips
☑ Anti–aliased Artwork
☐ Select Same Tint %
☑ Append [Converted] Upon Opening Legacy Files

☑ Double Click To Isolate
☐ Use Japanese Crop Marks
☑ Transform Pattern Tiles
☑ Scale Strokes & Effects
☑ Use Preview Bounds

Reset All Warning Dialogs

Selection & Anchor Display Preferences

Selection

Tolerance
Specify the range within which an anchor point becomes selected when you click near it with the Direct Selection tool (the default setting is 3 px).

Object Selection by Path Only
With this option checked, in order to select an object with the Selection or Direct Selection tool, you must click a path segment or anchor point. With this option unchecked, you can select a filled object in Preview view by clicking the fill area with a selection tool. We usually keep this option on.

Snap to Point
With this option checked, the pointer will snap to a nearby anchor point or guide, within the range of pixels that you specify in the adjacent field (the default setting is 2 px).

Anchor Point and Handle Display

Anchors
Choose a display style for anchor points: small selected and unselected points, large selected points and small unselected points, or large selected and unselected points. We recommend choosing the third option.

Handles
Choose a display style for direction points on direction handles: small, large, or hollow.

Highlight Anchors on Mouse Over
If this option is checked and you move the Direct Selection tool over an anchor point, the point will become highlighted (enlarged). We recommend checking this option, as it makes it easier to locate anchor points on a path.

Show Handles When Multiple Anchors Are Selected
Check this option to permit the display of dual direction handles on multiple anchor points when selected with the Direct Selection tool, or uncheck this option to allow a pair of direction handles to display on only one selected point at a time.

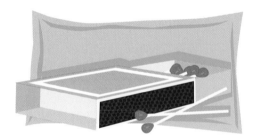

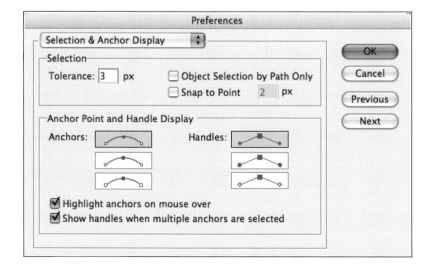

Type Preferences

Size/Leading, Baseline Shift, and Tracking
Selected text is modified by this increment each time a keyboard shortcut is executed for the respective command.

Type Object Selection by Path Only
With this option checked, to select a type object with a selection tool, you have to click right on its path. With this option unchecked, you can select a type object by clicking anywhere on or near it. Unless your artwork is very complex, we recommend keeping this option off.

Show Asian Options
Check this option to display options for Chinese, Japanese, and Korean language characters on the Character panel, Paragraph panel, and Font menu.

Show Font Names in English
When this option is checked, Chinese, Japanese, and Korean font names display in English on the Font menus. When this option is unchecked, two-byte font names display in the native characters for the font.

Number of Recent Fonts
Choose the maximum number of recently chosen fonts (1–15) to be listed on the Type > Recent Fonts submenu.

Font Preview
Check this option to have font family names display in their actual fonts, along with icons for each kind of font (e.g., TrueType, OpenType) for easy identification on the Type > Font menu, on the Character panel, and in the Find Font dialog. Also choose a Size for the font display of Small, Medium, or Large.

Enable Missing Glyph Protection
Check this option to let Illustrator preserve a glyph that's being used in your artwork if you switch to a font in which that glyph isn't supported.

Use Inline Input for Non-Latin Text
Check this option to be able to type non-Latin characters directly into Illustrator (rather than having to use a separate dialog outside Illustrator).

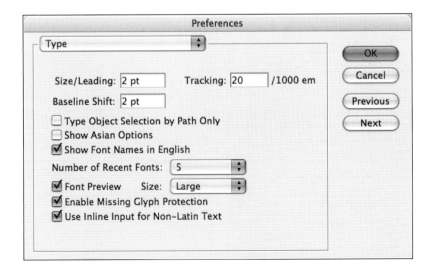

Units & Display Performance Preferences

To open this panel of the dialog quickly in the Mac OS, press Cmd-,/Ctrl-, (comma). ★

Units

General

This unit of measure is used in entry fields in most panels and dialog boxes, and on the rulers in the document window. (See also the instructions on the following page.)

Stroke

This unit of measure is used on the Stroke panel and in the Stroke Weight field on the Control and Appearances panels.

Type

This unit of measure is used on the Character and Paragraph panels. (We use points.)

Asian Type

This unit of measure is used for Asian type.

➤ When entering values in a dialog box or panel, you can use any unit that is listed in the sidebar below, regardless of the current default units. A value entered in a nondefault unit is converted to the default unit when you press Tab or Return/Enter.

Numbers Without Units Are Points

If Picas is the current Units: General setting and this option is checked, a value entered in a field will be listed as points instead of picas-and-points. For example, if you enter "99," it will stay that way instead of being translated to "8p3."

➤ To enter a combination of picas and points in a field, separate the two numbers with a "p". For example, 4p2 equals 4 picas plus 2 points, or 50 pt. (12 pt. = 1 pica; 6 picas = 1 inch).

Identify Objects By

When creating dynamic objects associated with XML-based variables, you can specify whether variables are assigned the Object Name or an XML ID number. Consult with your Web developer regarding this option.

Display Performance

Hand Tool

Drag the Hand Tool slider to the left toward Full Quality for better onscreen display as you move the document across the screen with the Hand tool; or move the slider to the right toward Faster Updates to allow the artwork to move more quickly but at a lower display quality.

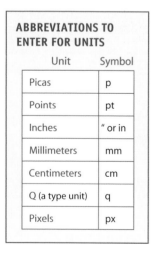

ABBREVIATIONS TO ENTER FOR UNITS

Unit	Symbol
Picas	p
Points	pt
Inches	" or in
Millimeters	mm
Centimeters	cm
Q (a type unit)	q
Pixels	px

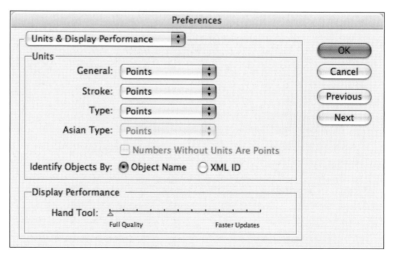

The measurement unit chosen for a document overrides the General unit specified for the application in Units & Display Performance Preferences.

To change the measurement unit for the current document:

Do either of the following:

If the rulers aren't showing, choose View > Show Rulers (Cmd-R/Ctrl-R). Control-click/right-click either **ruler** and choose a unit from the context menu.

Deselect all, then click **Document Setup** on the Control panel. Choose an option from the **Units** menu (Points, Picas, Inches, Millimeters, Centimeters, or Pixels), then click OK.

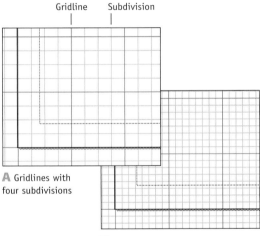

A Gridlines with four subdivisions

B Gridlines with eight subdivisions

Guides & Grid Preferences
Guides
Color
For guides, choose a color from the Color menu; or choose Other or double-click the color square to open the Colors/Color dialog and mix a color.

Style
For the guides, choose a Style of Lines or Dots.

Grid
Color
For the grid (View > Show Grid), choose a color from the Color menu; or choose Other or double-click the color square to open the Colors/Color dialog and mix a custom color. (If View > Snap to Grid is on, a guide or object will snap to a nearby gridline as it is created or moved.)

Style
Choose a Style of Lines or Dots for the grid. Subdivision lines don't display for the Dots Style.

Gridline Every
Enter the distance between gridlines.

Subdivisions
Enter the number of subdivision lines **A–B** to be drawn between the main (darker) gridlines when the Lines Style is chosen for the grid.

Grids in Back
Check Grids in Back (the default and recommended setting) to have the grid display behind all objects, or uncheck this option to have the grid display in front of all objects.

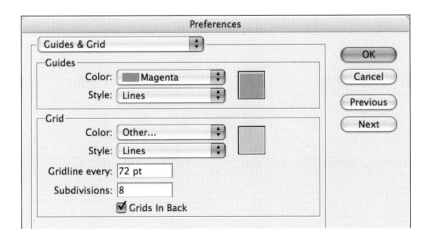

Smart Guides Preferences ★

To activate Smart Guides, choose View > Smart Guides (Cmd-U/Ctrl-U) and make sure View > Snap to Grid and View > Pixel Preview are off.

Display Options

Color

Choose a color for Smart Guides from the menu; or choose Other from the menu to open the Colors/Color dialog, and mix a custom color. (This color can differ from the Guide color for ruler guides, which is set in the Guides & Grid panel.)

Alignment Guides

If this option is on, as you create, drag, or transform an object, straight lines appear when the object's center point or edge meets the center or edge of another object, or the edge of the artboard or bleed region. For an irregularly shaped object, alignment guides appear for the object's bounding box. Alignment guides also appear when you use the Artboard tool to create or move an artboard.

Anchor/Path Labels

Check this option to allow a "path," "anchor," or "center" label to display as you pass the pointer over that part of an object, and an "intersect" label to display where two alignment guides intersect.

Object Highlighting

Check this option to have an object's path become highlighted as you pass the pointer over it. **A** This is helpful for locating unpainted paths (e.g., clipping mask objects) or paths obscured by other paths. Hidden objects (visibility off on the Layers panel) don't highlight. The highlight color matches the object's layer selection color.

Measurement Labels

With this option on, as you move the pointer (mouse button up) over an anchor point or the center point of a stationary object, the current x/y location of that point displays in a gray label. When an object is moved, the label displays the object's x/y distance from its original location. When a geometric drawing tool (e.g., Rectangle) or the Scale tool is used, a label displays the object's current width and height dimensions. When the Pen tool is used, a label displays the distance of the pointer from the last created anchor point. When an object is rotated, the label displays the current angle of rotation; when an object is sheared with the Shear tool, the label displays the shear angle.

Transform Tools

Check this option to have angle lines display as you transform an object with the Scale, Rotate, Reflect, or Shear tool. **B** Choose or create an angles set for the lines in the Angles area (see below).

Construction Guides

With this option checked, if you pass the mouse across an anchor point on a stationary object as you draw a new object or transform an existing one, a diagonal angle line emerges from that anchor point. **C** To choose or create an angles set for construction guides, see the next paragraph.

Angles

Choose a preset angles set from the Angles menu or enter custom angles in one or more of the six fields (press Tab to update the preview). If you enter custom angles, switch from Custom Angles to a predefined set, then later choose "Custom Angles" on the menu, the last custom angles will reappear in the fields.

Snapping Tolerance

The Snapping Tolerance is the distance (0–10 pt) within which an object's center point or edge must be from being aligned to the center or edge of a stationary object for a Smart Guide to appear, and for the active object to snap to the guide. The default value is 4 pt.

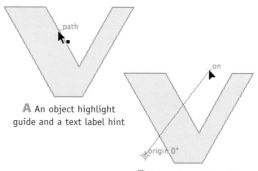

A An object highlight guide and a text label hint

B A transform tool guide

C A construction guide

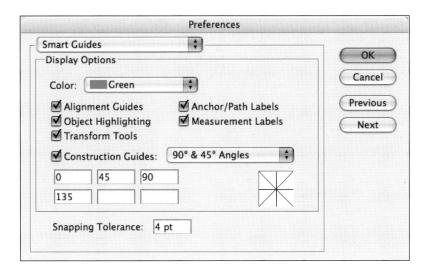

Slices Preferences ★

These preferences apply to creating slices for Web graphics, a topic that is not covered in this book.

Show Slice Numbers

Check this option to have slice numbers display onscreen.

Line Color

From the Line Color menu, choose a color for the slice numbers and for the lines that surround each slice.

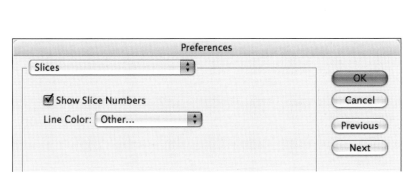

Hyphenation Preferences

Default Language

Choose the language dictionary for Illustrator to refer to when it inserts hyphen breaks. Note: From the Language menu on the Character panel, you can choose a different hyphenation language dictionary for the current document.

Exceptions

Enter words that you want hyphenated in a particular way. Type the word in the New Entry field, inserting hyphens where you would want them to appear (or enter a word with no hyphens to prevent Illustrator from hyphenating it), then click Add. To remove a word from the list, click it, then click Delete.

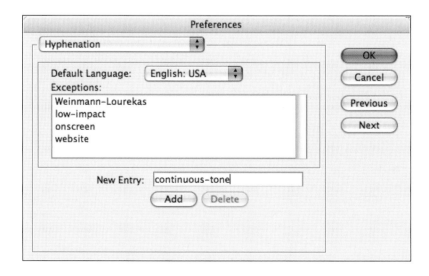

Plug-ins & Scratch Disks Preferences

Note: For changes made in this dialog to take effect, you must quit/exit and then relaunch Illustrator.

Additional Plug-ins Folder

The core and add-on plug-in files that are supplied with Illustrator provide additional functionality to the main application, and are installed automatically in the Plug-ins folder inside the Adobe Illustrator CS4 folder. If you have additional plug-ins that you want to use with Illustrator but want to keep in a separate folder, you must use this Preferences dialog to tell Illustrator where that folder is located. Click Choose. In the New Additional Plug-ins Folder dialog, locate and click the name of the desired plug-ins folder, then click Choose/OK to exit. The new location will be listed in this panel.

Scratch Disks

Primary

The Primary scratch disk is used as virtual memory when available RAM is insufficient for processing. From the Primary menu, choose an available hard drive, preferably your largest and fastest one. The default Primary scratch disk is Startup.

Secondary

As an optional step, choose an alternate Secondary hard drive to be used for extra virtual memory when needed. If you have only one hard drive, of course, you can have only one scratch disk.

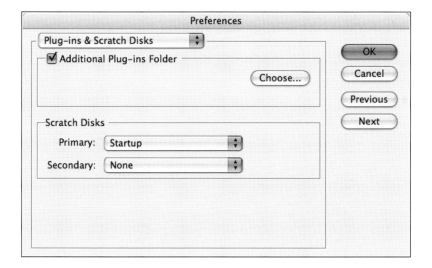

User Interface Preferences

Brightness
Choose a gray value, between Dark and Light, for the background in all the Illustrator panels, window title bars, etc.

Auto-Collapse Icon Panels
With this option checked, if you expand a panel that was collapsed to an icon, then click away from the panel, the panel will collapse back to an icon automatically. With this option unchecked, expanded panels stay expanded.

Open Documents as Tabs ★
With this option checked, documents dock automatically into a tabbed window when opened (whether the Application frame is displayed or not). With this option unchecked, documents open in individual floating windows.

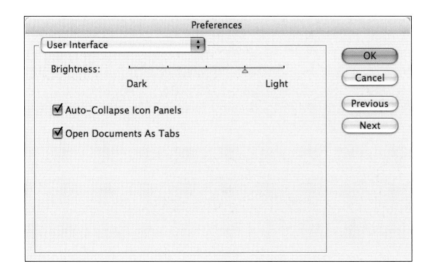

File Handling & Clipboard Preferences

Files

If you work with a lot of linked files, you can enhance Illustrator's performance by checking **Use Low Resolution Proxy for Linked EPS**. Placed images will display as low-resolution bitmap proxies (screen previews, in plain English). With this preference unchecked, linked EPS images will display at full resolution. Also, the Live Trace command uses this setting when tracing a linked EPS image.

To specify how linked images are updated when the original files are modifed, from the **Update Links** menu, choose one of the following:

Automatically to have Illustrator update a linked image automatically, with no dialog opening, when you edit the image and then click back in Illustrator.

Manually to leave the link unchanged when an original image file is modified. You can update the link at any time via the Links panel.

Ask When Modified to display a dialog when an original file is modified. (In the dialog, click Yes to update the linked image, or click No to leave it unchanged.)

Clipboard on Quit

These options affect how selections are copied to the Clipboard for transfer between Illustrator and other programs in the Adobe Creative Suite (e.g., Photoshop, Dreamweaver, and InDesign). Selections are copied in the PDF and/or AICB format, depending on the current **Copy As** setting:

PDF preserves transparency information in the selection and is designed for use with Adobe programs, such as Photoshop.

AICB (no transparency support) is a PostScript format that preserves the appearance of transparency through flattening (objects are divided into nonoverlapping objects). Click **Preserve Paths** to copy a selection as a collection of paths, or click **Preserve Appearance and Overprints** to preserve the appearance of the selection and any overprinting objects.

Note: It is best to check both PDF and AICB to allow the receiving application to choose between the two. The copying time will be longer and the memory requirements higher, but fills and effects will copy and paste more accurately.

➤ To learn about copying and pasting graphics from Adobe Illustrator into InDesign CS4, on the Adobe Illustrator Help and Support web page, search for "importing Illustrator graphics into InDesign CS4."

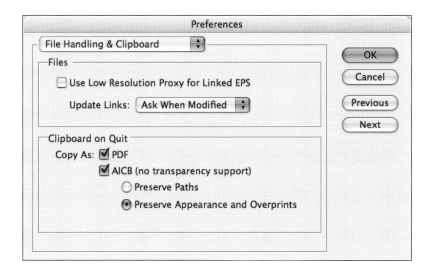

Appearance of Black Preferences

Sometimes printers use a combination of CMYK inks instead of 100K (only black ink) to produce a richer (more lustrous) black. Options in this preferences panel control whether blacks will be displayed onscreen and output using their actual values or as rich blacks. The examples of 100K Black and Rich Black as shown in the dialog are exaggerated intentionally to enable you to compare them.

Options for Black on RGB and Grayscale Devices

On Screen

Choose Display All Blacks Accurately to display blacks onscreen based on their actual values (pure CMYK black will display as dark gray), or choose Display All Blacks as Rich Black to display all blacks as rich black regardless of their actual CMYK values.

Printing/Exporting

Choose Output All Blacks Accurately to print blacks using their actual K or CMYK values on RGB and grayscale devices, or choose Output All Blacks as Rich Black to print blacks as a mixture of CMYK values (rich blacks) on RGB and grayscale devices. This setting affects print output data only, not values in the actual document (nor color separations). Output All Blacks as Rich Black produces the darkest possible black on an RGB printer.

Description

To learn about any option in the dialog, rest the pointer on it with the mouse button up, and read the pertinent information in the Description area.

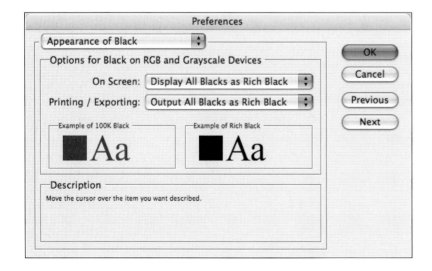

Output tasks are divided into two chapters in this book: print output in this chapter, and export from Illustrator to other applications in the next. The tasks you will learn here include how to print using basic settings, print multiple artboards, specify a bleed region for objects that extend beyond an artboard, prepare a file for color separation, choose flatness settings, choose settings for downloading fonts, use color management in printing, choose overprint options, create and edit print presets, create crop marks, choose a resolution for outputting effects, and use the Document Info panel to learn about a file.

Using the new Separations Preview panel, you will preview how the C, M, Y, and K color components in a CMYK document will separate to individual printing plates during the commercial printing process, check that any particular color is properly set to knock out or overprint other colors, and find out whether a specific black is a rich black (made from a mix of C, M, Y, and K) or a simple black containing only the K component.

Although Illustrator objects are described and stored as mathematical commands, when printed, they're rendered as dots. The higher the resolution of the output device, the more smoothly and sharply the lines, curves, gradients, and continuous-tone images in your artwork are rendered. To start, you can use just the basic settings in the Print dialog, as we show you on the following page, before delving into the many specialized or advanced controls. The Print dialog contains all the controls needed for outputting a color proof on a desktop printer, and for preparing and printing color separations.

PRINT

31

IN THIS CHAPTER

Print dialog: General options

There are seven option sets in the Print dialog, which are accessed by clicking a set name on the left. We'll show you how to print a document on a desktop color or grayscale printer using basic settings first.

To print a document on a black-and-white or color printer: ★

1. For printing on a desktop inkjet printer, choose File > Document Color Mode > **RGB Color**; for printing on a desktop color laser printer, check your printer documentation to determine the correct document color mode; for a grayscale printer, choose either of the two modes.

2. Choose File > **Print** (Cmd-P/Ctrl-P). The Print dialog opens (**A**, next page). Settings chosen in this dialog apply to all the artboards in the current document.

3. From the **Printer** menu, choose from the list of printers that are available in your system.

   If you chose a PostScript printer, the PPD menu will display the default PPD (PostScript printer description) file for that printer. If your commercial printer supplied (and you installed) a custom PPD file for the chosen printer, choose that file name from the menu.

4. On the list of option sets on the left side of the dialog, click **General**.

5. In the **Copies** field, enter the desired number of print copies.

   Click **All** to print all the artboards in the document; or click **Range** and enter an artboard number or a range of artboard numbers (separate the range with a hyphen), then press Tab. (To learn more about printing artboards, see page 376.)

6. In the **Media** area, from the **Size** menu, choose **Defined by Driver** or the desired paper size.

   Click one of the orientation buttons to print the artboards vertically or horizontally on their respective pages.

7. *Optional:* If you need to change the position of the artboards relative to the paper, in the Options area, do any of the following:

   Click a different point on the Placement icon to position all the artboards relative to that part of the paper.

Enter X and Y values to specify the position of the upper left corner of all the artboards relative to the paper.

Drag an artboard in the preview area. Note that this will reposition the page borders for all the artboards. Only objects that display within an artboard's page area will print.

8. For scaling, click **Do Not Scale** to print each artboard at its current size, even if it exceeds the paper size; or **Fit to Page** to scale all the artboards to the current paper size; or **Custom Scale**, then enter a W (width) or H (height) value to scale all the artboards proportionally. (For nonproportional scaling, deselect the Constrain Proportions button,⬚ then enter separate width and height values.)

9. From the **Print Layers** menu, choose which layers are to print:

   Visible & Printable Layers to print only the visible layers for which the Print option is checked in the Layer Options dialog. (To prevent an individual object from printing, you would have to uncheck the Print option for its layer before opening the Print dialog.)

   Visible Layers to print only those layers that display a visibility icon on the Layers panel.

   All Layers to print all layers, regardless of the current Layers panel settings.

10. Click **Print** to print the artboards you selected in the Copies area using the current settings (or to save the current settings with your document without printing, click Done, then save the file).

➤ Adobe recommends choosing all print settings from the Print dialog and bypassing the system options that display when you click the Page Setup or Printer button in the Mac OS, the Setup button in Windows.

SAVE YOUR PRINT SETTINGS!

Considering how many options you need to choose in the Print dialog, we recommend saving your settings as a preset so you don't have to reenter them each time you print to a particular output device: Click the Save Preset 💾 button at the top of the dialog,★ enter a name for the preset, then click OK. Saved presets are accessed from the Print Preset menu at the top of the Print dialog. To edit a print preset, see page 391.

Access to the option sets

Print preview

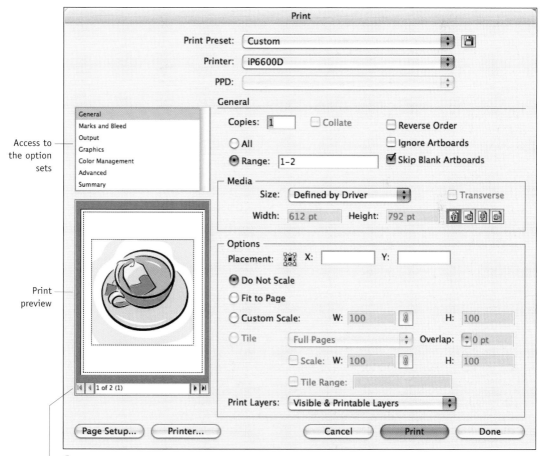

A In the General option set in the Print dialog, choose basic print settings.

Use these arrows to navigate between multiple artboards.

Printing multiple artboards ★

There are two approaches to printing multiple artboards. In the first task below, oversized artboards are printed on multiple tiled pages; and in the second task, all the artboards in a document are printed on a single page.

To print multiple artboards as a collection of tiled pages:

1. Choose File > **Print** (Cmd-P/Ctrl-P), then click **General** on the list of option sets (**A**, next page).

2. Under General, check **Ignore Artboards**. You are going to use other options to position the artwork.

3. Choose a **Media** (page) **Size** and an **orientation** setting.

4. Click **Tile**, then from the **Tile** menu, choose either of the following:

   Full Pages to divide the artwork into whole pages, including the margins, based on the printer media size (**B**, next page).

   Imageable Areas to divide the artwork into a grid of pages based on the printer media size (**C**, next page).

5. *Optional:* For the Tile option, you can do any of the following.

   To reposition the artwork on a different part of the paper or grid of pages, click that corresponding point on the Placement icon (or click the center point to recenter the artwork).

   To reposition the artwork on the grid of pages, place the pointer over the preview and drag.

   If you chose Full Pages from the Tile menu, you can change the Overlap value for the amount of overlap between pages.

To scale the artwork proportionally, check **Scale** and enter a **W** (width) or **H** (height) value, then press Tab. (For nonproportional scaling, deselect the Constrain Proportions button, ⬚ then enter separate W and H values.) To restore the default Scale value at any time, enter 100%.

6. *Optional:* To print select tiled pages, check Tile Range, then enter the desired range of pages (separate consecutive numbers with a hyphen, or non-consecutive numbers with a comma).

7. Choose print settings, if necessary, from the other option sets (see pages 378–385).

8. Click **Print** to print the document (or to save the current settings with the document without printing, click Done, then save your file).

➤ To save a file containing multiple artboards as a multipage PDF file, see page 398.

The Fit to Page option in the instructions below applies to all the artboards in a document. All oversized artboards are reduced to fit the paper, and similarly, all undersized artboards are enlarged.

To print multiple artboards on one page:

1. Follow steps 1–3 in the preceding instructions.

2. Under **Options**, click **Fit to Page**. The artwork will be scaled, if necessary, to fit the page (**D**, next page).

3. Choose print settings, if necessary, from the other option sets (see the pages 378–385).

4. Click **Print** to print the document (or to save the current settings with the document without printing, click Done, then save your file).

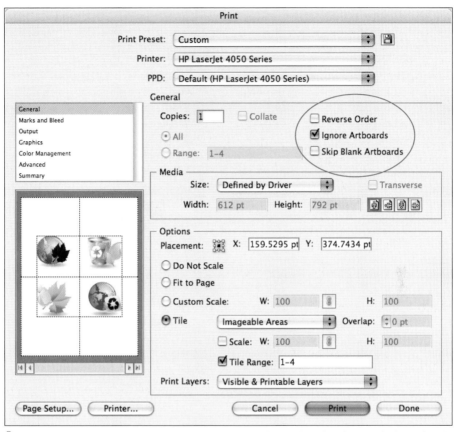

A In the General option set in the Print dialog, you can specify that the artboards are to be ignored, and you can control the position of all the artwork on the printed page or pages manually.

B The Full Pages setting is previewed.

C The Imageable Areas setting is previewed.

D The Fit to Page setting is previewed.

Next, we'll explore settings in the six other option sets of the Print dialog.

Marks and Bleed options

Use the Marks and Bleed set of the Print dialog to create printer's marks at the edges of each artboard or the overall printable area, or to set bleed parameters for objects that extend beyond that area. Commercial printers use trim marks to trim the final printout, registration marks to align the printing plates, and color bars to judge the print colors.

To include printer's marks in your printout:

1. To ensure that printer's marks will fit within the respective page sizes for the artboards, in the General option set, do either of the following:

   Make sure the output **Media: Size** is large enough to accommodate printer's marks for the largest artboard in the document.

   Click **Fit to Page** to allow the artboards to scale, if necessary.

2. Click **Marks and Bleed** on the left side of the Print dialog (**A**, next page).

3. Under Marks, check **All Printer's Marks**, then keep checked or uncheck any of these options:

   Trim Marks adds thin lines that designate where the printed pages are to be trimmed. The trim marks align with the horizontal and vertical edges of each artboard or, if Ignore Artboards is checked (General option set), with the tiled artwork.

   Registration Marks adds small circles outside the corner of each artboard or, if Ignore Artboards is checked, outside the corner of the bounding box for the tiled artwork.

   Color Bars adds color swatches outside each artboard or tiled artwork area.

   Page Information adds a text label of specs for the print shop at the top of the printout.

4. From the **Printer Mark Type** menu, choose a printer's marks style of Roman or Japanese.

5. *Optional:* Via the Trim Mark Weight menu, change the thickness for trim marks. You can also enter an Offset value (0–72 pt) for the distance between the trim marks (and other printer's marks) and the edge of each artboard or the bounding box of the tiled artwork. If Fit to Page is checked, the artboard will be scaled downward to accomodate a large offset value.

If you position objects on any artboard so they extend into the bleed region (the area just beyond the edge of the artboard), they will print to the very edge of the final trimmed page. You should ask your commercial printer what bleed values to enter for their specific printer.

To choose bleed values:

1. Follow steps 1–2 in the instructions at left.

2. In the **Bleeds** area, uncheck **Use Document Bleed** settings, then do either of the following:

   With the link icon activated, ▣ enter a single bleed value (then press Tab) for all four sides of each artboard.

   To specify asymmetrical bleed values, deactivate the link icon, ▣ then enter **Top**, **Left**, **Bottom**, and **Right** values (0–1 inch, or 0–72 pt).

   Enter a low bleed value to move the edge of each artboard and its trim marks closer to the edges of the page, or a higher bleed value to move the artboard edge farther away from the page edge and thereby print more of any objects that extend into the bleed region (say, if you chose Fit to Page in the General option set or if the page size is much larger than the artboards). If Ignore Artboards is checked and Tile: Imageable Areas is chosen in the General options, more tile pages may be added to accommodate a wide bleed region.

3. Choose any other print settings, then click **Print** to print the document; or to save the current settings with the document without printing, click Done, then save your file.

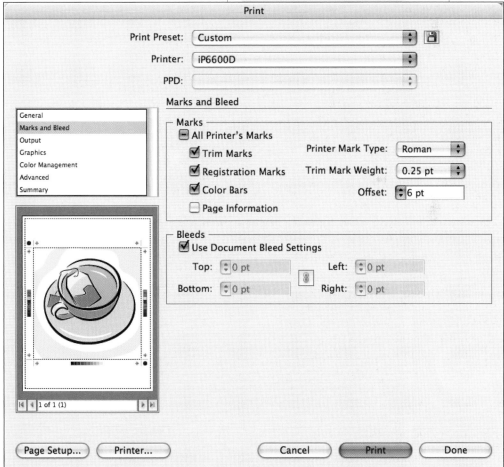

A In the Marks and Bleed option set in the Print dialog, choose marks for commercial printing and set values for the bleed region.

Output options

During color separation, each color prints to a separate plate or piece of film. Settings in the Output option set of the Print dialog are used primarily by prepress operators to produce color separations for commercial printing (a separate plate is made for each process and spot color used in the file).

To output a composite print or color separations:

1. *Optional:* To preview how colors in your artwork will overprint and/or separate onto individual plates, click Done to exit the Print dialog, then follow the instructions for the Separations Preview panel on pages 386–387.

2. Make sure your file is in CMYK Color mode, then in the Print dialog, click Output on the list of option sets.**A**

3. On the **Printer** menu, choose the PostScript color or grayscale printer that's available to your system.

   Before choosing other settings (steps 4–7), consult with your commercial printer.

4. From the **Mode** menu, choose one of the following:

   Composite to print all the colors on one sheet (for desktop printing).

   Separations (Host-Based) to allow Illustrator to prepare the separations data and send it to the printing device.

   In-RIP Separations to have Illustrator send PostScript data to the printer's RIP* for that device to perform the separations. (Available options will vary depending on the type of printer you chose in step 3.)

5. Choose **Emulsion: Up (Right Reading)** or **Down (Right Reading)**.

6. Choose **Image: Positive** or **Negative**.

7. From the **Printer Resolution** menu, choose a halftone screen ruling (lpi)/device resolution (dpi), as suggested by your commercial printer.

   For more Output options, see the next page.

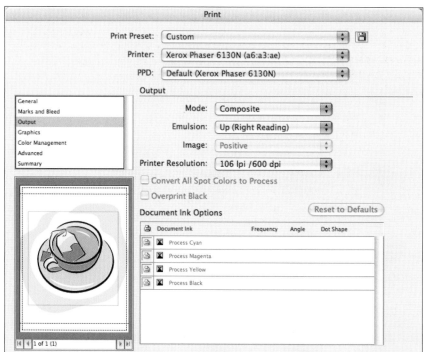

A Use the Output option set in the Print dialog to choose settings for color separations.

*The RIP (short for "raster image processor") converts vector data into printable dots.

You can also use the Output option set to turn printing on or off for individual colors or to convert individual spot colors to process colors.

To change the print setting for, or convert, individual colors in a document:

1. In the **Output** option set of the Print dialog, choose a separation **Mode**.

2. The colors used in the document are listed in the **Document Ink Options** area.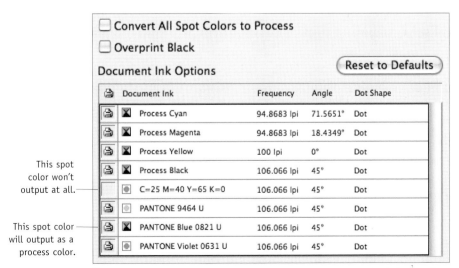**A** To prevent a particular process or spot color from outputting, click the printer icon in the left column.

3. Do either of the following:

   Check **Convert All Spot Colors to Process** to convert all spot colors in the document to process colors.

   To convert specific spot colors to process colors, uncheck **Convert All Spot Colors to Process**, then click the spot color icon on the list; the process color icon will appear in its stead.

4. *Optional:* To allow black fills and strokes to overprint any colors below them, check Overprint Black. To learn more about overprinting, see page 387.

5. Choose other print settings, then click **Print**.

➤ Don't change the Frequency, Angle, or Dot Shape settings unless your commercial printer advises you to do so. Click Reset to Defaults at any time to restore all the default ink settings.

➤ The Adobe Illustrator, Illustrator EPS, and Adobe PDF (1.4 or later) file formats preserve spot colors and apply overprinting correctly. Spot colors that are applied to objects, raster effects, and grayscale images will appear on separate plates, whether the file is output from InDesign or directly from Illustrator.

COLOR-SEPARATING A GRADIENT

➤ To color-separate a gradient containing one spot color and white onto one plate, make sure the gradient uses the spot color as the starting color and a 0% tint of the same spot color as the ending color.

➤ To color-separate a gradient containing one spot color as the starting color and another spot color as the ending color, uncheck Convert All Spot Colors to Process, and ask your output service provider to assign the screen angles for those colors.

➤ To convert a spot color in a gradient to a process color, click that color stop on the Gradient panel, then on the Color panel, click the Spot Color button. The color will convert to the current document color mode (RGB or CMYK). Repeat for the other color stops.

A In the Output option set in the Print dialog, you can prevent individual colors from outputting and convert spot colors to process colors.

Graphics options

The Flatness setting in the Graphics option set of the Print dialog controls how precisely all the objects in a document print on a PostScript printer. If your document doesn't print, one possible solution is to raise the Flatness setting.

To change the flatness setting for a file to facilitate printing:

1. Open the file that stubbornly refuses to print, choose File > **Print**, then click **Graphics** on the list of option sets (**A**, next page).

2. If **Automatic** is checked (under Paths), Illustrator will choose an optimal Flatness value for the chosen printing device. If you have encountered a printing error, uncheck Automatic, drag the **Flatness** slider a notch or two to the right, then try printing the file. If it prints, but with noticeably jagged curve segments, you raised the Flatness value too much. Lower it by dragging the slider slightly to the left, and print once more.

➤ To display a numeric readout of the current Flatness setting, rest the pointer on the slider.

To choose settings for downloading fonts:

1. To manage how fonts are downloaded to the printer, open the Print dialog and display the **Graphics** option set.

2. From the **Download** menu in the **Fonts** area, choose one of the following options:

   None to have no fonts download. This is the preferred setting when fonts are permanently stored in the printer.

   Subset to download only the characters (glyphs) used in the document.

   Complete to have all the fonts used in the document download at the beginning of the print job. This is effective when printing multiple artboards that use the same fonts.

3. Click **Print** to print the document; or to save your settings with the document without printing, click Done, then save the file.

FLATTENING VERSUS FLATNESS

Upon output, Illustrator flattens overlapping shapes to preserve the look of transparency. This is a different process from setting a Flatness value to control how precisely the curve segments in a document will print. The higher the Flatness value, the less precisely those curves will print.

GRAPHICS CHOICES

Normally, Illustrator sets the PostScript (LanguageLevel 2 or 3) and Data Format (Binary or ACSII) options in the Graphics option set of the Print dialog based on what features the chosen printer supports, and you can ignore them. However, if your printer supports multiple options for those features, you will need to choose settings (decisions, decisions!). For PostScript, we recommend choosing LanguageLevel 3, because it contains the latest definitions for printing transparency and facilitates smooth shading to prevent banding in gradients.

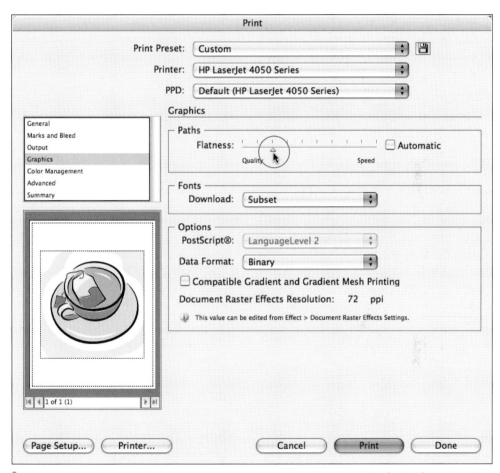

A In the Graphics option set of the Print dialog, choose a Flatness setting and an option for how fonts are to be downloaded.

Color Management options

Use the Color Management option set of the Print dialog to control how color conversions will be handled. Note: If you haven't learned about profiles and color settings yet, read Chapter 2 first.

To print using color management:

1. In the **Print** dialog, display the **Color Management** option set.**A**

2. Do either of the following:

   From the Color Handling menu, choose **Let Illustrator Determine Colors** (the preferred choice) to let Illustrator convert document colors to the printer gamut based on the chosen printer profile and send the converted data to the printer. The quality of the conversion depends on the accuracy of the chosen printer profile. From the **Printer Profile** menu, be sure to choose the correct ICC profile for your printer, ink, and paper. Click **Printer/Setup**, then turn off color management for the printer driver (see Adobe Illustrator CS4 Help).

   From the **Color Handling** menu, choose **Let PostScript Printer Determine Colors** (if available) to send the color data to the printer and have the printer convert the colors to its gamut.

If your printing device requires it, click **Printer/Setup**, then locate and turn on color management for the printer driver.

3. If you chose Let PostScript Printer Determine Colors and the document color mode is CMYK, check **Preserve CMYK Numbers** to preserve the color values of native objects and type in your artwork. For RGB documents, Adobe recommends leaving this option unchecked.

4. Leave the **Rendering Intent** on the default setting of Relative Colorimetric unless you or your output specialist have a specific reason to change it. (To learn more about the rendering intents, see the sidebar on page 20.)

5. Choose other print options, then click **Print** to print the document; or to save the current settings with the document without printing, click Done, then save your file.

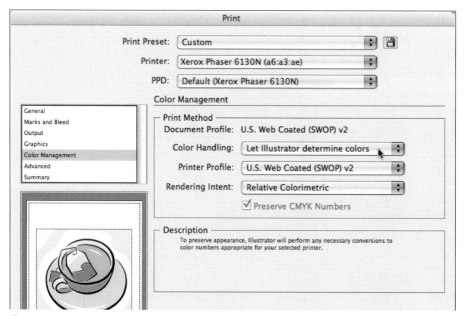

A Use the Color Management option set in the Print dialog to control whether Illustrator or your PostScript printer will handle the color conversion.

Advanced options

In the Advanced option set of the Print dialog, you can choose overprint options for fills and strokes, for color separation or composite printing.

To choose overprint and flattening options for output:

1. In the **Print** dialog, display the **Advanced** option set.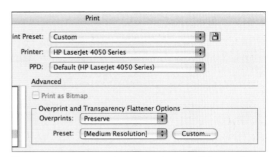

2. Choose an option from the **Overprints** menu:

   Preserve to keep the file's overprint settings, for color separations.

   Discard to ignore a file's overprint settings when printing.

   Simulate to create the visual effect of overprinting on a composite printer, for the purpose of proofing.

   Note: The Overprints setting doesn't override the current Overprint Fill or Stroke settings on the Attributes panel.

3. To specify how transparent objects are flattened for printing, choose a preset from the **Preset** menu (see step 2 on page 388), or click Custom to create and save a custom preset that will save with the current file (see page 391).

4. Choose other print settings, then click **Print** or **Done**.

Summary options

In the Summary option set, you can read a summary of the current Print dialog settings.

To view a summary of the current print settings:

1. In the Print dialog, display the **Summary** option set.**B**

2. Expand any listings in the **Options** window to view the settings, and read any related alerts in the Warnings window.

3. *Optional:* Click Save Summary to save the current settings to a separate file.

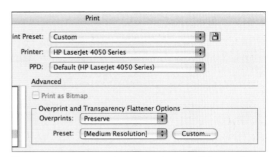

A Use the Advanced option set in the Print dialog to choose overprint settings.

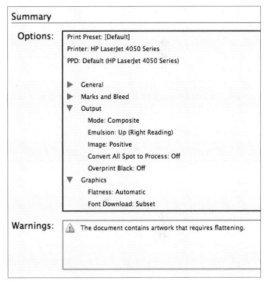

B In the Summary option set in the Print dialog, you can view a listing of the current print settings.

GOT A NON-POSTSCRIPT PRINTER?

If your document contains complex objects (such as gradients or soft-edged effects) and it generates a printing error from a non-PostScript or low-resolution printer, instead of printing the file as vectors, in the Advanced option set in the Print dialog, check Print as Bitmap. Note that the driver for the chosen printer controls whether this option is available, and most Macintosh printer drivers don't include it.

Using the Separations Preview panel

The new Separations Preview panel lets you see how the C, M, Y, and K color components in a CMYK document will separate to individual printing plates during the commercial printing process. You can use the panel to check that a color is properly set to knock out colors beneath it in the artwork, or to check whether a color is properly set to overprint on top of the other colors. You can monitor the use of spot colors in the artwork and verify that any spot color is set to knock out colors beneath it. And you can determine whether a specific black is a rich black (a mixture of C, M, Y, and K inks) or a simple black comprising only the K component.

To view individual color plates in a CMYK document: ★

1. Open a CMYK document, A and display the **Separations Preview** panel.

2. Check **Overprint Preview** at the top of the panel to make the list of process and spot colors accessible. With this option on, knockouts and overprints are simulated onscreen.

3. To view a single color plate, Option-click/ Alt-click the visibility icon 👁 for a color listing.B Only the objects in which that color will print are now visible in the document. If an object contains 0 percent of that particular color, it will display as a white area.

   To redisplay all the process and spot color plates, Option-click/Alt-click the same visibility icon.👁

4. To restore the normal view of your artwork, uncheck Overprint Preview.

➤ The Separations Preview panel lists all the spot colors that are currently on the Swatches panel, whether they are being used in your document or not.

A We will preview color separations for this artwork.

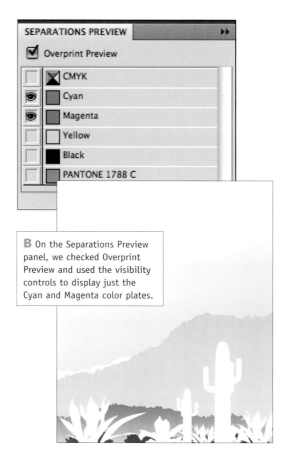

B On the Separations Preview panel, we checked Overprint Preview and used the visibility controls to display just the Cyan and Magenta color plates.

By default, when color-separating a CMYK document for commercial printing, Illustrator knocks out colors below an upper object so its colors won't mix on press with any colors it overlaps. Because black ink is opaque (and is normally printed last), it may be preferable to set black fills or strokes to overprint on top of other inks. This will help prevent any potential gaps from showing due to the misregistration of printing plates.

Note: Colors overprint on a commercial press but not on a composite print (proof) from a PostScript color printer.

To preview and change black knockouts to overprints: ★

1. Open a CMYK document.

2. Display the **Separations Preview** panel, and check **Overprint Preview**.

3. Click the visibility icon 👁 for **Black** to hide that color plate.

4. In Overprint Preview view, if a black object is previewing as white, it means that object is set to knock out any colors below it and that black won't mix with other inks on press. **A** Any black objects that aren't previewing as white are going to overprint on top of other colors, meaning their colors will mix with other inks.

5. To make a black object overprint, with the Selection tool (V), click the white knockout area or the hidden object (use Smart Guides to locate its path). Display the **Attributes** panel, then check **Overprint Fill** or **Overprint Stroke** (whichever part of the object you want to enable overprinting for). **B**

➤ Any object set to overprint will display differently in Overprint Preview view if it contains a percentage of 0 of at least one of the four process colors.

➤ Checking Overprint Preview on the Separations Preview panel also checks View > Overprint Preview, and vice versa. And when this feature is on, "Overprint Preview" is listed in the document window tab.

➤ For an RGB document, only spot colors can be set to overprint.

To identify rich and process blacks in a document: ★

1. Display the **Separations Preview** panel, and check **Overprint Preview**.

2. Click the visibility icon 👁 for **Black** to hide that color plate. Objects containing just a percentage of K (black) ink will now be hidden; objects containing a rich black (made from a mixture of C, M, Y and K) will display as a shade of gray. If you want to confirm this, click a gray object with the Selection tool and view the CMYK settings on the Color panel.

3. Click the visibility square for Black to redisplay that plate.

A With the Black color plate hidden, black objects preview as white, indicating that they will knock out colors below them.

B Overprint Fill is checked for the black objects and the Black plate is hidden. Now those objects don't preview as white, and they will overprint other colors.

Printing and exporting semitransparent objects

Nondefault transparency settings* in objects, groups, and layers are preserved when a document is saved in a native Adobe Illustrator format (CS through CS4) or in the Adobe PDF format (Compatibility: Acrobat 5 or higher).

When you print a file that contains nondefault transparency settings or when you export it in a nonnative format, Illustrator uses the current transparency flattener settings to determine how objects will be flattened and rasterized, in an effort to preserve the appearance of semitransparency.

In the course of flattening, if Illustrator detects a semitransparent object that overlaps an underlying object, it converts the overlapping area into a separate flat, opaque shape and leaves the remaining, nonoverlapping parts of the original objects as is.

Although Illustrator tries to keep flattened shapes as vector objects, if the look of the transparency settings can't be preserved in the flattened vector object, the program will rasterize it instead. This will happen, for example, when two gradient objects containing nondefault transparency settings overlap; the resulting flattened shape will be rasterized in order to preserve the complex appearance of transparency.

To control how transparency is flattened for exported files:

1. Deselect all, then check **Document Setup** on the Control panel. ★

2. Do either of the following:

   In the Transparency area, **A** choose from the **Preset** menu: [**High Resolution**] for high-quality color separations or film-based color proofs, [**Medium Resolution**] for desktop PostScript color prints or proofs, or [**Low Resolution**] for a black-and-white desktop printer. Click OK.

   Click **Custom** to create a custom preset that saves with the file, then follow the instructions on the next page.

> **TRANSPARENCY TO ADOBE INDESIGN**
>
> When saving artwork for InDesign CS4, use the native Adobe Illustrator (ai) format, which preserves the editability of transparency. Illustrator objects containing nondefault transparency settings will interact correctly with the content of, and any transparency in, the InDesign layout, and InDesign will perform any needed transparency flattening when printing.

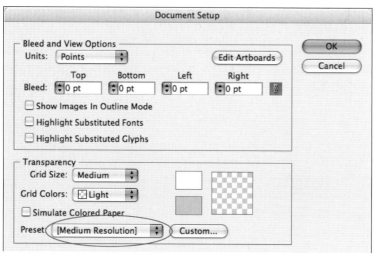

A Using the Transparency controls in the Document Setup dialog, you can either choose an existing transparency flattener preset or create a custom preset.

*Blending modes other than Normal and opacity levels below 100%.

To choose custom transparency flattener options:

1. When you click **Custom** in the Transparency area of the Document Setup dialog or in the Advanced option set of the Print dialog, the Custom Transparency Flattener Options dialog opens.**A** Perform any of the following steps.

2. Move the **Raster/Vector Balance** slider to control the percentage of flattened shapes that will remain as vectors versus the percentage of shapes that will be rasterized. This setting applies only to flattened shapes that represent transparency. Vector shapes print with cleaner, higher-quality color and crisper edges as compared with rasterized shapes.

   Higher values (to the right) produce a higher percentage of flattened shapes as vectors, though complex flattened areas may still be rasterized. A higher percentage of vector shapes will result in higher-quality output, but at the expense of slower, more memory-demanding output processing.

   The lowest (leftmost) value won't necessarily produce poor output quality. In fact, if a document is very complex and contains a lot of transparency effects, this may be the only setting that produces acceptable output. Low settings produce fast output at a low resolution.

3. During the rasterization process, the output quality is calculated based on two resolution settings. To specify the resolution for rasterized line art and text, choose or enter a **Line Art and Text Resolution** value. For most purposes, the default resolution setting of 300 ppi will be adequate, but for small text or thin lines, you should increase this value to 600 ppi.

Transparent text is flattened and preserved as text objects; clipping and masking are used to preserve the look of transparency.

4. For the **Gradient and Mesh Resolution**, choose or enter the resolution for rasterized gradients and mesh objects. Gradients and meshes, like continuous-tone imagery, don't contain sharp details. The default value of 150 ppi is usually adequate; a value of 300 ppi would be considered high.

   When the Raster/Vector Balance value is below 100, due to transparency flattening, Illustrator may rasterize placed or embedded images at the current Gradient and Mesh Resolution value. This value will be used only for portions of an image that are overlapped by a transparent object; the remainder of the image will print at the original image resolution.

   When an EPS image is overlapped by an object that contains transparency, to ensure an accurate printout of the image and the transparency effect, embed the image into the Illustrator document by clicking the **Embed** button on the Control panel.

5. With the Raster/Vector Balance slider between 10 and 90, portions of type that are overlapped by an object containing transparency will be rasterized or converted to outlines, and may be thickened slightly. If those areas look noticeably different from type that isn't overlapped by transparency, try checking **Convert All Text to Outlines** to make all the type within a given font print in the same width, or move the type into its own layer above the transparent object.

Continued on the following page

A Choose custom settings for your file in the Custom Transparency Flattener Options dialog.

6. With the Raster/Vector Balance slider at a setting between 10 and 90, any strokes that are overlapped by a semitransparent object will convert to outlines. As a result, very thin strokes may be thickened slightly and may look noticeably different from parts of strokes that don't overlap transparency. If you check **Convert All Strokes to Outlines**, the look of each stroke will be preserved for its entire length, but this option also increases the number of paths in the file. An alternative to using this option is to apply Object > Path > Outline Stroke to selected strokes in the artwork.

7. When a file is sent to print, any areas of semi-transparent objects that overlap other objects are flattened and rasterized. The flattened areas, however, won't match the exact path shapes of the objects. Also, the resulting flattened object may contain a combination of pixel and vector areas, and color discrepancies (called "stitching") between adjacent pixel and vector areas may result. With **Clip Complex Regions** checked, boundaries between raster and vector flattened shapes fall exactly on object paths. This helps eliminate the signs of stitching but also slows down printing because the resulting paths are more complex. (Note: When an entire document is rasterized, no stitching occurs.)

8. Click OK.

Via the Flattener Preview panel, you can see ahead of time which semitransparent areas of a document are going to be flattened.

To preview the flattening settings:

1. Display the **Flattener Preview** panel. ✔ **A**

2. Click **Refresh** on the panel, and choose **Show Options** from the panel menu.

3. Move the **Raster/Vector Balance** slider, if desired; check the appropriate options; then click Refresh again.

4. From the **Highlight** menu, choose which type of object is to be displayed in the highlight color.

5. *Optional:* Save your settings as a preset by choosing Save Transparency Flattener Preset from the panel menu.

➤ To learn more about flattening, in the Search for Help field on the right side of the Application bar, enter "transparency flattening."

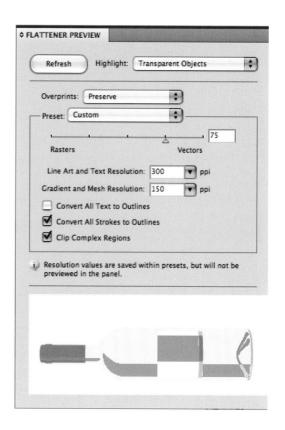

A Use the Flattener Preview panel to preview different flattening settings for semitransparent objects in a document.

FLATTENING SELECTIVELY

In addition to setting flattening options for a whole document, you can also set them for individual objects. When your artwork is ready to be output, save a copy of the file. Select a semitransparent object and any objects that it overlaps, choose Object > Flatten Transparency, then follow the instructions on pages 389–390. The command will flatten (divide) the areas where selected objects overlap into separate, nonoverlapping objects. Although the objects will still look semitransparent, the transparency settings will no longer be editable.

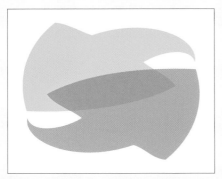

The yellow object has a fill color and a stroke of None; the green object has a semitransparent fill and a stroke of None.

The Flatten Transparency command produced three objects from the original two. (We moved the flattened objects apart.)

Creating and editing presets

By creating a preset for your custom transparency flattener or Print dialog settings, you'll be able to apply the same settings to multiple files quickly. For example, instead of tediously choosing custom flattener settings via the Print dialog (Advanced option set) or the Document Setup dialog (Transparency area) for individual files, you can create presets for different printing scenarios, to be used with any file. Presets can also be exported as files for use by other users.

To create or edit a transparency flattener, tracing, print, or PDF preset:

1. From the Edit menu, choose **Transparency Flattener Presets**, **Tracing Presets**, **Print Presets**, or **Adobe PDF Presets**. A preset dialog opens.

2. *Optional:* Click New to create a new preset; or click an existing preset, then click New to create a variation (copy) of that preset.

3. Enter a descriptive Name.

4. Choose settings. For the Transparency Flattener Preset Options dialog, see the instructions on the previous two pages; for the Tracing Options dialog, see pages 213–215; for the Print Presets Options dialog, see pages 374–385; or for the Adobe PDF Presets dialog, see pages 398–401. Click OK.

5. To edit an existing user-created preset (one not listed in brackets), click the preset name, click Edit, change any of the settings, then click OK. Note: You can also edit the [Default] print preset, but not the predefined transparency flattener, tracing, or Adobe PDF presets.

6. Do any of the following optional steps:

   To view a summary of settings for a preset, click the preset name, then look at any expandable category in the **Preset Settings** window.

   Click **Delete** to delete the currently selected user-created preset.

   Click **Export** to save the settings for the currently selected preset as a separate text file.

   Click **Import** to locate and open an exported settings file.

7. Click OK.

Producing crop marks

The Crop Marks effect places eight (four pairs of) crop marks around a selected object or group, which a print shop uses as guidelines when trimming the paper. This effect lets you create multiple sets of crop marks on a single artboard. And best of all, since the crop marks are an effect, they will move and transform with the object they are applied to.

To create crop marks for an object or group:

1. Select the object or group that crop marks are to be created for.

2. From the **Add New Effect** menu *fx.* on the Appearance panel ★ or from the **Effect** menu on the Illustrator menu bar, choose **Crop Marks**. Crop marks will appear at the corners of the selection.**A**

➤ To delete the crop marks, on the Appearance panel, click the Crop Marks effect listing, then click the Delete Selected Item button.

➤ Trim marks that are assigned via the Marks and Bleed option set (in the Print dialog) will align with the edges of each artboard or the tiled artwork, and are independent of any marks that are created via the Crop Marks effect.

A We applied the Crop Marks effect to the whole group of objects.

Choosing a resolution for effects

All the Photoshop effects in the lower half of the Effect menu will rasterize upon export or output, as will the following effects on the Illustrator Effects > Stylize submenu: Drop Shadow (if the Blur value is greater than 0), Inner Glow, Outer Glow, and Feather. By following these instructions, you can choose a resolution value for all the raster effects in a document.

To choose a resolution for raster effects:

1. With your Illustrator file open, choose Effect > **Document Raster Effects Settings.**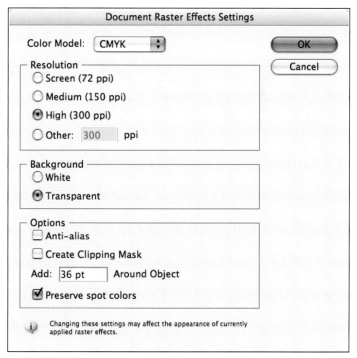

2. In the dialog, click another **Resolution** option, or click **Other** and enter a custom resolution value. Choose the resolution needed for output —72 ppi for onscreen or Web output, or 300 ppi (usually) for print output. The higher the resolution, the slower the output processing time, but the higher the quality of the rasterized effects. (The current setting is also listed in the Graphics option set of the Print dialog.)

➤ To learn more about the options in this dialog, see page 198.

A In the Document Raster Effects Settings dialog, choose a Resolution setting for raster effects.

Using the Document Info panel

On the Document Info panel, you can view data about the entire document or about just a selected object or objects.

To display information about an object or a whole document:

1. *Optional:* Select the object (or objects) that you want to read info about.

2. Display the **Document Info** panel. 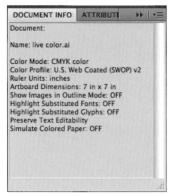 **A**

3. To display information about a currently selected object, on the panel menu, make sure Selection Only has a check mark, **B** or uncheck that option to display information pertaining to all the objects in the document.

4. Do either of the following:

   Choose **Objects** from the panel menu to list a tally of various kinds of items in the document, such as paths, compound paths, clipping masks, opacity masks, transparent groups, transparent objects, gradients, etc., as well as information about the colors, fonts, and linked images used.

   Choose another category from the panel menu to view data about graphic styles; brushes; objects containing spot colors, patterns, or gradients; fonts; linked or embedded images; or font details (PostScript name, font file name, language, etc.).

5. *Optional:* If Selection Only is checked on the panel menu, you can click any other object in the document to view data about that object in the currently chosen category.

6. *Optional:* Choose Save from the panel menu to save the currently displayed information as a text document. Choose a location in which to save the text file, rename the file, if desired, then click Save. Use the system's default text editor to open the text document. You can print this file and refer to it when preparing the document for high-resolution printing.

A Document information is always available on the Document Info panel, whether the Selection Only option is on or off.

B The Selection Only and Objects options are checked on this Document Info panel menu.

In this chapter, you'll learn how to save files in various formats for export to other applications. You can export your file to the EPS format for layout and drawing applications; the PDF format for a variety of output media; the GIF or JPEG format for a Web layout application; or the PSD format for Adobe Photoshop.

To export your artwork to a CS version of InDesign, we recommend sticking with the native Adobe Illustrator (ai) format; check Create PDF Compatible File in the Illustrator Options dialog, which opens from the File > Save As dialog. This format includes both an Illustrator and a PDF version of the file and preserves transparency and live features.

To prepare an Illustrator file for a drawing or page layout application that doesn't read native AI files (such as QuarkXPress versions 7 and earlier), save it in either the Illustrator EPS format (see below) or the PDF format (see pages 398–401).

Saving files in the EPS format

The EPS (Encapsulated PostScript) format saves both vector and bitmap objects and is supported by most illustration and page layout programs. EPS files can be reopened and edited in Illustrator.

To save a file as EPS:

1. With the file open in Illustrator, choose File > **Save As** or **Save a Copy**.

2. From the **Format/Save as Type** menu, choose **Illustrator EPS (eps)**. Choose a location for the file. To save the artboards as separate files, check **Use Artboards**, then click All (to save each artboard plus a master EPS file containing all the artboards) or click Range and enter a range. ★ Or to combine all the artboards into one file, uncheck Use Artboards. Click Save.

Continued on the following page

A This prompt appears if you save a file in the Illustrator EPS format and objects containing spot colors in the file are either semi-transparent or are stacked below other semitransparent objects.

If the file contains spot colors that aren't fully opaque, an alert dialog will appear (**A**, preceding page). If you allow those spot colors to be converted to process colors by another application, the results may be unpredictable. Click Cancel and convert the spot colors in Illustrator (or click Continue if you know the spot color conversion won't be an issue).

3. The EPS Options dialog opens (**A**, next page). Keep the Version as **Illustrator CS4 EPS.** (Or to save the file in an earlier version, read the sidebar on the next page.)

4. Choose a **Preview Format**:

None for no preview. The image won't display onscreen in any other application, but it will print.

TIFF (Black & White) for a black-and-white preview.

TIFF (8-bit Color) for a color preview.

For a layout program in the Mac OS, alternative options are **Macintosh (Black & White)** for a black-and-white PICT preview, or **Macintosh (8-bit Color)** for a color preview in the PICT format. These previews don't display transparent backgrounds.

Note: Regardless of which preview option you choose, color information will be saved with the file, and it will print normally from Illustrator or any other application that it is imported into.

If you chose the TIFF (8-bit Color) format, click **Transparent** to save the file with a transparent background, or **Opaque** to save it with a solid background.

5. If the artwork contains overprints (applied via the Attributes panel), from the **Transparency: Overprints** menu, choose **Preserve** to record overprint information in the EPS file, or **Discard** to save the EPS file without overprint information.

If the artwork uses blending modes or contains transparency, those areas will be flattened before the file is printed. From the **Preset** menu, choose **[High Resolution]**, **[Medium Resolution]**, or **[Low Resolution]** as the preset to be used for flattening transparency (see page 388). The [High Resolution] preset will produce the best-quality printout.

Take a moment to read any messages 🛈 that you see in the Warnings area for the current settings. For example, you may learn that the document contains transparency, which requires flattening, or learn how overprinting in transparent areas will be handled.

6. Under Fonts, check **Embed Fonts (for Other Applications)** to save any fonts being used as a part of the file so they'll display and print properly on any system, even where they aren't installed. Check this option if your Illustrator file contains type and will be imported into a layout application.

7. Check any of these optional boxes, if available:

Include Linked Files to embed a copy of any linked images used in the artwork into the Illustrator EPS file. This option increases the file size but allows you to print the EPS file from another program without the original (linked) image. (In any case, don't discard the original file that the image is linked to; you will still need it to edit or print the file from Illustrator.)

Include Document Thumbnails to include a thumbnail of the file for previewing in the Open or Place dialog in Illustrator.

Include CMYK PostScript in RGB Files to convert RGB objects in the EPS file to CMYK colors. This makes it possible to print the file from programs that output only CMYK colors. Note: If you reopen the EPS file in Illustrator, RGB colors will be preserved as RGB.

Compatible Gradient and Gradient Mesh Printing to include instructions to enable older PostScript devices to print gradients and gradient meshes. Unless you're getting a printing error when printing gradients or meshes, leave this option unchecked.

8. Choose whichever **Adobe PostScript** option conforms to your printing device: **LanguageLevel 2** or **LanguageLevel 3**. (Choose LanguageLevel 3 if the file contains meshes and will be output to a Level 3 printer.)

9. Click OK. If you didn't check Include Linked Files and your file contains placed, linked images, an alert dialog will appear (**B**, next page); click **Embed Files** or **Preserve Links**.

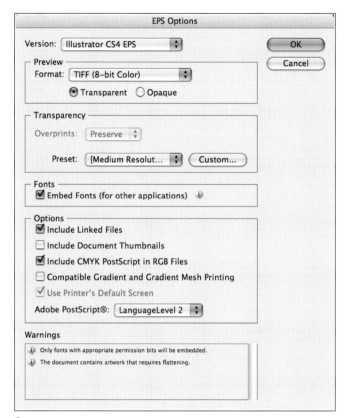

A Choose Preview, Transparency, Font, and other options in the EPS Options dialog.

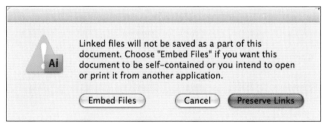

B This alert dialog will appear if you didn't check Include Linked Files in the EPS Format Options dialog and your file contains placed, linked images. This is your second chance to include those placed files.

SAVING TO EARLIER EPS FORMATS

If you need to save a copy of a file to an earlier Illustrator EPS format, in step 3 on the preceding page, choose the desired Illustrator CS EPS option, and be sure to read the messages in the Warnings area at the bottom of the dialog. The CS EPS, CS2 EPS, and CS3 EPS formats preserve transparency, effects, and type features; the latter two formats also preserve live features, such as live blends and live paint. However, saving a file in any of these earlier formats may cause changes to area type and some loss of editability.

Understandably, saving a file to one of the Legacy Formats (Illustrator version 10 or earlier), will result in an even greater loss of editability.

Saving files in the Adobe PDF format

The versatile Adobe PDF (Portable Document Format) is a good choice for output to the Web, or to other applications and platforms. This format is also useful for showing Illustrator artwork to clients, as the only software a user needs in order to view a PDF file is Adobe Reader 6 or later (which is available as a free download) or, in Mac OSX, the Preview application; Adobe Illustrator isn't required. Plus, your artwork will look as it was originally designed, because this format preserves all object attributes, groups, fonts, and type.

PDF files can also be viewed in Adobe Acrobat, where edits and comments can be applied. Acrobat versions 5 and later support transparency; Acrobat versions 6, 7, and 8 also preserve layers; and Acrobat 8 offers support for 3D features. The PDF format also supports document text search and navigation features.

Note: The instructions below are long-winded (yawn). If you like, you can stop at the end of step 3 by choosing one of the default presets.

To save a file as Adobe PDF:

Save as PDF using a preset

1. With your file open in Illustrator, choose File > Save As or Save a Copy.

2. From the Format menu, choose **Adobe PDF (pdf)**, and choose a location for the file. To save every artboard as a separate page, click **All**; or to save only specific artboards as pages, click **Range** and enter a range. ★ Click Save. The Save Adobe PDF dialog opens (**A**, next page).

3. From the **Adobe PDF Preset** menu, choose a preset that best suits the intended output medium (the Compatibility menu will display the default Acrobat version for the chosen preset):

   ➤ You can read about the currently chosen preset in the Description window.

   Illustrator Default creates a PDF file that can be reedited in Illustrator or placed into InDesign or QuarkXPress. Fonts are embedded, and bitmap images aren't downsampled or compressed.

   High Quality Print creates PDF files for desktop printing and proofing devices.

   PDF/X-1a: 2001, PDF/X-3: 2002, PDF/X4 2007, and PDF/X-4: 2008 create Acrobat-compatible

PDF files that will be checked for compliance with specific printing standards to help prevent printing errors. PDF/X-1a and PDF/X-3 don't support transparency (files are flattened); PDF/X-3 and both of the PDF/X-4 presets support embedded color profiles and color-managed workflows; and the PDF/X-4 presets provide support for transparency (files aren't flattened). If you need your file to remain fully editable in Illustrator, don't choose a PDF/X preset.

Press Quality is for high-quality prepress output. This preset embeds all fonts automatically, uses JPEG compression and Maximum quality, and preserves custom color and high-end image options. To accommodate all this data, however, the resulting file size will be large.

Smallest File Size creates compact, low-resolution PDF files for output to the Web, e-mail, or other onscreen uses. Fonts are embedded and colors are converted to RGB.

If you're satisfied with the settings in the chosen preset, click Save PDF, or if you want to choose custom settings, proceed with any or all of the remaining steps.

Save as PDF using custom settings

1. Via the **Standard** menu, you can apply a PDF/X compliance standard to any non-PDF/X preset to ensure printing compliance. If you don't choose a PDF/X compliance standard, choose which version of Adobe Acrobat you want your file to be compatible with from the **Compatibility** menu. Note that not all applications can read Acrobat 7 or 8 files.

   If you choose any nondefault settings for a preset, the word "(Modified)" is added to the preset name on the Adobe PDF Preset menu.

2. Under **Options**, check any of the following:

   Preserve Illustrator Editing Capabilities to embed a copy of the Illustrator file into the PDF file. This option will enable the file to be reopened and edited in Illustrator but also limits how much it can be compressed.

   Embed Page Thumbnails to save a thumbnail of the artboard for display in the Open and Place dialogs.

Optimize for Fast Web View to enable the file to display quickly in a Web browser.

View PDF After Saving to have your system's default PDF viewer (most likely Adobe Reader or Acrobat) launch automatically and display the file after you click Save PDF (in step 9).

If the Compatibility option is Acrobat version 6, 7, or 8, check **Create Acrobat Layers from Top-Level Layers**. This will preserve the edit-ability of top-level layers if the file is opened in one of those versions of Acrobat.

To choose even more custom options, follow the remaining steps, starting on the next page.

SAVE YOUR PRESET!

► Once you've chosen custom settings in the Save Adobe PDF dialog, you should save them as a user-created preset by clicking Save Preset in the lower left corner. You can then choose your custom preset from the Adobe PDF Preset menu for any file.

► To edit a user-created preset, choose Edit > Adobe PDF Presets, click your user-created preset on the Presets scroll list, then click Edit.

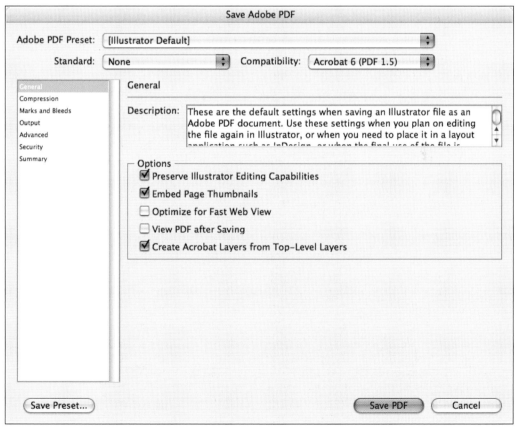

A These are the [Illustrator Default] settings in the General option set of the Save Adobe PDF dialog.

3. For online (not print) output, click **Compression** on the list of option sets on the left side of the dialog, then choose options to control how your artwork will be compressed (downsampled) to reduce the file size.**A** From the menus under Color Bitmap Images, Grayscale Bitmap Images, and Monochrome Bitmap Images, choose an interpolation method for downsampling:

Do Not Downsample preserves the current image size.

Average Downsampling To divides the image into sample areas, averages the pixels in each area, and substitutes the average values for the original values.

Subsampling To replaces a sampled area with pixel data taken from the middle of that area, producing a smaller file but not necessarily an accurate one.

Bicubic Downsampling To replaces the sampled area with an average of the area's values, and is often more accurate than average downsampling.

For the chosen interpolation methods, enter the desired **ppi** resolution and the minimum resolution threshold an image must have in order to be downsampled.

Other settings in the Compression option set:

Choose a compression type from the **Compression** menus: **None** for no compression, a **JPEG** option, or the **ZIP** option. All the JPEG options are lossy (cause data loss). The ZIP option is usually lossless (see Adobe PDF Options in Illustrator Help). If you choose an Automatic option, Illustrator will choose the appropriate compression settings for the artwork—Automatic (JPEG) for the widest

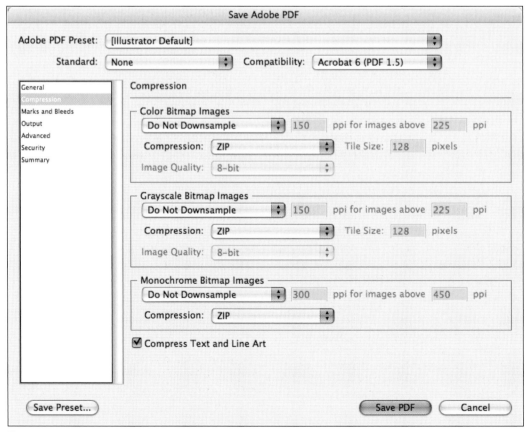

A Choose Compression options in the Save Adobe PDF dialog.

compatibility, or Automatic (JPEG2000) for the best compression.

4. For information about the **Marks and Bleeds** option set, see pages 378–379.

5. Click **Output** on the left side of the dialog to control color conversion and profile inclusion in the PDF file:

Note: Unless you're knowledgeable about setting up a color-managed workflow, it's best to leave the Color menus on the default settings.

In the **Color** area, choose color conversion settings. Choose from the **Color Conversion** menu: **No Conversion** to preserve color data and let the printer or the program that outputs the PDF convert the colors; or a **Convert to Destination** option to let Illustrator do the conversion. If the file has the same color space and embedded profile as the destination profile (e.g., when converting a CMYK file to a CMYK profile), choose Convert to Destination (Preserve Numbers). For the conversion options, choose a destination profile from the **Destination** menu.

The **PDF/X** options are available for the PDF/X presets. Unless your press shop instructs you otherwise, leave the Output Intent Profile Name menu and fields on the default settings.

Note: For Web output, we suggest choosing Smallest File Size from the preset menu, in which case the Output options will be set correctly for you.

6. Click **Advanced** on the left side of the dialog to access font, overprint, and flattening options.

By default, the PDF presets automatically embed all the characters in each font used in the file. If only a portion of the characters in those fonts is being used in your artwork, you can embed just that subset to reduce the file size. Enter a percentage in the **Subset Fonts When Percentage of Characters Used Is Less Than** field. If you enter 50%, for example, the entire font will be embedded only if you use more than 50% of the font's characters in the file, and the Subset option will be used if you use fewer than 50% of those characters.

Acrobat versions 5 through 8 preserve overprinting and transparency automatically. If Acrobat 4 is chosen as the Compatibility option and the document contains overprints, choose whether to Preserve or Discard Overprints. Similarly, if the artwork contains transparency, choose Transparency Flattener options (see pages 388–390).

7. Click **Security** on the left side of the dialog if you want to restrict user access to the PDF. The following options are available only for non-PDF/X files:

Check **Require a Password to Open the Document** to make the file password protected, and type a password in the Document Open Password field.

➤ Since the password can't be recovered from the document, jot it down in a separate location.

Check **Use a Password to Restrict Editing Security and Permissions Settings** if you want to maintain control over those options. Type a password in the Permissions Password field. The following Acrobat Permissions become available:

The **Printing Allowed** menu lets you control whether users can print the file. Options are None, Low Resolution (150 dpi), and High Resolution.

The **Changes Allowed** menu lets you specify precisely which parts of the document users may alter.

Check **Enable Copying of Text, Images, and Other Content** to permit users to alter text or images.

Check **Enable Text Access of Screen Reader Devices for the Visually Impaired** to permit screen readers to view and read the file.

Check **Enable Plaintext Metadata** if you want the file metadata to be searchable by other applications (available only for Acrobat versions 6 through 8).

8. Click **Summary** on the left side of the dialog to see an expandable list of the settings you've chosen for each category.

9. Click **Save PDF**, then give yourself a nice pat on the back.

Using the Export command

The Export dialog gives you access to other file formats besides EPS and PDF. Some of them are discussed briefly on the next page.

To export a file:

1. With the file open, choose File > **Export**. The Export dialog opens.

2. *Optional:* Change the file name in the Save As/ File Name field. Illustrator will automatically append the proper file extension (e.g., .bmp, .psd, .tif) to the file name for the format you will choose in the next step.

3. Choose from the **Format/Save as Type** menu, **A–B** and choose a location for the new file.

   ► To create a new folder for the file in the Mac OS, choose a location, click New Folder, enter a name, then click Create. In Windows, click Create New Folder, then enter a name.

4. If the Use Artboards options are available for the chosen format and you want to save the artboards as separate files, check **Use Artboards**, then click All or click Range and enter a range. ★ Or to combine all the artboards into one file, uncheck Use Artboards.

5. Click Export/Save. Choose settings in any additional dialog that opens, then click OK. A few file formats are discussed briefly on the facing page; following that, the GIF, JPEG, and PSD formats are discussed in depth.

✓ PNG (png)
BMP (bmp)
AutoCAD Drawing (dwg)
AutoCAD Interchange File (dxf)
Enhanced Metafile (emf)
Flash (swf)
JPEG (jpg)
Macintosh PICT (pct)
Photoshop (psd)
TIFF (tif)
Targa (tga)
Text Format (txt)
Windows Metafile (wmf)

A These choices are available on the Format menu in the Mac OS.

AutoCAD Drawing (*.DWG)
AutoCAD Interchange File (*.DXF)
BMP (*.BMP)
Enhanced Metafile (*.EMF)
Flash (*.SWF)
JPEG (*.JPG)
Macintosh PICT (*.PCT)
Photoshop (*.PSD)
PNG (*.PNG)
Targa (*.TGA)
Text Format (*.TXT)
TIFF (*.TIF)
Windows Metafile (*.WMF)

B These choices are available on the Save as Type menu in Windows.

USING ILLUSTRATOR FILES IN ADOBE FLASH

The Adobe Flash application is used for Web animations and interactive graphics. The simplest way to get Illustrator objects into Flash is by opening the Adobe Illustrator (ai) file in that program. All paths, strokes, gradients, type (designated as Flash Text), masks, effects, and symbols are preserved. And you can specify whether layers are converted to individual Flash layers, keyframes, or a single Flash layer.

A few file formats, in brief

Rasterize

If you choose a raster (bitmap) file format in the Export dialog, such as BMP, the Rasterize Options dialog opens.**A** Choose a Color Model for the resulting file. For the file Resolution, choose Screen (72 dpi), Medium (150 dpi), or High (300 dpi), or enter a custom resolution (Other). Check Anti-Alias to allow pixels to be added along curved edges to make them look smoother.

BMP (bmp)

BMP is the standard bitmap image format on Windows and DOS computers. When you choose rasterization settings and click OK, the BMP Options dialog opens. Choose the Windows or OS/2 format for the target operating system, specify a bit (color) depth, and choose whether you want to enable RLE compression, if available.

TIFF (tif)

TIFF, a bitmap image format, is supported by virtually all paint, image-editing, and page layout applications. It supports RGB, CMYK, and grayscale color, and offers LZW as a compression option.

When you choose the TIFF file format in the Export dialog, the TIFF Options dialog opens.**B** Choose a Color Model; choose a Resolution of Screen (72 dpi), Medium (150 dpi), or High (300 dpi) or enter a custom resolution; and turn Anti-Alias on or off. Check LZW Compression if

you need to compress the file; this lossless method doesn't discard or degrade image data. Choose your target platform in the Byte Order area, and check Embed ICC Profile if you've assigned such a profile to your file.

Enhanced metafile (emf) and Windows metafile (wmf)

A metafile describes a file, and functions as a list of commands for drawing a graphic. Typically, a metafile is made up of commands for drawing objects such as straight lines, polygons, and text, and commands to control the style of the objects. Use these formats to export simple artwork only. Windows Metafile (WMF), a 16-bit metafile format, is used on Windows platforms; Enhanced Metafile (EMF), a 32-bit metafile format that is also used on Windows platforms, can store a wider range of commands than WMF.

Microsoft Office

Choose File > Save for Microsoft Office to save your document in a PNG format that is readable by Microsoft Word, PowerPoint, and Excel; transparent areas will become opaque. If you want to specify a resolution and background color, with the option to preserve transparency, use File > Export instead, choosing PNG from the Format/Save as Type menu.

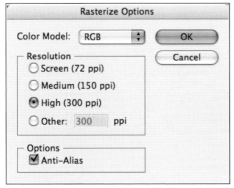

A The Rasterize Options dialog opens if you choose a raster format in the Export dialog.

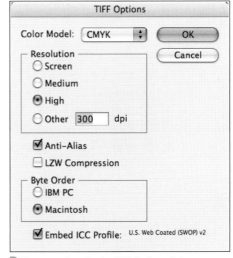

B Choose options in the TIFF Options dialog.

Optimizing files for the Web

You can use Illustrator to create graphics for a Web page, such as a logo or an illustration, or maybe buttons, graphics, or text to be used as navigation devices. Before placing such elements into a Web page creation program, such as Adobe Dreamweaver, you need to convert them from vector art into pixels. In this section, you'll learn how to optimize the conversion to pixels for efficient transmission and display online.

When preparing an Illustrator file for online viewing, you will choose an appropriate format, then choose compression options for that format. When choosing compression options for a graphic, your goal is to optimize its speed of transmission on the Web while preserving an acceptable level of quality.

Image size

The length of time it takes for an image to load into a Web page is directly related to its file size. The file size, in turn, is governed by the dimensions of the image in pixels and the amount and kind of compression that is applied to it. When choosing dimensions for your image, keep in mind that the Web page your graphics will be viewed on is smaller than the 1024 x 768-pixel area of a typical monitor.

➤ Before optimizing your file, choose View > Pixel Preview to see how your vector artwork will look when rasterized for the Web.

Although the GIF and JPEG formats cause a small reduction in image quality as they compress a file, the resulting smaller size allows the file to download more quickly on the Web. Vector graphics, in particular, tend to compress well because they're usually composed of solid-color shapes. For your Web design, resist the urge to add patterns or gradients, which can't be compressed as much as solid colors.

File format

Your choice of file format also affects how much an image is compressed. **GIF** and **JPEG**, the two file formats most commonly used for optimizing Web graphics, are suitable for different types of graphics:

➤ GIF is an 8-bit format, meaning it can save a maximum of 256 colors. It's a good choice when color fidelity is a priority, such as for artwork that contains type or solid-color vector shapes. Graphics like these contain far fewer colors than continuous-tone (photographic) images, so the color restriction won't have an adverse impact. If your artwork contains transparency, you must choose this format, because unlike the JPEG format, it supports transparency.

When you optimize an Illustrator file in the GIF format, the solid colors in your artwork translate into just a small portion of the maximum 256 possible colors (this set of colors is referred to as the file's color table). Reducing the number of colors shrinks the file size and enables the file to download more quickly.

➤ If your Illustrator file contains continuous-tone images (e.g., raster images that you've imported into it), the JPEG format, which saves 24-bit color, will do a better job of preserving color fidelity than GIF. Another advantage of JPEG is that its compression scheme can shrink an image significantly without lowering its quality. When saving an image in this format, you can choose a quality setting; the higher the quality setting, the larger the file size.

Unfortunately, the JPEG format, unlike GIF, doesn't preserve transparency or the sharp edges of vector objects. Furthermore, each time you optimize an image as JPEG, some image data is lost; the greater the compression, the greater the loss. (Always remember to optimize a copy of your file, not the original!)

You'll learn the actual optimization steps next.

In the Save for Web & Devices dialog, you'll find everything you need to optimize your Illustrator graphics for the Web. Experiment with the multiple previews in this dialog first to test the effects of different optimization settings.

To use the previews in the Save for Web & Devices dialog:

1. Via the Artboard Navigation controls at the bottom of the Application Frame or tabbed window, display the artboard that optimization settings are to be previewed for.

2. Choose File > **Save for Web & Devices** (Cmd-Option-Shift-S/Ctrl-Alt-Shift-S). The chosen artboard will display in the dialog.**A**

3. Do either of the following:

   Click the **4-Up** tab to display the original image and three previews simultaneously. Illustrator will use the current optimization options to generate the first preview (to the right of the original), then generate two other preview variations of the current optimization settings. You

can click any preview and change the optimization settings for just that preview. As you choose options in the Save for Web & Devices dialog, note the change in image size, which is listed below each preview.

For a more definitive test preview (at any time), click the **Preview in Default Browser** button at the bottom of the dialog. Your optimized image will open in the default Web browser application that is installed in your system. Or if you'd rather choose a different browser that's installed in your system, from the **Select Browser** menu, choose a browser name; or choose Other, then locate and open the preferred browser.

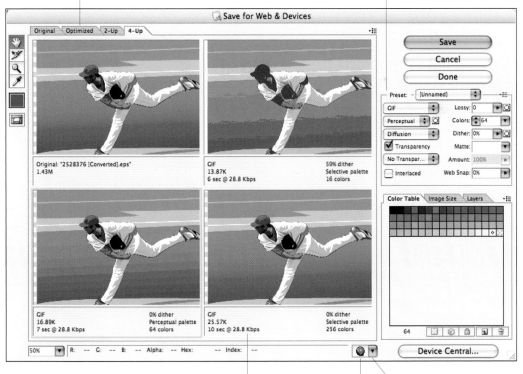

A Use the Save for Web & Devices dialog to choose and preview optimization settings for a file.

We'll show you how to optimize files in the GIF format first, because it does a better job of optimizing vector objects and type than JPEG.

To optimize a file in the GIF format:

1. Save your file and display the artboard to be optimized.

2. Choose File > **Save for Web & Devices** (Cmd-Opt-Shift-S/Ctrl-Alt-Shift-S).

3. Click the **2-Up** tab at the top of the dialog box to display the original and optimized previews of the image.

4. Do either of the following:

   From the **Preset** menu, choose one of the **GIF** options. Leave the preset settings as is, then click Save. The Save Optimized As dialog opens. Keep the current name, choose a location, and then click Save.

   Follow the remaining steps to choose custom optimization settings.

Choose GIF settings

1. From the **Optimized File Format** menu, choose GIF.**A**

2. From the **Color Reduction Algorithm** menu, choose a method for reducing the number of colors in the image. We recommend the Selective (default) option because it preserves solid and Web-safe colors.

3. Next, to remove some colors from the document's color table, choose **16** from the **Colors** menu. If it looks (in the optimized preview) as though some colors have been substituted, you can raise the Colors value to **32**.

4. *Optional:* Dithering is a process by which Illustrator mixes dots of a few different colors to simulate a greater range of colors. This option increases the file size slightly but is helpful for artwork that contains gradient or soft-edged effects, such as drop shadows. Choose the Diffusion method from the Dither Algorithm menu, and on the right, choose a Dither value between 50% and 75%. (If you choose No Dither, gradients may have noticeable banding.)

5. Check **Transparency** to preserve fully transparent pixels in the artwork. By default, the background becomes transparent. With Transparency checked, you have the option to define which colors in the artwork are to become transparent. Choose the Eyedropper tool, click a color in the optimized preview area, then click the **Maps Selected Colors to Transparent** button ▨ at the bottom of the Color table.

6. If your artwork contains any soft-edged effects (such as a drop shadow) on top of transparent areas and you know the background color of the target Web page, click the **Matte** color swatch and use the Color Picker to choose that color. This will help your artwork blend in. If that color is unknown, set Matte to None; this will create a hard, jagged edge.

   Another option is to choose Matte: None, then check Transparency and choose one of the three options on the Transparency Dither Algorithm menu. With one of these options chosen, the art will look the same on any background.

7. Click Save. In the Save Optimized As dialog, keep the current name, choose a location, and then click Save.

➤ To save the current (Unnamed) options, see the tip on the following page.

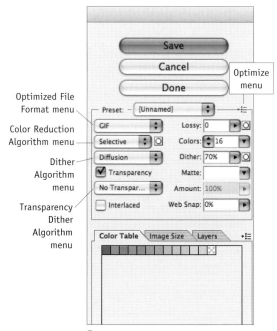

Optimized File Format menu
Color Reduction Algorithm menu
Dither Algorithm menu
Transparency Dither Algorithm menu
Optimize menu

A Choose optimization options for a GIF file in the Save for Web & Devices dialog.

JPEG is the format of choice for optimizing continuous-tone imagery (gradients, blends, and placed raster images). When optimized in this format, your file's 24-bit color will be preserved, and its colors will be seen and enjoyed by most viewers (provided their display is set to thousands or millions of colors). Two drawbacks to JPEG are that its compression method eliminates image data and that it doesn't preserve transparency.

To optimize a file in the JPEG format:

1. Save your file and display the artboard to be optimized.

2. Choose File > **Save for Web & Devices** (Cmd-Opt-Shift-S/Ctrl-Alt-Shift-S). The Save for Web & Devices dialog opens.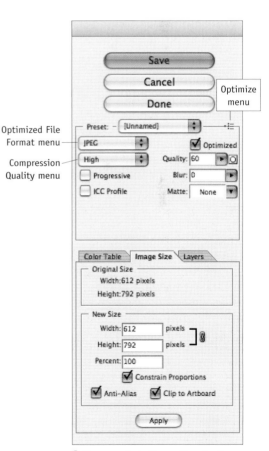

3. Click the **2-Up** tab at the top of the dialog to display the original and optimized previews of the image.

4. Do either of the following:

   From the **Preset** menu, choose one of the **JPEG** options. Leave the preset settings as is, then click Save. The Save Optimized As dialog opens. Keep the current name, choose a location, and then click Save.

   Follow the remaining steps to choose custom optimization settings.

Choose JPEG settings

1. From the Optimized File Format menu, choose **JPEG**.

2. Do either of the following:

   From the **Compression Quality** menu, choose a quality level for the optimized image.

   Move the **Quality** slider to the desired compression level.

   ➤ The higher the compression quality, the higher the image quality—and the larger the file size.

3. Increase the **Blur** value to lessen the prominence of JPEG artifacts that may arise from the chosen JPEG compression method, and to reduce the file size. Be careful not to blur the artwork to the point that the sharp vector shapes become too soft.

4. Choose a **Matte** color to be substituted for areas of transparency in the artwork (see step 6 on the preceding page). If you choose None, transparent areas will display as white.

Note: The JPEG format doesn't support transparency. To have the Matte color simulate transparency, make it the same solid color as the background of the Web page (if you know what that color is).

5. Leave **Progressive** and **ICC Profile** unchecked.

6. *Optional:* Check Optimized to produce the smallest possible file size.

7. Click Save. The Save Optimized As dialog opens. Leave the name as is, choose a location, then click Save.

➤ To save the current (Unnamed) options, choose Save Settings from the Optimize menu, enter a name, then click Save. Your saved set is now available on the Preset menu in the Save for Web & Devices dialog for any file.

A Choose optimization options for the JPEG file format in the Save for Web & Devices dialog.

Exporting files to Adobe Photoshop

There are several ways to get an Adobe Illustrator file into Adobe Photoshop.

➤ For the greatest ease in future editing, make use of the Smart Object layer feature in Photoshop. A Smart Object layer is created automatically when you place an Adobe Illustrator (ai) file into Photoshop CS4 via the Place command in Photoshop or Bridge; drag an object from Illustrator into Photoshop; or choose Smart Object in the Paste dialog when copying and pasting an object into Photoshop. When you double-click a Smart Object layer in Photoshop, the Illustrator artwork that you embedded into the Photoshop file opens in Illustrator for editing. Save the temporary file and the Smart Object layer updates in Photoshop—an effortless round trip!

➤ Copy and paste an object into Photoshop as pixels, as a path, or as a shape layer by choosing that option in the Paste dialog. To ensure that the Paste dialog displays in Photoshop, in Illustrator, go to Illustrator/Edit > Preferences > File Handling & Clipboard and check both the PDF and AICB options. If you copy a compound path or compound shape from Illustrator and paste it into Photoshop (click Shape Layer in the Paste dialog), it will show up as multiple paths on a shape layer.

➤ Drag and drop an Illustrator object as a plain, unstroked path into Photoshop by holding down Cmd/Ctrl as you drag. The path will be listed on the Paths panel in Photoshop.

➤ Export your Illustrator file in the Photoshop (psd) format (see the following page).

CREATING SMART OBJECTS

If you create artwork containing editable type or other objects in Adobe Illustrator CS4 and import the file into Photoshop by using the Place command, it becomes a Smart Object layer in Photoshop. In Illustrator, save the file in the Adobe Illustrator (ai) format. With a document open in Photoshop, use the File > Place command to import the file (or select the file thumbnail in Bridge, then use the Place > In Photoshop command). The object will appear as a new Smart Object layer on the Layers panel.

The contents of the Smart Object layer (which are now embedded in the Photoshop file) can be edited in the original application at any time. Double-click the Smart Object layer, and a temporary file opens in Illustrator. Edit, resave, then close the file, and the object will update in the Photoshop document.

Last but not least, the Photoshop (psd) format, available as an option in the Export dialog, converts Illustrator objects into pixels and preserves layers and transparency (well, pretty much; see the sidebar at right).

To produce a Photoshop (psd) file:

1. Choose File > **Export**. The Export dialog opens.

2. Type a name and choose a location for your file, then choose Format/Save as Type: **Photoshop (psd)**. To save the artboards as separate files, check **Use Artboards**, then click All or click Range and enter a range. ★ Or to combine all the artboards in one file, uncheck Use Artboards, and click Export/Save. The Photoshop Export Options dialog opens. **A**

3. Choose a **Color Model**.

4. Click a preset or custom **Resolution** option.

5. In the Options area, do any of the following:

   To have all layers in the artwork import as one flattened layer in Photoshop, click **Flat Image**. Or to export the unflattened layers to Photoshop, click **Write Layers** and check **Maximum Editability**. If the Illustrator file contains type that doesn't have a stroke or effects applied to it, checking Preserve Text Editability will allow the text to be edited in Photoshop.

   Notes: Although the Write Layers option preserves the stacking appearance of objects nested within a layer, only top-level layers will become layers in Photoshop. Hidden layers and empty artboards in the Illustrator file won't be included in the export file. Live Paint groups will be included, but will be expanded.

   Check **Anti-alias** to soften the edges of any curved shapes.

   Check **Embed ICC Profile** to embed the current color profile in the file, if one was assigned.

6. Click OK.

➤ When File > Export is used to export an Illustrator file in the Photoshop (psd) format, a layer-level clipping set or an object-level clipping set group will export as a layer group with a vector mask; the mask will clip all the objects in the group.

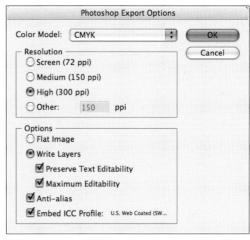

A Choose options in the Photoshop Export Options dialog.

USING THE PHOTOSHOP (PSD) FORMAT

➤ The Photoshop (psd) export format preserves opacity masks and layers, and editable type that doesn't contain a stroke or effects. Blending modes and transparency will look the same in Photoshop, although on the Layers panel in Photoshop, the imported layers will have a blending mode of Normal and an Opacity of 100%.

➤ If an Illustrator layer contains an object that Photoshop can't import in its current state (such as a stroke or an effect), that layer and any layers below it will be merged into one layer in Photoshop.

➤ Opacity masks from Illustrator are converted to layer masks in Photoshop. The opacity mask feature is not covered in this book.

➤ Compound shapes translate easily between the two programs.

Appendix A: Artwork by Illustrator pros

Michael Bartalos

©Michael Bartalos (created for the United States Postal Service)

Michael Bartalos

©Michael Bartalos (created for Savoir-Faire)

Michael Bartalos

©Michael Bartalos (created for the California Academy of Sciences)

Michael Bartalos

©Michael Bartalos (created for the California Academy of Sciences)

Daniel Pelavin

Daniel Pelavin

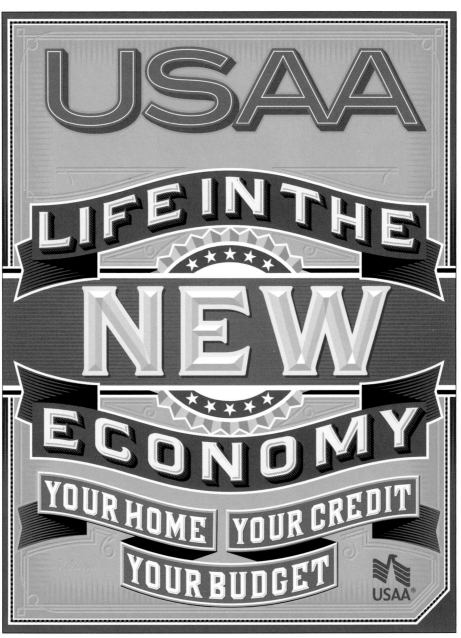

©Daniel Pelavin

Koichi Fujii

©Koichi Fujii (some work was done in Adobe Photoshop)

J.D. King

©J.D. King

J.D. King

Chris Lyons

©Chris Lyons

Chris Lyons

©Chris Lyons

Chris Lyons

©Chris Lyons

Chris Lyons

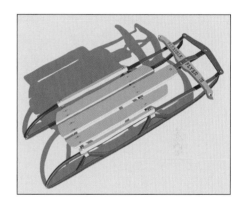

All artwork above ©Chris Lyons

Nancy Stahl

©Nancy Stahl

Nancy Stahl

©Nancy Stahl

Appendix B: Credits

Artists

Michael Bartalos
bartalosillustration.com
bartalos.com
Pages 410–413

Koichi Fujii
www.illustrationweb.com/KoichiFujii
Rep: 888-645-5878
us@illustrationweb.com
Pages 416–417

J.D. King
Rep: Gerald & Cullen Rapp 212-889-3337
www.jdkingillustration.com
Pages 418–419

Chris Lyons
14 East Park Road
Pittsford, NY 14534
Studio 585-615-2781
www.chrislyonsillustration.com
Pages iv, x, 420–423

Daniel Pelavin
80 Varick Street, #3B
New York, NY 10013
Studio 212-941-7418
www.pelavin.com
Pages 143 (hat), 414–415

Nancy Stahl
www.nancystahl.com
Pages 424–425

Vector art and photography

Shutterstock.com
Pages i, v, 1, 6, 13, 21, 24, 35, 36, 53, 55, 57, 58, 59, 61, 63, 65, 66, 67, 71, 72, 73, 75, 77, 78, 79, 80 (figure B), 81*, 82, 83*, 85, 90, 93, 95*, 96, 107, 110, 119, 129, 130, 131*, 133, 134*, 136, 140, 142*, 144*, 145, 146, 147*, 149*, 150*, 152*, 153*, 160, 161*, 162*, 163, 167, 181, 182*, 184, 188*, 189, 190, 194, 195, 196, 197, 199, 201*, 208*, 209*, 211, 212, 225*, 227*, 230*, 231, 237, 265, 273, 274*, 276*, 277*, 280*, 283, 291*, 294, 296, 298*, 303*, 305*, 306*, 311, 313*, 315*, 316*, 317*, 320*, 321*, 325*, 326*, 331*, 332*, 333*, 342*, 359, 361, 362, 367, 368, 370, 372, 373, 377, 386, 390*, 395, 405, 426

*This artwork was modified by the authors.

All other artwork © Peter Lourekas and Elaine Weinmann

INDEX

The entries in this index pertain to Illustrator, except where Bridge is listed.